WHAT'S YOUR IQ?

Thunder Bay Press
An imprint of Printers Row Publishing Group
10350 Barnes Canyon Road, Suite 100, San Diego, CA 92121
www.thunderbaybooks.com

All notations of errors or omissions should be addressed to Thunder Bay Press, Editorial Department, at the above address. All other correspondence (author inquiries, permissions) concerning the content of this book should be addressed to Carlton Books Ltd, 20 Mortimer Street, London, W1T 3JW, United Kingdom.

Publisher: Peter Norton
Associate Publisher: Ana Parker
Publishing/Editorial Team: April Farr, Kelly Larsen, Kathryn C. Dalby
Editorial Team: JoAnn Padgett, Melinda Allman, Dan Mansfield

ISBN: 978-1-68412-935-5

Printed in Dubai

23 22 21 20 19 1 2 3 4 5

WHAT'S YOUR IQ?

Challenge your IQ with over 400 formidable puzzles

Tim Dedopulos
& Richard Cater

San Diego, California

CONTENTS

INTRODUCTION

INTRODUCTION

Welcome to this book of puzzles. The ultimate goal of the tests contained within these pages is to give those little gray cells that belong exclusively to you a good old-fashioned testing session. By quizzing you on factors such as logical deducation, spatial reasoning, conceptual thinking and concentration (among other things), your brain will be pushed to the limits of its powers. This will hopefully be a rewarding experience, and help you in your quest for further knowledge. We very much hope that by the end of this book, you'll know more about your intelligence—and your brain's limits—than you did before.

Intelligence is found in all humans, to a greater or lesser degree. Your own level of intelligence has a maximum and there is really no way to increase that all of a sudden and become a genius. Neither is it possible to increase your IQ (Intelligence Quotient) either; you're born a genius or you're not. However, a very high IQ puts you into the top 2 percent of the world's population, and if you are up there, hopefully you are doing something to keep your brain busy. After all, having a high IQ is meaningless; it's what you do with it that counts, right?

Many people fail to realize their full mental potential. One reason for this is because they never test themselves. This is one of the many reasons why this book could change your life for the better. At the very least, it should make you aware of your IQ potential, if you don't know it already. After all, how do you know how intelligent you are if you never test yourself?

HOW TO USE THIS BOOK

This book is made up of 20 separate tests, each one containing 20 thought-provoking puzzles. Each test has the

correct answer referenced in the Answers section that starts on page 258. In order to mazimize the most of this book's content, do one test at a time. Proceed through each one as quickly as possible and answer those questions you find easiest, then return to the more difficult ones. The tests will help you discover what your cognitive strengths and weaknesses are, but they will not result in a conventional IQ score (you will need to test for that under certain strict conditions). When you take the tests, try to simulate actual test conditions: set aside a time when you will not be interrupted, time yourself, and try to work calmly and efficiently. Should you ever wish to take an IQ test, the questions you have answered in this book will help you to be well prepared for some of the types of questions you will encounter.

SCORE	PERCENTILE
20	95
19	94
18	93
17	92
16	91
15	90
14	85
13	80
12	75
11	70
10	65
9	60
8	55
7	50
6	45
5	40

When you have finished, check your answers and total them up. You can use the scores opposite as an indicator of how you have been performing mentally. If you consistently achieve top scores, you should think about taking an official test, which can be arranged by contacting an accredited intelligence society directly.

50 percent of the population have an IQ between 90 and 110. Only 2 percent have an IQ lower than 53 or higher than 147.

THE IMPORTANCE OF INTELLIGENCE

This book can't help you change your IQ—no one can—but it can help you get your best score possible. But why is testing your IQ so important?

Puzzles, brainteasers, riddles, and tests designed to make us scratch our chins are as old as humankind. They have helped us expand our minds, far beyond our early ancestors working out basic survival skills. By pushing our brains' abilities to the very edge, our world has opened up to us, from the invention of fire to the creation of the wheel, from supercomputers to the Large Hadron Collider, from exploring the oceans to manned missions to Mars. This has been taxing work. But our brains haven't begged for mercy, they have pushed back, evolved, got bigger, grown leaner, become smarter and, by doing so, have developed into the most finely tuned organism in the known universe.

Our brains make sense of the world around us by looking at the pieces that combine to make up our environment. Each piece is then compared to everything else we have encountered. We compare it by shape, size, color, texture, a thousand different qualities, and place it into the mental category it seems to belong to. Our brains, for example, can deduce that the fast-moving object in the corner of the street is a car, without actually seeing the car. It fills in the gaps not supplied by our eyes and ears. We keep on following this web of connections until we have enough understanding of the object of our attention to allow us to proceed in the current situation. Most of the time, just basic recognition is good enough, but every time we perceive an object, it is cross-referenced, analyzed, pinned down, and puzzled out.

This capacity for logical analysis—for reason—is one of the greatest tools in our mental arsenal, on a par with creativity and lateral induction. Without it, science would be nonexistent, and mathematics no more than a shorthand for counting items. In fact, although we might have made it out of the caves, we wouldn't have gotten far.

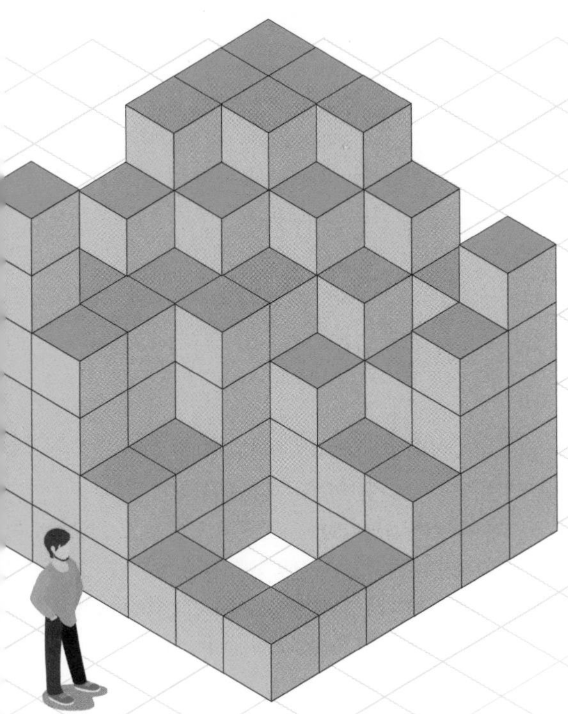

Furthermore, we automatically compare ourselves to each other—we place ourselves in mental boxes along with everything else. We like to know where we stand. It gives us an instinctive urge to compete, both against our previous bests and against each other. Experience, flexibility, and strength are acquired through pushing personal boundaries, and that's as true of the mind as it is of the body. Deduction is something that we derive satisfaction and worth from, part of the complex blend of factors that go into making up our self-image. We get a very pleasurable sense of achievement from succeeding at something, particularly if we suspected it might be too hard for us. The brain gives meaning and structure to the world through analysis, pattern recognition, and logical deduction—and our urge to measure and test ourselves is an unavoidable reflex that results from that. So what could be more natural than spending time puzzling?

Intelligence is difficult to nail down. Broadly speaking, it can be considered as the ability to gather and keep information, and to apply that information in new ways. Obviously, that's a very vague statement, but even so, there are potential problems with it. When you attempt to get to a more precise definition, it gets downright controversial.

In the *Wall Street Journal* in 1994, a team of researchers jointly described intelligence as a "general mental capability that ... involves the ability to reason, plan, solve problems, think abstractly, comprehend complex ideas, learn quickly, and learn from experience ... a capability for comprehending our surroundings." Fifty-one scientists signed on to agree with this definition—but another seventy-nine who were invited to do so declined to accept it.

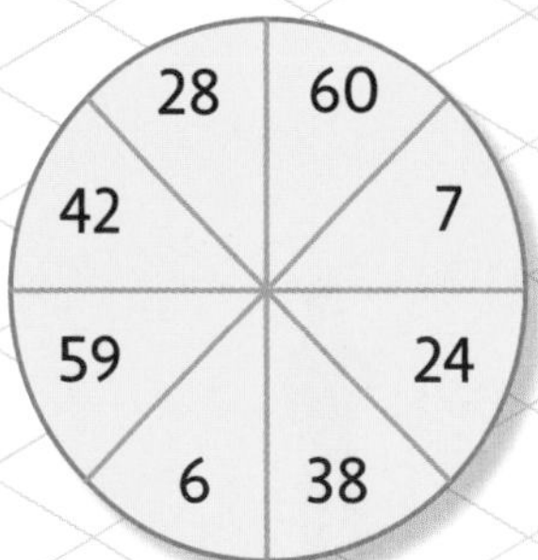

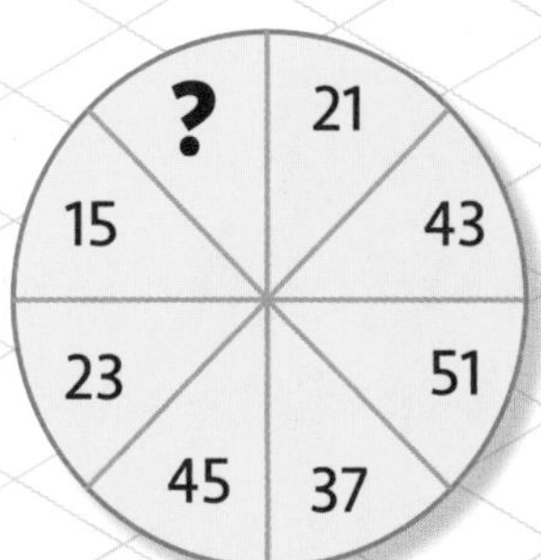

Of course, it doesn't help that people can have wildly different abilities to comprehend and learn in different areas of human interest and endeavor. It is entirely possible for the same person to be a near-genius in one field, and a dunce in another. Everything we do or communicate is expressed through the physicality of our bodies, and modulated through our senses, as understood by the linguistic and cultural strata that give our thoughts meaning and structure.

Some schools of thought regarding intelligence split it down into a (varying) number of interrelated fields. One current popular formulation, the Cattel-Horn-Carroll (CHC) theory, suggests ten broad categories of intelligence:

- Auditory Processing, including speech recognition and audio pattern manipulation
- Crystallized Intelligence, including learned knowledge, communication of information, and utilizing learned procedures
- Fluid Intelligence, including reasoning, conceptualization, and problem-solving
- Long-Term Memory, learning information and retrieving it fluently
- Quantitative Reasoning, including numerical reasoning and symbol manipulation
- Reading and Writing
- Processing Speed, performing automatic mental processing under time pressure
- Short-Term Memory, holding and using information for a few seconds
- Decision Speed, how quickly a stimulus can be reacted to
- Visual Processing, including analysis and manipulation of visual patterns

A pure abstract intellect may be under there somewhere, but it is nigh-impossible to get to. So when attempting to analyze and measure intelligence, the best option has proven to be to test a number of different aspects, and to apply those scores comparatively by looking at the population at large,

rather than absolutely by looking at some abstract scoring key.

One of the more successful attempts to measure intelligence has been the Intelligence Quotient, or IQ, invented by the German psychologist William Stern in 1912. Stern's innovation was to divide the effective mental age of a person, as measured by testing, by the person's actual age. Although there remains some academic disagreement regarding IQ as a measurement, it has been shown to be associated with income, job performance, mortality rate, and other important indicators of the quality of life.

IQ is defined in such a way that the average score across the whole population is set to 100. So 100 IQ is the same intelligence level as an average citizen of your country. Most tests are then calibrated so that a difference of 15 in the score is equal to one standard deviation. This is a statistical term that can be thought of as an umbrella encompassing a certain percentage of the results of any test—a way of looking at how much one given result differs from the usual. For our purposes here, roughly speaking, 68 percent of all people are within 1 standard deviation from average, 95 percent are within 2 standard deviations, and 99.7 percent are within 3 standard deviations. Since in many IQ tests, one standard deviation is equal to a difference of 15 points of score, under this scoring system, an IQ of 116 means that your test results are better than (50 percent + the top half of 68.3 percent) around 85 percent of the population. As the scores get higher, your relative position changes less. So if 100=top 50 percent and 116=~top 15 percent, then 131=~top 4 percent, and 145=~top 0.3 percent.

Official societies use a range of certified industry-standard IQ tests to analyze applicants. Great care is taken to ensure that these tests are standardized with a sample group of the same nationality as the person taking the test. Only by removing as many cultural variables as possible can intelligence fairly be

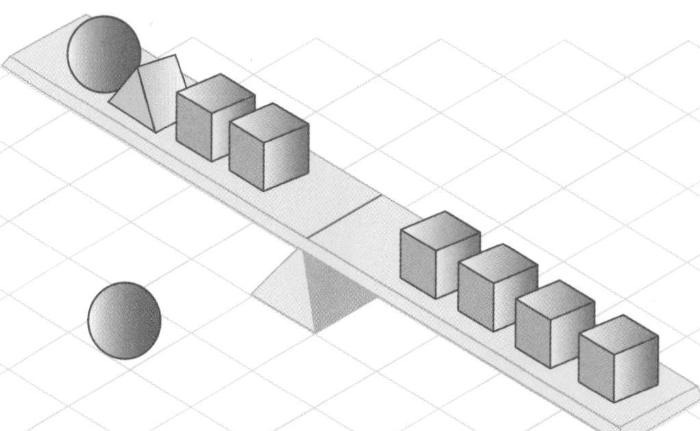

compared. Because of this, these societies gives test results in terms of comparison to percentage of the rest of the population. The admission criterion is to do better in the test than 98 percent of the standardized sample group.

To get past cultural and educational variance as much as possible, it is common for IQ tests to strongly feature abstract reasoning challenges. The tests that you will find in this book attempt to draw on some of the same types of abstract reasoning that you will encounter in IQ tests—namely pattern analysis, visual processing, fluid reasoning, quantitative reasoning, logical deduction, and more. They're not actual IQ tests, of course. By definition, it is impossible to analyze IQ without a huge database of previous test-takers' results, as measured under very careful circumstances. However, they do draw on some of the same skills.

As you go through the book, you'll find that the tests get tougher. This will help to provide you with a chance to get used to the styles of question involved, as well as to challenge yourself to improve. Remember to keep an open mind. Two questions might look quite similar, but in fact be about vastly different things.

A WORK OUT FOR THE BRAIN

It turns out that working out a complex puzzle is one of the most important things the human psyche can achieve. Recent advances in the scientific fields of neurology and cognitive psychology have hammered home the significance of puzzles and mental exercise like never before. Today, arithmetic and language puzzles, such as sudoku and crosswords, have infiltrated our daily lives. Even computer games are built on puzzle-solving algorithms, where completing one puzzle means we can progress to the next.

We now understand that the brain continually builds, shapes and organizes itself all through our lives. It is the only organ to be able to do so. Our brain continually rewrites its own operating instructions and alters its very structure

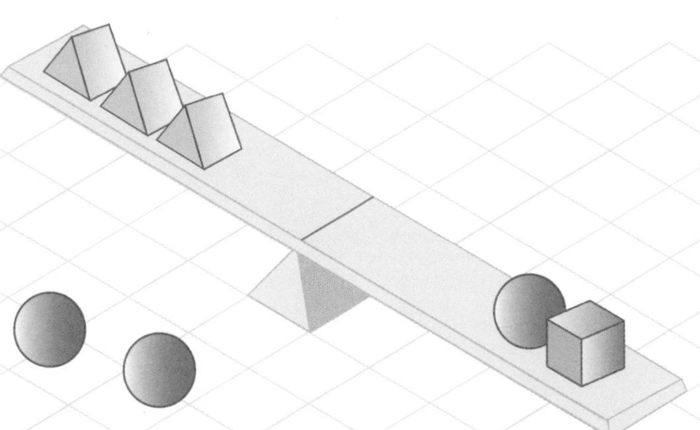

in response to our experiences. Just like the muscles of the body, our minds can respond to exercise, allowing us to be more retentive and mentally fitter. And while exercise can often be a chore for many of us, a good brain workout can often be acheived from the comfort of your own sofa.

The goal here is to have fun, of course. Afterwards, if you're not already a member, why not get a practice test from an official society to get an estimate of how you'd do at one of their supervised IQ tests? There are lots of benefits to being a member of an official branch, including the chance to make new friends, attend special events, join groups dedicated to particular interests, and receive the society's publications. Though perhaps see how you fare with this book, first...

Happy Puzzling!

TESTS

Test 1

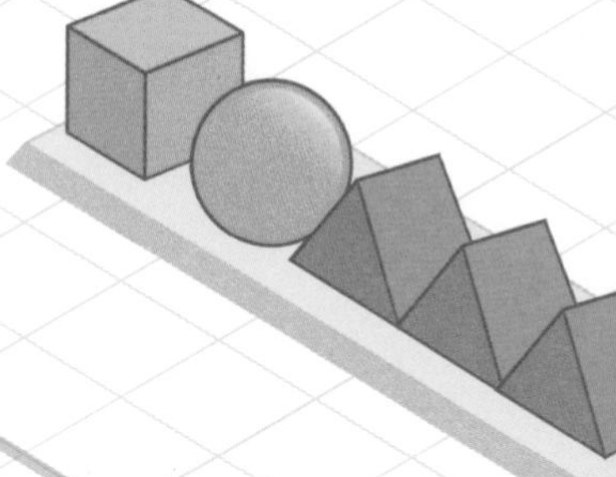

01

Which of the pentagons at the bottom should replace the question mark?

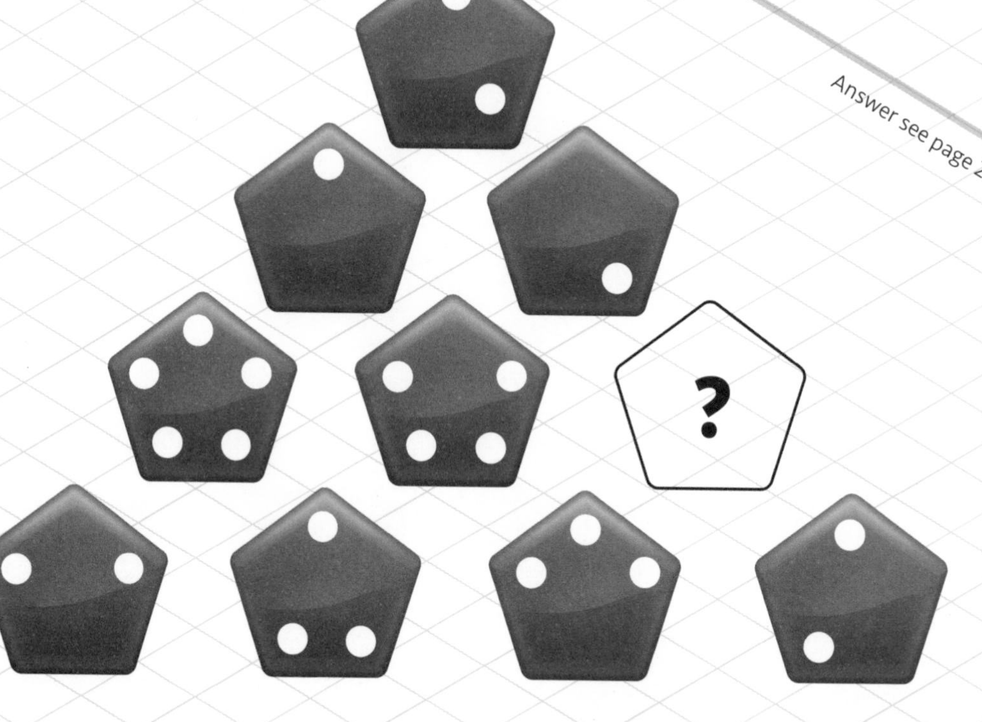

A B C D E

Answer see page 260

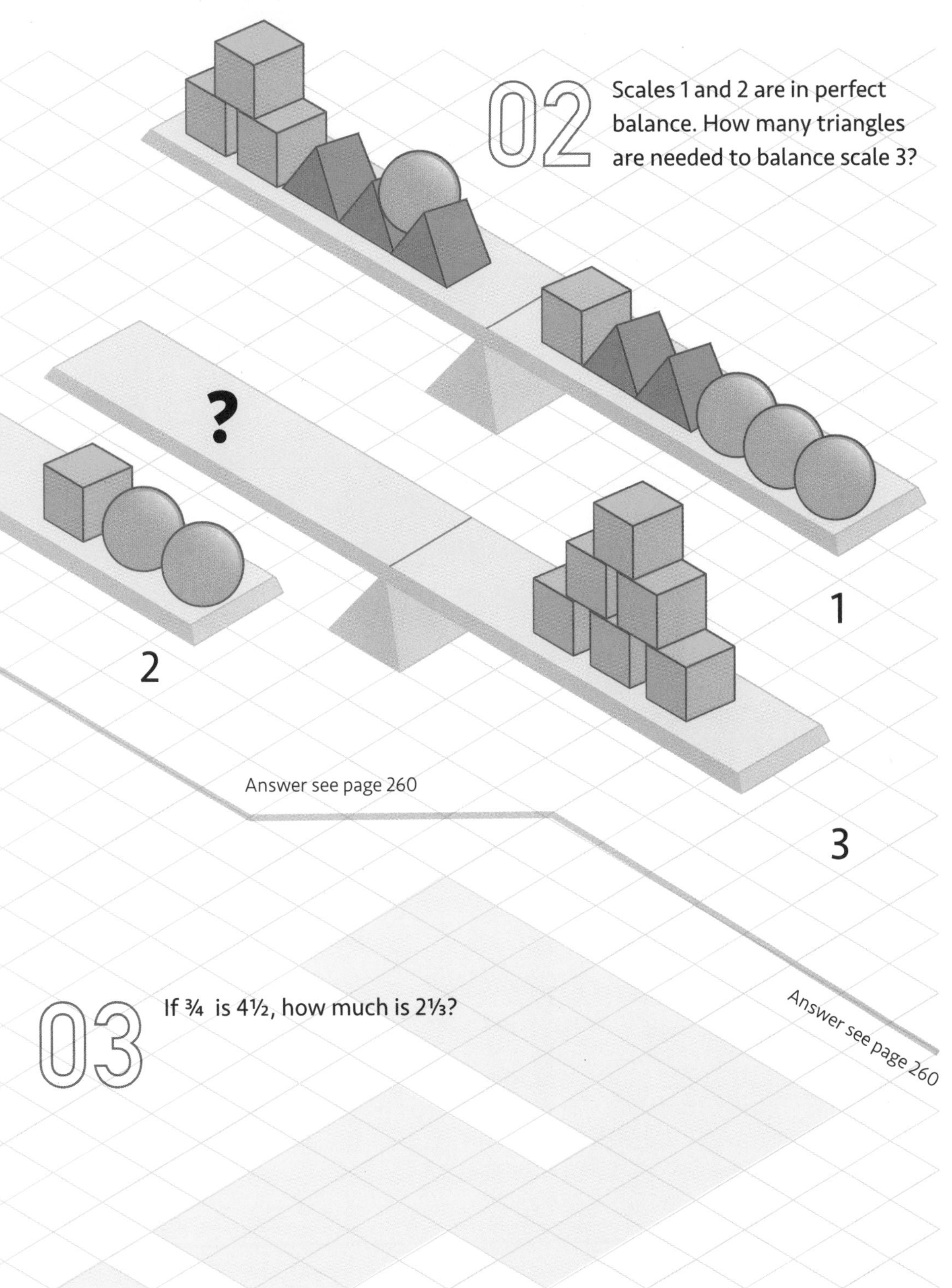

02

Scales 1 and 2 are in perfect balance. How many triangles are needed to balance scale 3?

Answer see page 260

03

If ¾ is 4½, how much is 2⅓?

Answer see page 260

Which shape below can be put with the one above to form a perfect square?

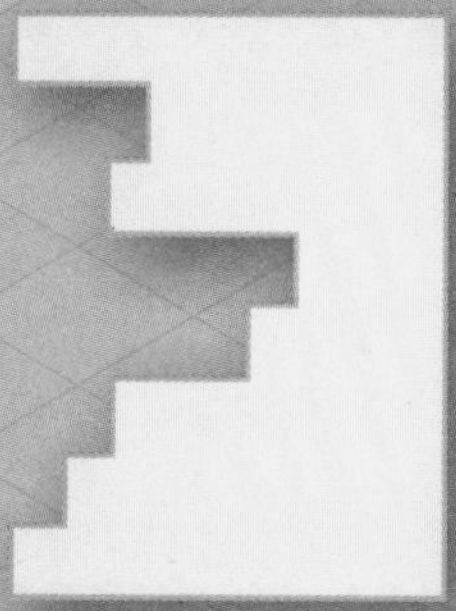

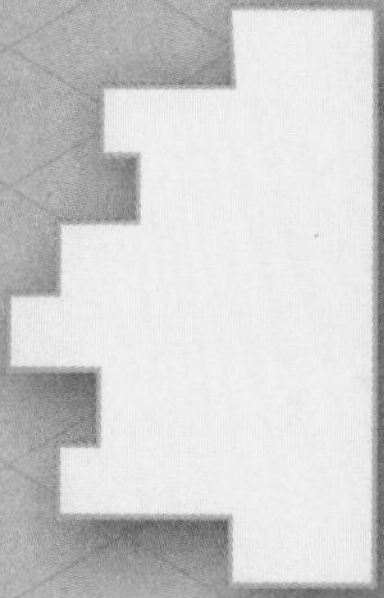

A

B

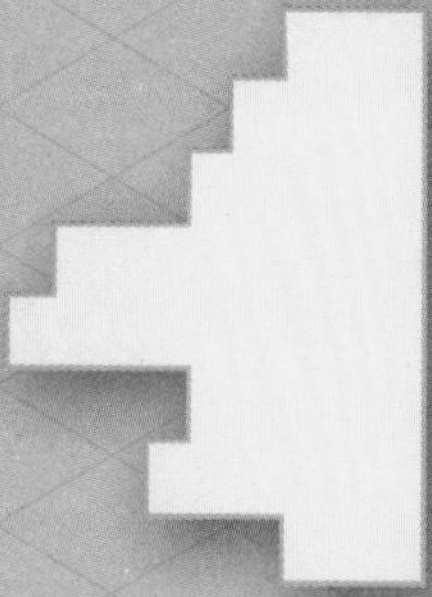

C

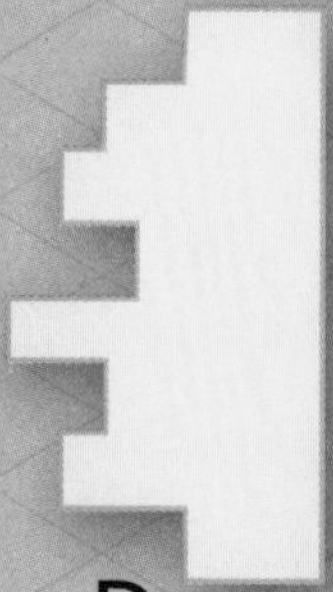

D

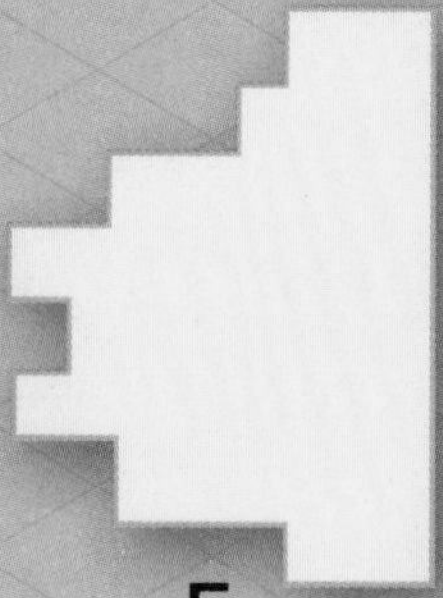

E

Answer see page 260

Select the correct figure from the numbered ones below to replace the question mark.

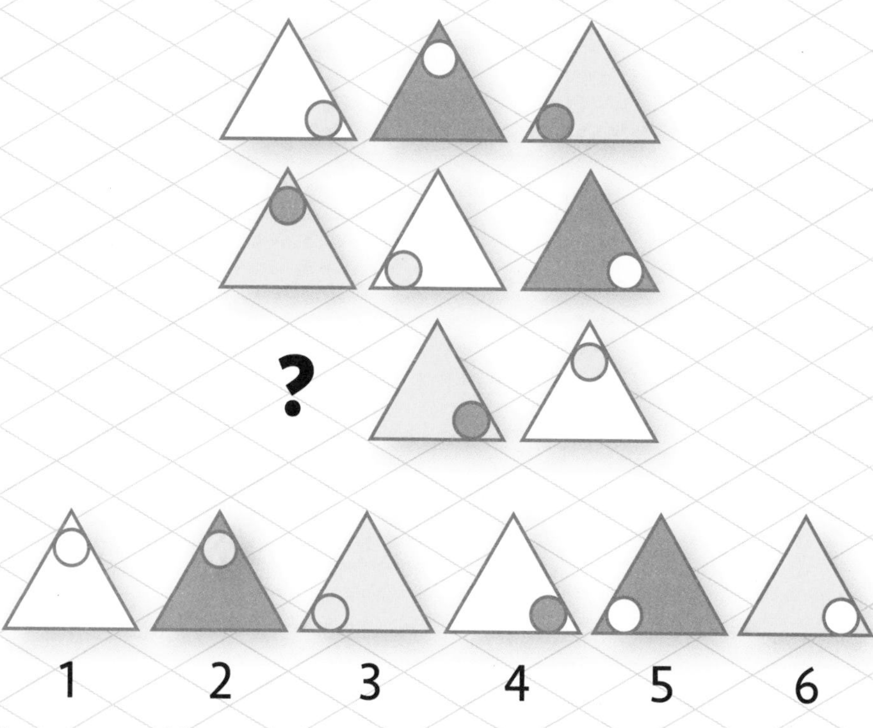

Answer see page 260

Answer see page 260

06

Complete the square using nine consecutive numbers, so that all rows, columns, and large diagonals add up to the same total.

07

Each of the nine squares in the grid marked 1A to 3C should incorporate all of the items that are shown in the squares of the same letter and number, at left and top. For example, square 2A should incorporate all of the items in squares 2 and A. One square however, is incorrect. Which is it?

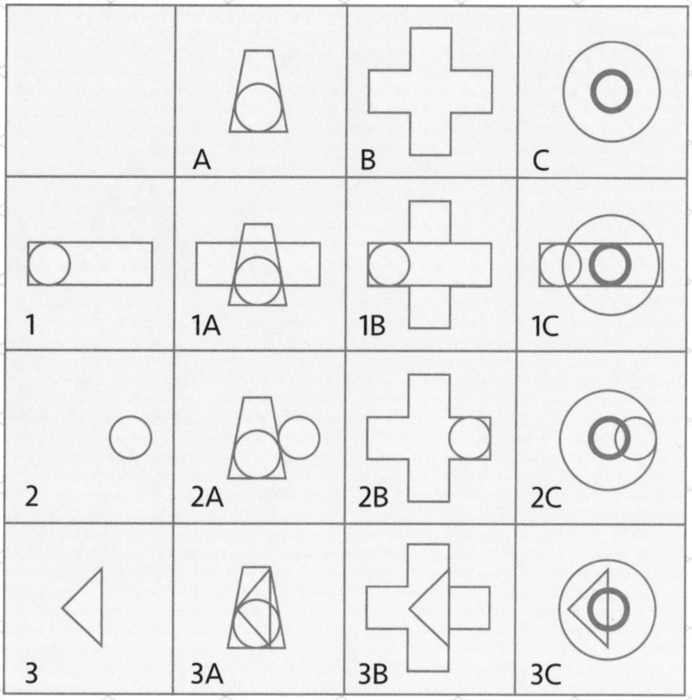
A
B
C
1
1A
1B
1C
2
2A
2B
2C
3
3A
3B
3C

Answer see page 260

08

Which is the odd one out?

56	104	32
42	64	96

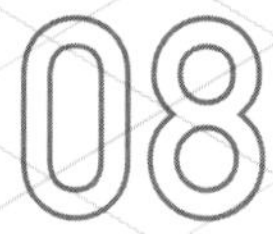

Answer see page 260

09

Which are the three odd ones out?

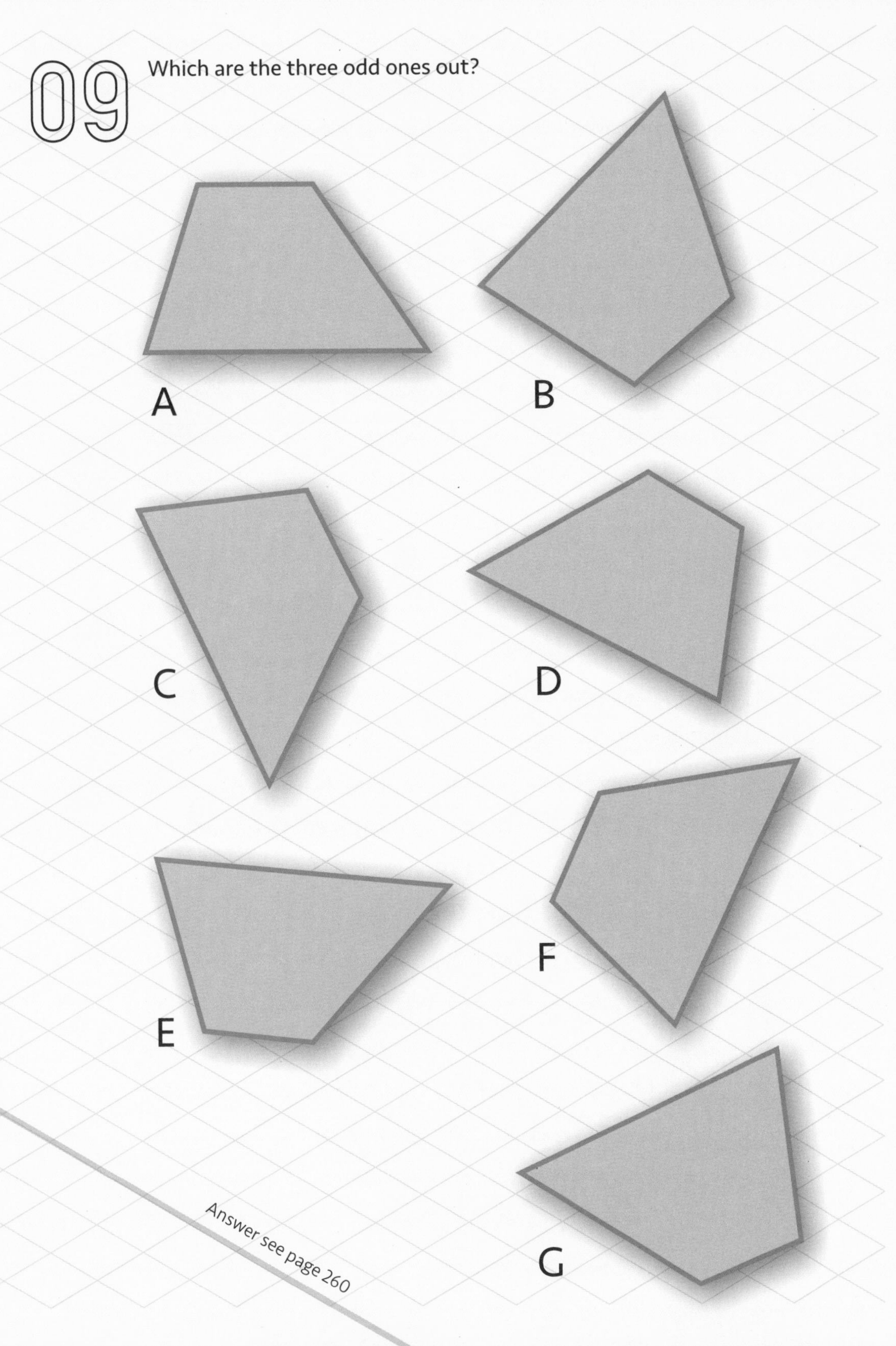

Answer see page 260

10

What number should replace the question mark?

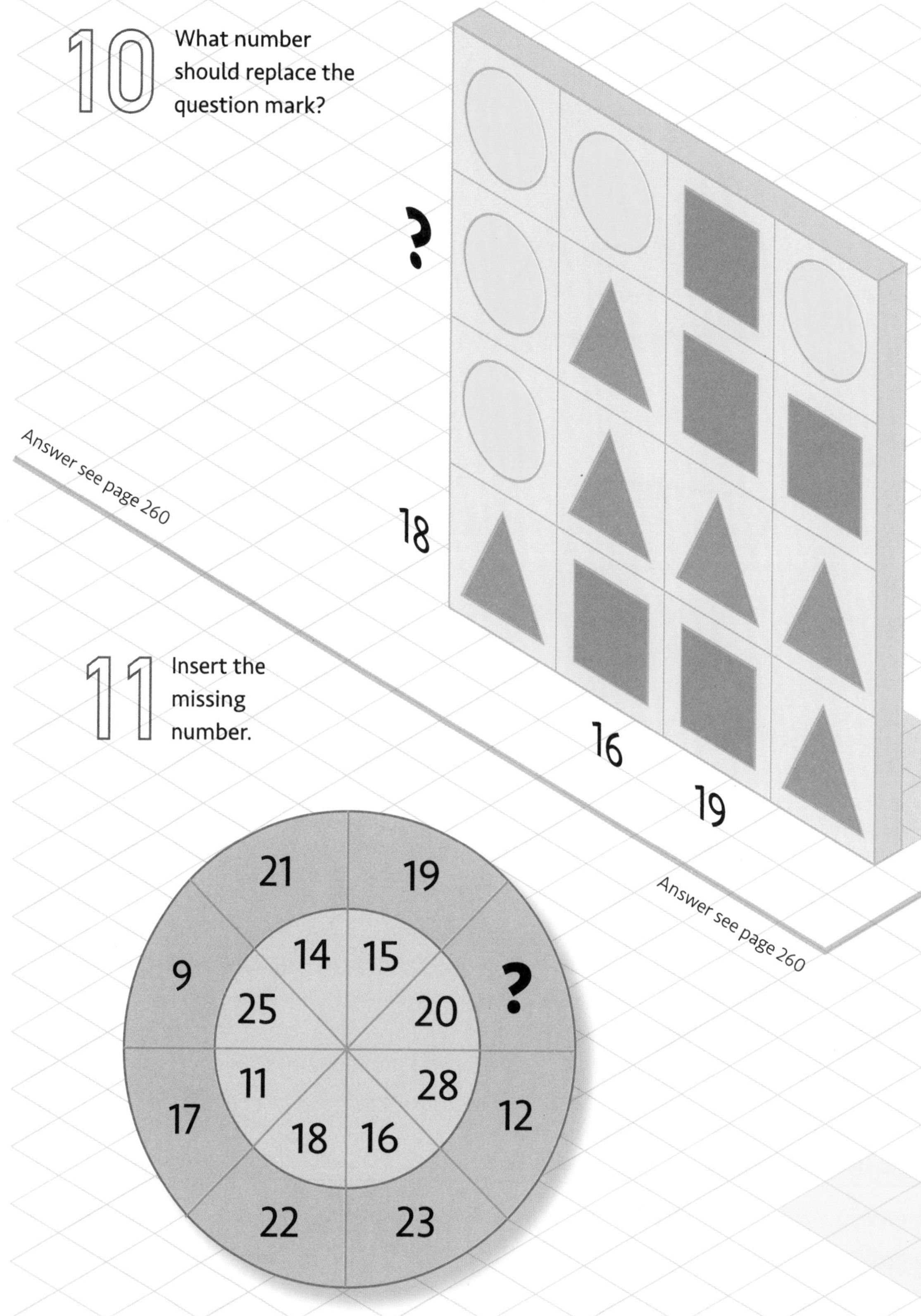

Answer see page 260

11

Insert the missing number.

Answer see page 260

12 Which of the constructed boxes below cannot be made from the given shape?

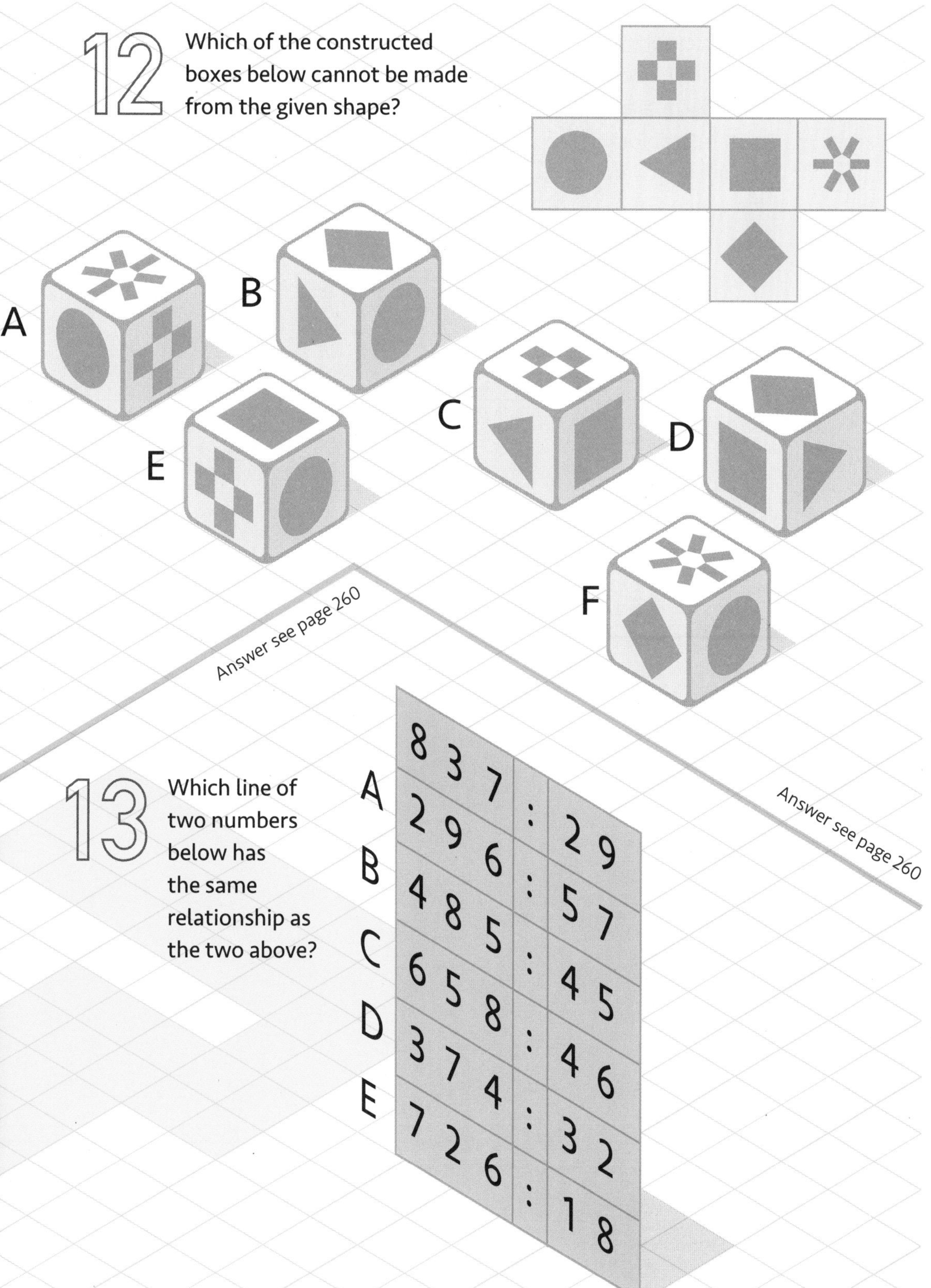

Answer see page 260

13 Which line of two numbers below has the same relationship as the two above?

Answer see page 260

14

When complete, this 6 x 6 x 6 cube contains 216 individual blocks. How many blocks are required to complete the cube?

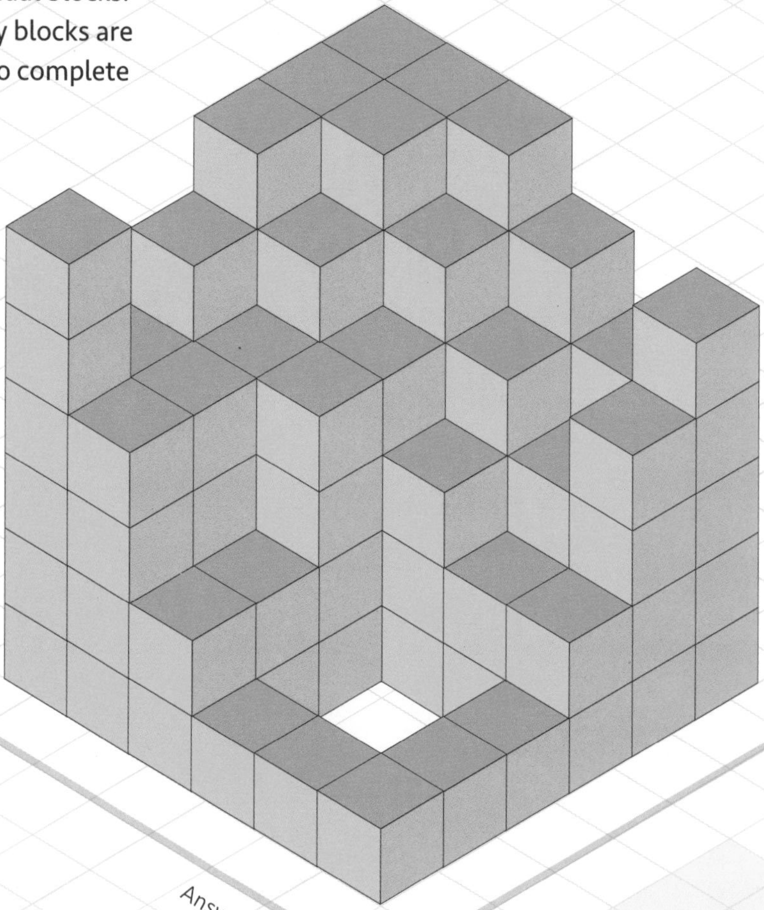

Answer see page 260

15

Insert the missing numbers.

Answer see page 260

16

Tokyo is 4½ hours ahead of Kabul, which is 2½ hours behind Hanoi. It is 4:45 a.m. on Saturday in Tokyo, what time is it in the other two cities?

TOKYO

KABUL

HANOI

Answer see page 261

17

What number should replace the question mark?

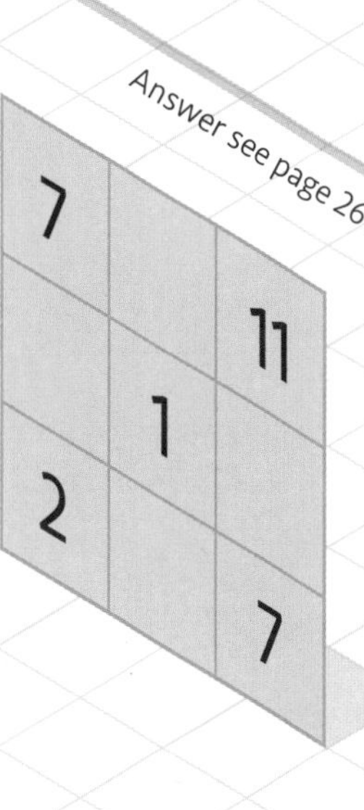

Answer see page 261

18

Which of these dice is not like the others?

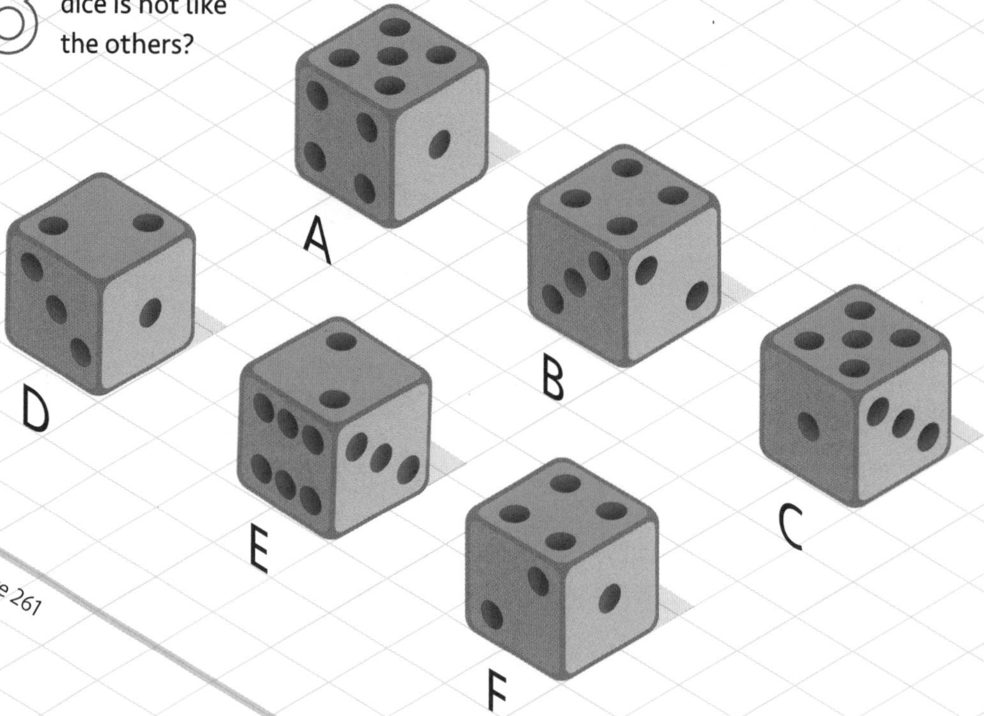

A

B

C

D

E

F

Answer see page 261

Answer see page 261

19

Which number is the odd one out?

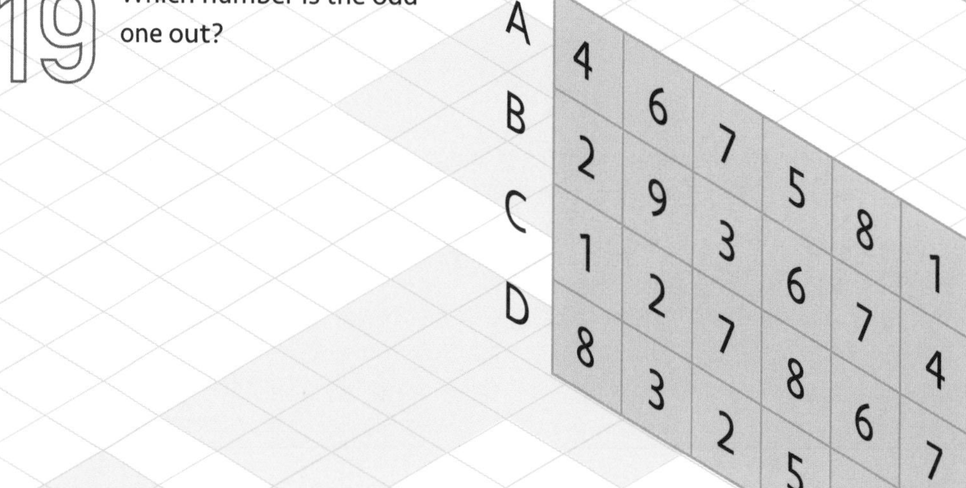

Which of the lettered clocks below continues the numbered series?

1 2 3 4 5

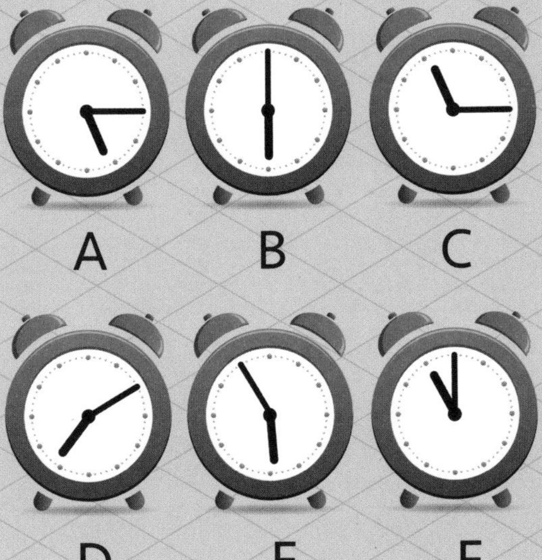

A B C

D E F

Answer see page 261

Test 2

01

The pieces can be assembled into a regular geometric shape. What is it?

Answer see page 261

Answer see page 261

02

How many are required to balance the final scale?

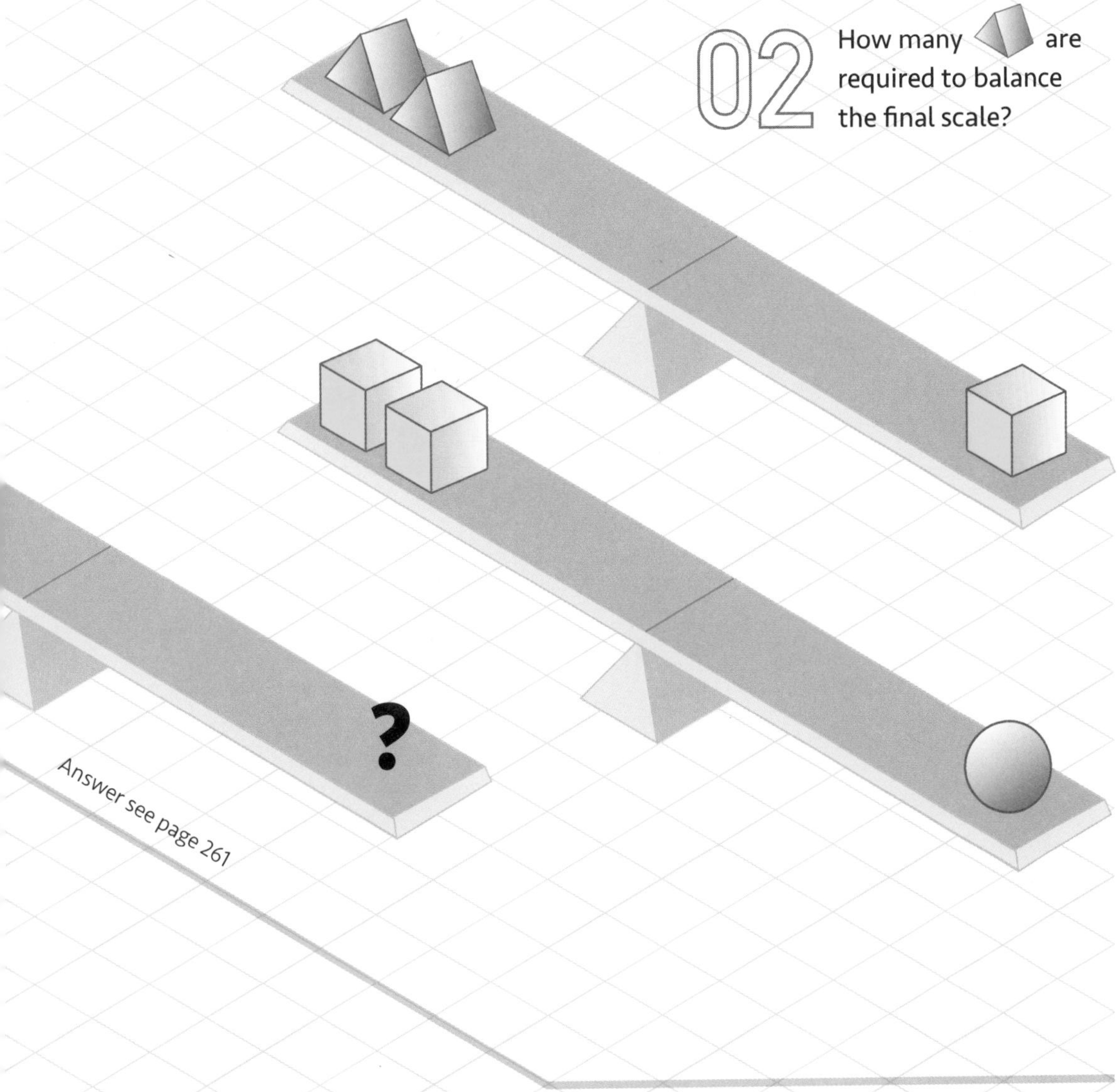

?

Answer see page 261

03

Fill in the missing plus and minus signs to make the equation below correct, performing all calculations strictly in the order they appear on the page.

5 7 2 8 = 35

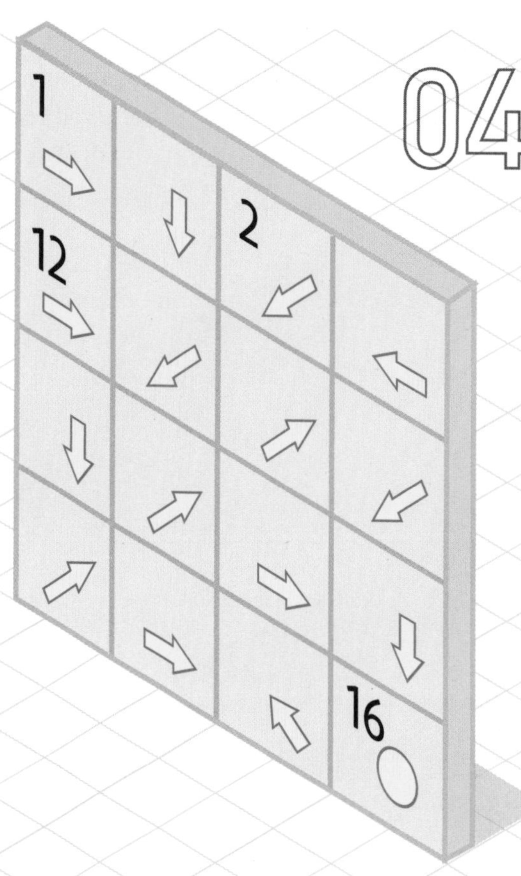

04

In each square, the arrow shows the direction you must move in. The numbers in some squares show that square's position in the correct sequence of moves. Move from top left to bottom right, visiting each square in the grid exactly once.

Answer see page 261

Answer see page 261

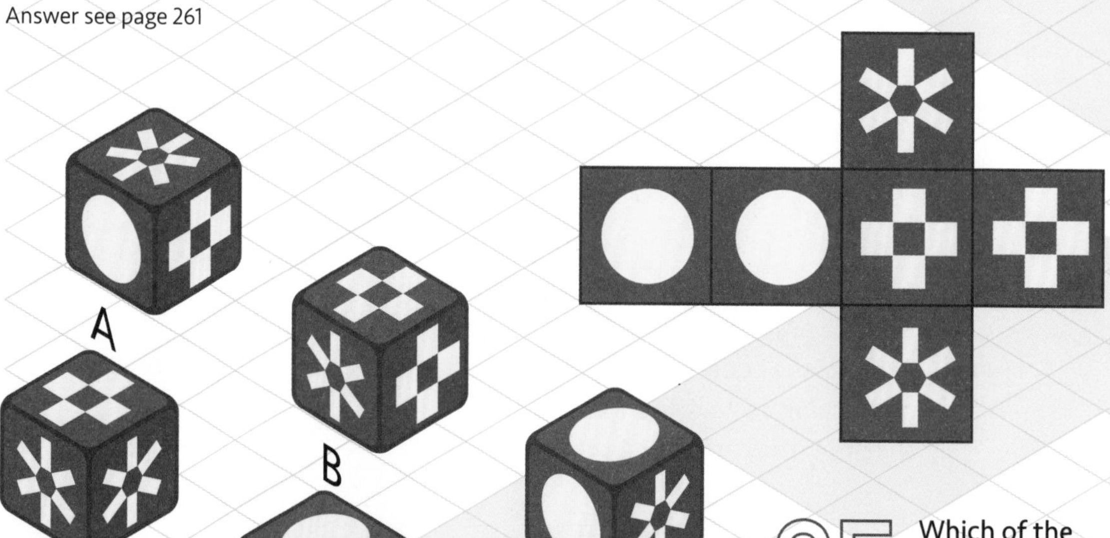

05

Which of the cubes A to E cannot be made using the layout shown?

06

Which of the options A to C most accurately continues the sequence?

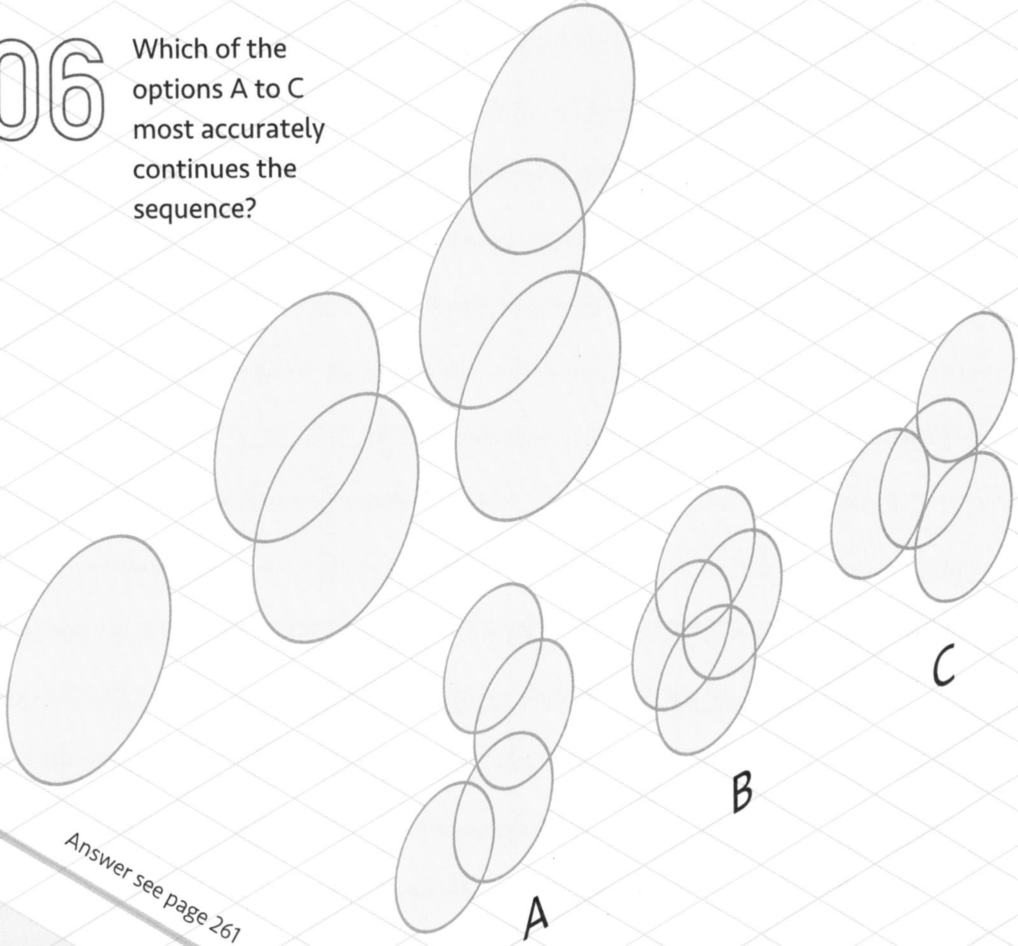

A

B

C

Answer see page 261

07

What number should replace the question mark?

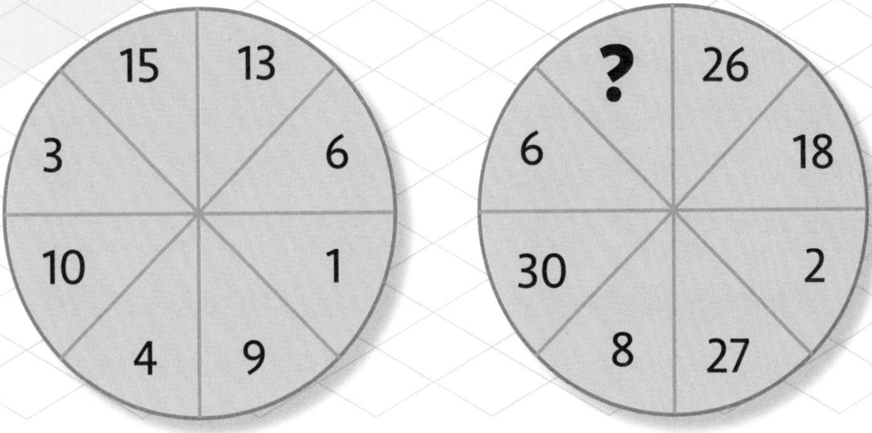

Answer see page 261

15
13
6
1
9
4
10
3

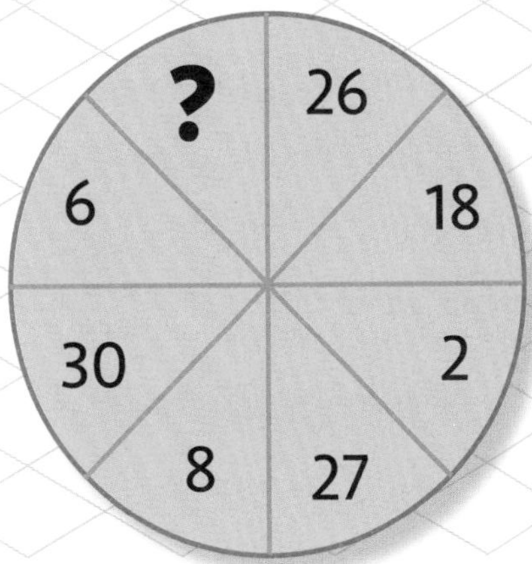

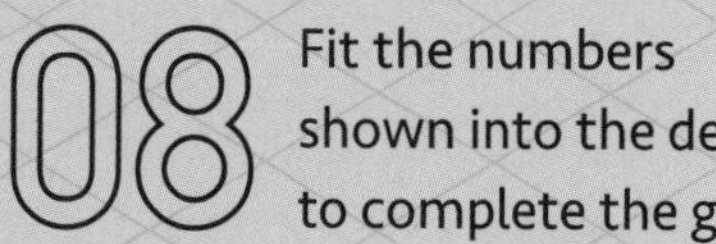

Fit the numbers shown into the design to complete the grid.

Answer see page 261

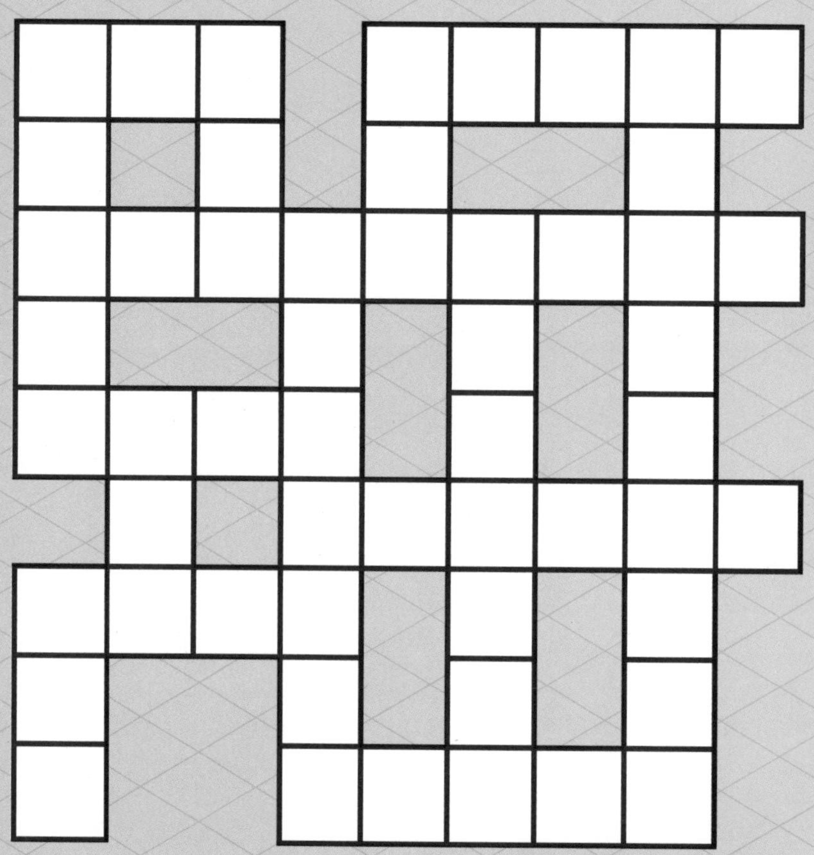

3 digits	4 digits	5 digits	6 digits	7 digits	9 digits
328	5844	76451	115261	1215440	508361402
533	7694	78517		3541488	570406111
658		88021			
763					
776					

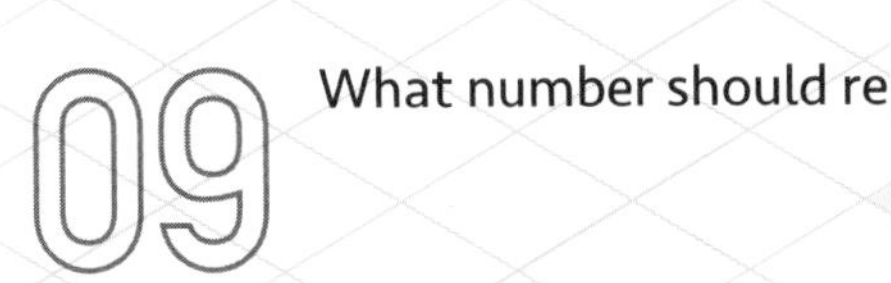

09

What number should replace the question mark?

1 2 3 5 8 13 ?

Answer see page 261

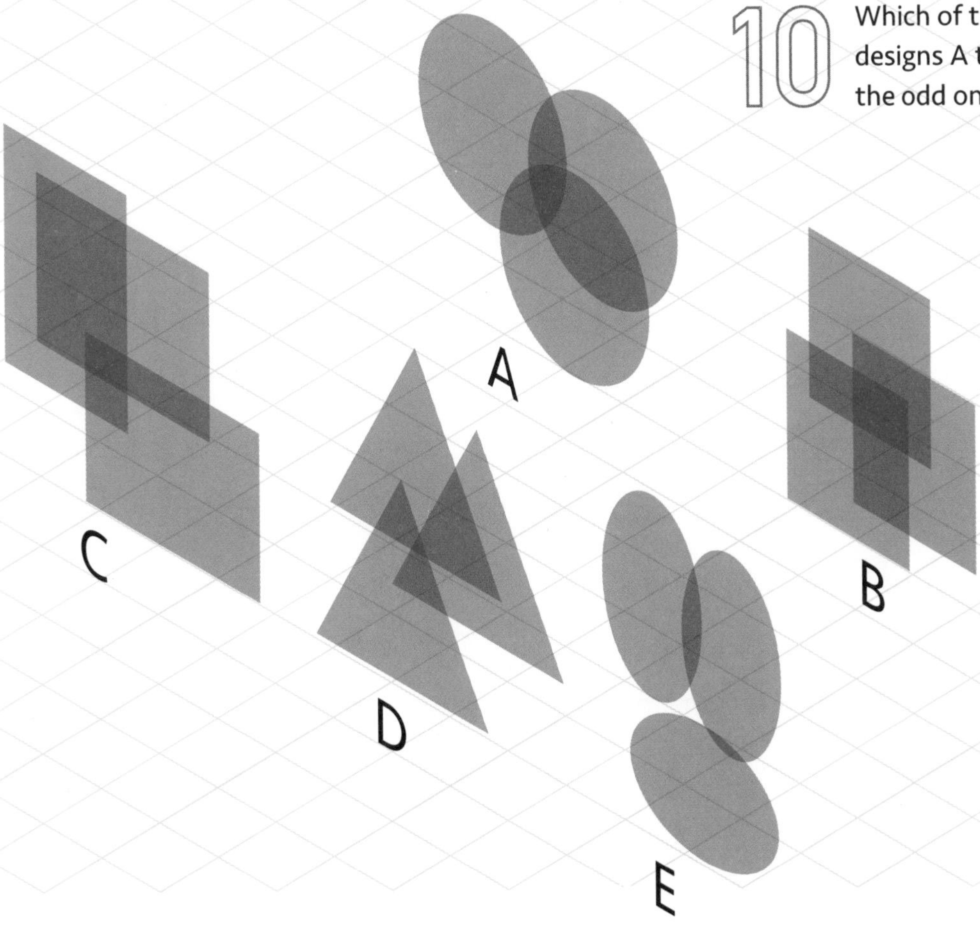

Answer see page 261

10

Which of the designs A to E is the odd one out?

A B C D E

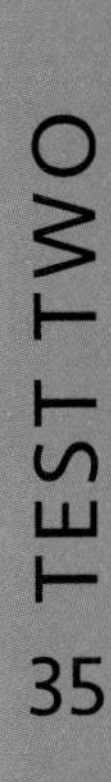

11

Which option A to E most accurately completes the pattern?

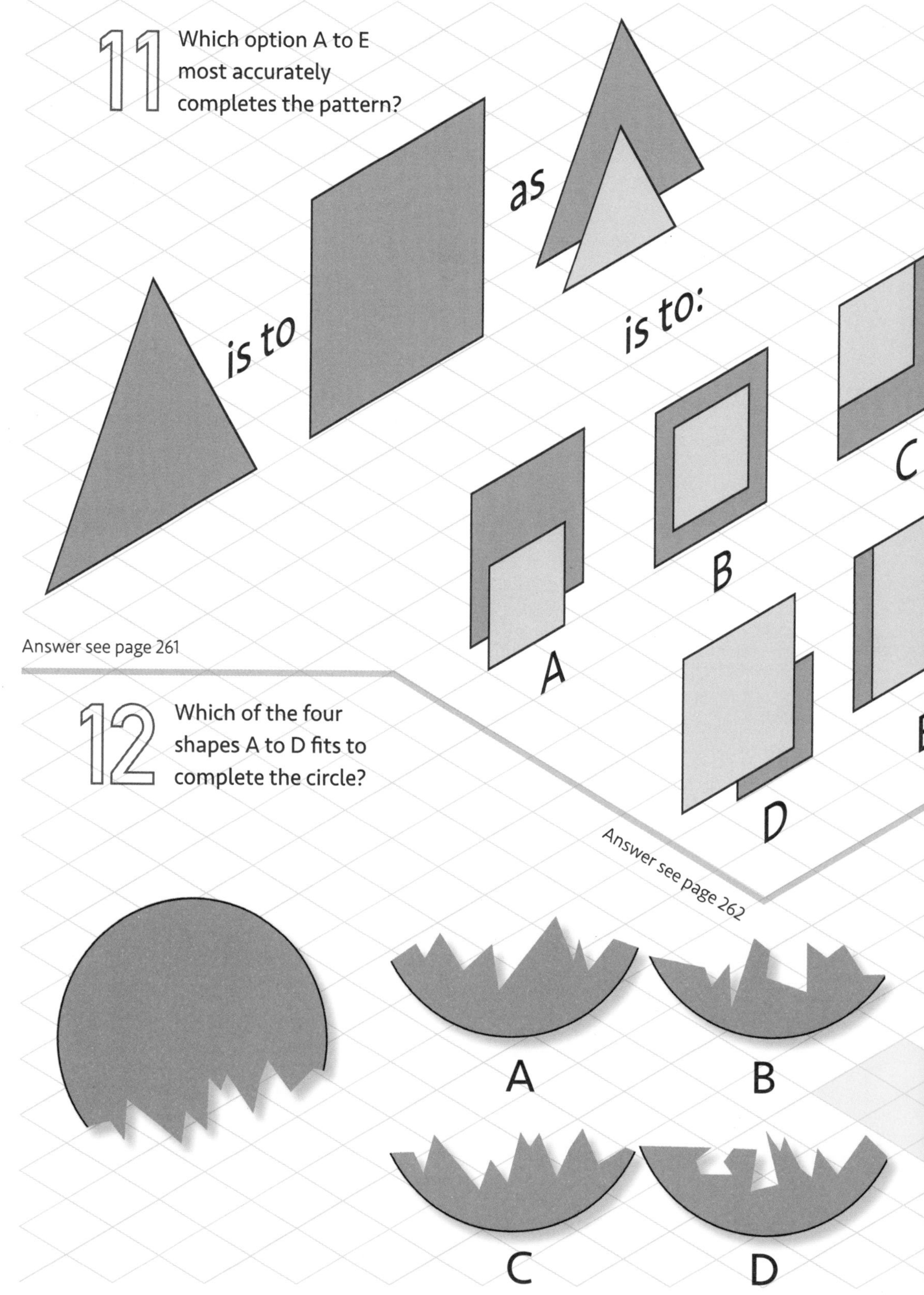

Answer see page 261

12

Which of the four shapes A to D fits to complete the circle?

Answer see page 262

13

Using six straight lines, divide up the field below into six sections, each containing seven stars of assorted sizes. Five of the six lines touch at least one border.

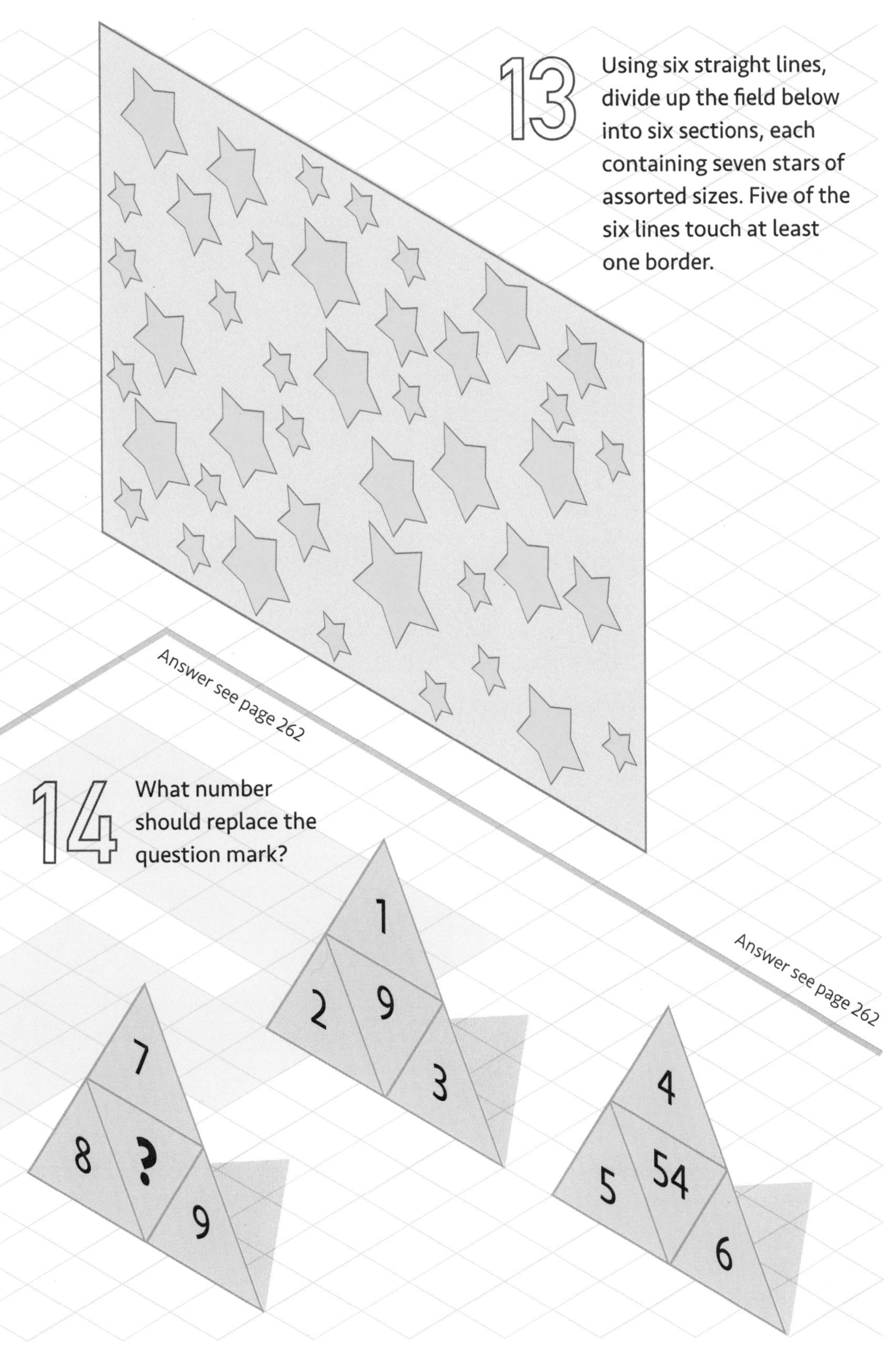

Answer see page 262

14

What number should replace the question mark?

Answer see page 262

15

In the grid below, how much is each symbol worth?

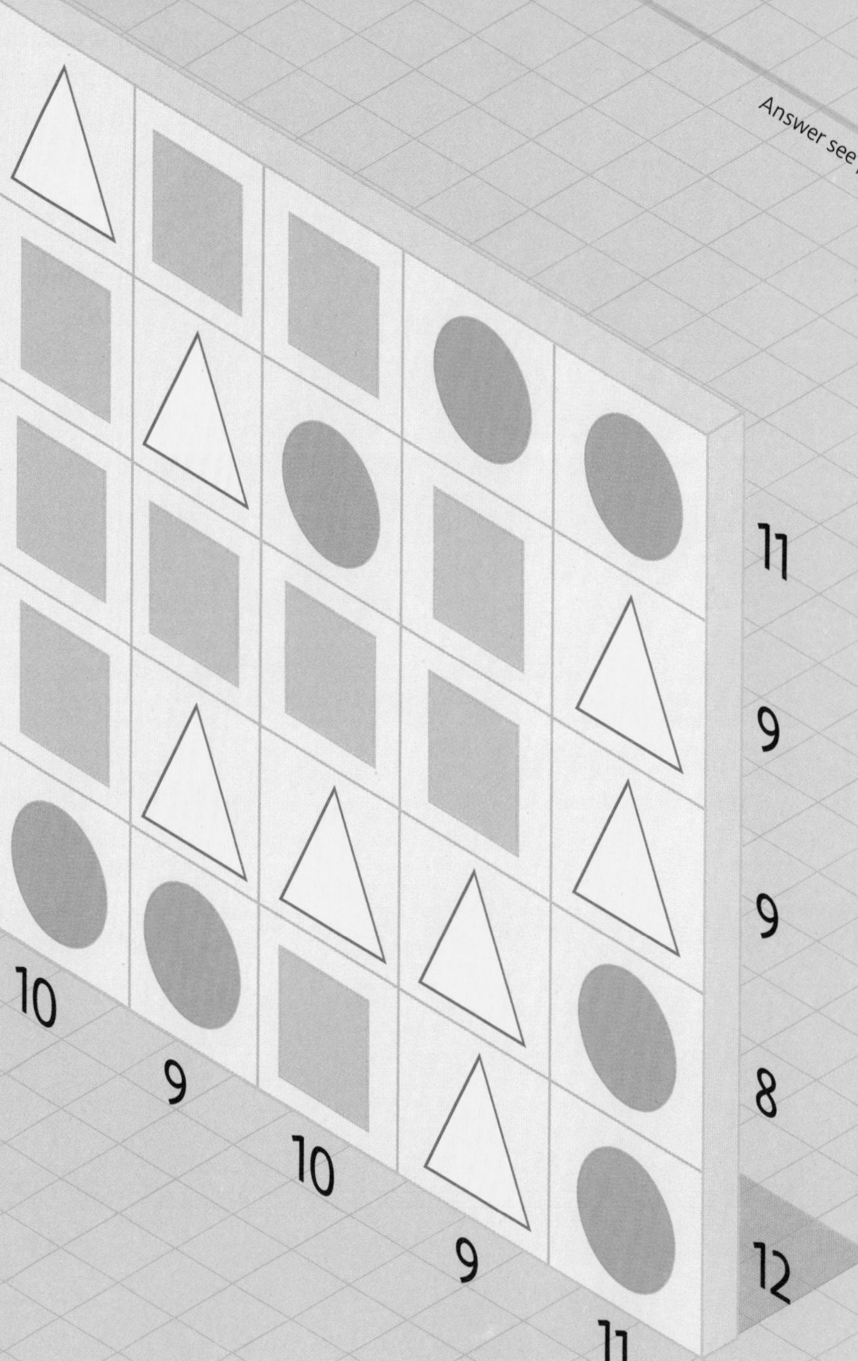

Answer see page 262

16

What number should replace the question mark?

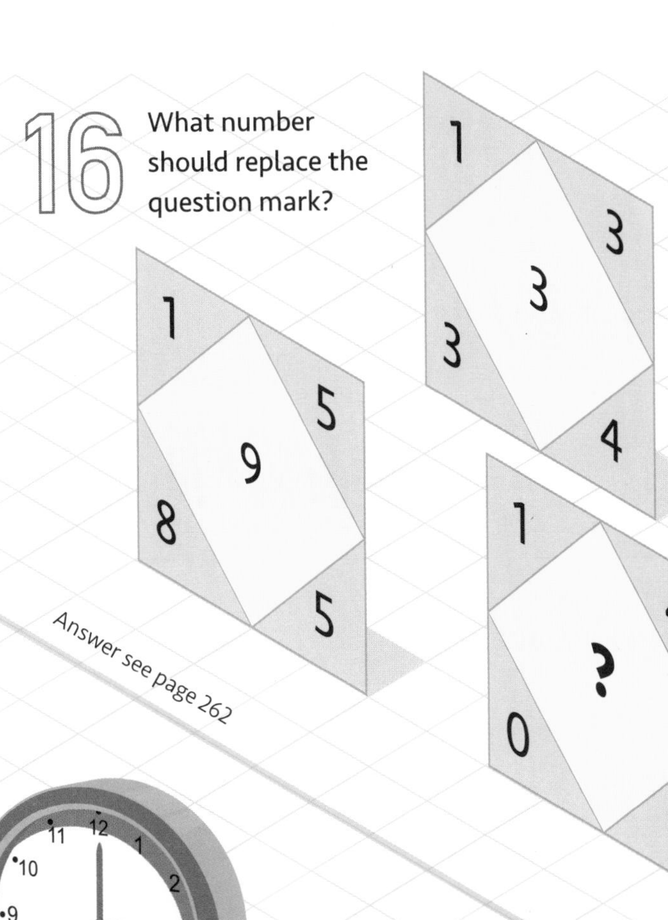
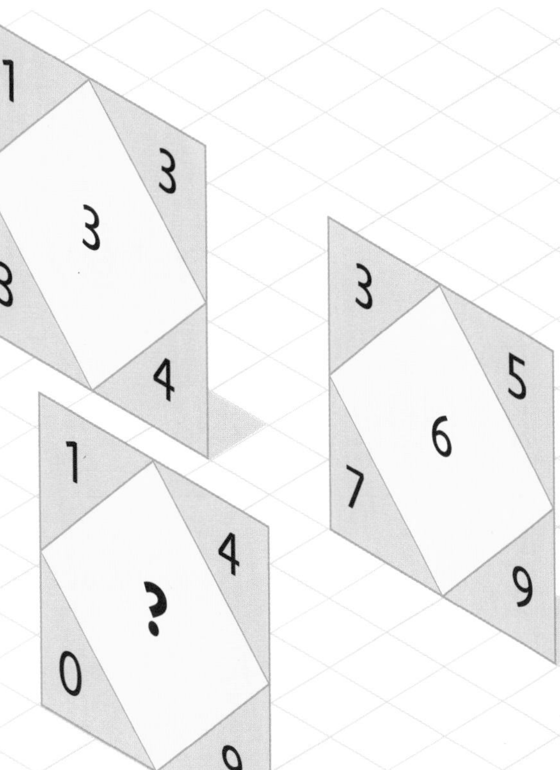

Answer see page 262

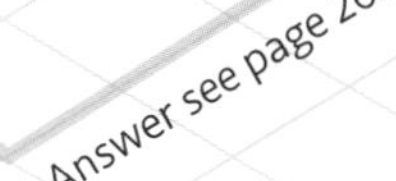

6:00

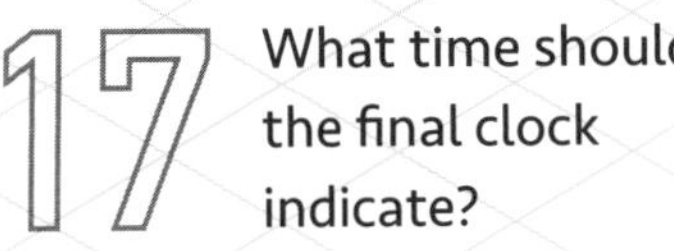

17

What time should the final clock indicate?

9:00

18

Combine the segments below to find the names of ten celebrities.

FREY	OCK	KOBE	STE
BRY	DRA	BERG	SPRING
RAH	BULL	OP	BRIT
JAM	JOLIE	WOODS	ER
JENN	VEN	LINA	ANGE
WIN	ANT	ES	SPE
ANIS	NEY	SPIEL	CAM
STEEN	BRUCE	ARS	SAN
ERON	IFER	TIG	TON

Answer see page 262

Answer see page 262

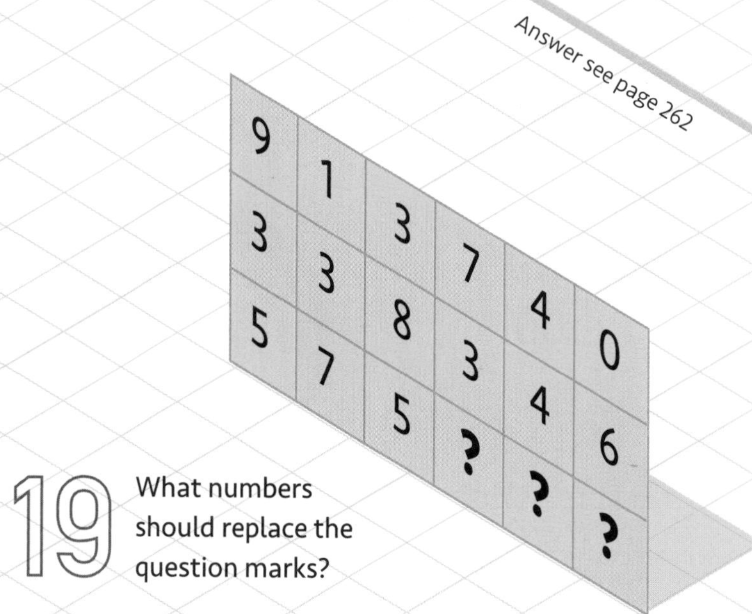

19

What numbers should replace the question marks?

20

Which symbols are missing from the blue squares in the grid below?

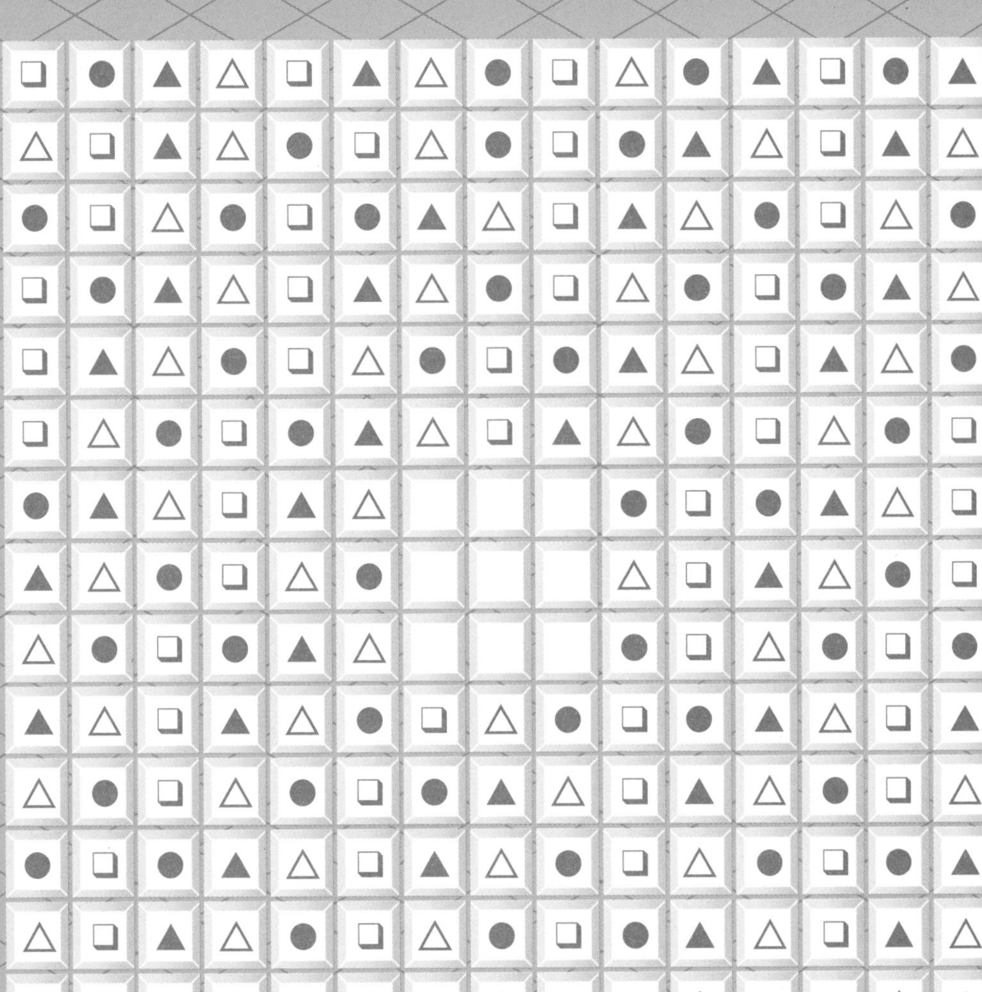

Answer see page 262

Test 3

01

Which of the pentagons at the bottom should replace the question mark?

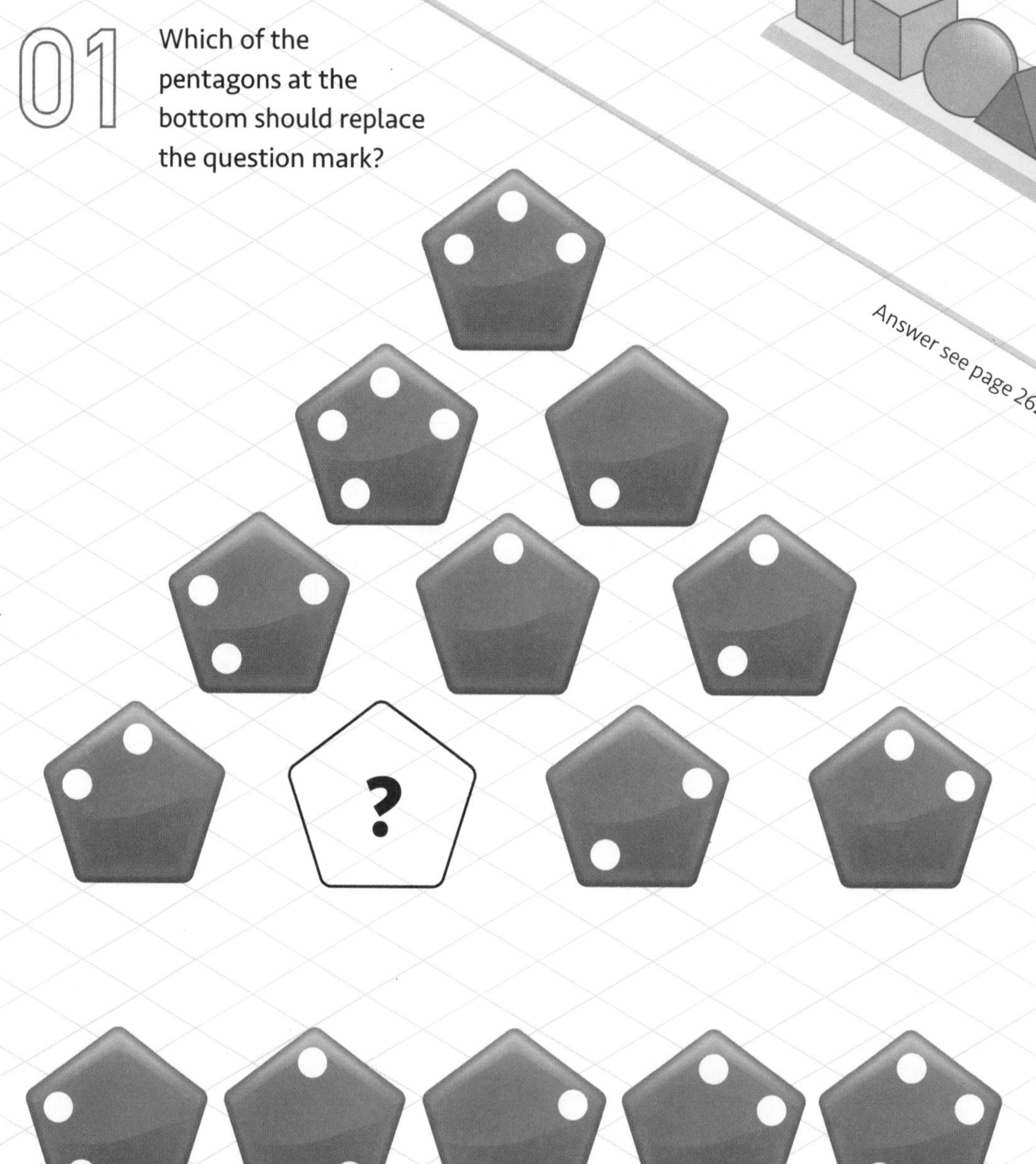

Answer see page 262

02

Scales 1 and 2 are in perfect balance. How many circles are needed to balance scale 3?

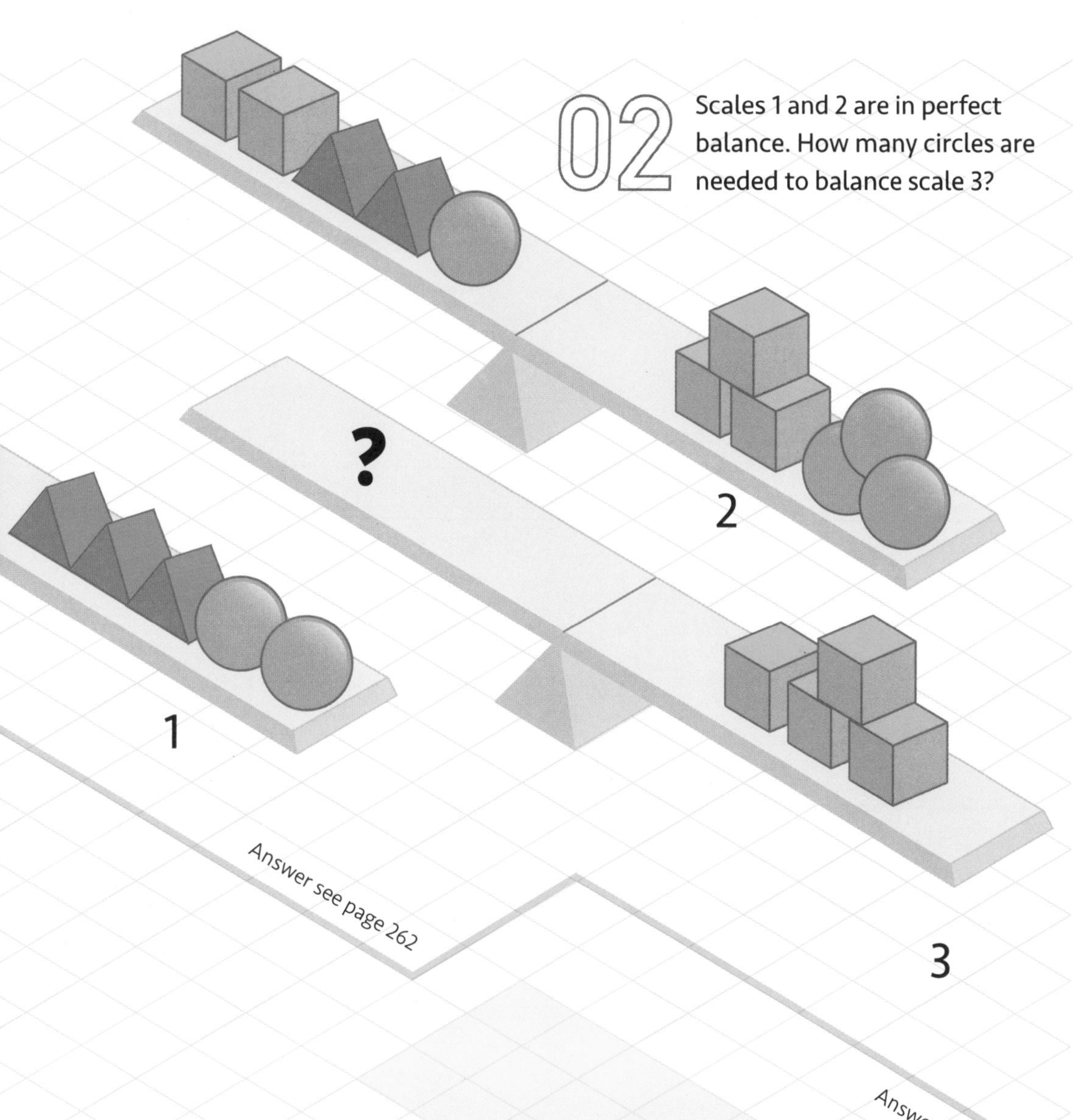

Answer see page 262

Answer see page 262

03

If ⅓ is 7, how much is 5?

04

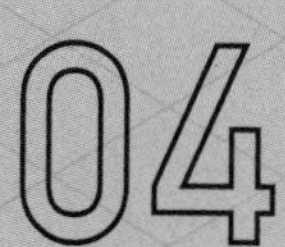

Which shape below can be put with the one above to form a perfect square?

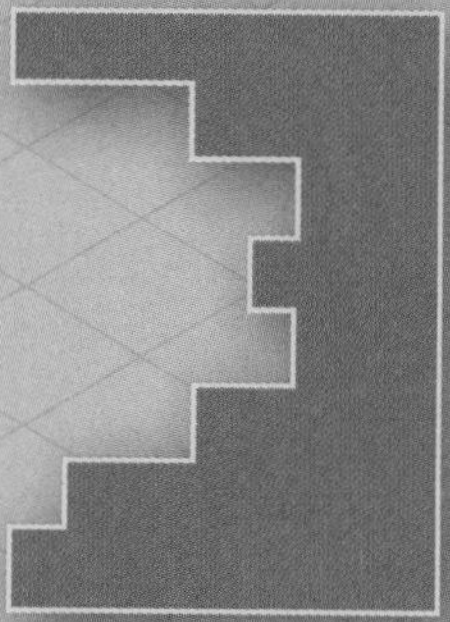

A

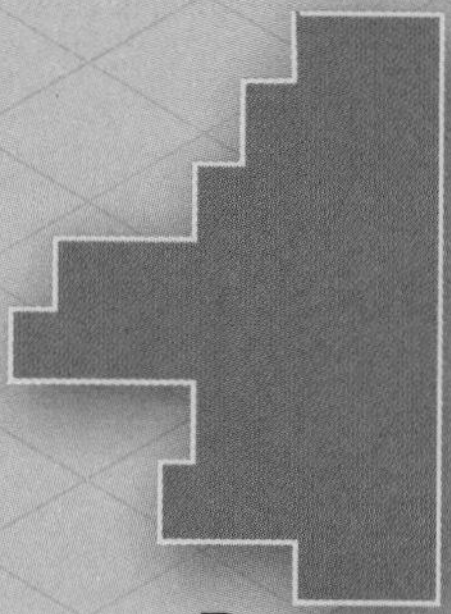

B

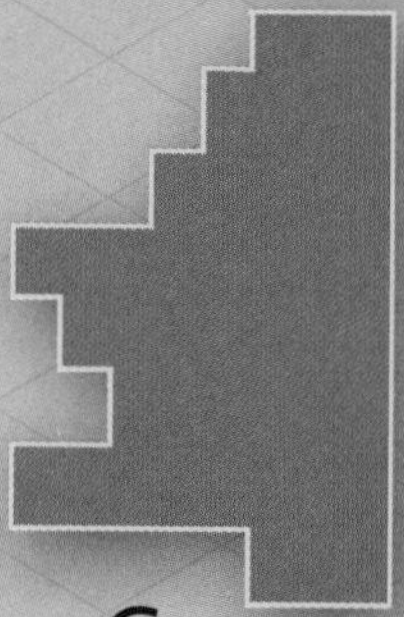

C

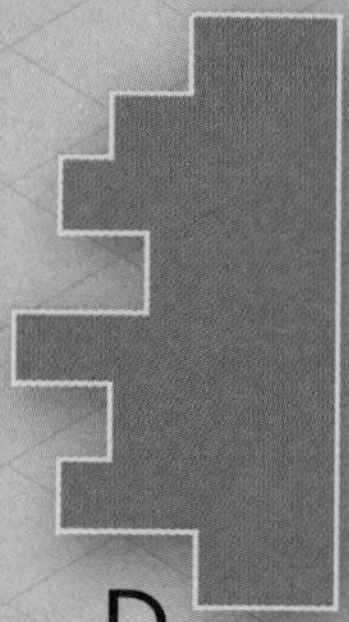

D

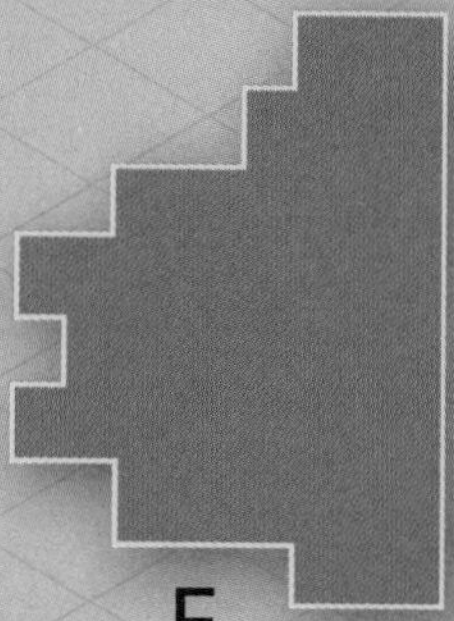

E

Answer see page 262

Select the correct figure from the numbered ones below to replace the question mark.

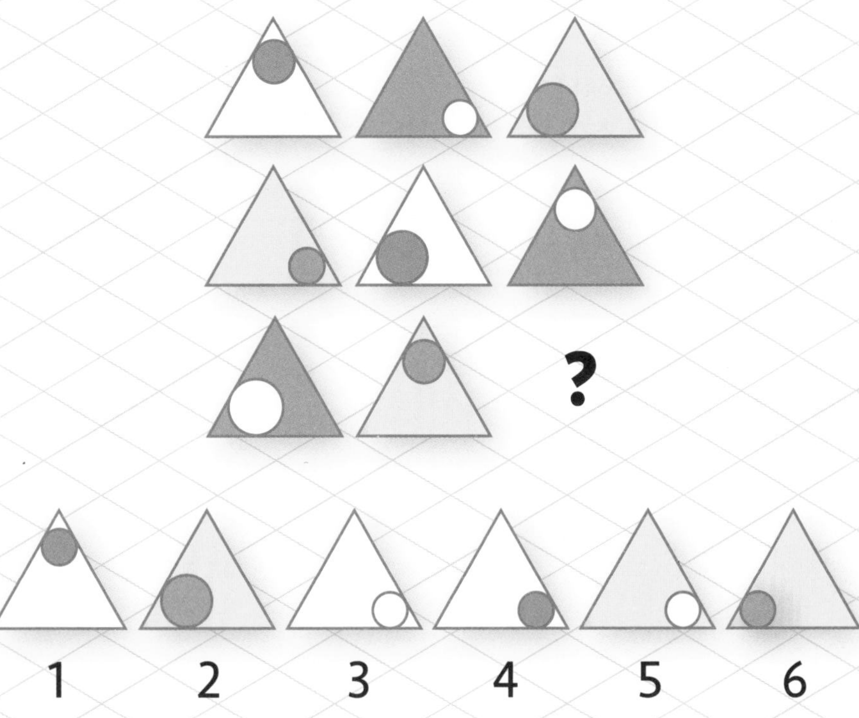

Answer see page 262

Which is the odd one out?

Answer see page 262

07

Each of the nine squares in the grid marked 1A to 3C should incorporate all of the items that are shown in the squares of the same letter and number, at left and top. For example, square 2A should incorporate all of the items in squares 2 and A. One square however, is incorrect. Which is it?

	A	B	C
1	1A	1B	1C
2	2A	2B	2C
3	3A	3B	3C

Answer see page 262

Answer see page 263

08

Complete the square using nine consecutive numbers, so that all rows, columns, and large diagonals add up to the same total.

Which are the odd ones out?

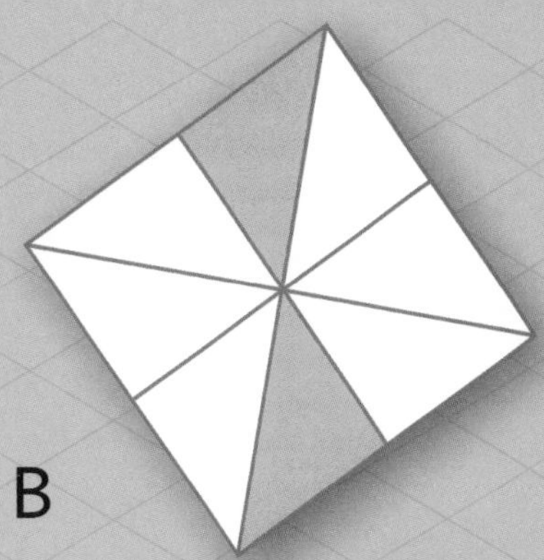

B

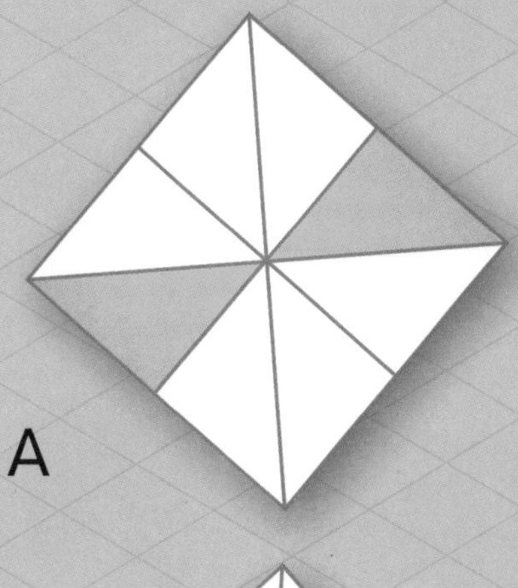

A

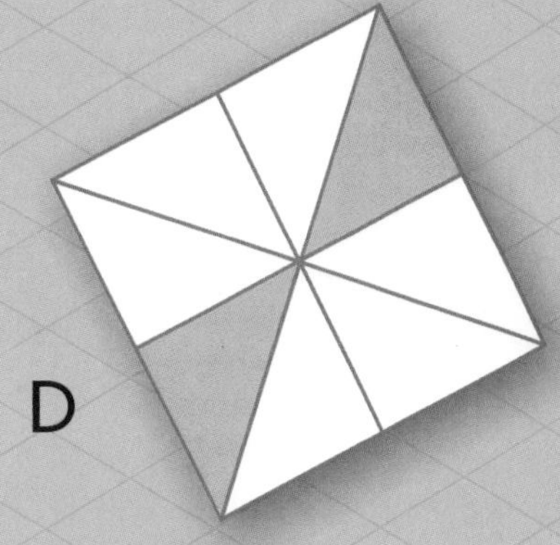

D

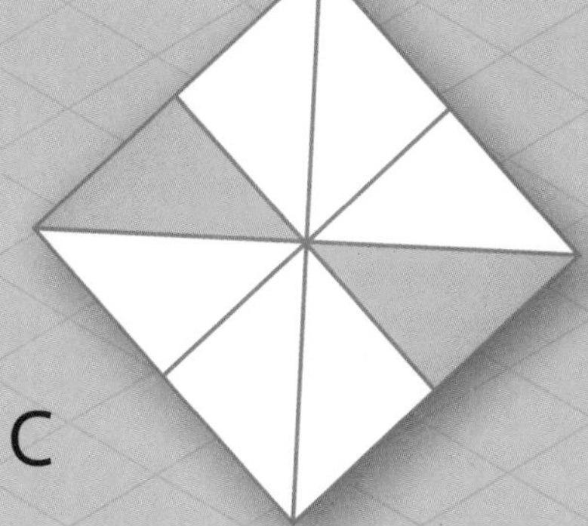

C

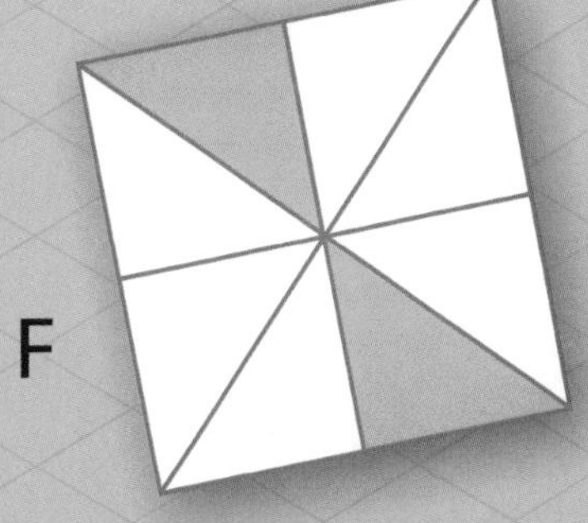

F

E

G

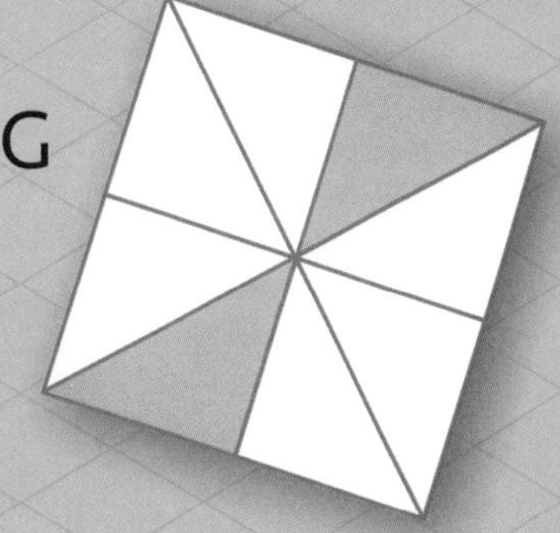

Answer see page 263

10

What number should replace the question mark?

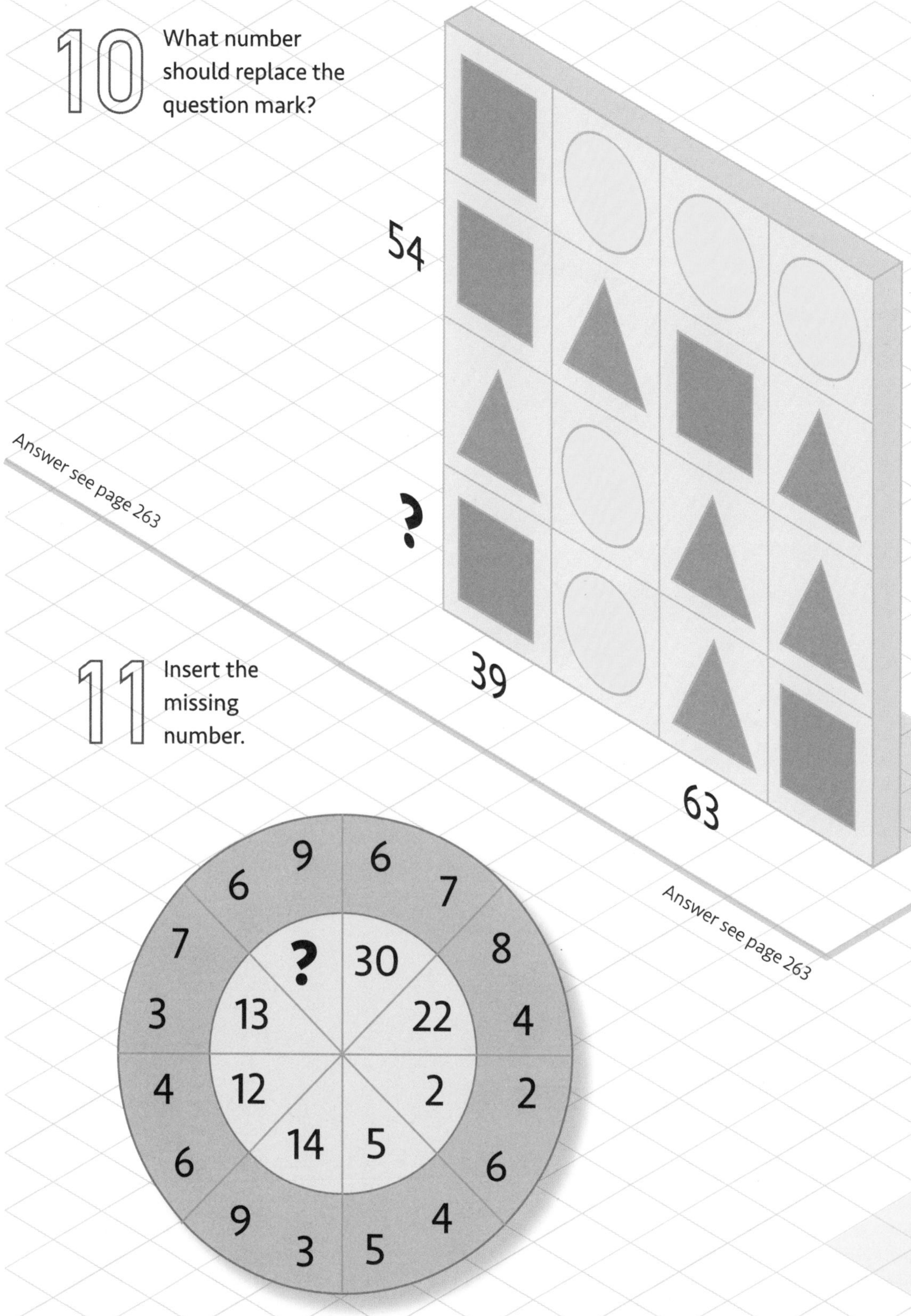

Answer see page 263

11

Insert the missing number.

Answer see page 263

12

Which of the constructed boxes below cannot be made from the given shape?

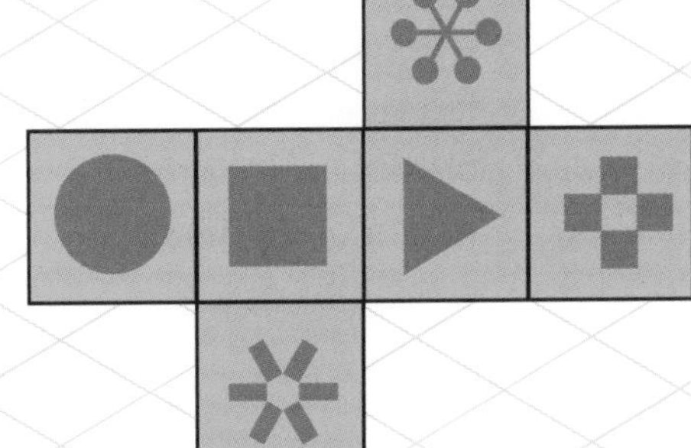

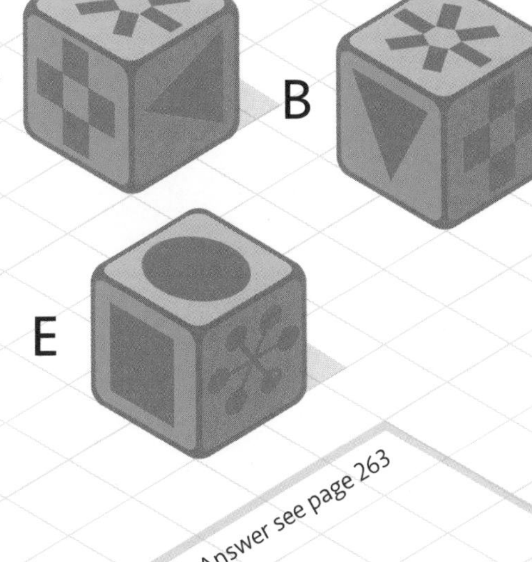

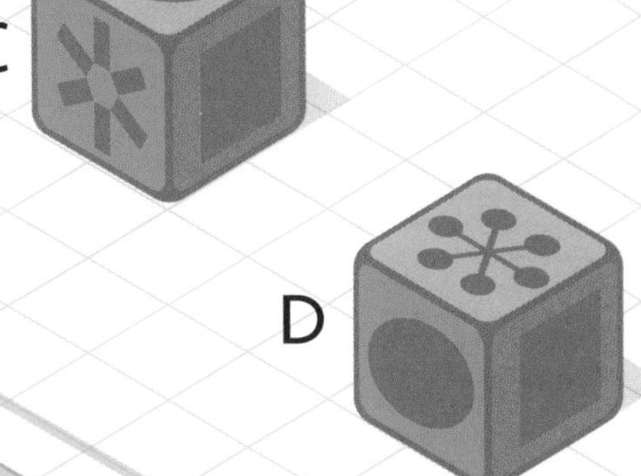

Answer see page 263

13

Which line of two numbers below has the same relationship as the two above?

	752	:	45
A	483	:	56
B	637	:	38
C	495	:	79
D	537	:	32
E	378	:	76

Answer see page 263

14 When complete, this 6 x 6 x 6 cube contains 216 individual blocks. How many blocks are required to complete the cube?

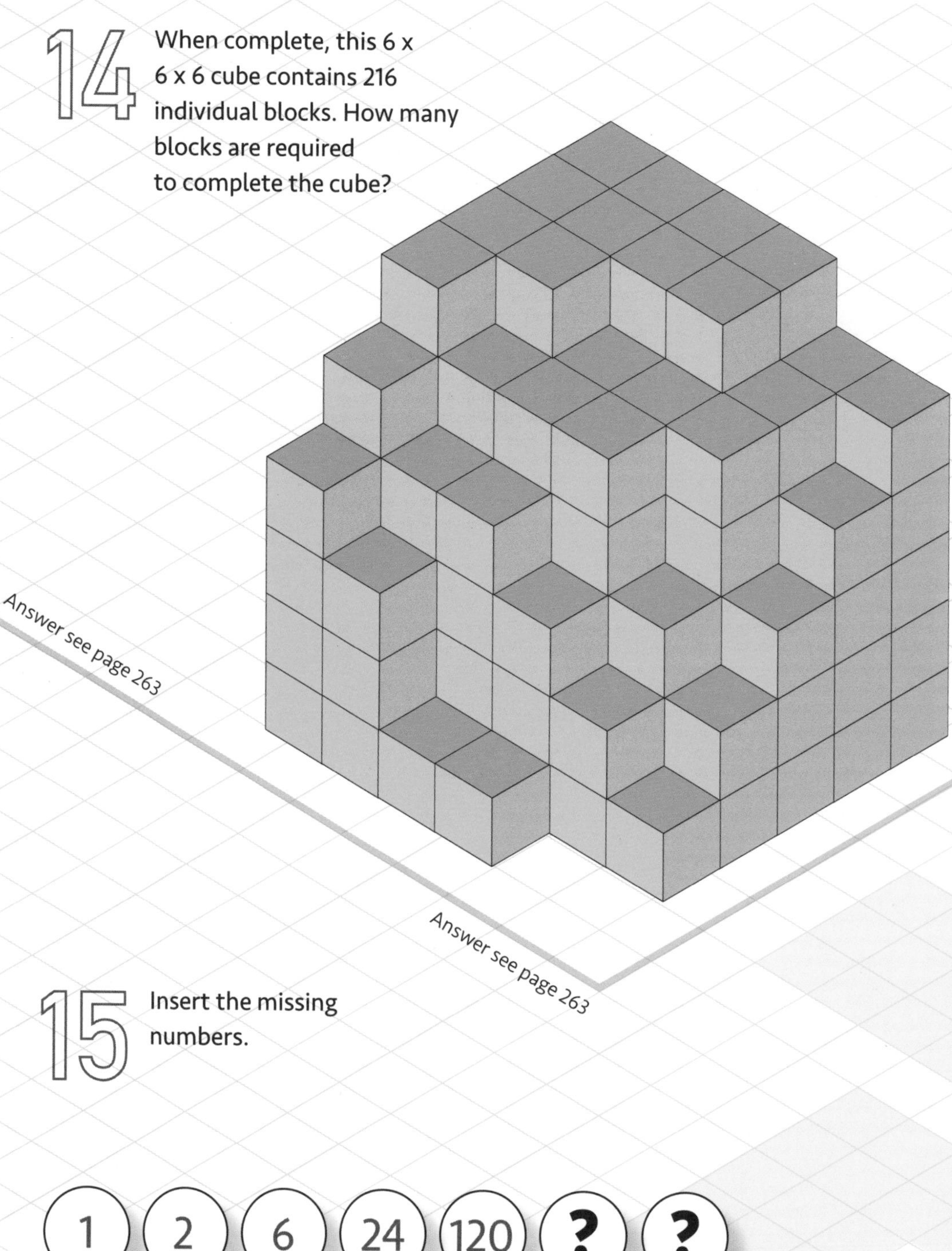

Answer see page 263

Answer see page 263

15 Insert the missing numbers.

1 2 6 24 120 ? ?

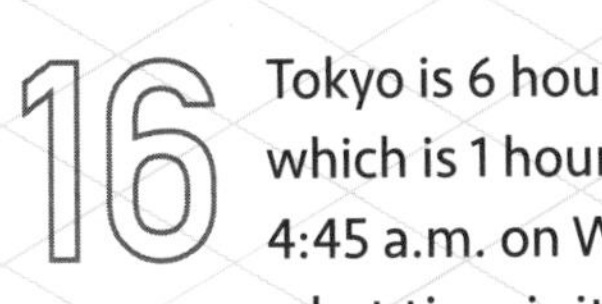

Tokyo is 6 hours ahead of Moscow, which is 1 hour ahead of Cairo. It is 4:45 a.m. on Wednesday in Moscow, what time is it in the other two cities?

Answer see page 263

17

What number should replace the question mark?

2
6 16 3

6
8 26 4

8
5 27 7

Answer see page 263

18

Which of the lettered clocks below continues the numbered series?

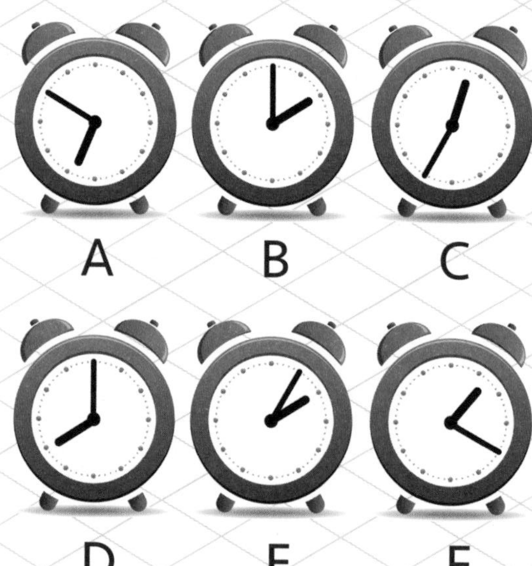

Answer see page 263

Which of these dice is not like the others?

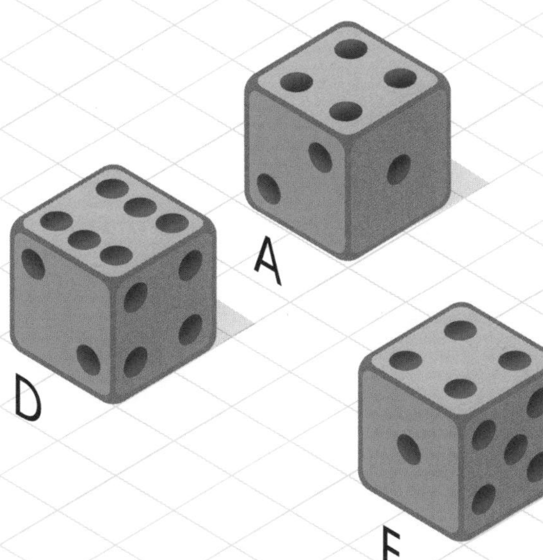

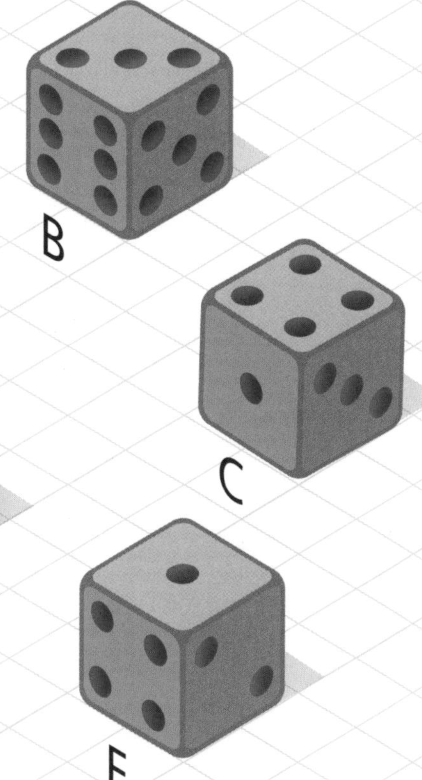

Answer see page 263

20

Which number is the odd one out?

A	8	7	6	4	3	2
B	7	1	7	6	4	3
C	7	6	5	3	2	1
D	9	6	5	4	3	2

Answer see page 263

Test 4

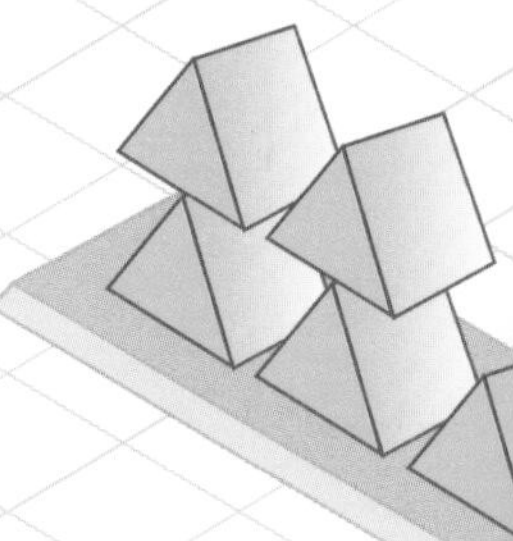

01

Which option A to E most accurately completes the pattern?

Answer see page 263

is to

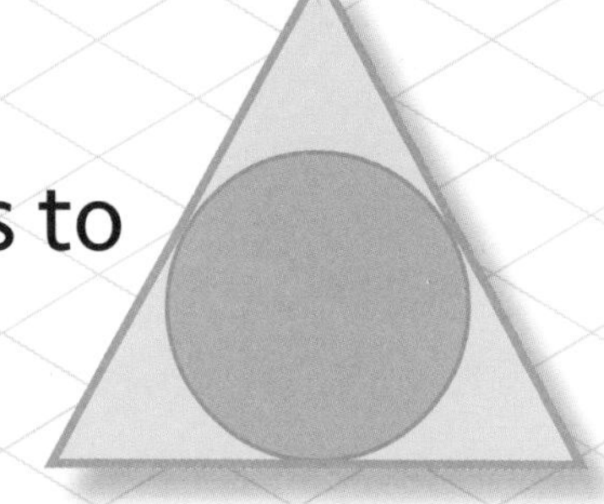

as

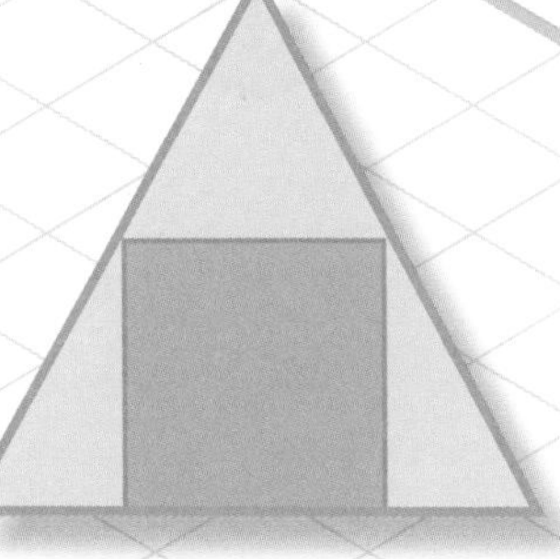

is to:

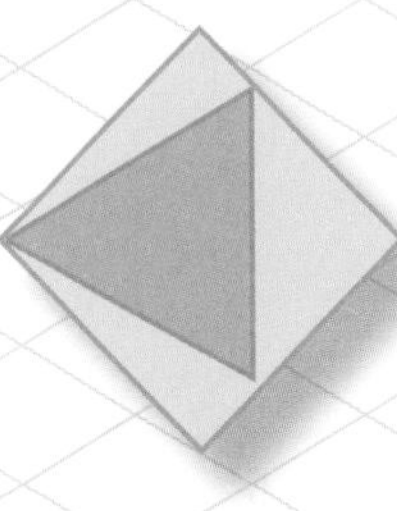

A

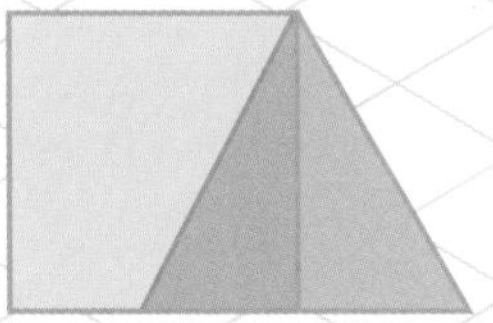

B

C

D

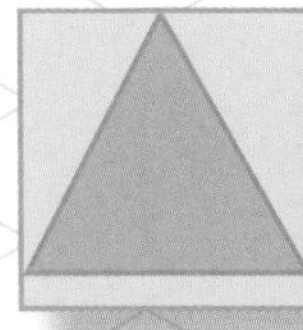

E

02

How many [cube] are required to balance the final scale?

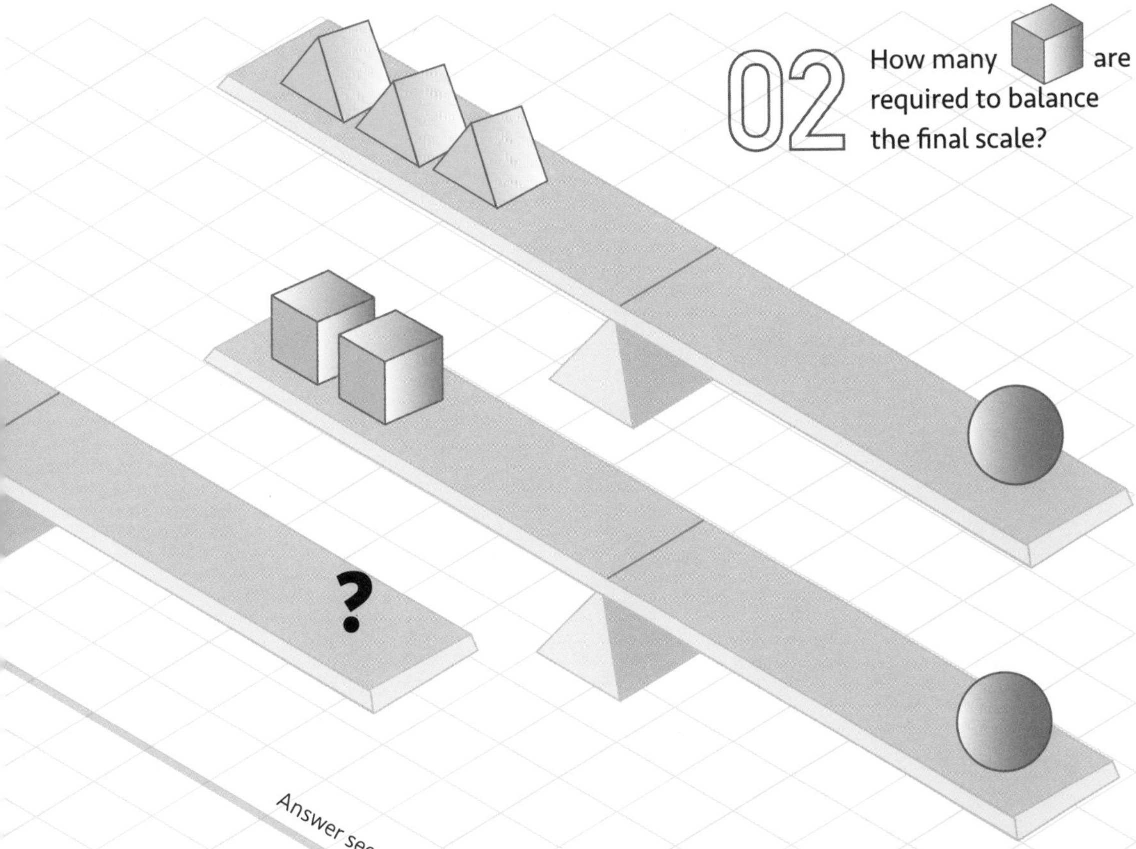

?

Answer see page 263

Answer see page 263

03

What number should replace the question mark?

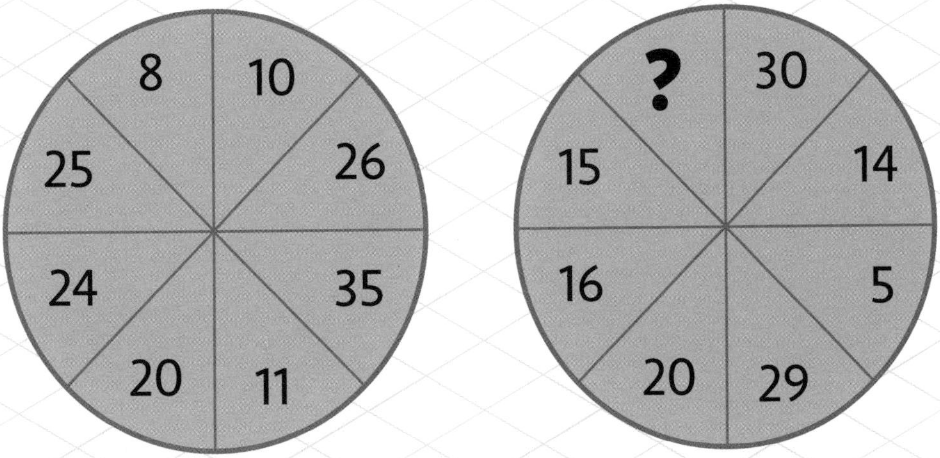

8
10
26
35
11
20
24
25

04

The pieces can be assembled into a regular geometric shape. What is it?

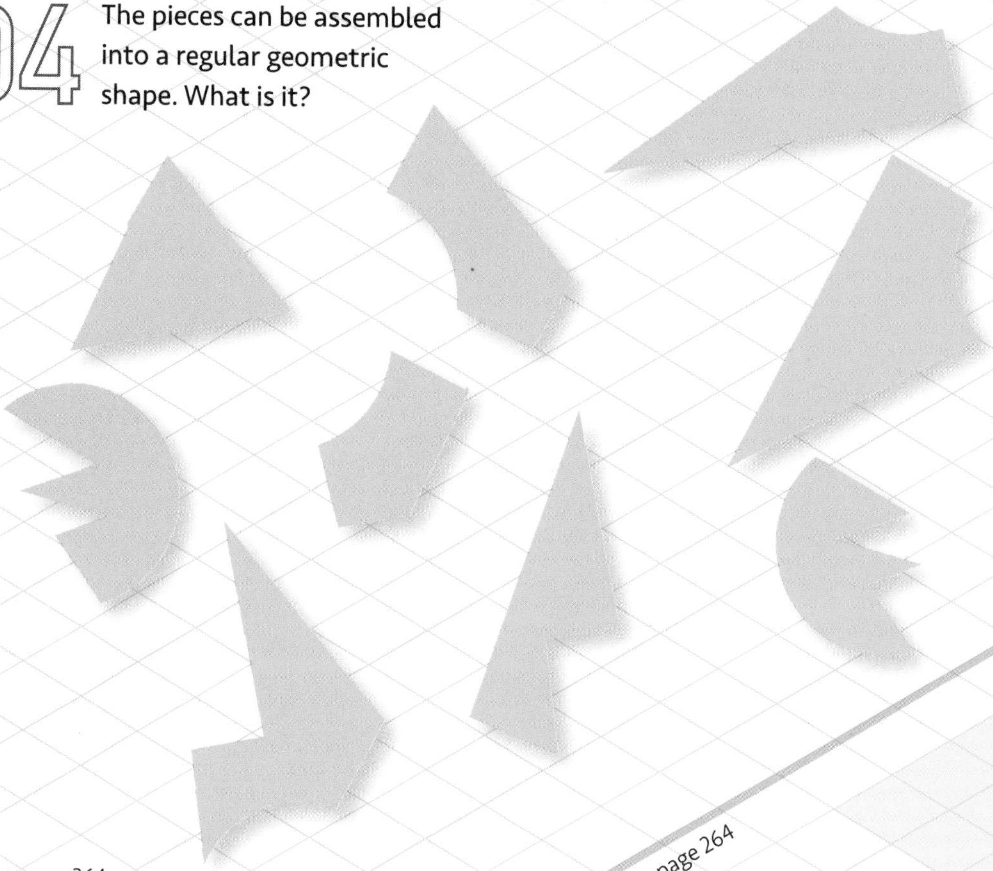

Answer see page 264

Answer see page 264

05

Fill in the missing plus and minus signs to make the equation below correct, performing all calculations strictly in the order they appear on the page.

40 9 5 14 12 32 = 20

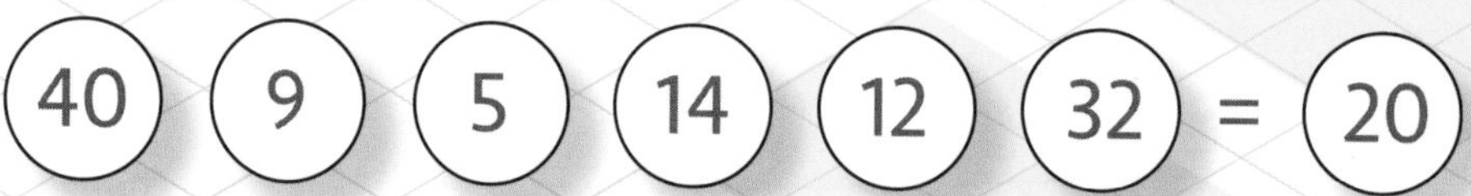

06

Which of the options A to E most accurately continues the sequence?

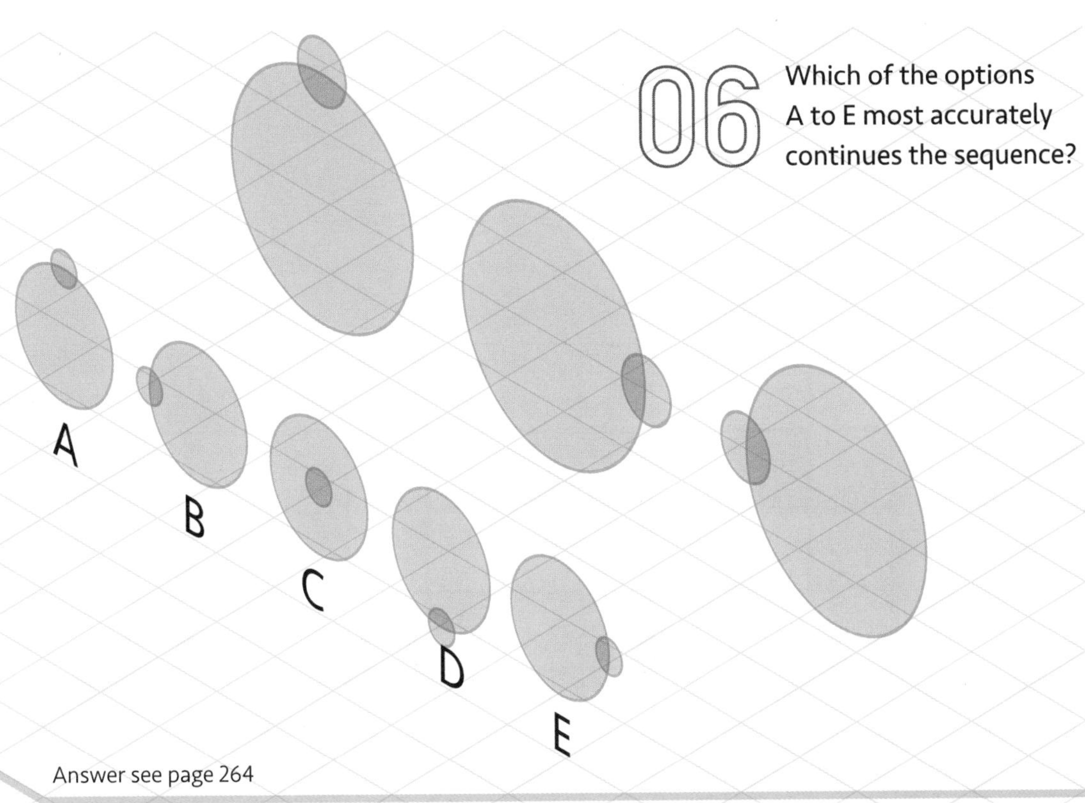

Answer see page 264

Answer see page 264

07

Which of the cubes A to E cannot be made using the layout shown?

A

B

D

C

E

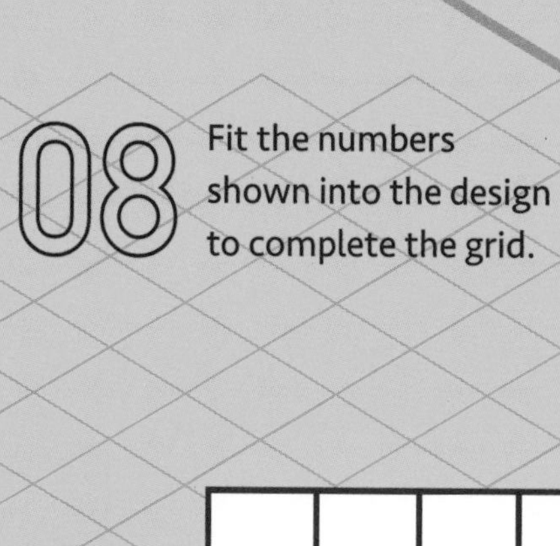

08

Fit the numbers shown into the design to complete the grid.

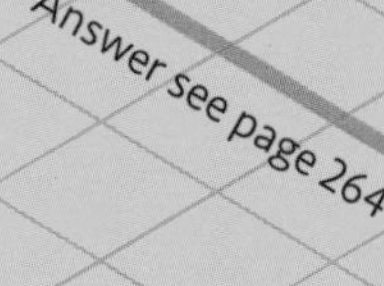

Answer see page 264

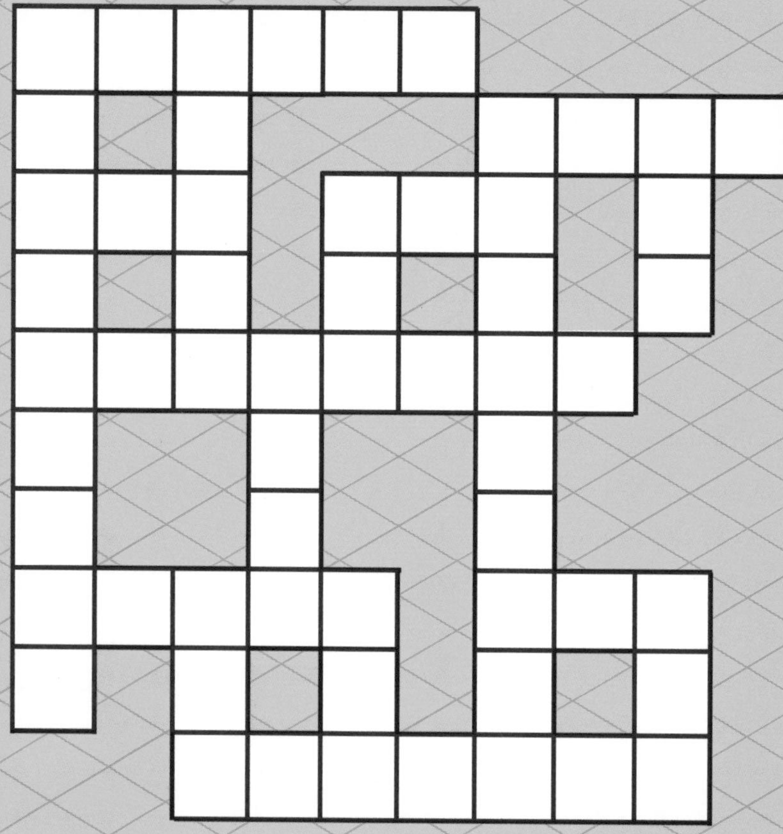

3 digits	4 digits	5 digits	6 digits	7 digits	8 digits	9 digits
107	6721	65513	476467	3044957	26165316	475327161
225	9066	67791				950199739
265						
394						
503						
597						
662						
731						

09

What number should replace the question mark?

2 8 18 32 50 72 ?

Answer see page 264

Answer see page 264

10

In each square, the arrow shows the direction you must move in. The numbers in some squares show that square's position in the correct sequence of moves. Move from top left to bottom right, visiting each square in the grid exactly once.

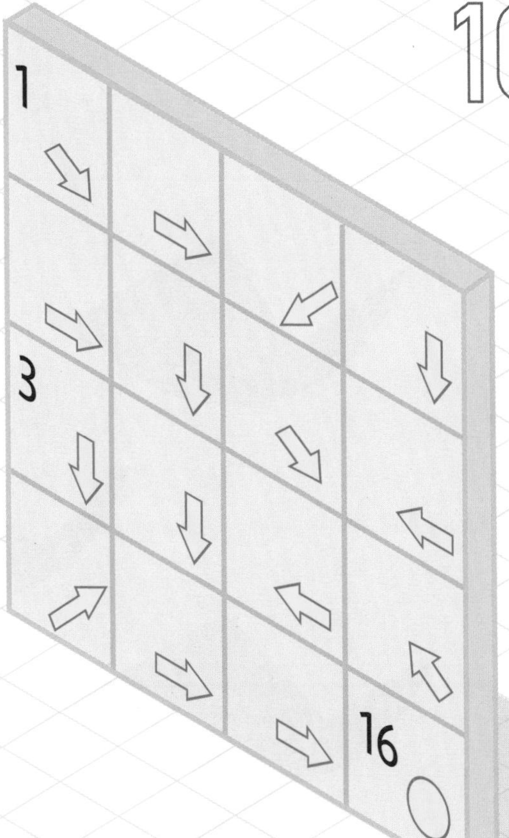

11

Which of the designs A to E is the odd one out?

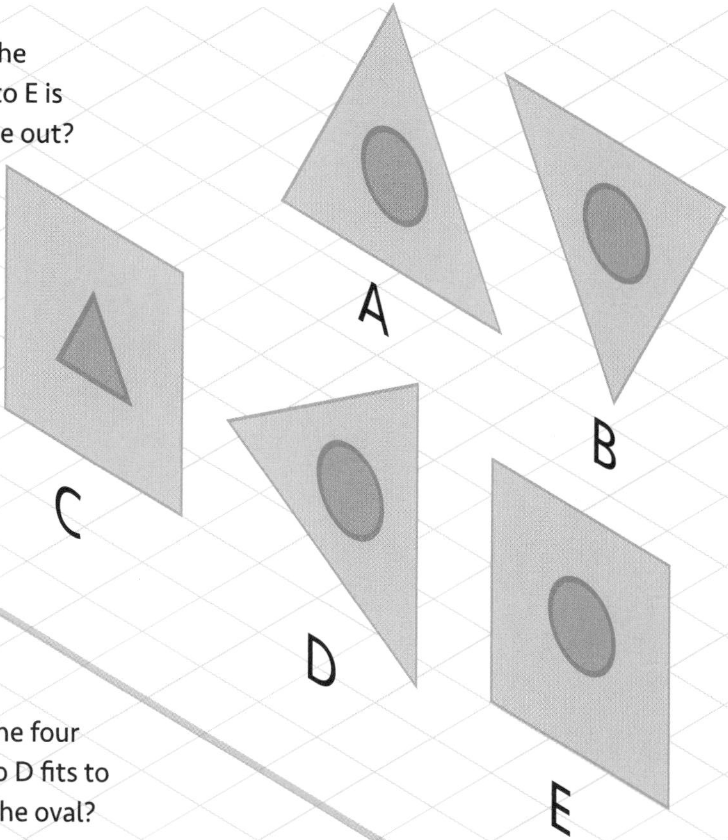

A

B

C

D

E

Answer see page 264

12

Which of the four shapes A to D fits to complete the oval?

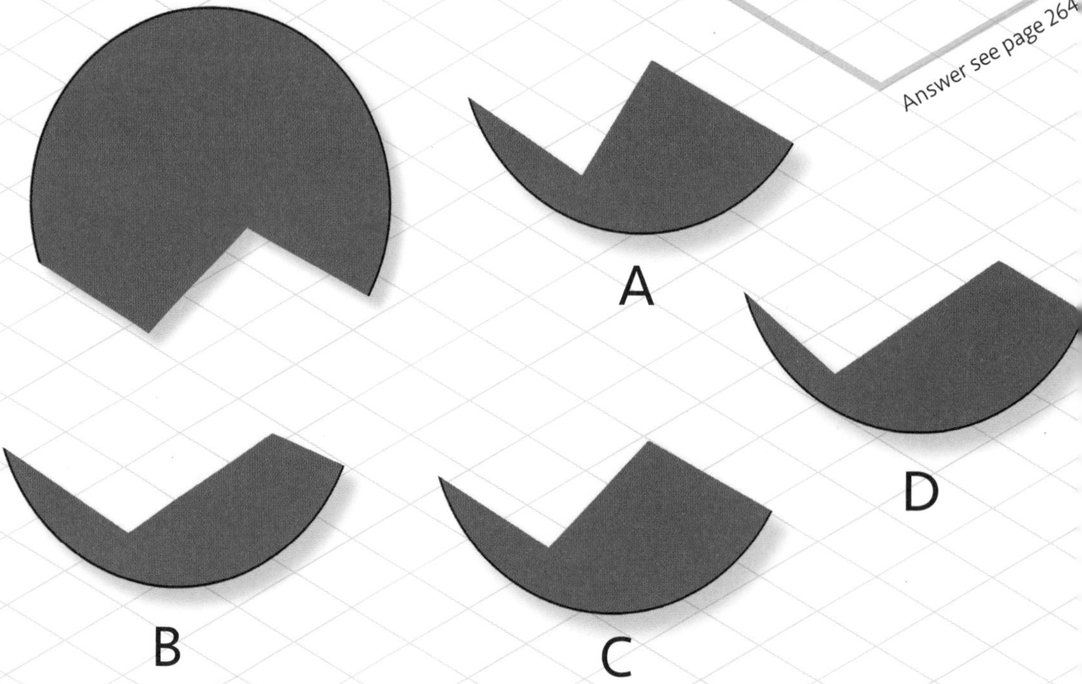

A

B

C

D

Answer see page 264

13

Use six straight lines, each touching the border, to divide the field below into six sections containing 3, 4, 5, 6, 7 and 8 circles.

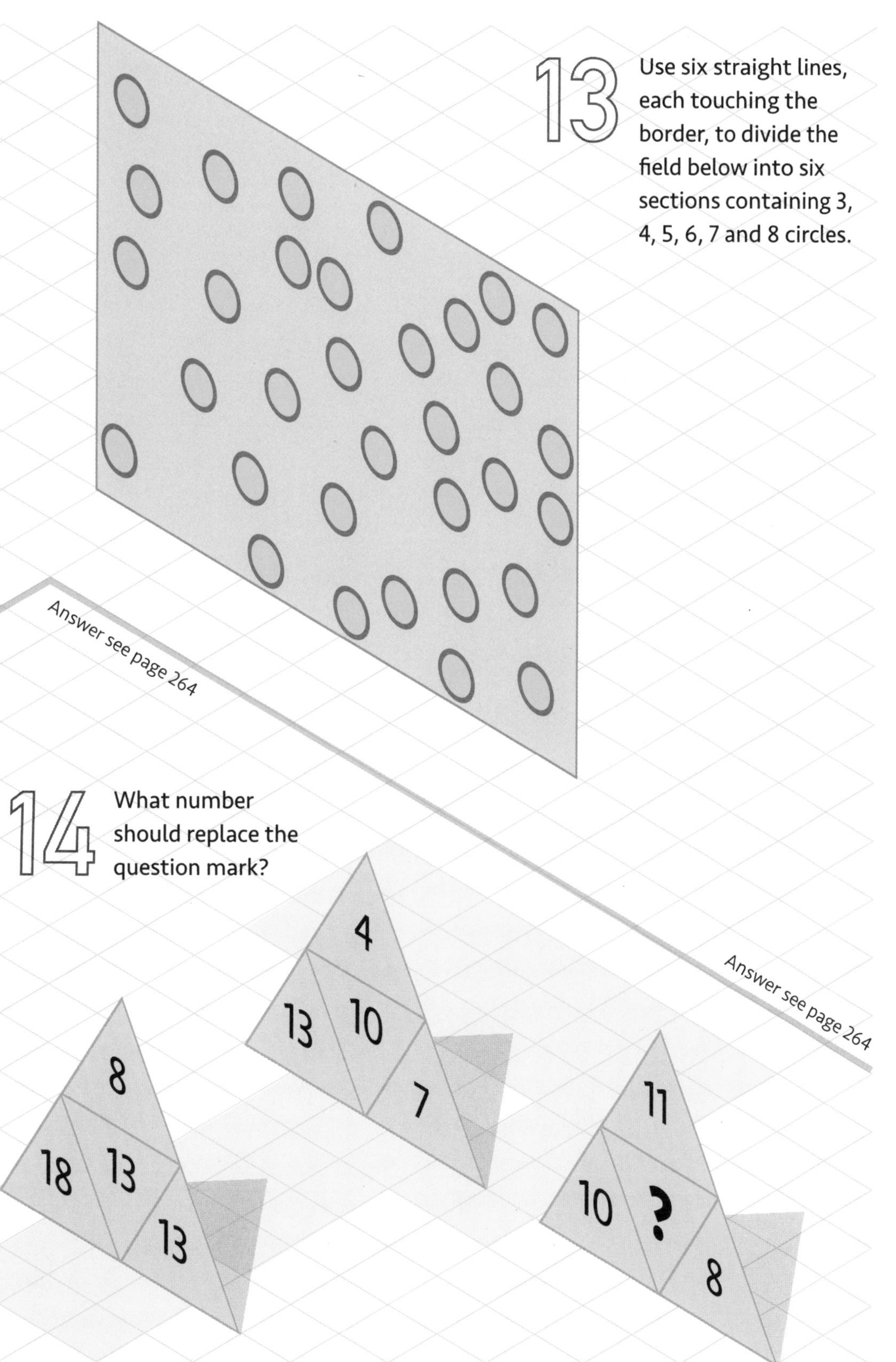

Answer see page 264

14

What number should replace the question mark?

Answer see page 264

15 In the grid below, how much is each symbol worth?

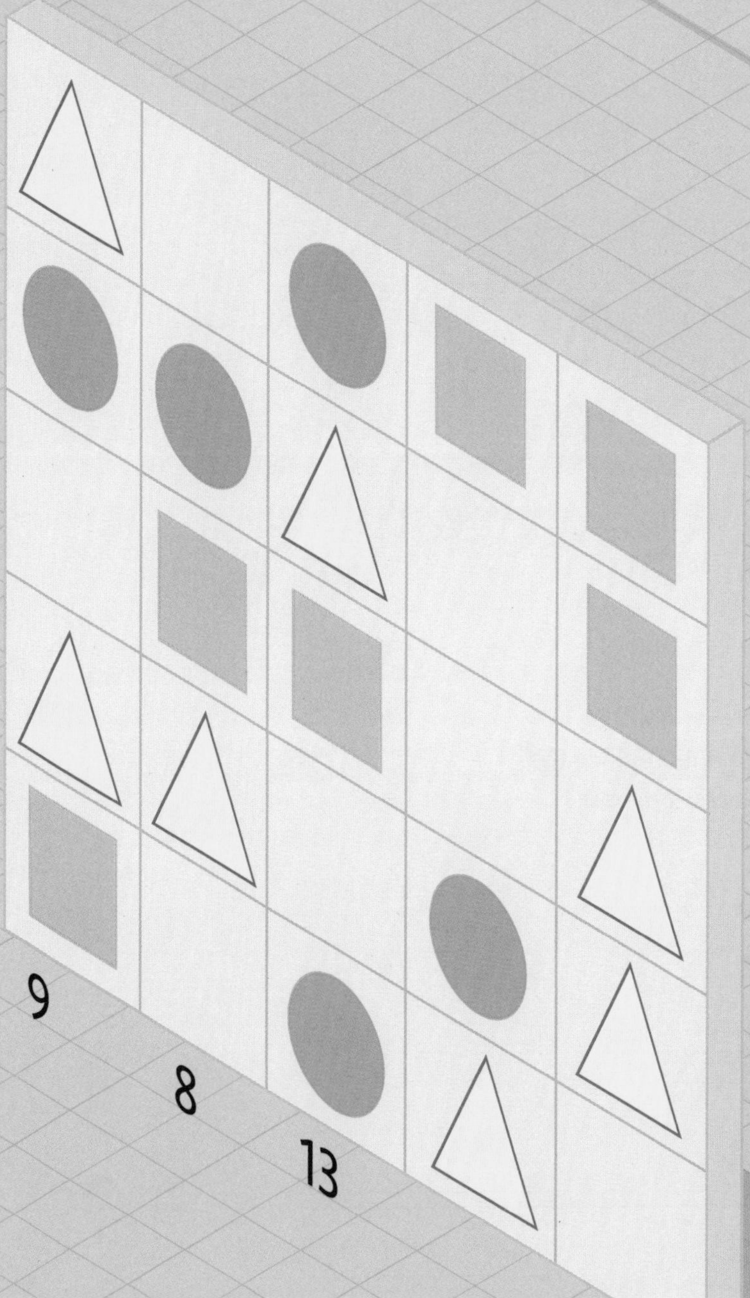

Answer see page 264

16

What number should replace the question mark?

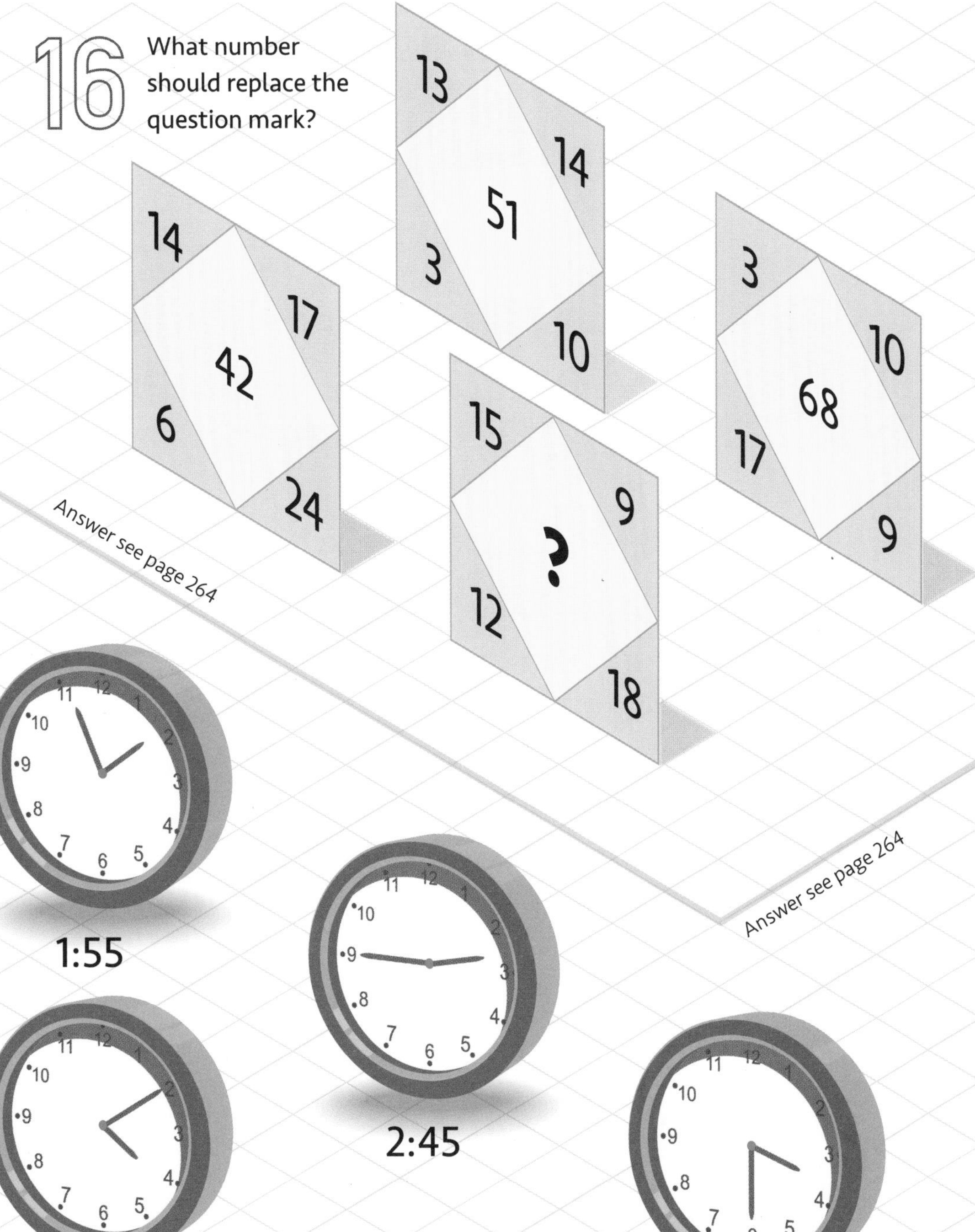

Answer see page 264

17

What time would the next clock indicate?

Answer see page 264

Combine the segments below to find the names of ten celebrities.

FREE
LAB
RRY
BE
JONES
SHIA
BRAN
JOHN
NY

GAN
HALLE
MOR
MAN
CUL
LIE
MACAU
EARL
LAY

LIN
MAR
EOUF
LON
CHAR
MAN
JOHN
CHAP
VOLTA

JACK
JAMES
TRA
HUGH
DEPP
DO
KIN

Answer see page 264

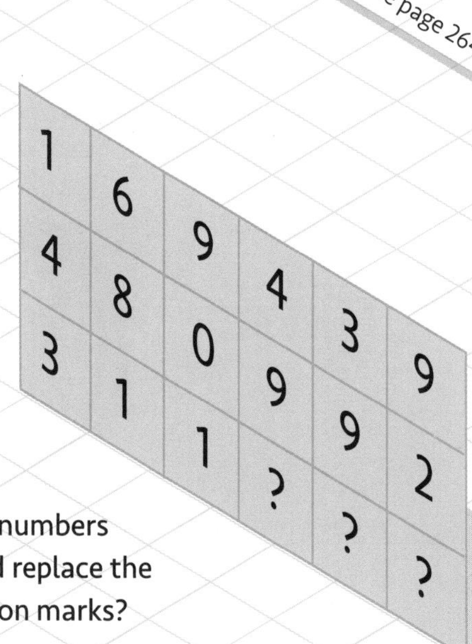

19

What numbers should replace the question marks?

Answer see page 264

20

Which symbols are missing from the grid below?

Answer see page 264

Test 5

01

Which of the pentagons at the bottom should replace the question mark?

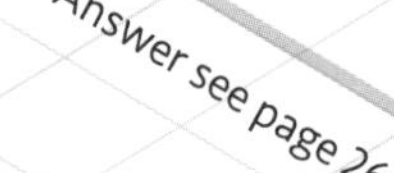
Answer see page 265

02

Scales 1 and 2 are in perfect balance. How many circles are needed to balance scale 3?

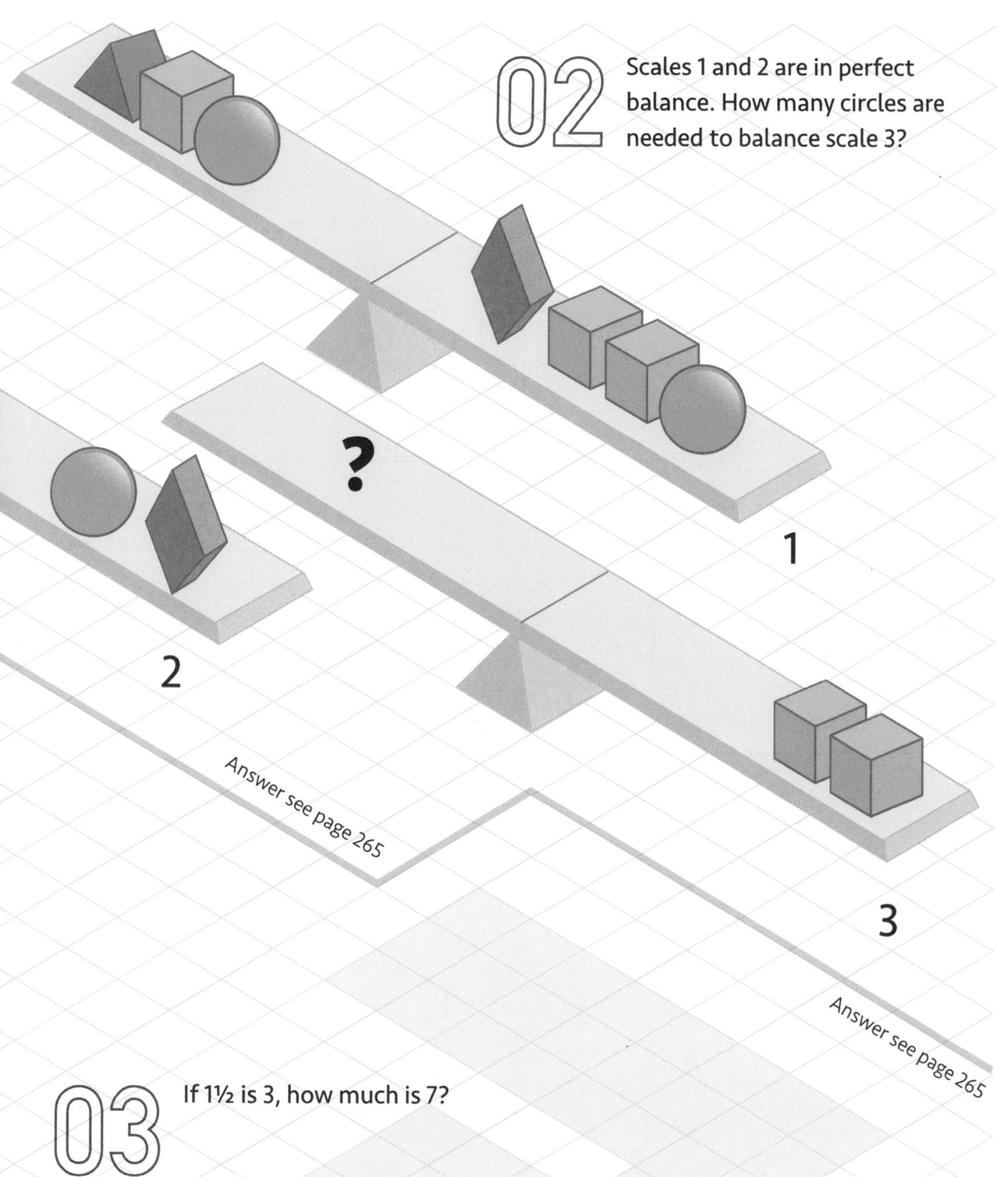

Answer see page 265

03

If 1½ is 3, how much is 7?

Answer see page 265

04

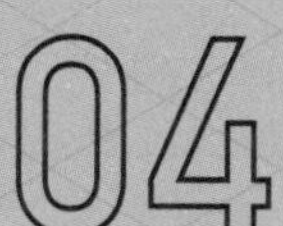

Which shape below can be put with the one above to form a perfect square?

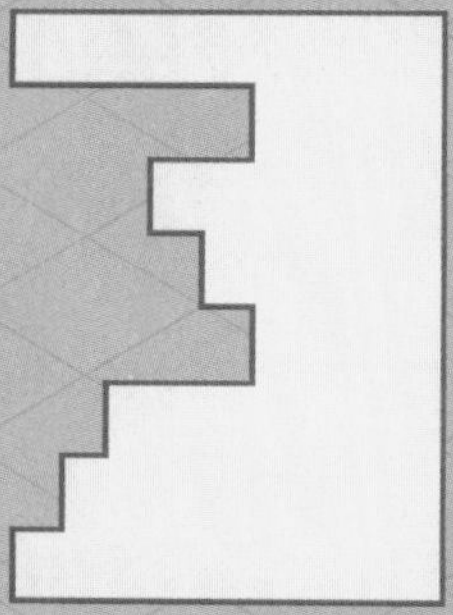

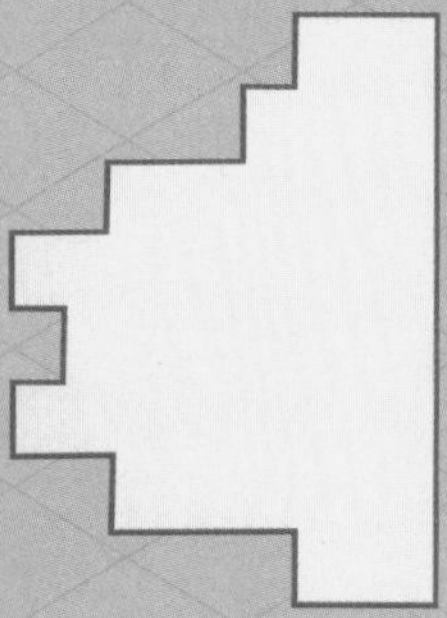

A

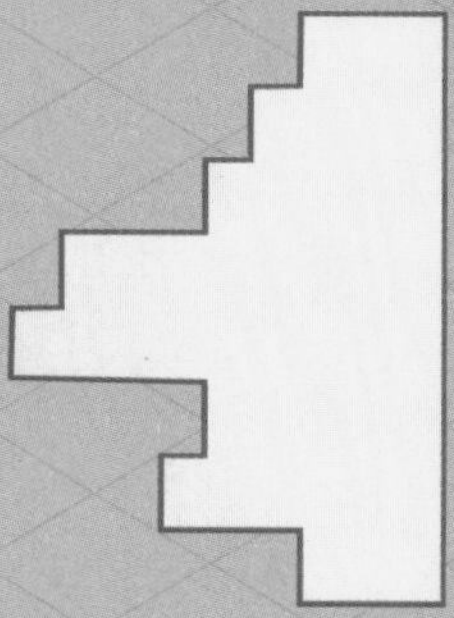

B

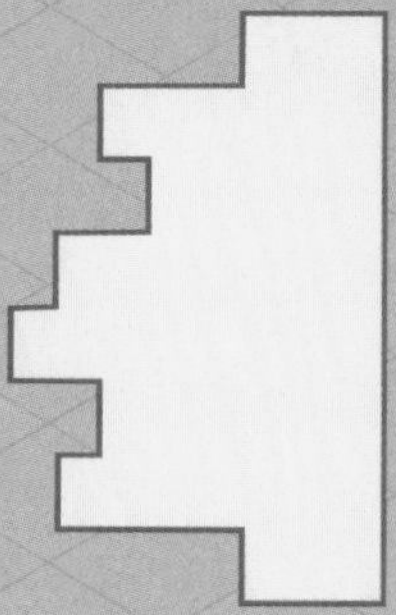

C

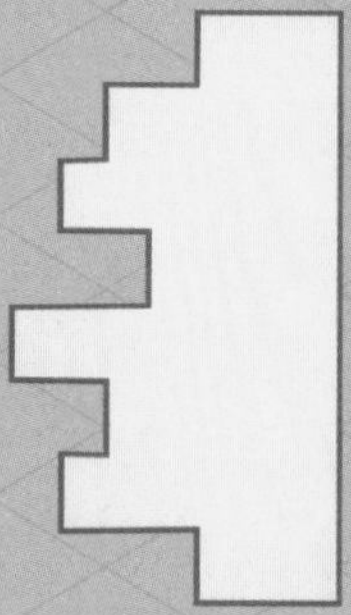

D

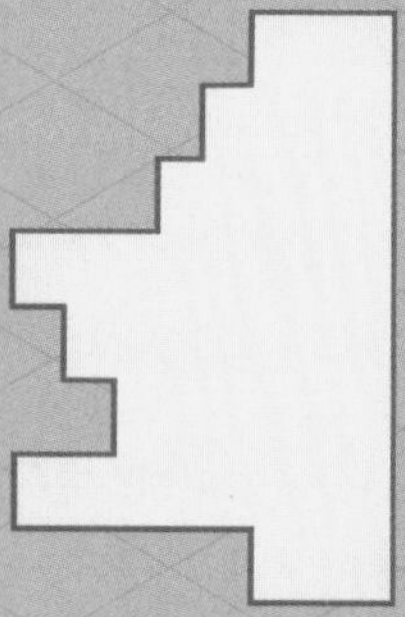

E

Answer see page 265

Select the correct figure from the numbered ones below to replace the question mark.

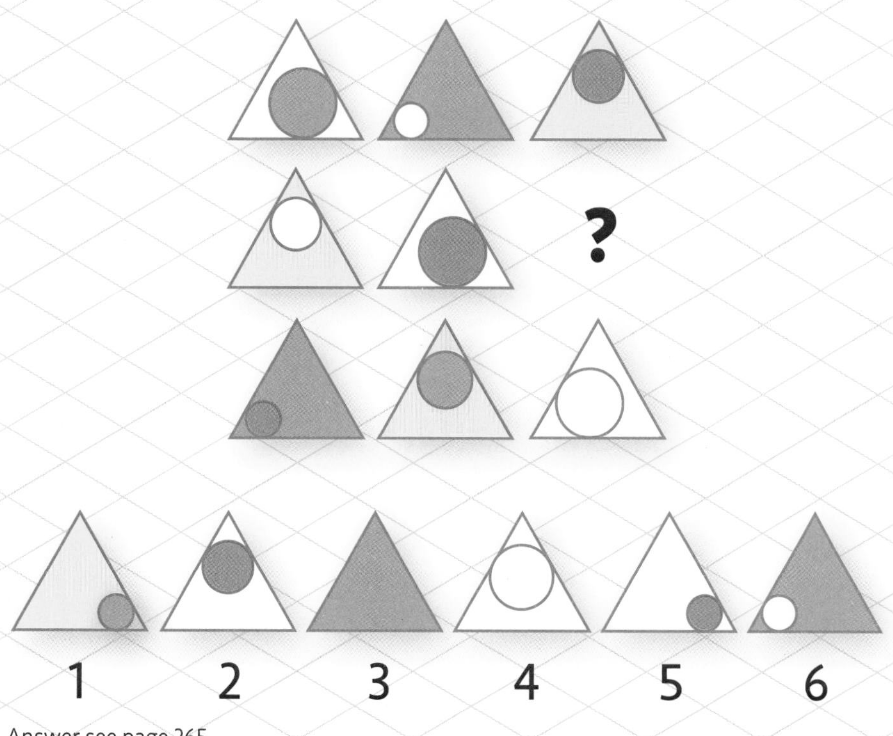

Answer see page 265

Answer see page 265

Complete the square using nine consecutive numbers, so that all rows, columns, and large diagonals add up to the same total.

07

Each of the nine squares in the grid marked 1A to 3C should incorporate all of the items which are shown in the squares of the same letter and number, at left and top. For example, square 2A should incorporate all of the items in squares 2 and A. One square however, is incorrect. Which is it?

	A	B	C
1	1A	1B	1C
2	2A	2B	2C
3	3A	3B	3C

Answer see page 265

Which is the odd one out?

Answer see page 265

Which are the odd ones out?

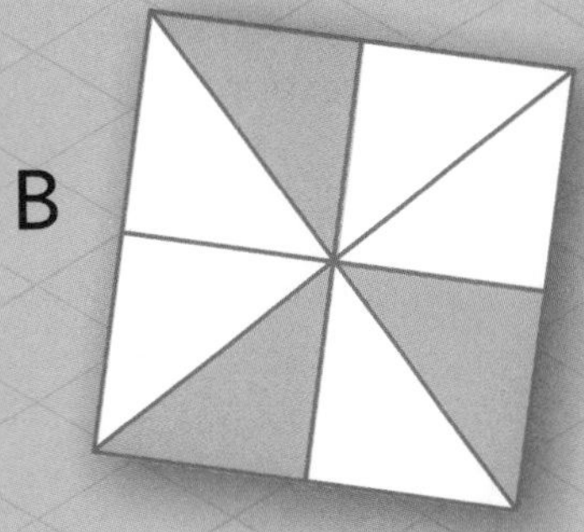

B

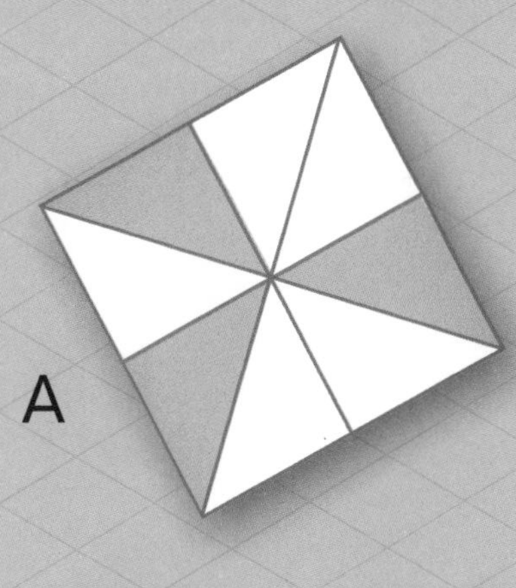

A

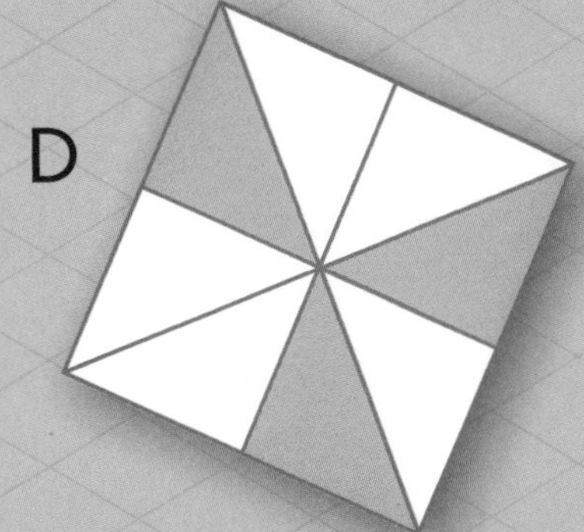

D

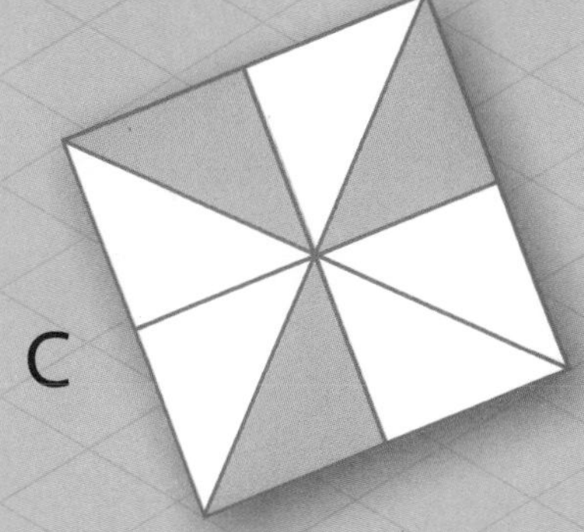

C

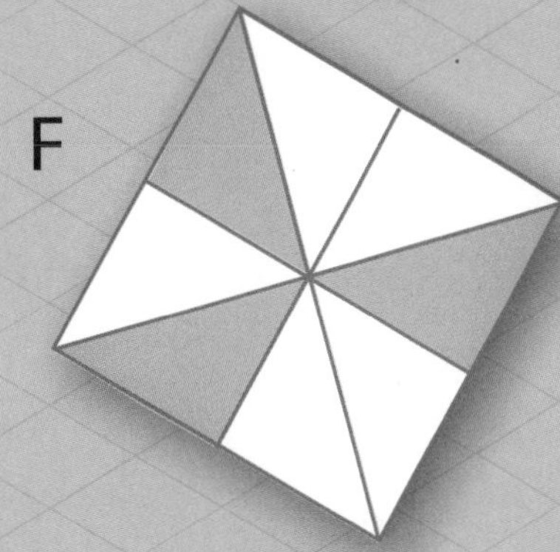

F

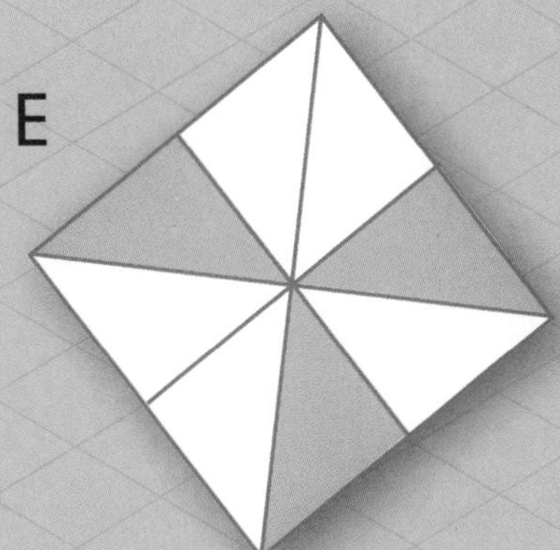

E

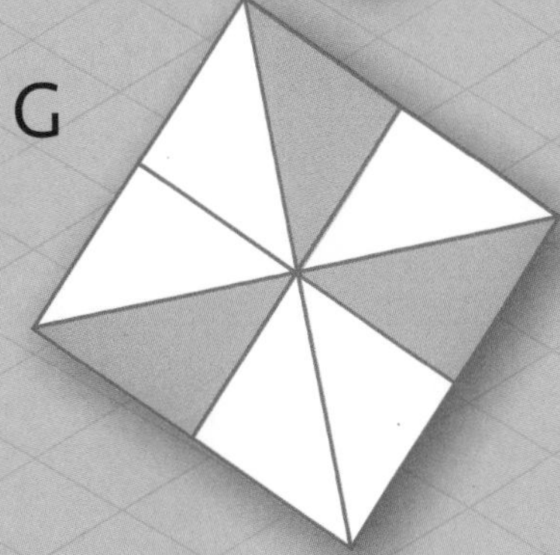

G

Answer see page 265

10

What number should replace the question mark?

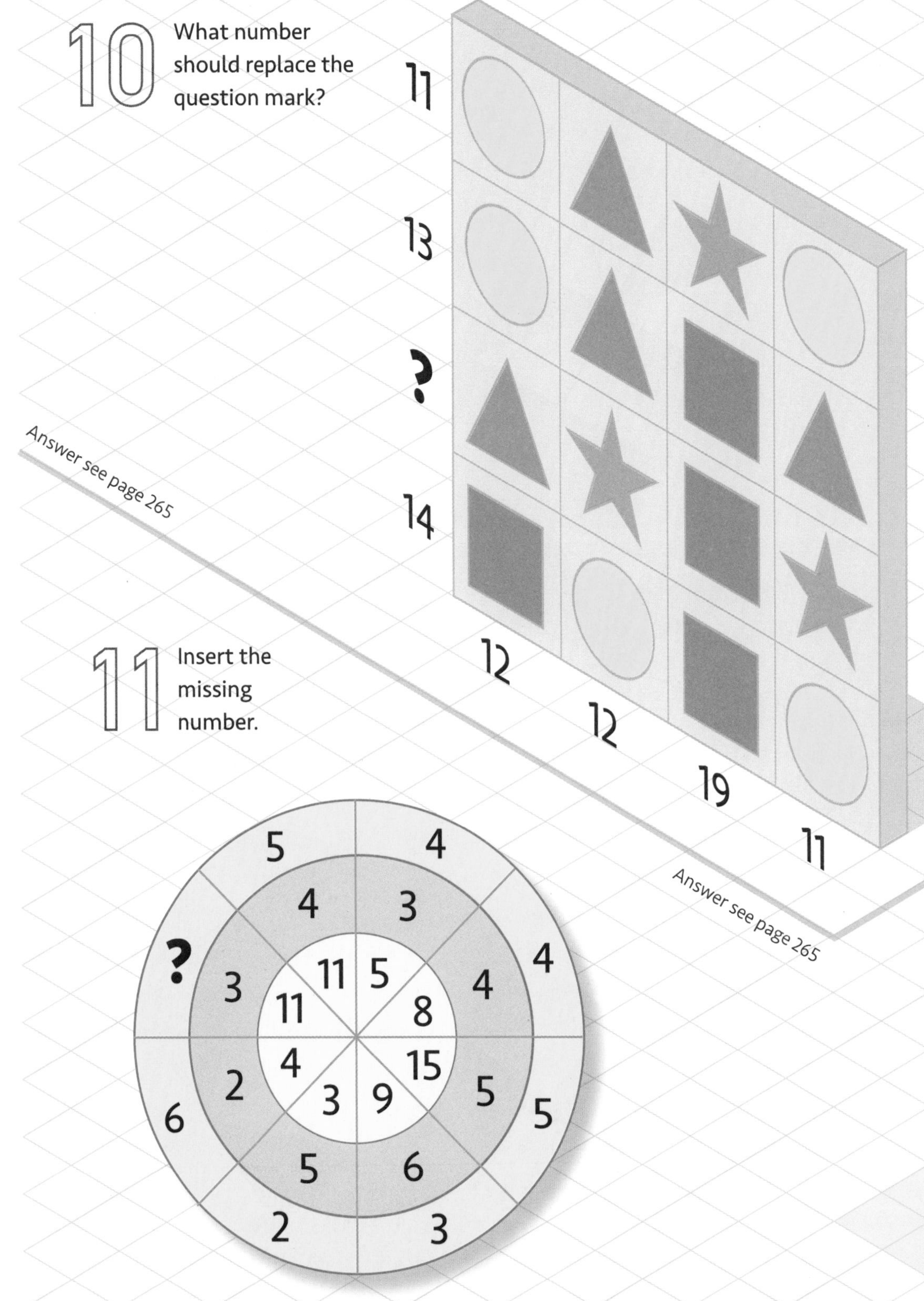

Answer see page 265

11

Insert the missing number.

Answer see page 265

12

Which of the constructed boxes below cannot be made from the given shape?

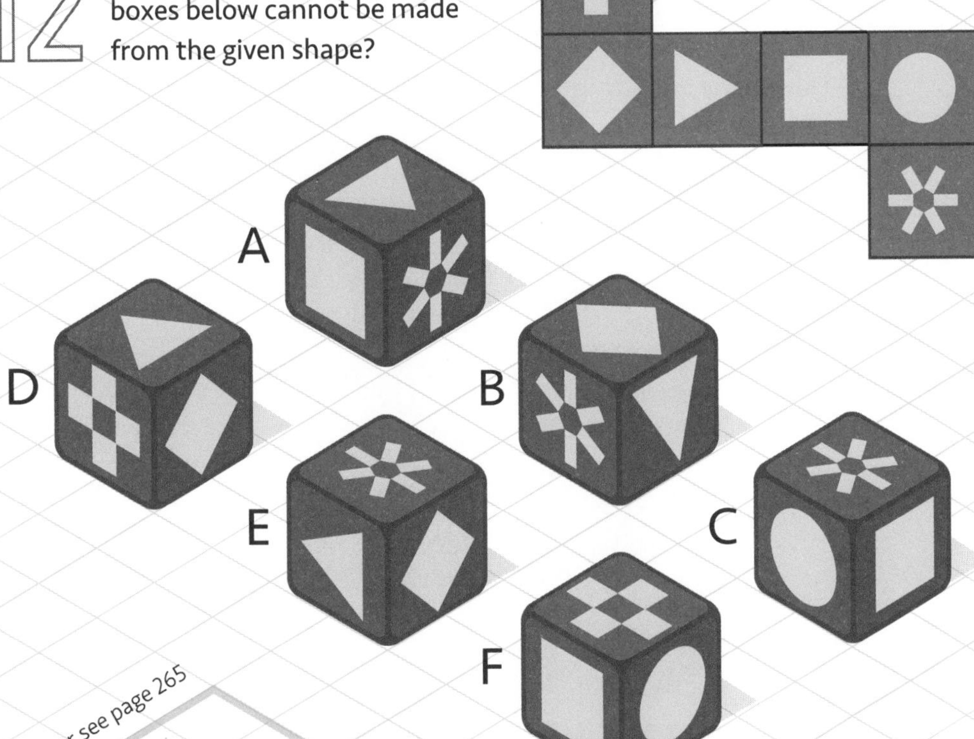

Answer see page 265

13

Which number is the odd one out?

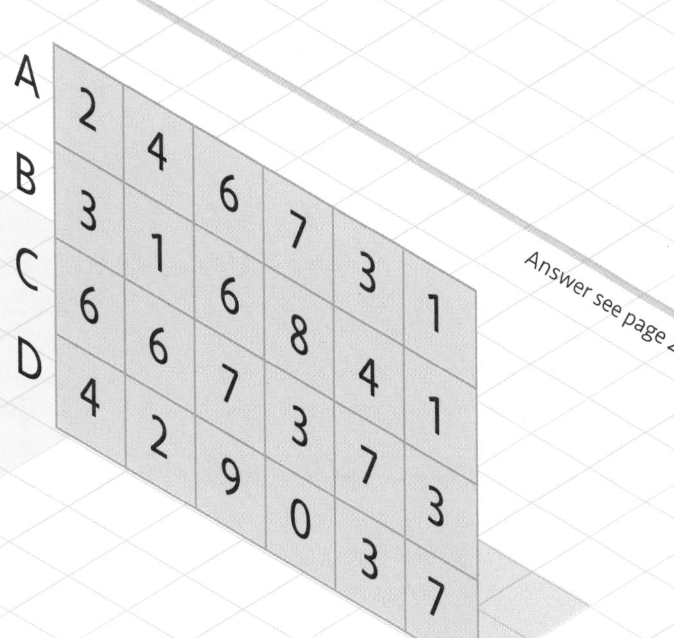

Answer see page 265

14

When complete, this 6 x 6 x 6 cube contains 216 individual blocks. How many blocks are required to complete the cube?

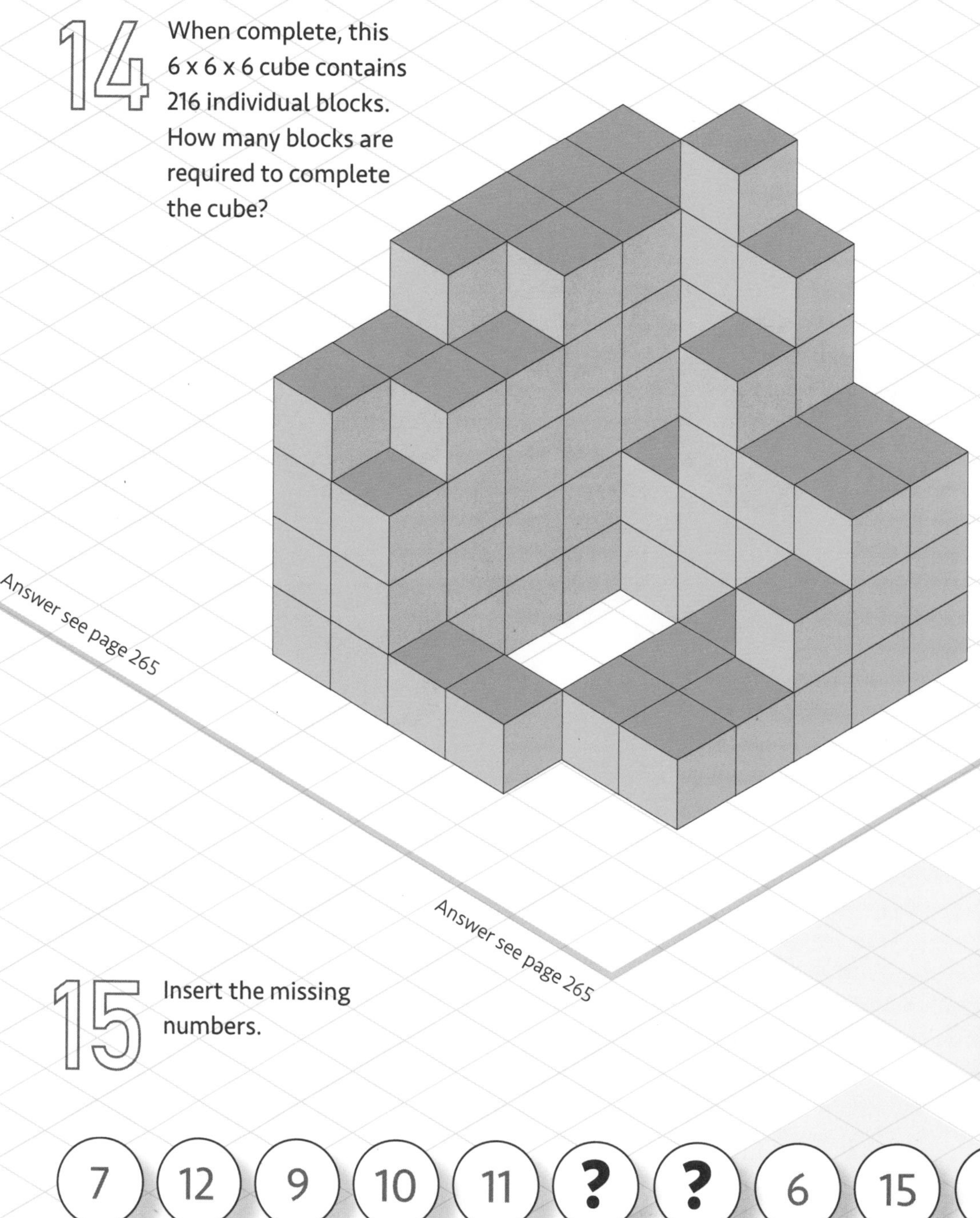

Answer see page 265

Answer see page 265

15

Insert the missing numbers.

7 12 9 10 11 ? ? 6 15 4

16

Havana is 12 hours behind Perth, which is 6 hours ahead of Cairo. It is 2:45 p.m. on Wednesday in Perth, what time is it in the other two cities?

PERTH

CAIRO

HAVANA

Answer see page 266

17

What number should replace the question mark?

Top	Left	Centre	Right
2	6	18	3
6	2	48	6
3	7	33	4
5	5	?	9

Answer see page 266

Answer see page 266

18 Which of the lettered clocks below continues the numbered series?

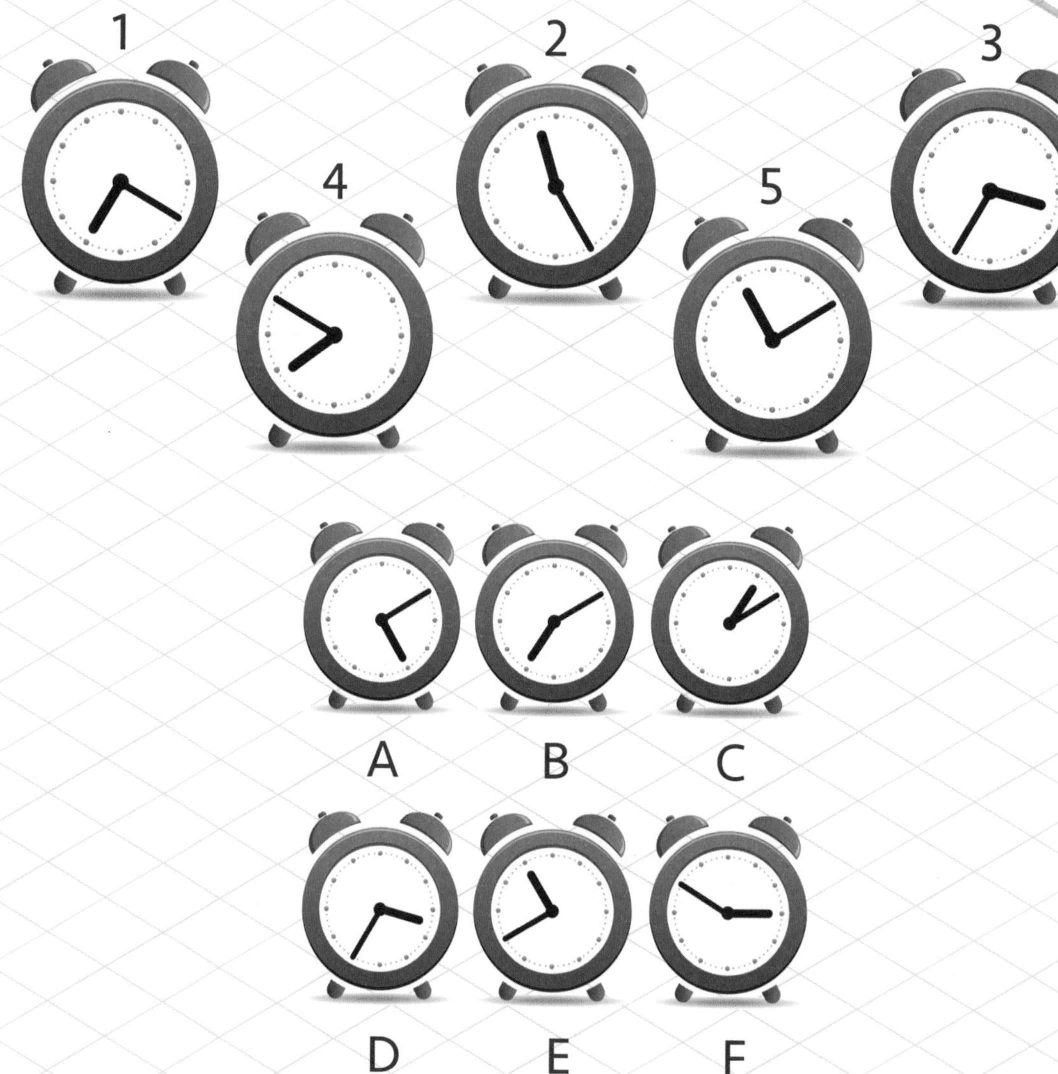

Which line of two numbers below has the same relationship as the two above?

	364	22
A	729	24
B	642	26
C	527	15
D	486	37
E	835	28

Answer see page 266

20

Which of these dice is not like the others?

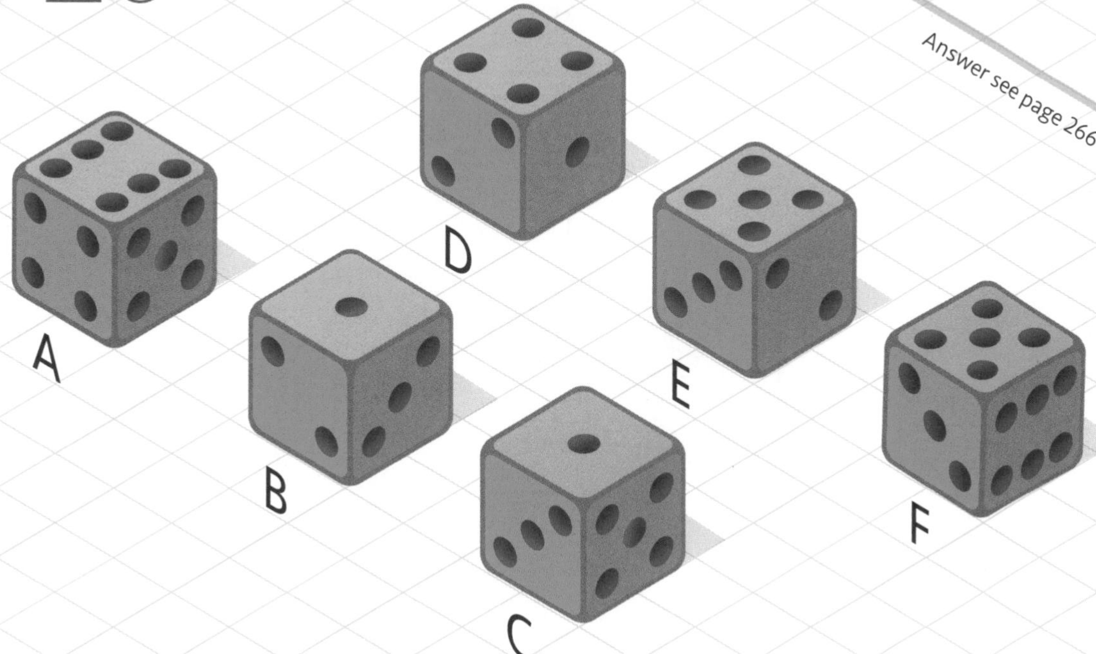

Answer see page 266

Test 6

01

Which option A to E most accurately completes the pattern?

Answer see page 266

is to as is to:

A B C

D E

02

How many [triangular prism] are required to balance the final scale?

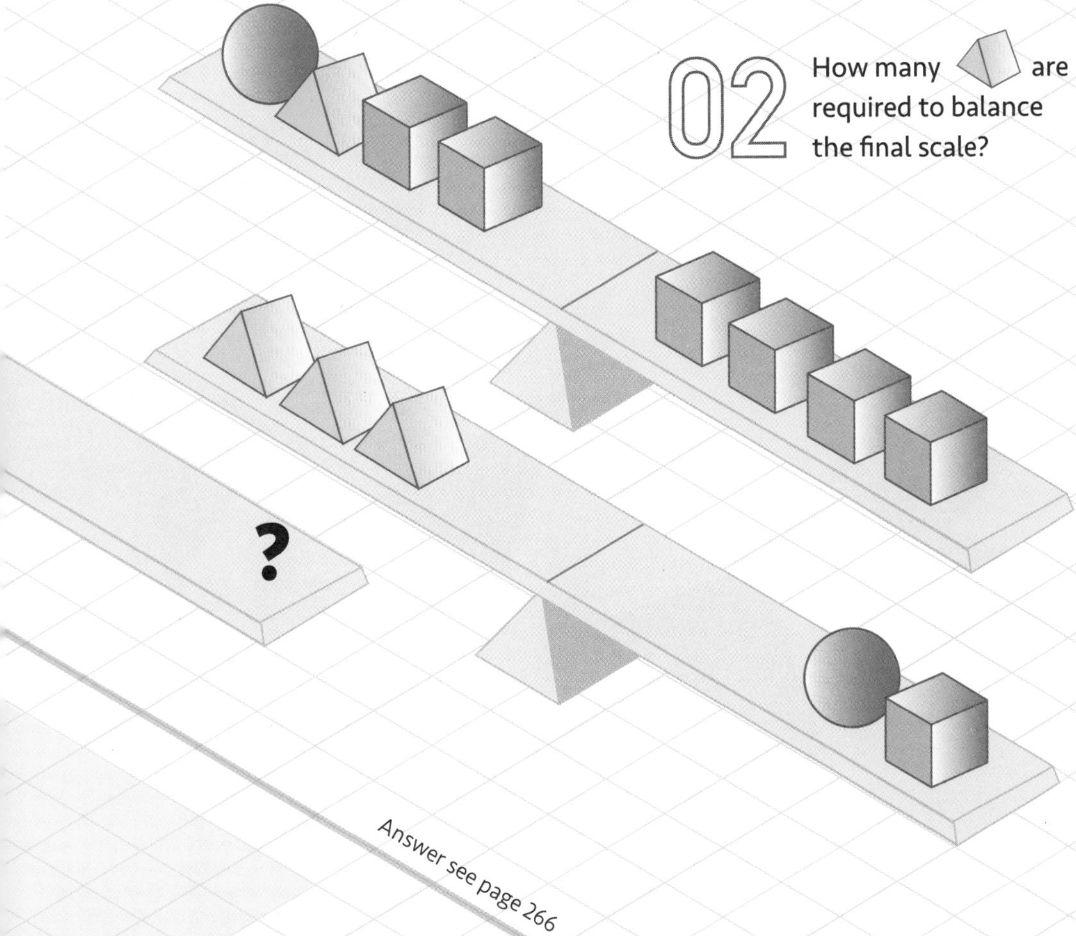

?

Answer see page 266

Answer see page 266

03

Fill in the missing plus, minus, and multiplication signs to make the equation below correct, performing all calculations strictly in the order they appear on the page.

04

The pieces can be assembled into a regular geometric shape. What is it?

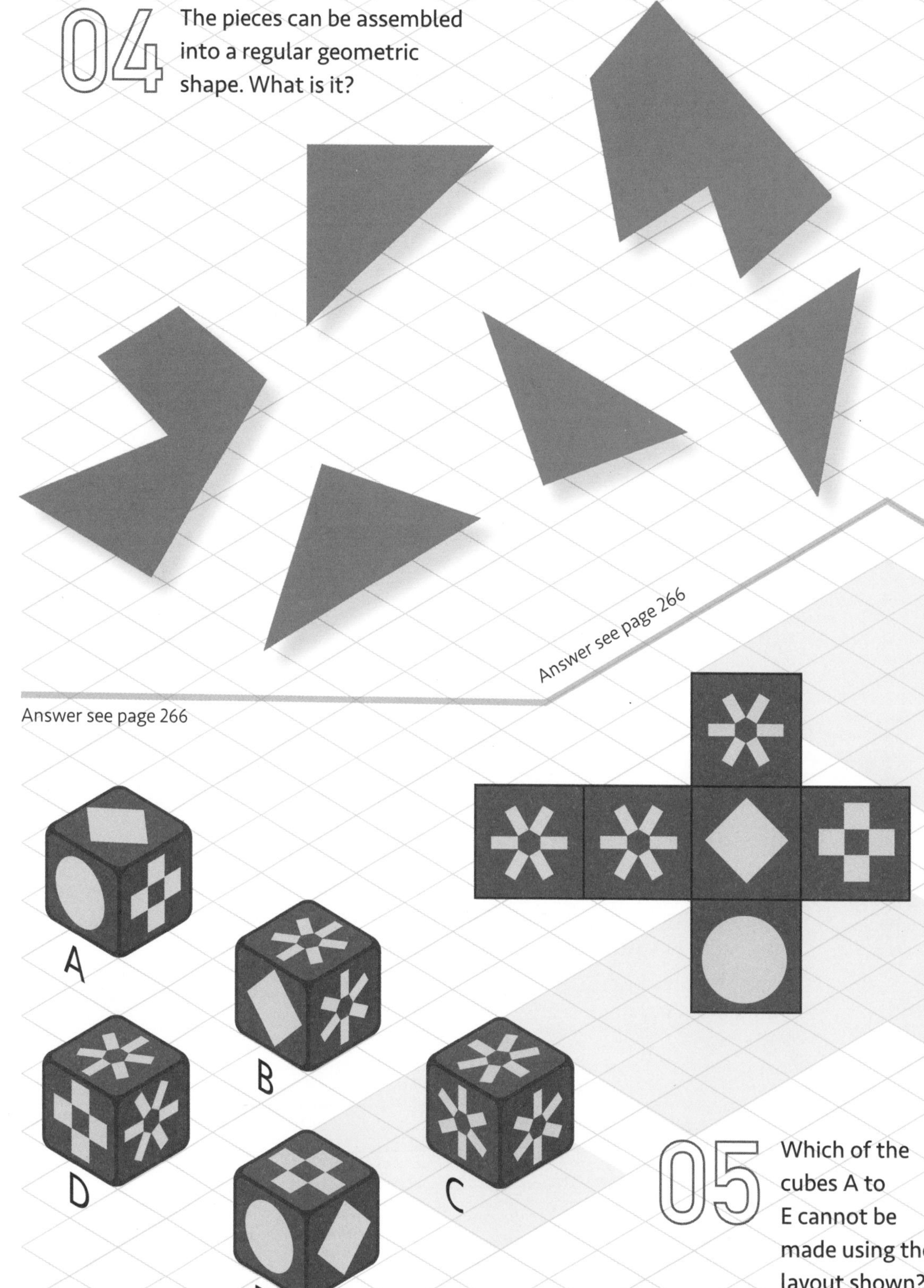

Answer see page 266

Answer see page 266

05

Which of the cubes A to E cannot be made using the layout shown?

06

Which of the options A to E most accurately continues the sequence?

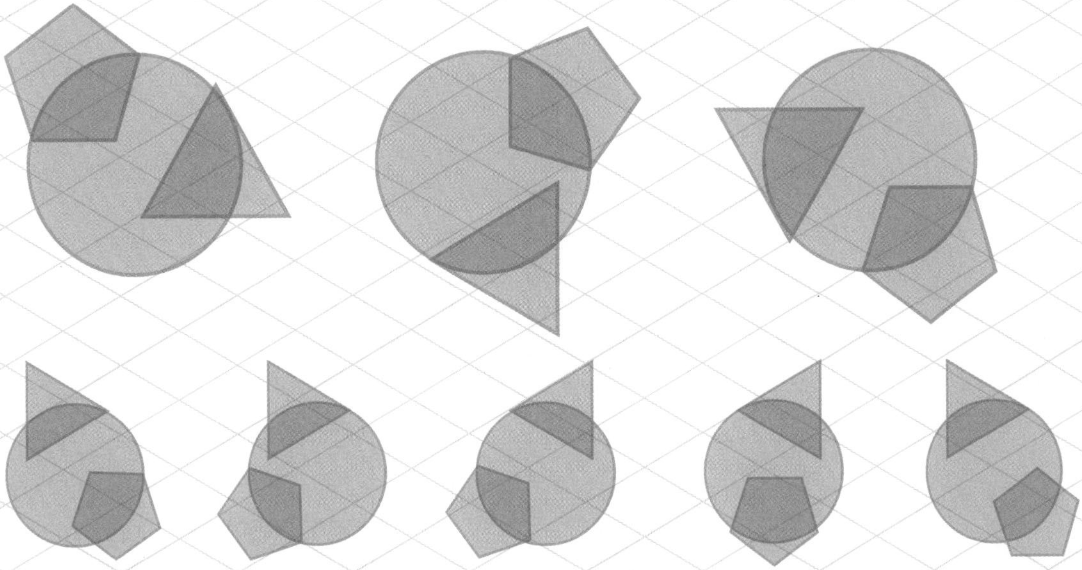

A B C D E

Answer see page 266

07

What number should replace the question mark?

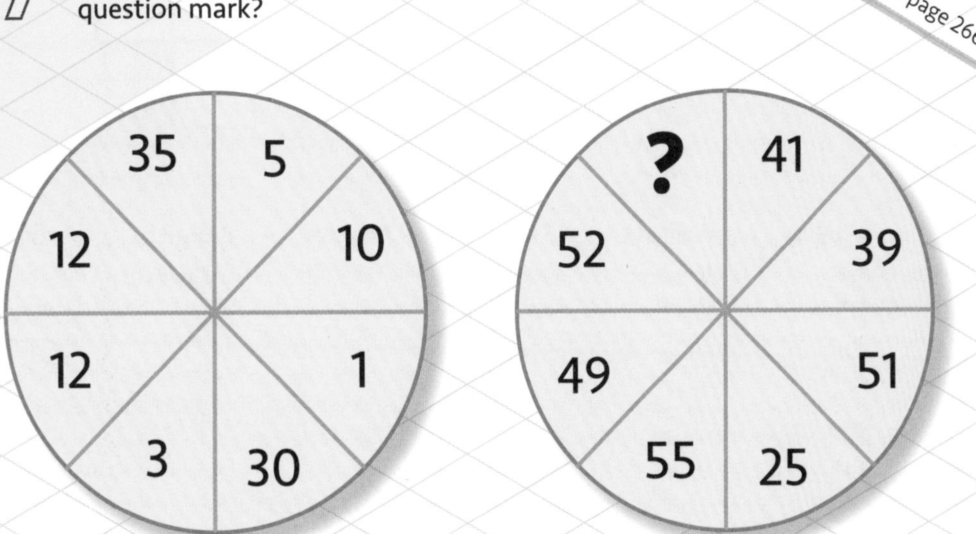

Answer see page 266

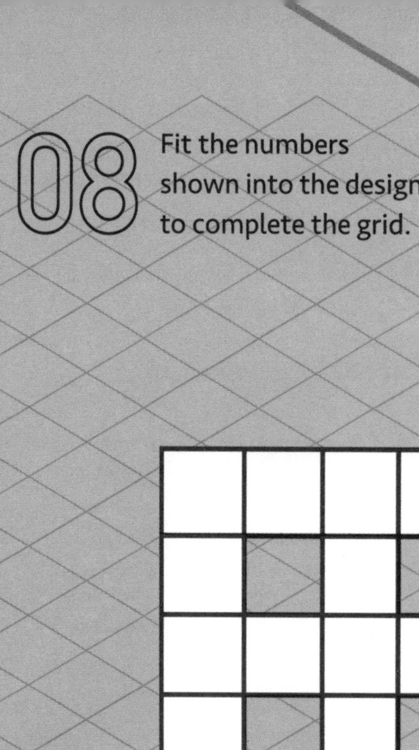

08

Fit the numbers shown into the design to complete the grid.

Answer see page 266

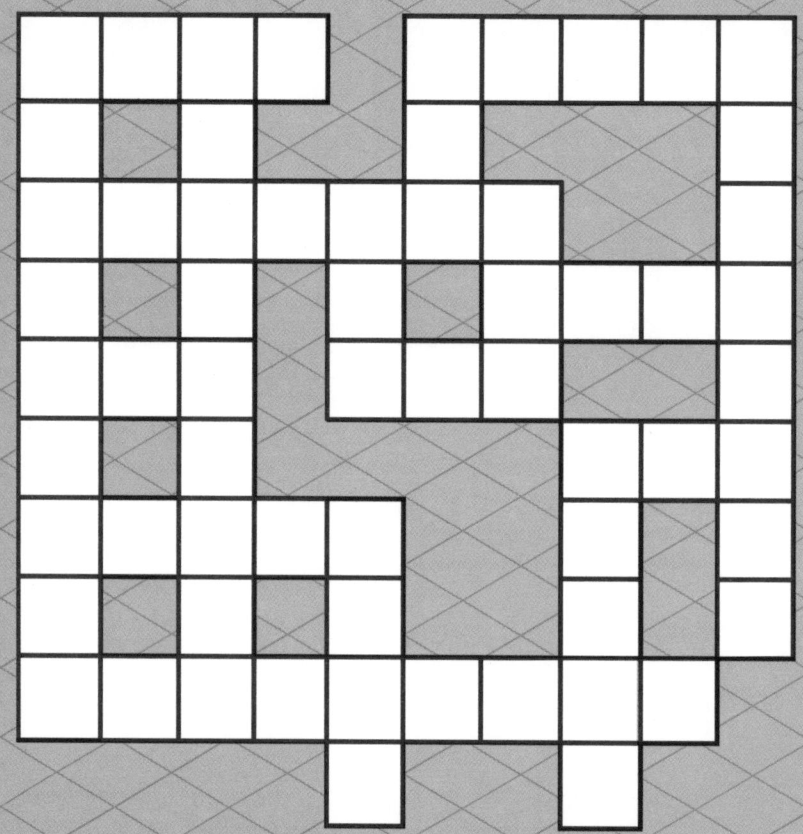

3 digits	4 digits	5 digits	7 digits	8 digits	9 digits
312	1642	36157	7034723	71230908	197896485
315	1993	46126			423738130
395	6325	87587			500524182
753					
889					
943					

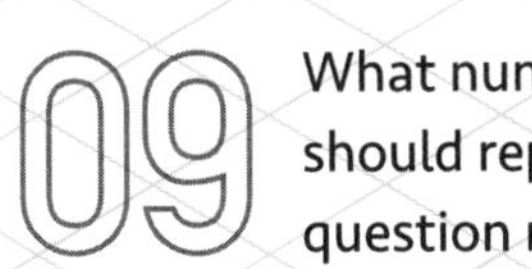

What number should replace the question mark?

Answer see page 266

Answer see page 266

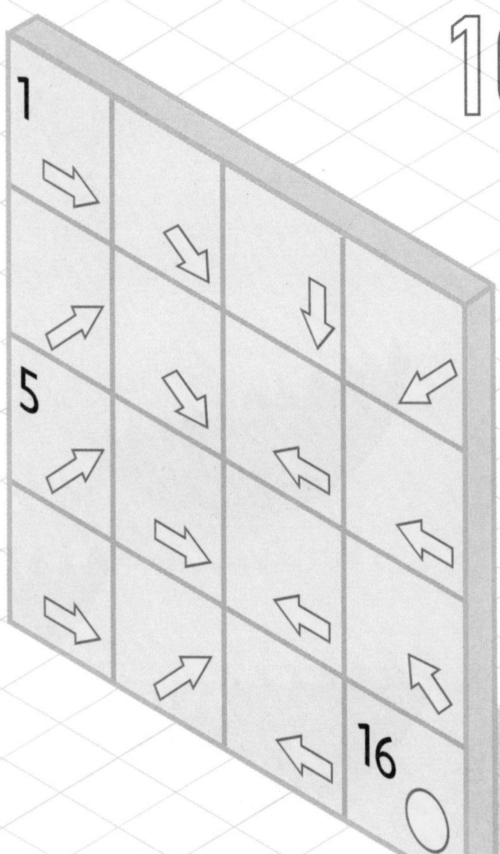

10 In each square, the arrow shows the direction you must move in. The numbers in some squares show that square's position in the correct sequence of moves. Move from top left to bottom right, visiting each square in the grid exactly once.

11 Which of the designs A to E is the odd one out?

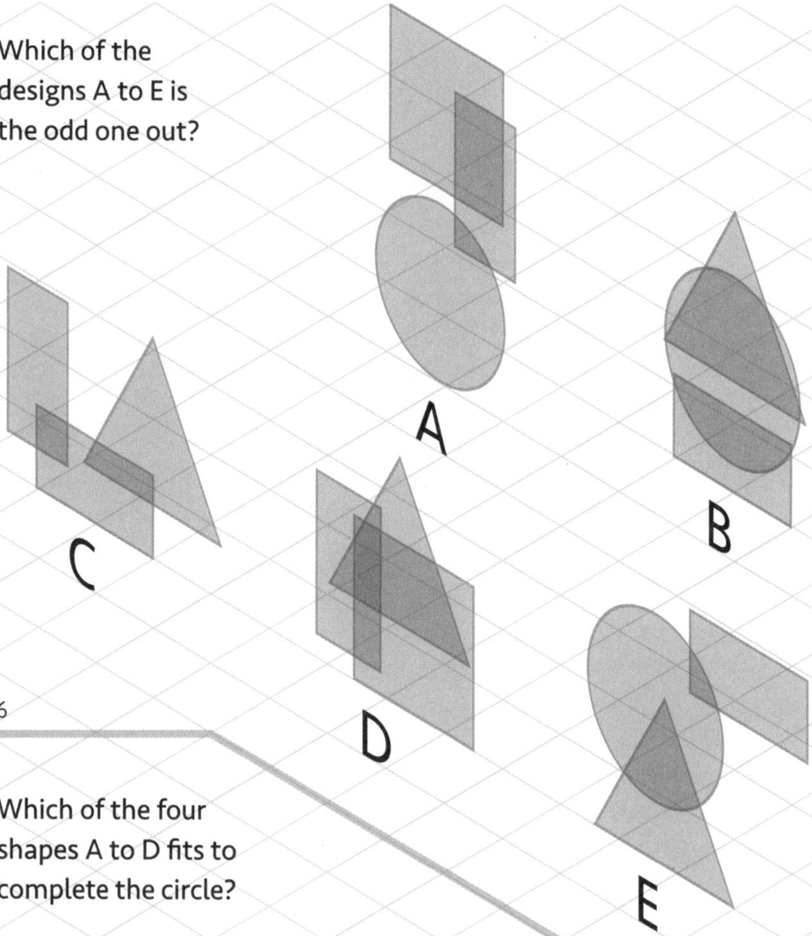

A

B

C

D

E

Answer see page 266

12 Which of the four shapes A to D fits to complete the circle?

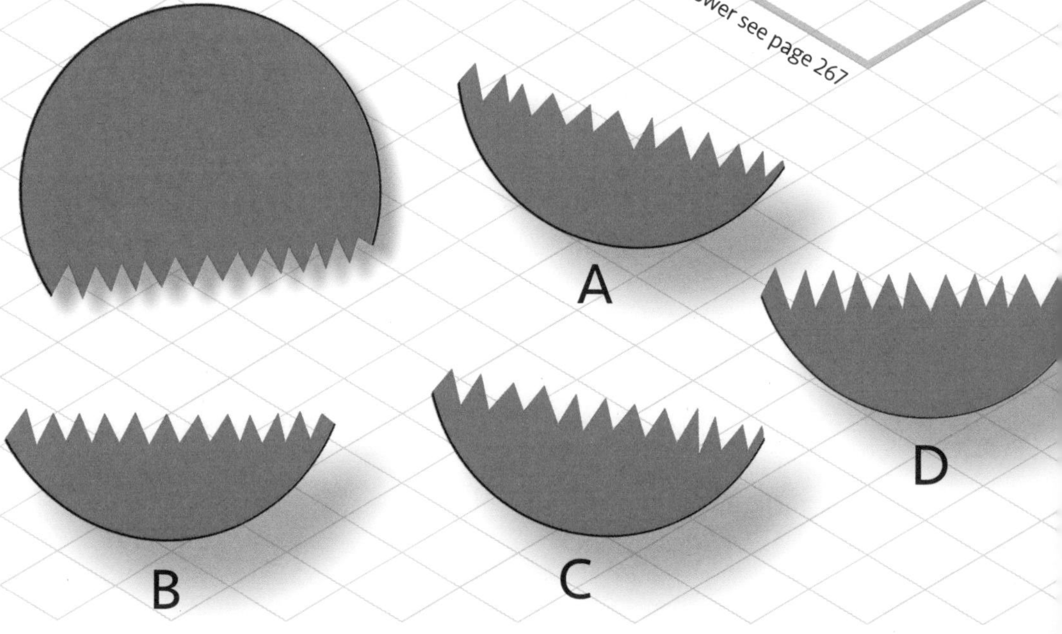

Answer see page 267

A

D

B

C

13

Use six straight lines to divide the field below into six sections each containing five squares.

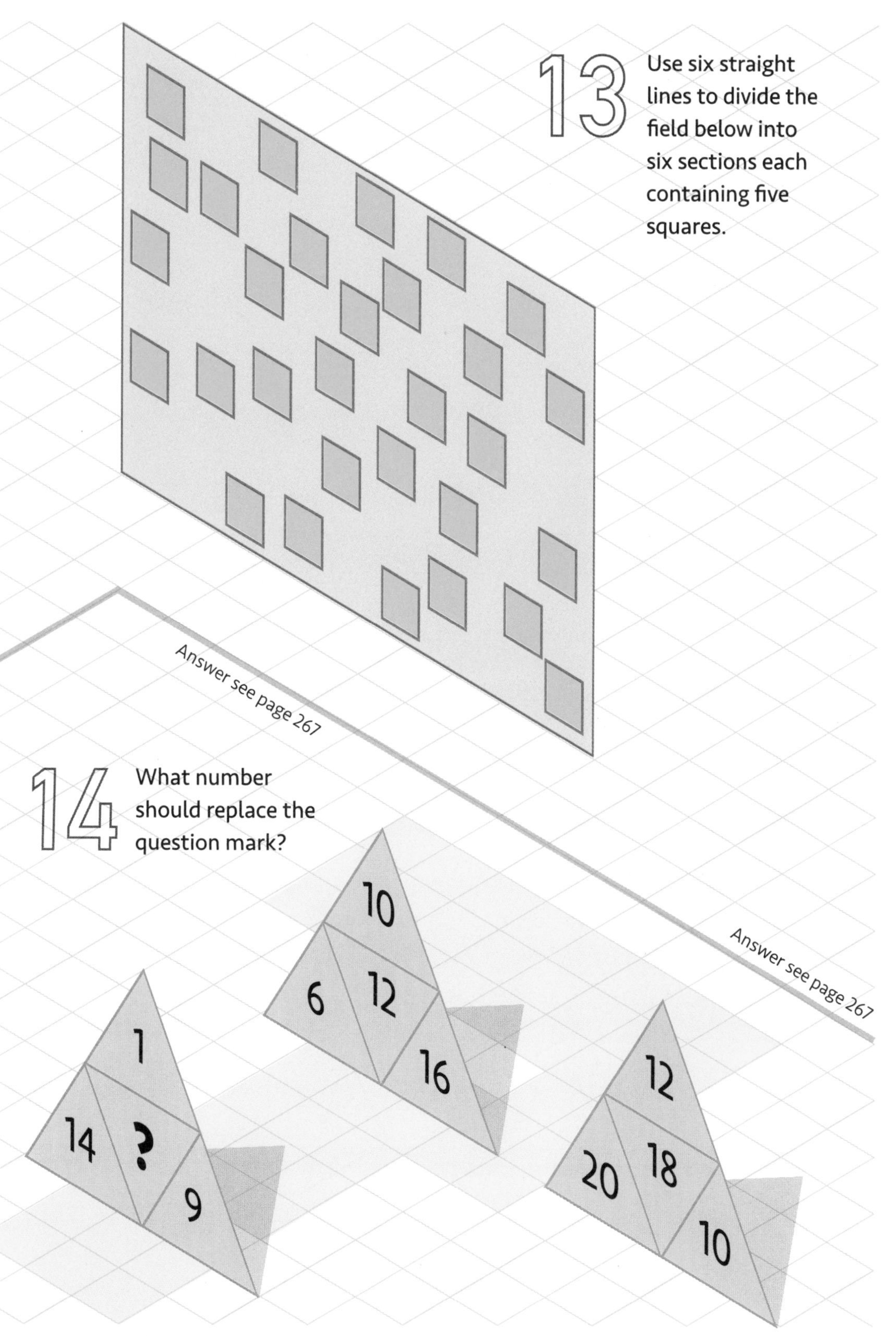

Answer see page 267

14

What number should replace the question mark?

Answer see page 267

15

In the grid below, how much is each symbol worth?

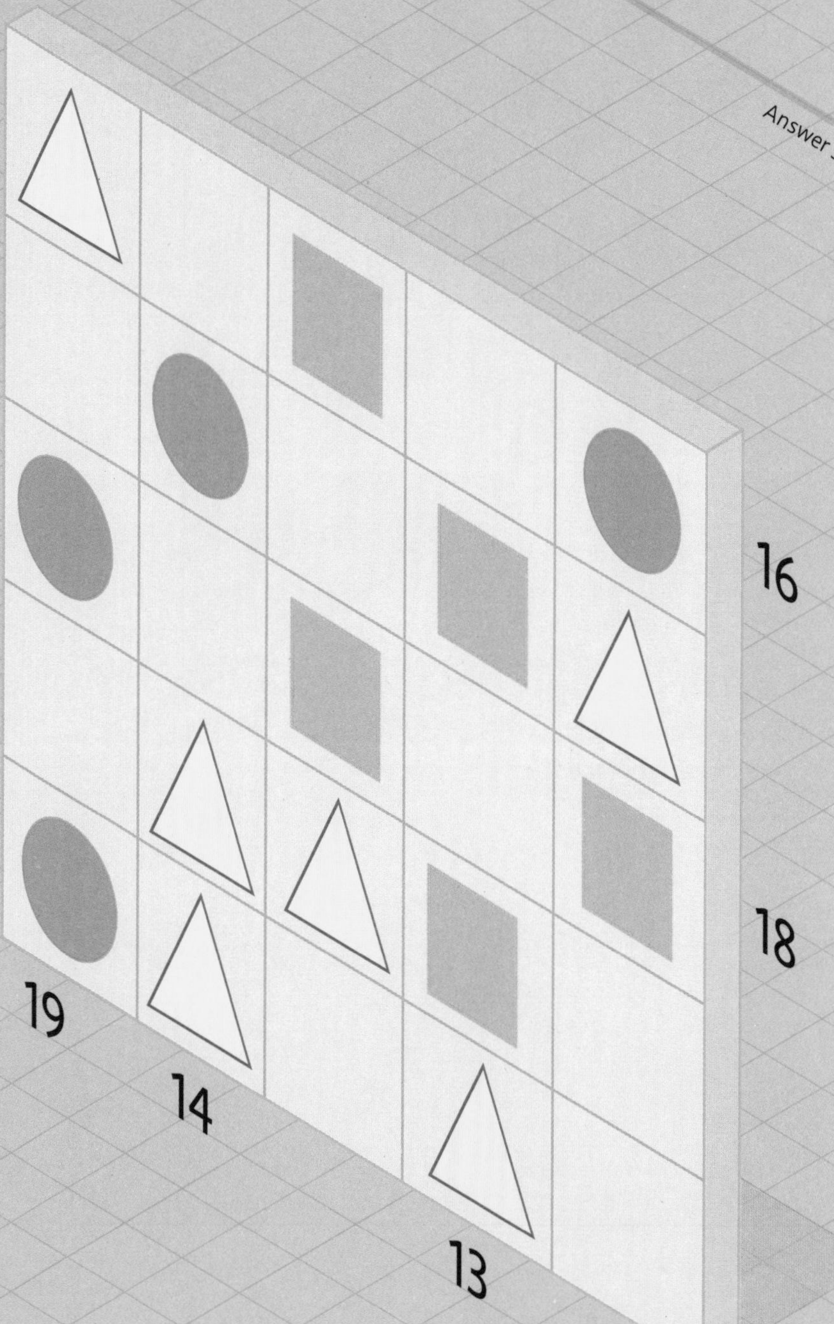

Answer see page 267

16

What number should replace the question mark?

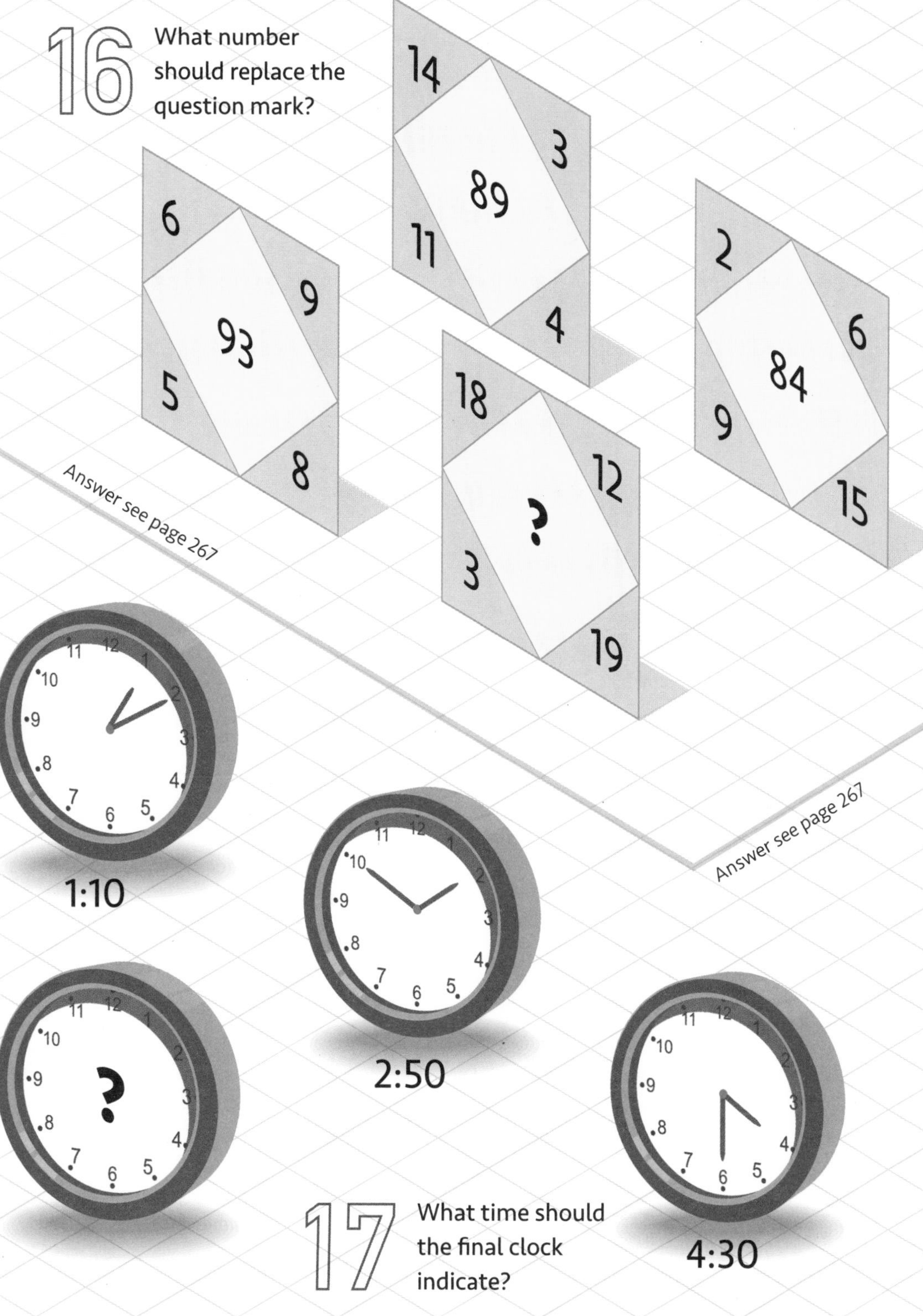

Answer see page 267

17

What time should the final clock indicate?

Answer see page 267

18

Combine the segments below to find the names of ten celebrities.

NING	ORE	YNE	NU
HIDD	TON	KEA	VES
TER	CHAN	LEN	CAGE
LES	AL	BEN	SON
VES	AFF	TIM	SYL
LONE	LECK	LAS	REE
RUS	WE	TAT	TOM
DWA	NICO	BAR	SELL
UM	CRO	STAL	
JOHN	DREW	RYM	

Answer see page 267

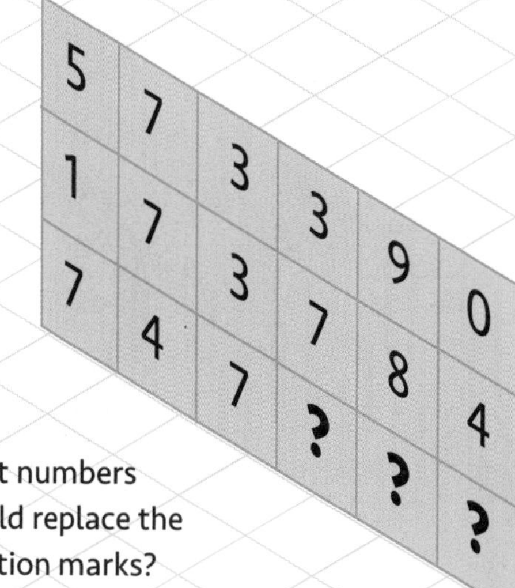

Answer see page 267

19

What numbers should replace the question marks?

20

Which symbols are missing from the grid below?

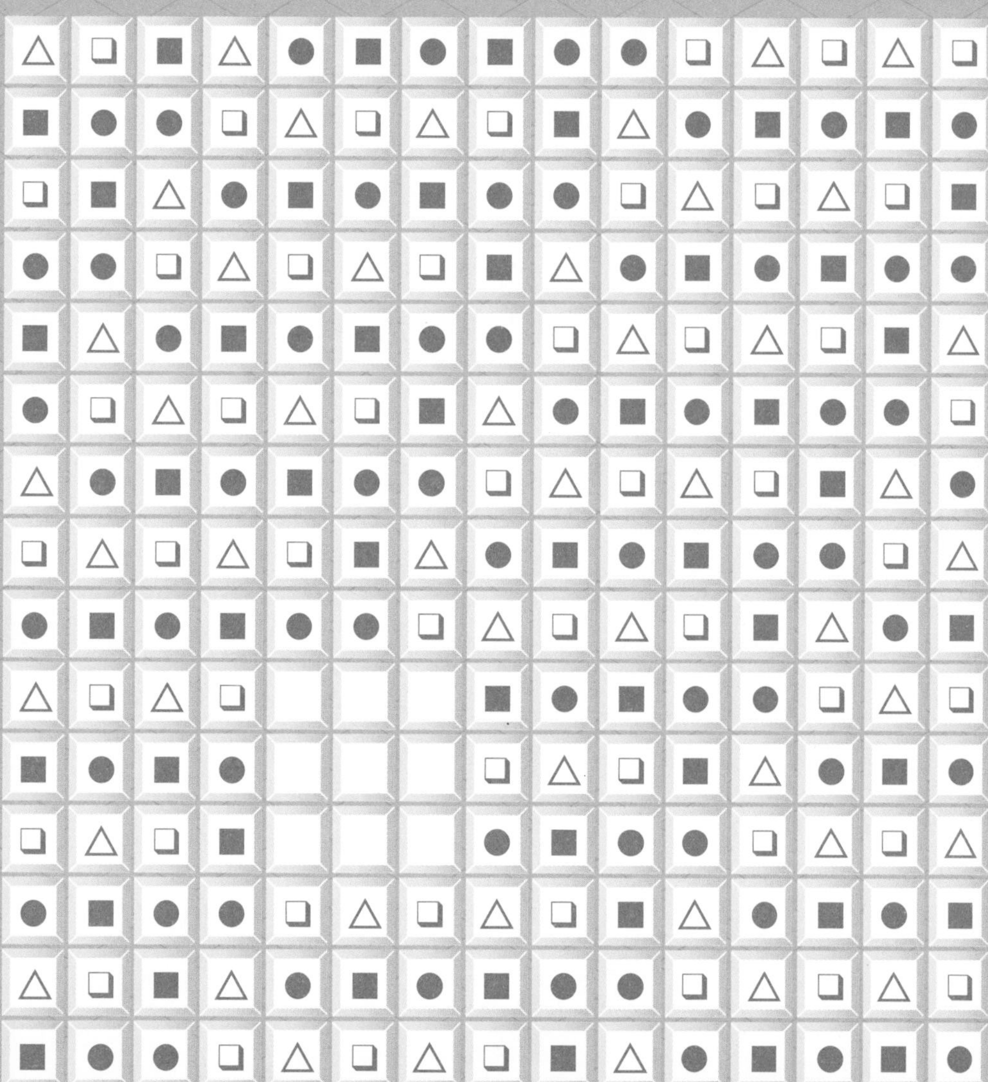

Answer see page 267

Test 7

01

What sequence should replace the question mark to maintain a perfect balance?

Answer see page 267

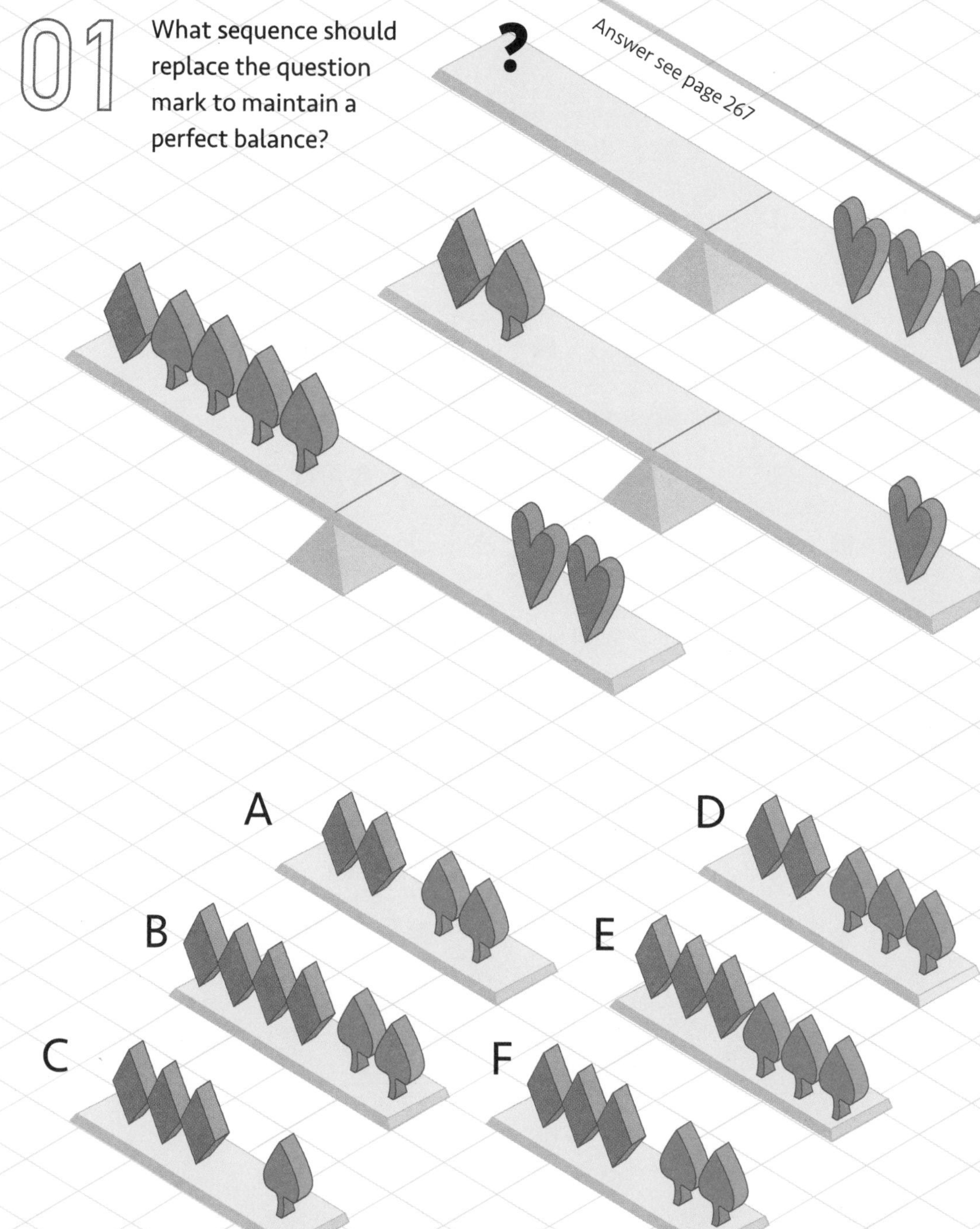

Answer see page 267

02 Which of the pentagons at the bottom should replace the question mark?

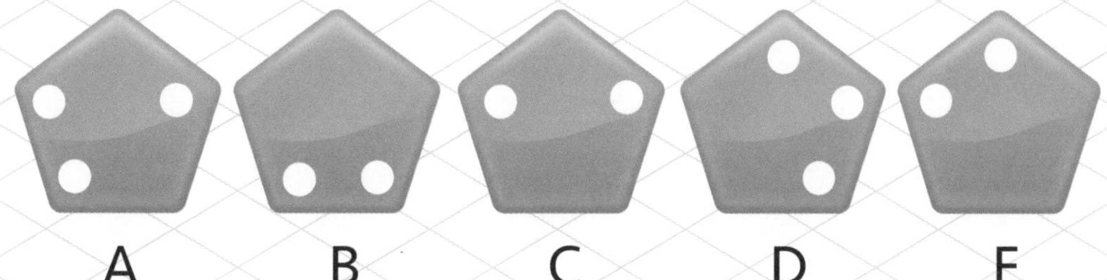

03

Which shape below can be put with the one above to form a perfect square?

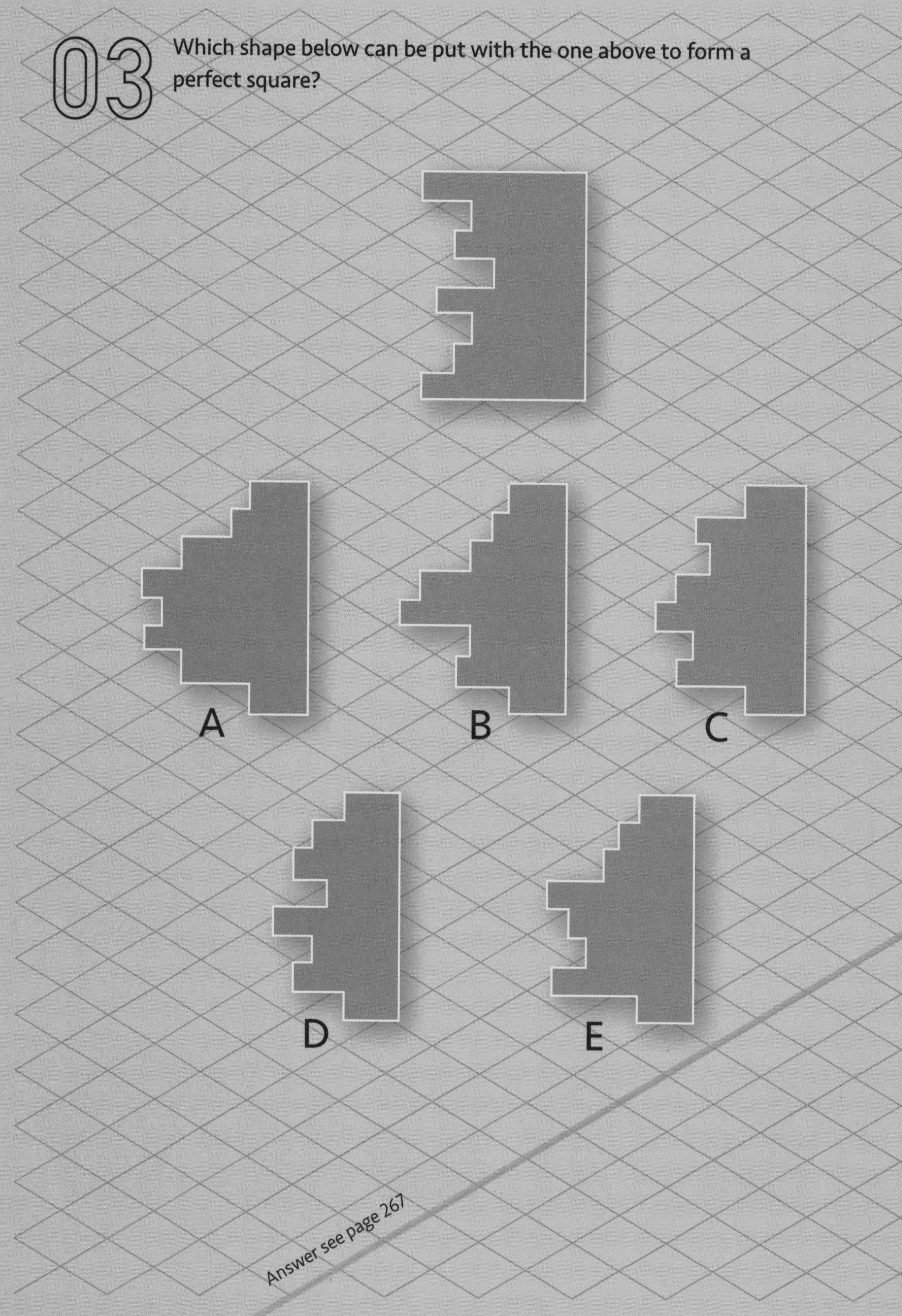

Answer see page 267

Select the correct figure from the numbered ones below to replace the question mark.

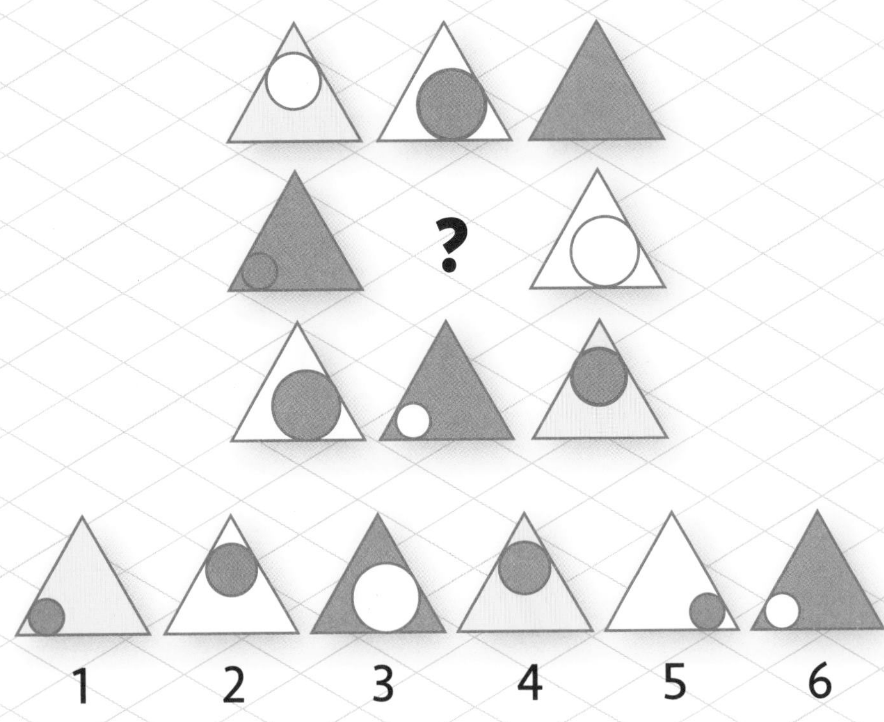

Answer see page 267

Which is the odd one out?

Answer see page 267

169 64 196

Each of the nine squares in the grid marked 1A to 3C should incorporate all of the items that are shown in the squares of the same letter and number, at left and top. For example, square 2A should incorporate all of the items in squares 2 and A. One square however, is incorrect. Which is it?

	A	B	C
1	1A	1B	1C
2	2A	2B	2C
3	3A	3B	3C

Answer see page 267

Answer see page 267

07

Complete the square using nine consecutive numbers, so that all rows, columns, and large diagonals add up to the same total.

08

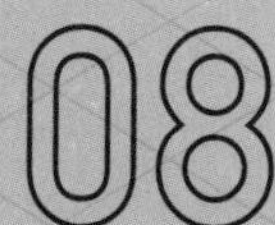

Which is the odd one out?

A

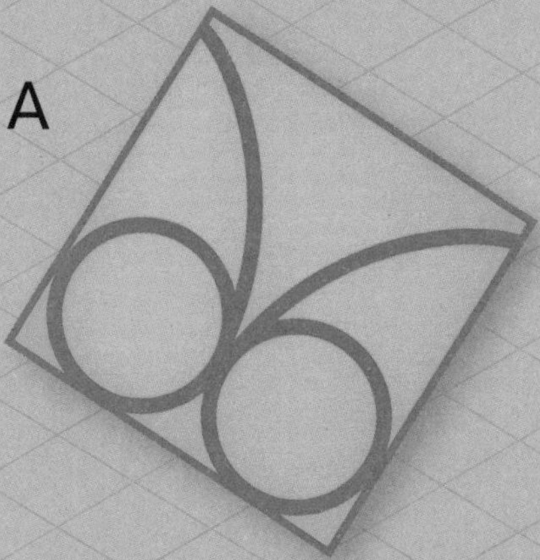

B

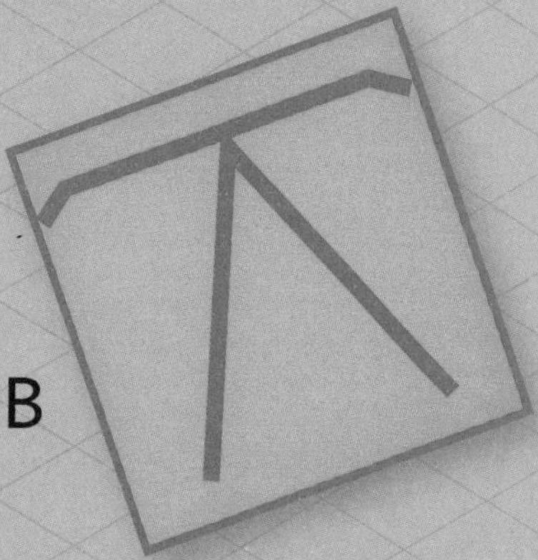

C

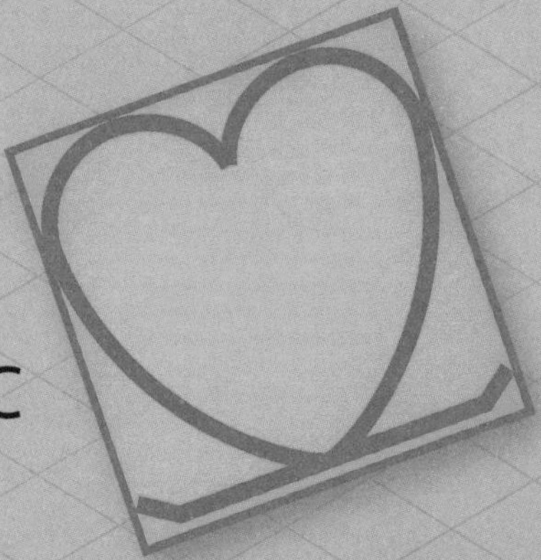

D

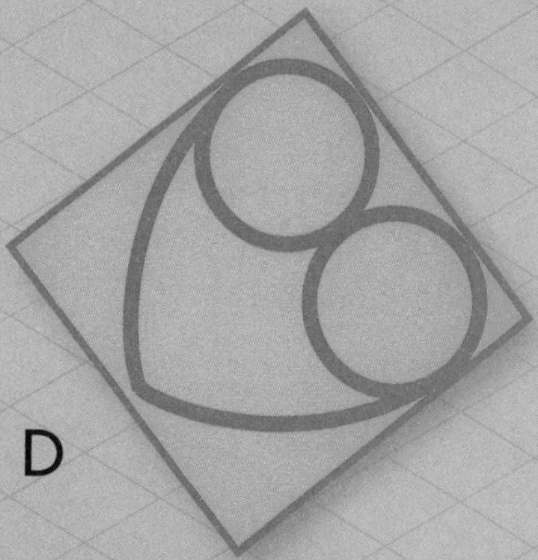

E

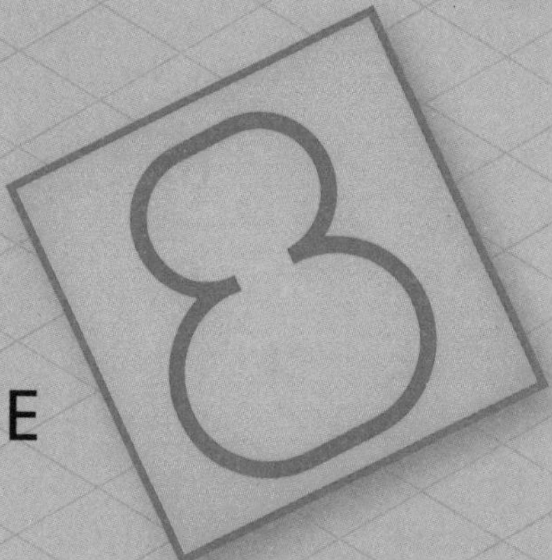

Answer see page 267

09

What number should replace the question mark?

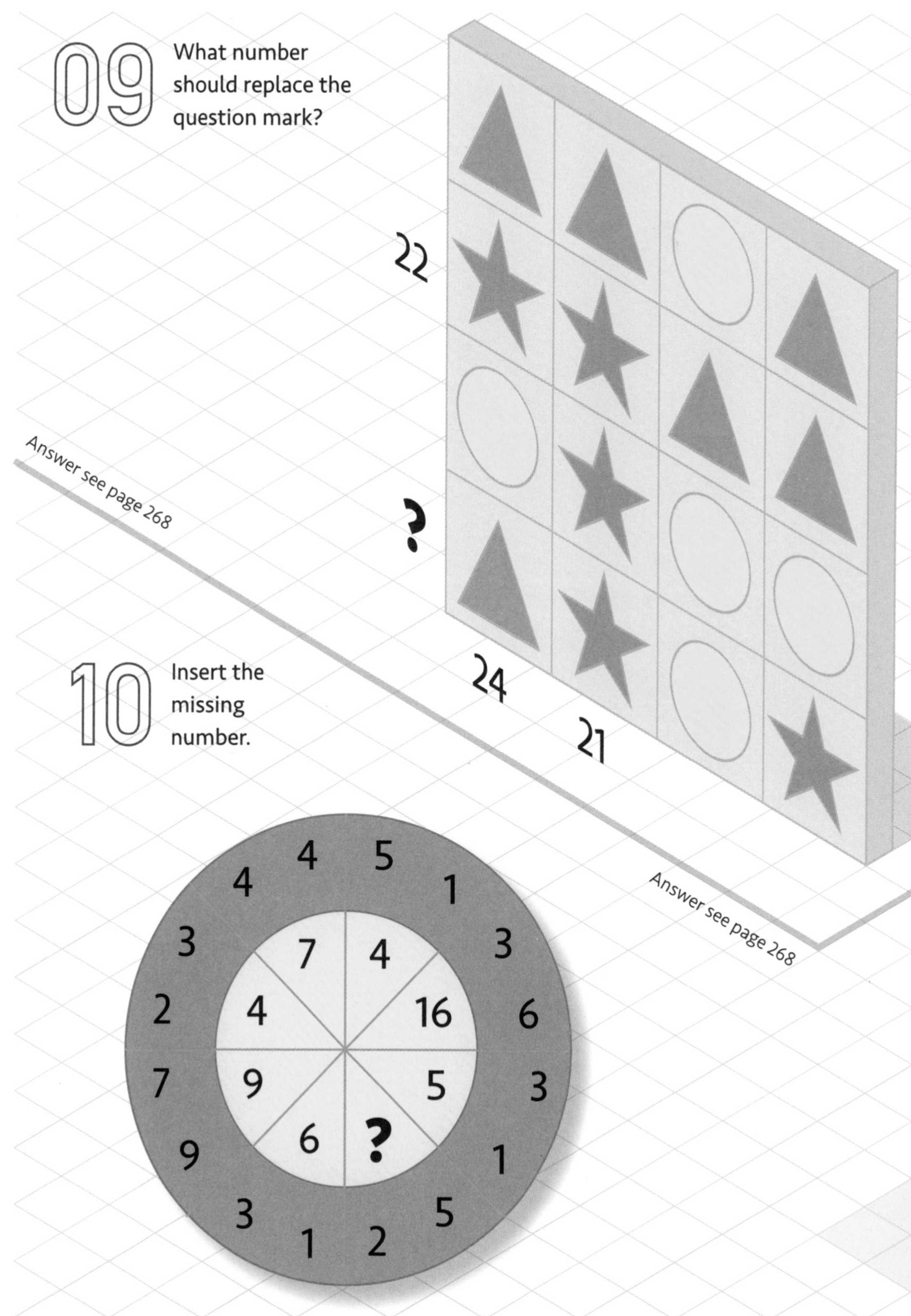

Answer see page 268

10

Insert the missing number.

Answer see page 268

11

Which of the constructed boxes below cannot be made from the given shape?

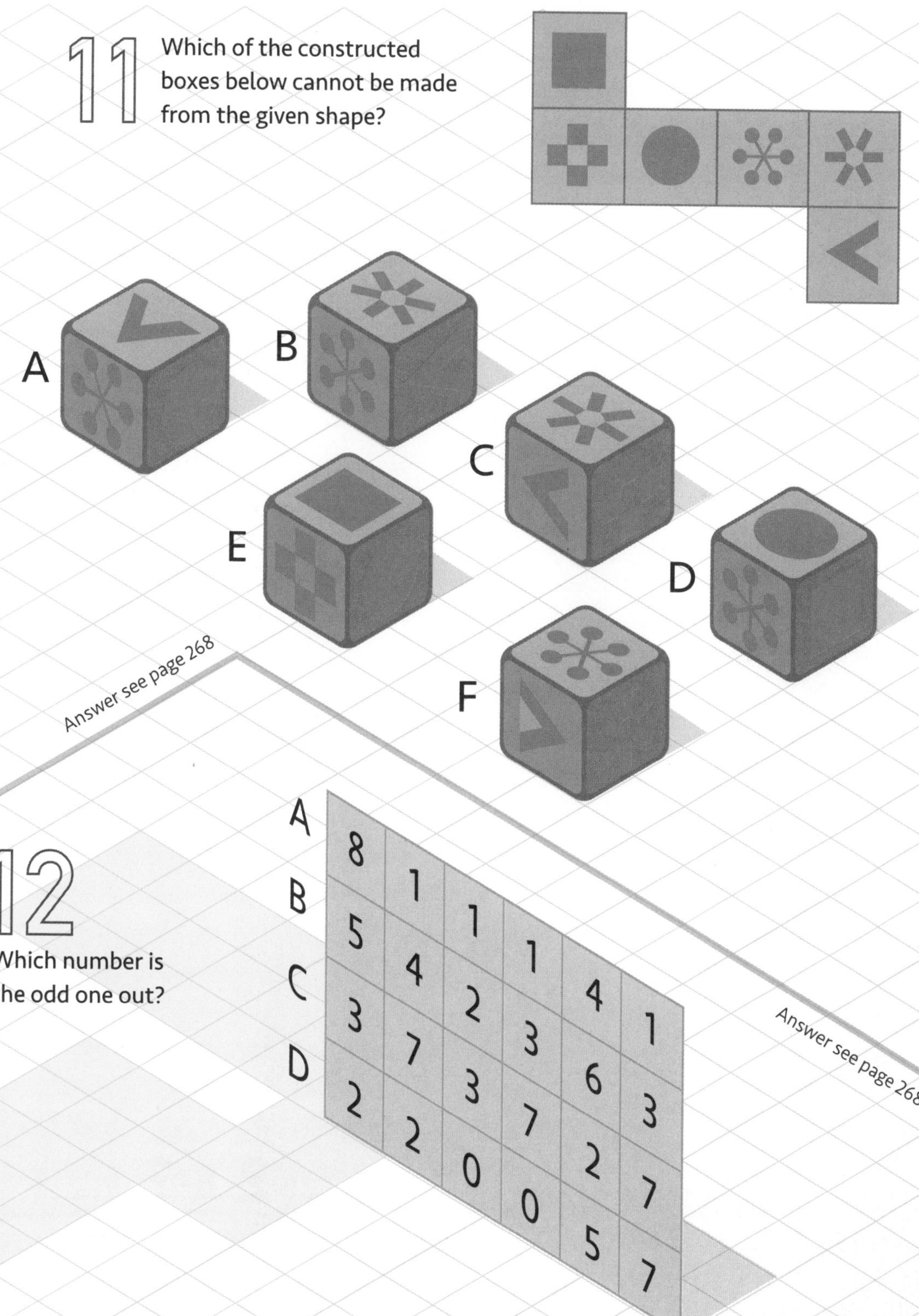

Answer see page 268

12

Which number is the odd one out?

A	8	1	1	1	4	1
B	5	4	2	3	6	3
C	3	7	3	7	2	7
D	2	2	0	0	5	7

Answer see page 268

13

When complete, this 6 x 6 x 6 cube contains 216 individual blocks. How many blocks are required to complete the cube?

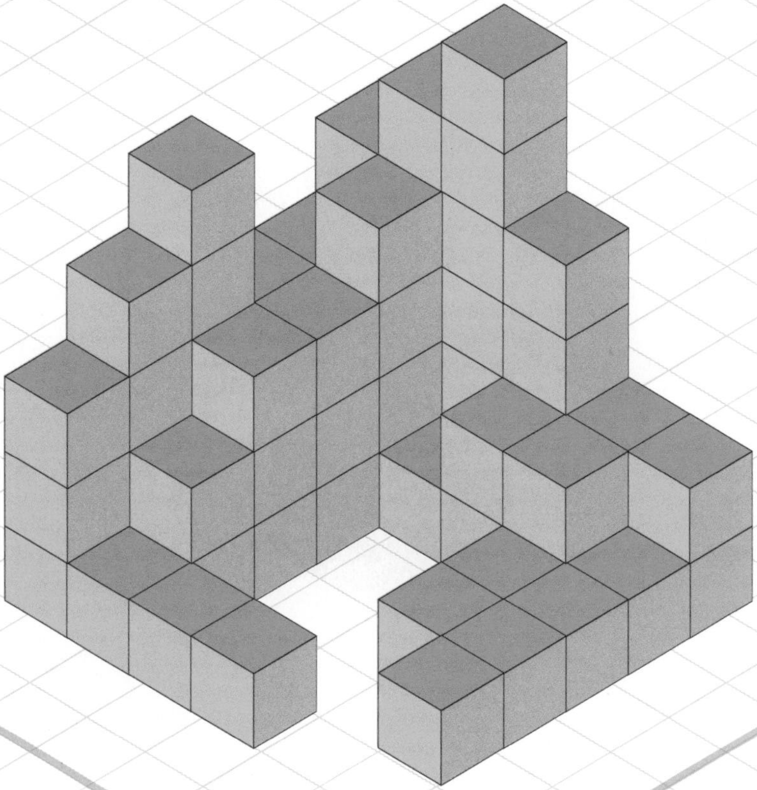

Answer see page 268

14

Insert the missing numbers.

5 7 12 19 31 50 ? ?

Answer see page 268

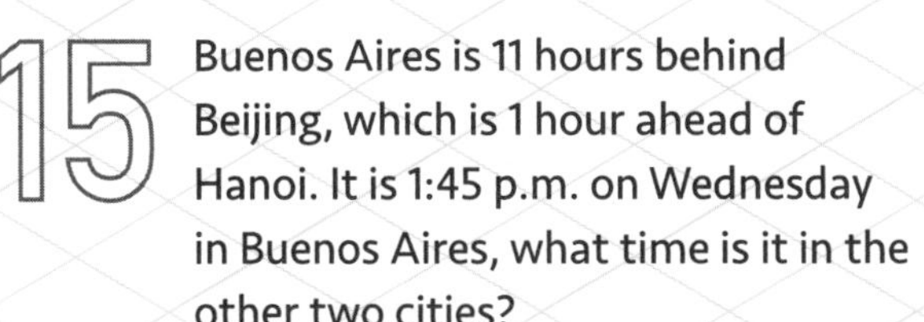

15

Buenos Aires is 11 hours behind Beijing, which is 1 hour ahead of Hanoi. It is 1:45 p.m. on Wednesday in Buenos Aires, what time is it in the other two cities?

Answer see page 268

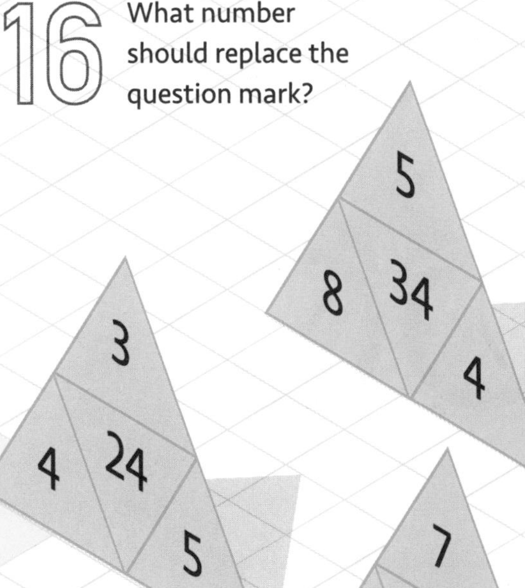

16

What number should replace the question mark?

Answer see page 268

17

Which of the lettered clocks below continues the numbered series?

1 2 3 4 5

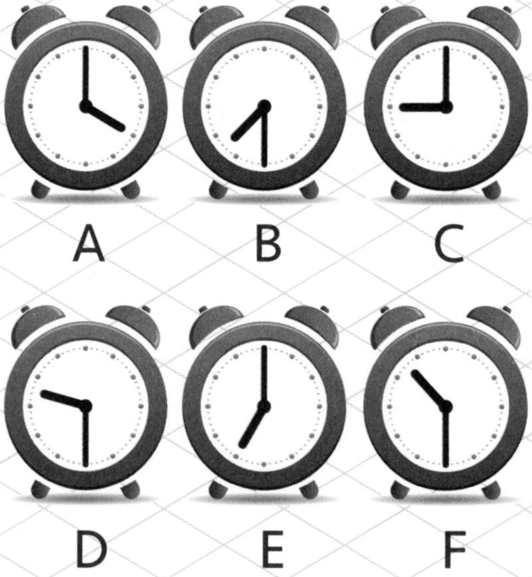

A B C

D E F

Answer see page 268

Answer see page 268

18

If $^3/_7$ is 9, how much is 4?

19

Which of these dice is not like the other five?

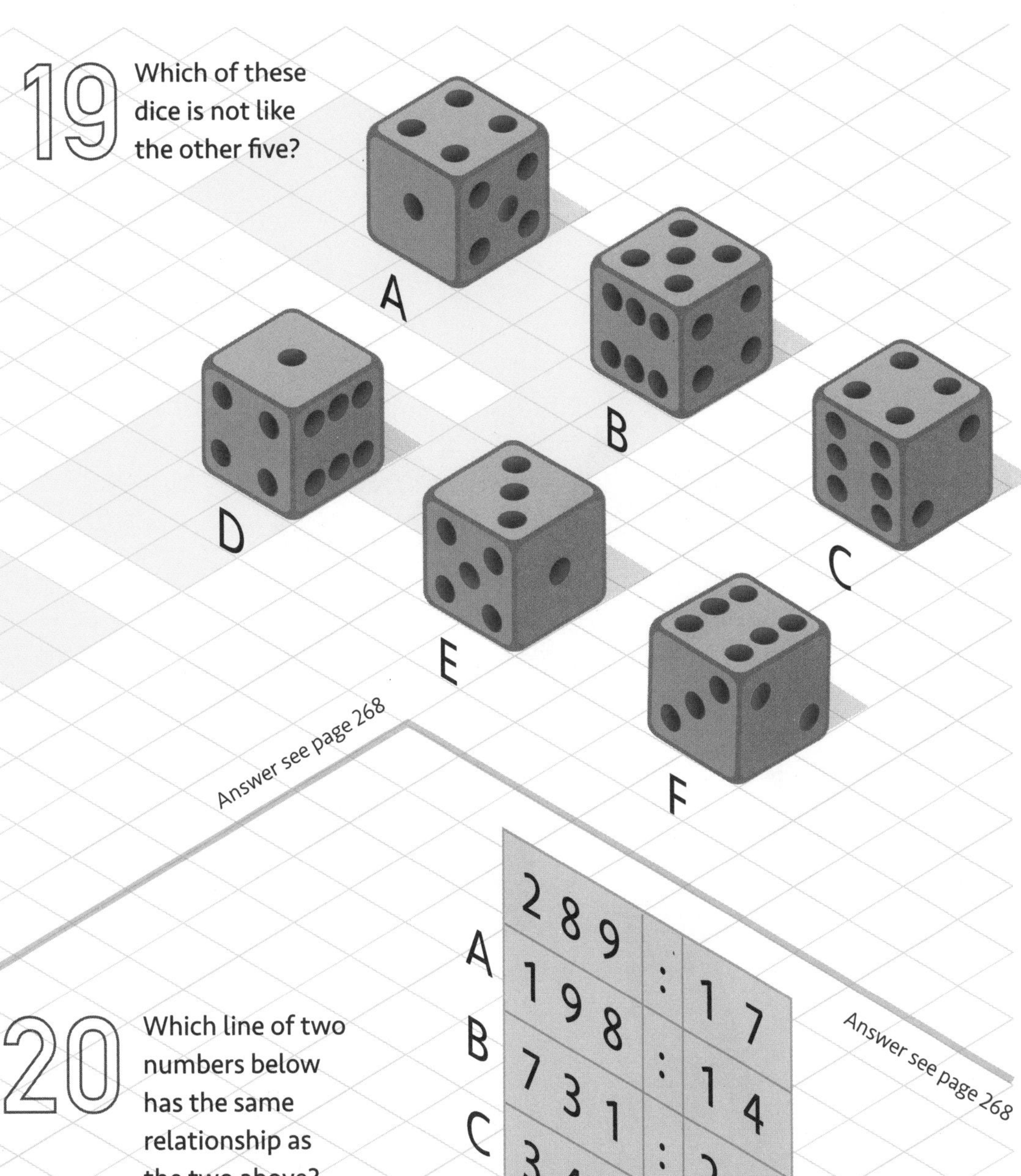

Answer see page 268

20

Which line of two numbers below has the same relationship as the two above?

	289	:	17
A	198	:	14
B	731	:	27
C	342	:	18
D	841	:	28
E	441	:	21

Answer see page 268

Test 8

01

The pieces can be assembled into a regular geometric shape. What is it?

Answer see page 268

02

How many 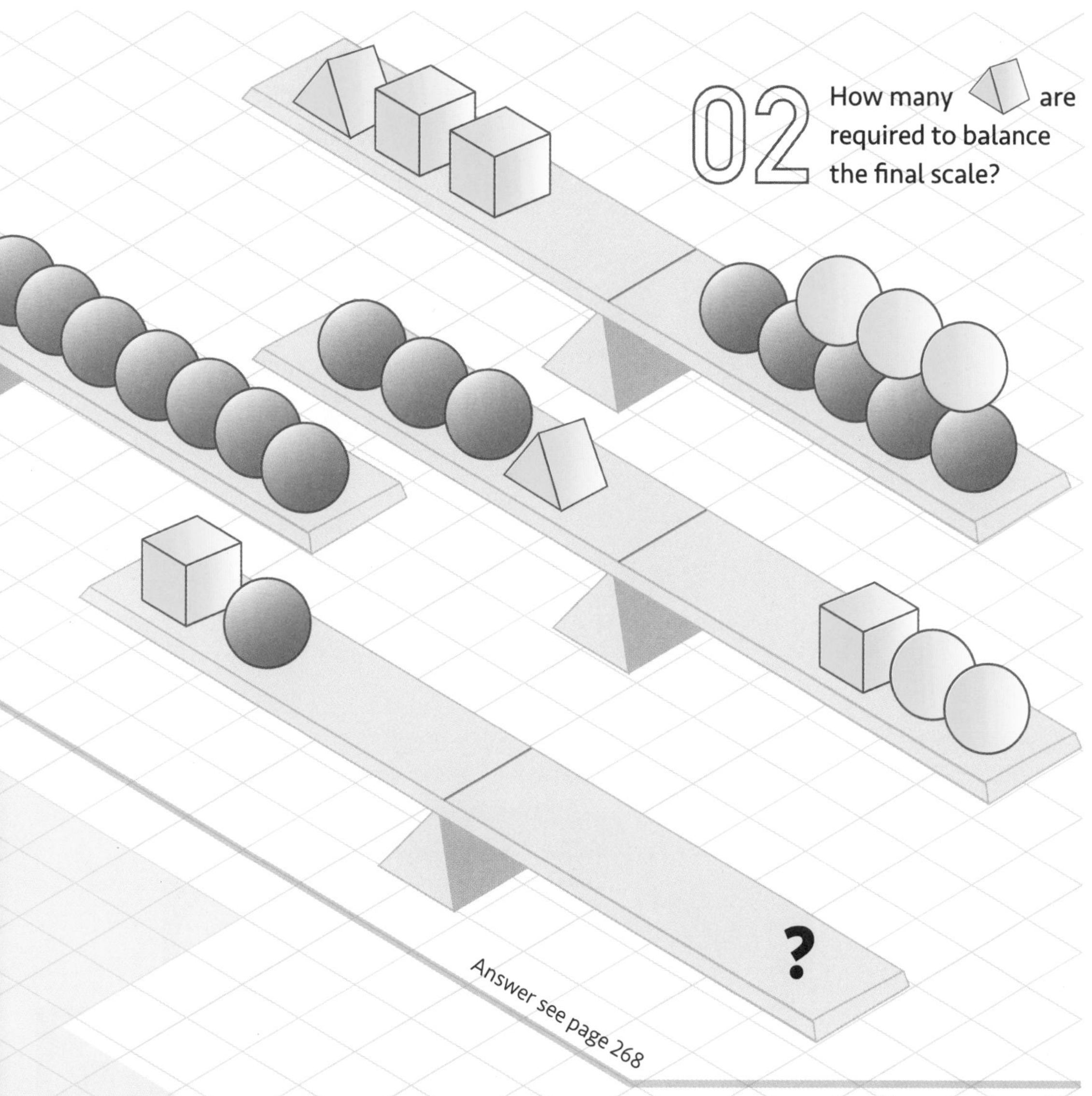 are required to balance the final scale?

Answer see page 268

Answer see page 268

03

Fill in the missing plus, minus, multiplication, and division signs to make the equation below correct, performing all calculations strictly in the order they appear on the page.

28 38 41 5 6 5 = 55

04

In each square, the arrow shows the direction you must move in. The numbers in some squares show that square's position in the correct sequence of moves. Move from top left to bottom right, visiting each square in the grid exactly once.

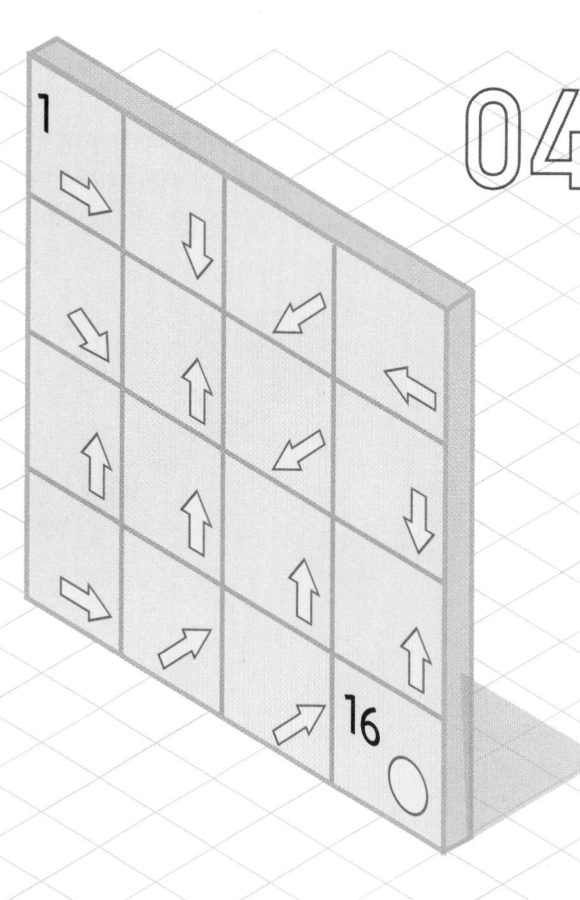

Answer see page 268

Answer see page 268

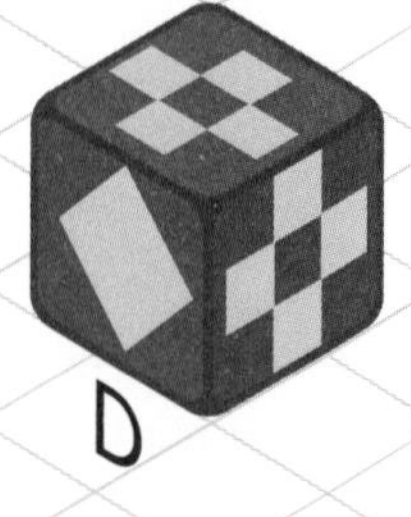

05

Which of the cubes A to E cannot be made using the layout shown?

06

Which of the options A to E most accurately continues the sequence?

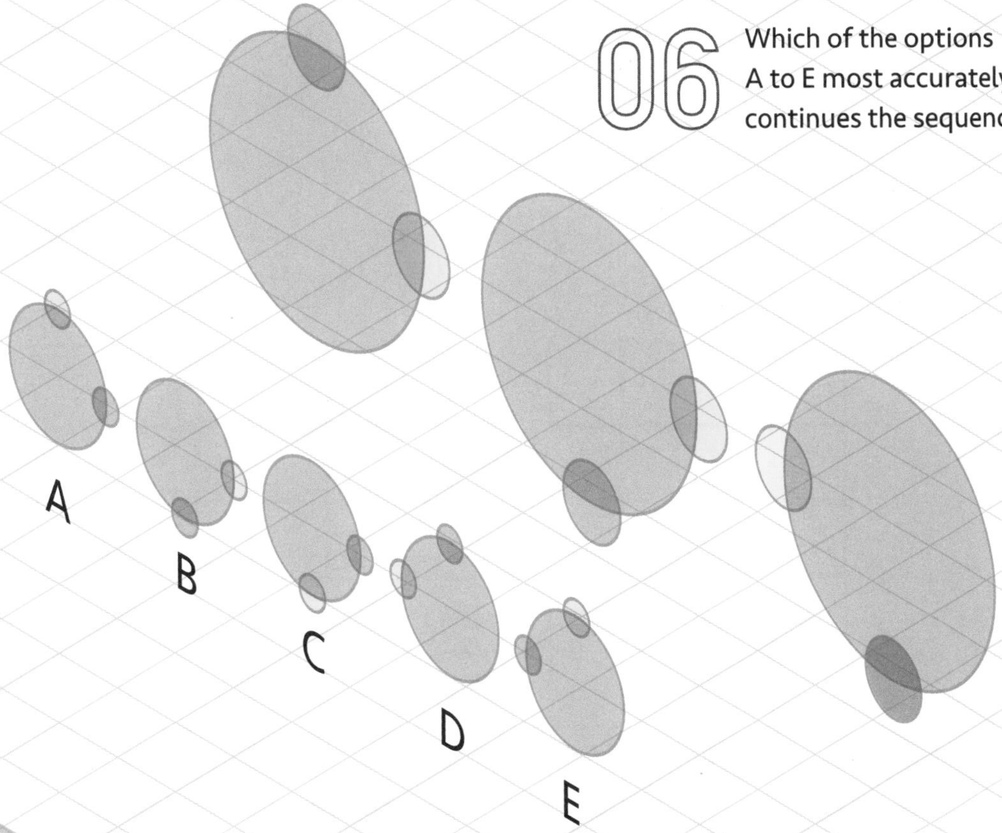

A

B

C

D

E

Answer see page 269

07

What number should replace the question mark?

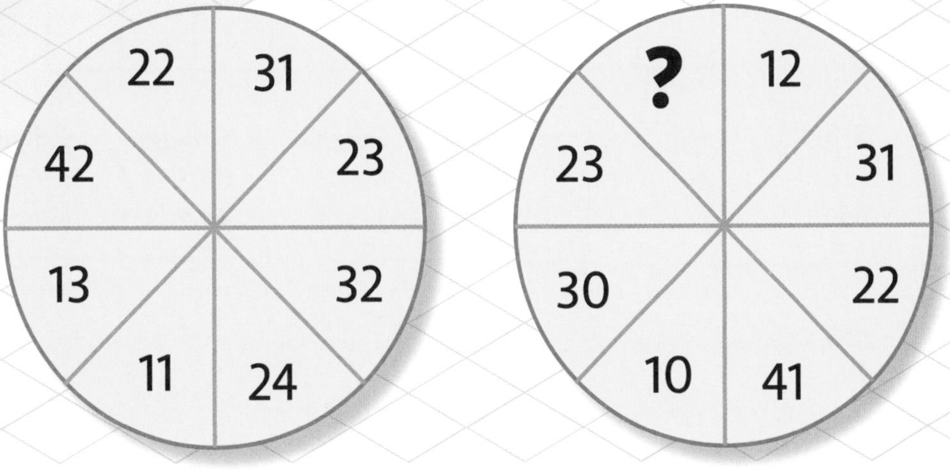

Left circle	Right circle
22	?
31	12
23	31
32	22
24	41
11	10
13	30
42	23

Answer see page 269

Fit the numbers shown into the design to complete the grid.

Answer see page 269

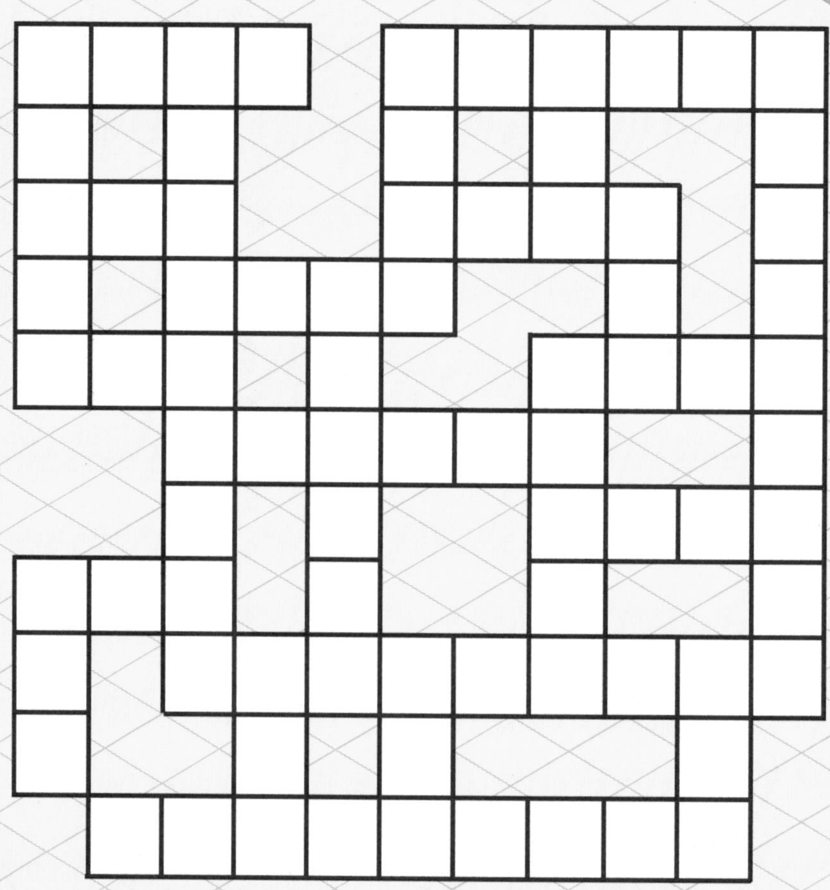

3 digits		4 digits	5 digits	6 digits	9 digits
187	814	1662	16871	862098	371837789
434	851	2599	88584	902091	541484449
471	875	5917		907063	625278445
478		7424			818354914
495		8113			
792		9879			

What number should replace the question mark?

Answer see page 269

Answer see page 269

10 Which of the designs A to E is the odd one out?

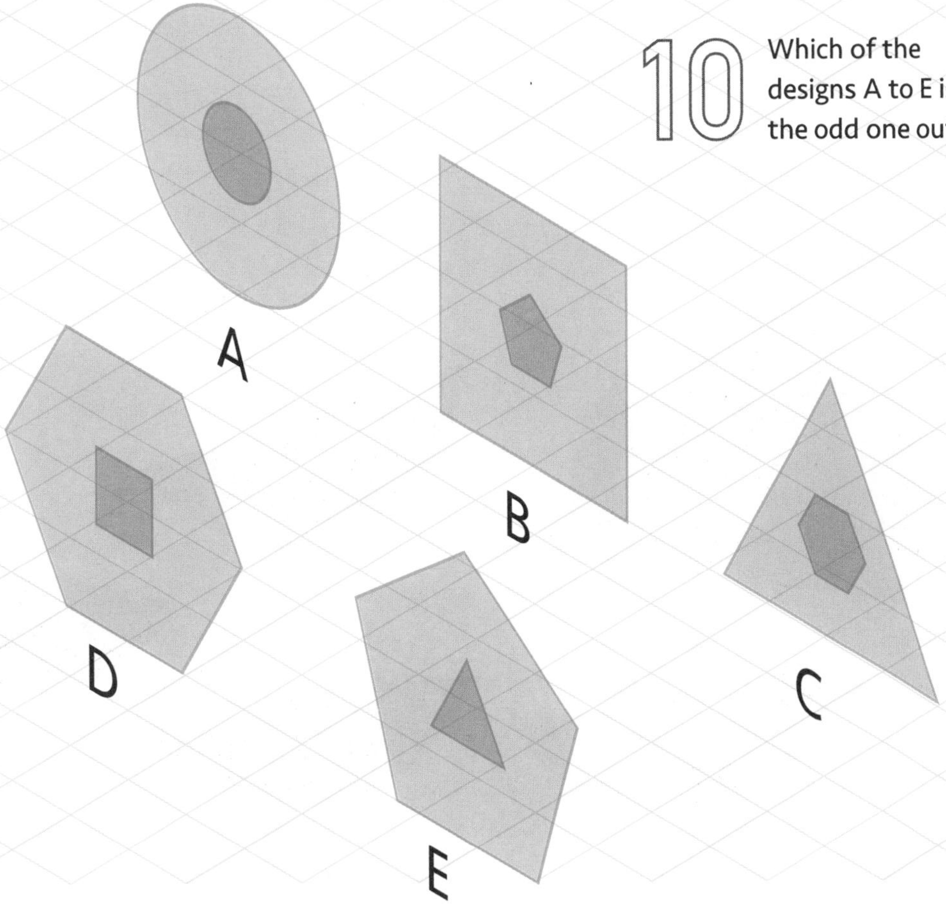

A

B

C

D

E

11 Which option A to E most accurately completes the pattern?

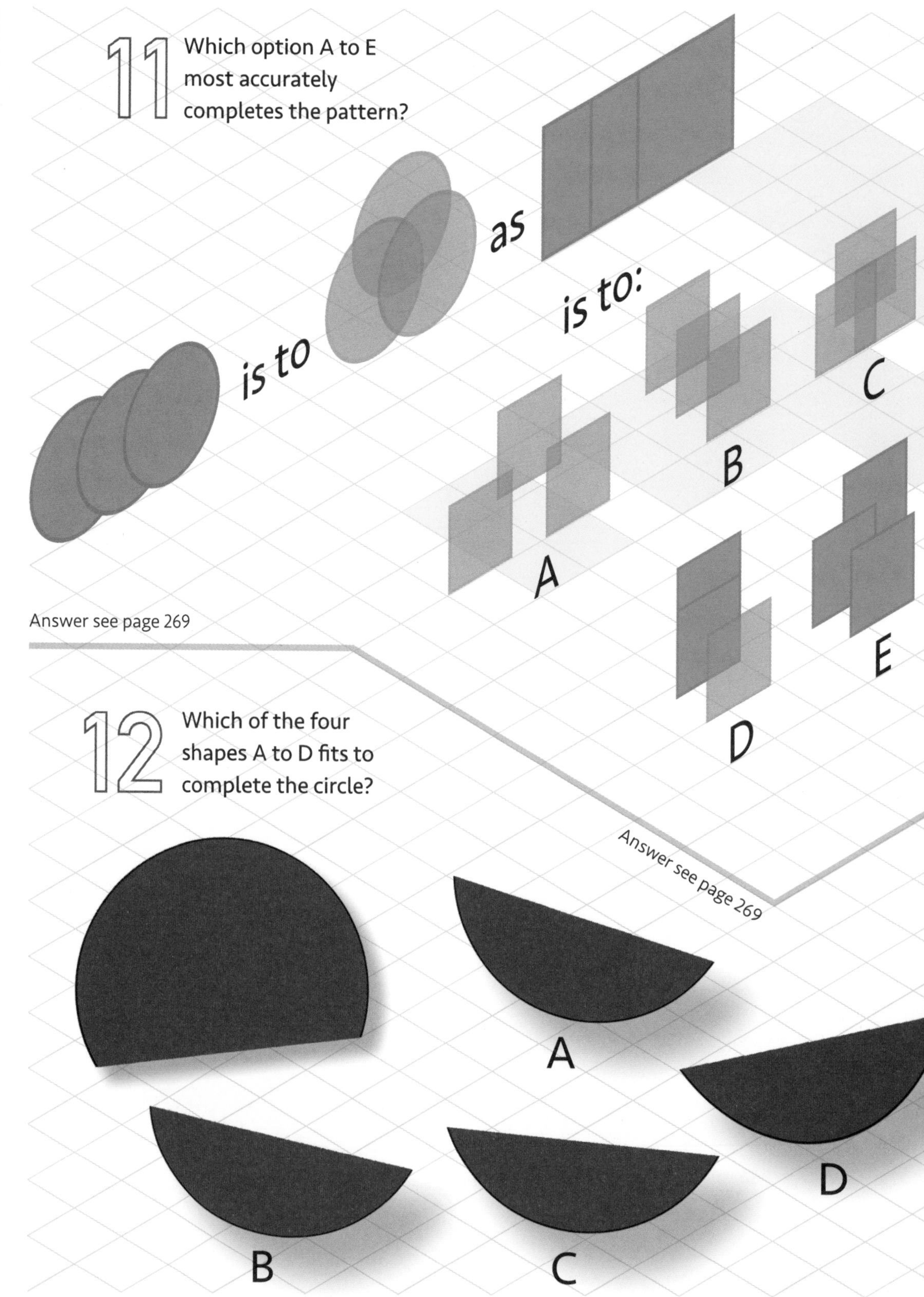

Answer see page 269

12 Which of the four shapes A to D fits to complete the circle?

Answer see page 269

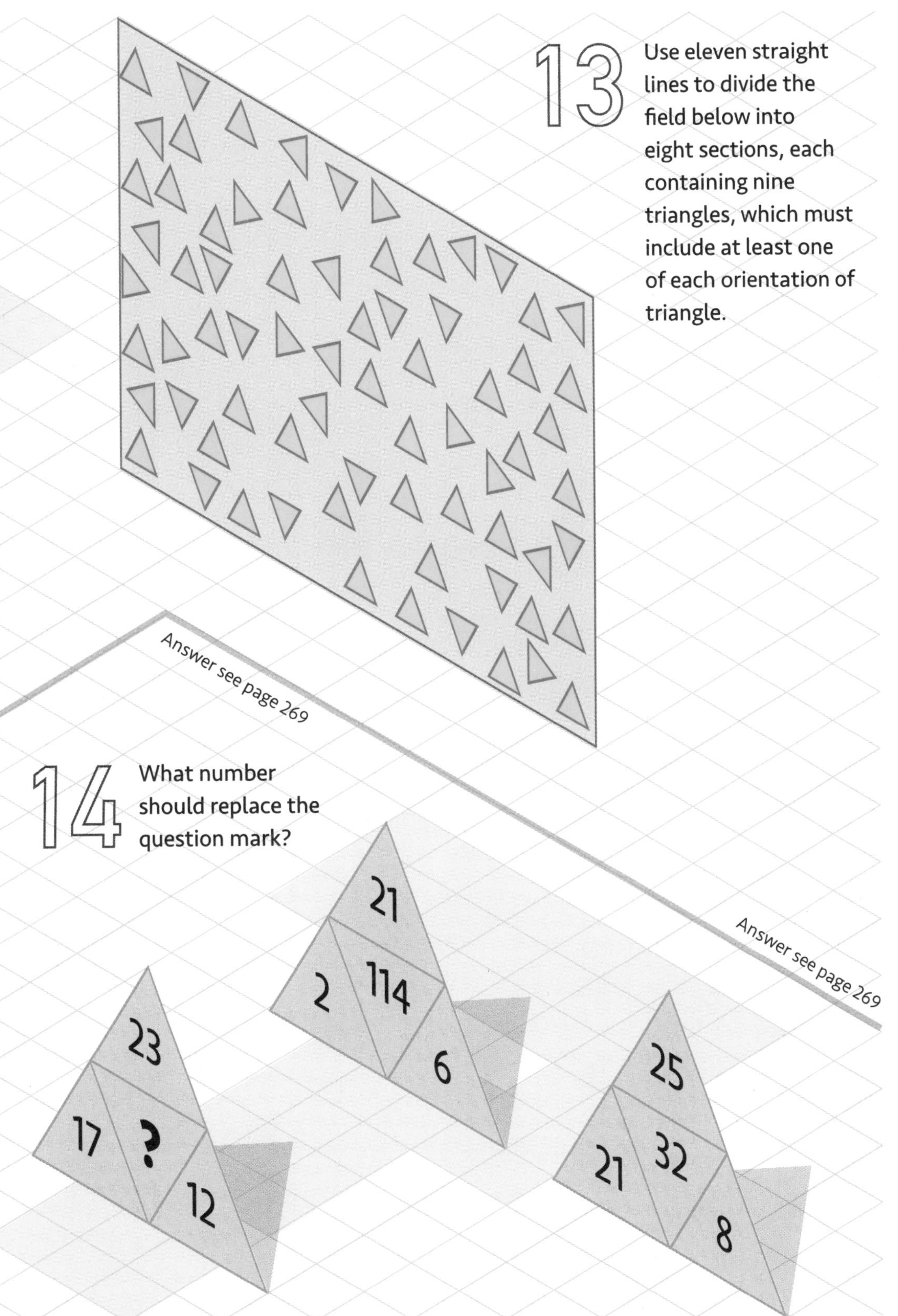

13

Use eleven straight lines to divide the field below into eight sections, each containing nine triangles, which must include at least one of each orientation of triangle.

Answer see page 269

14

What number should replace the question mark?

Answer see page 269

15 In the grid below, how much is each symbol worth?

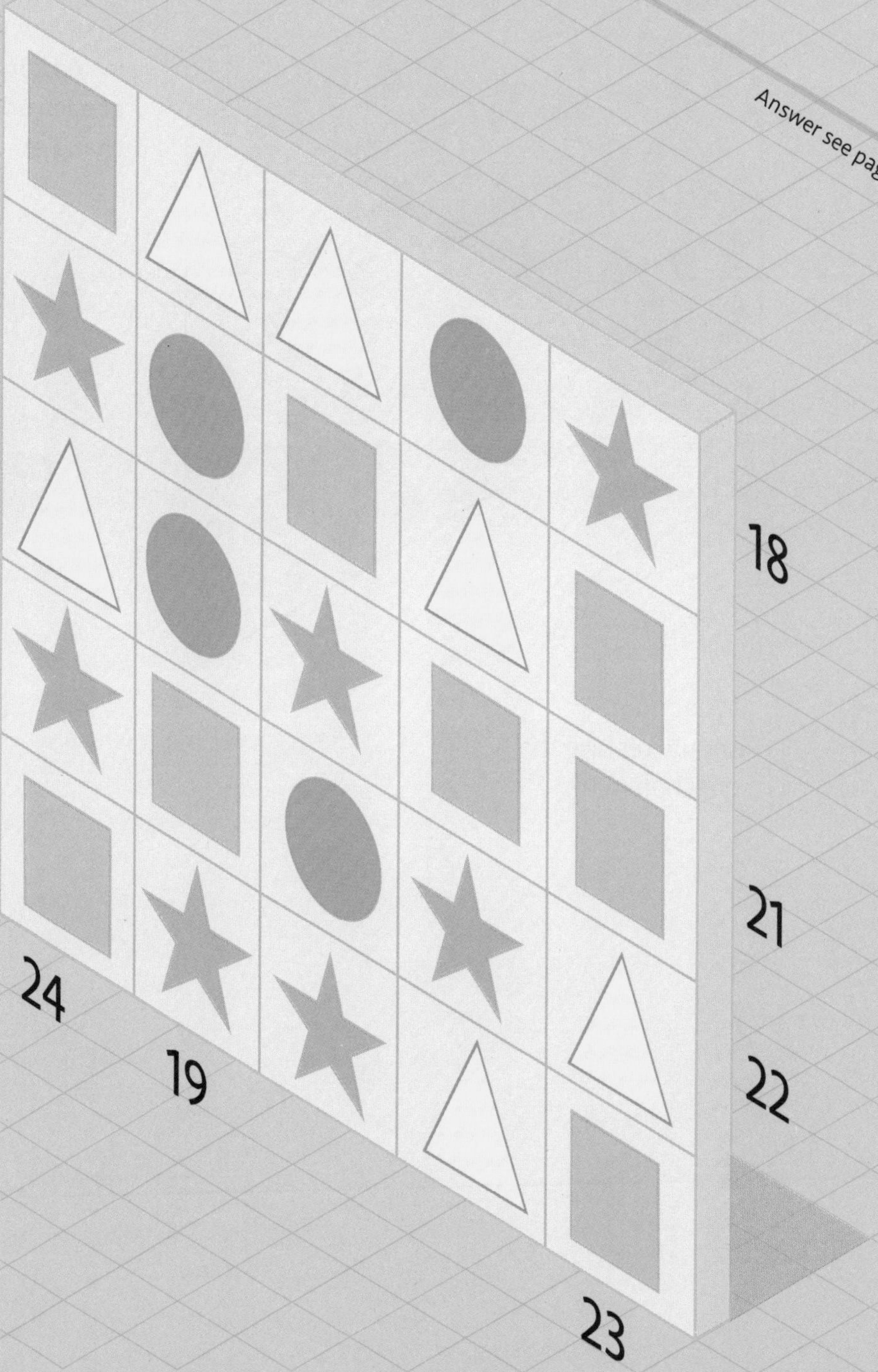

Answer see page 269

16

What number should replace the question mark?

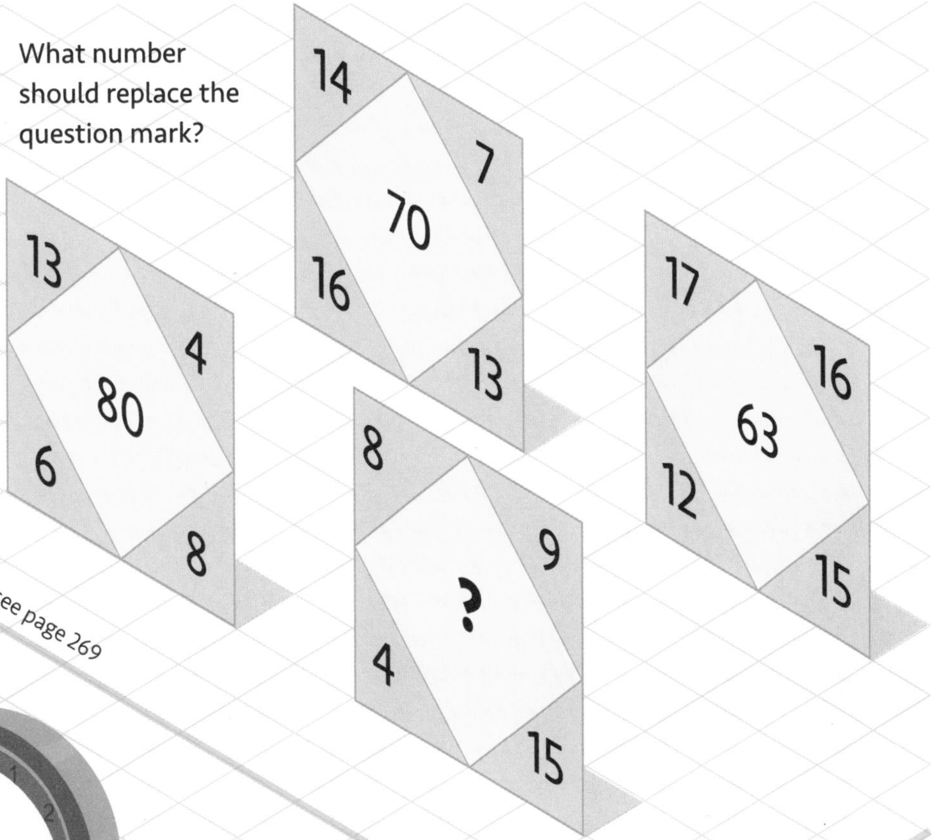

13	4	6	8	80
14	7	16	13	70
8	9	4	15	?
17	16	12	15	63

Answer see page 269

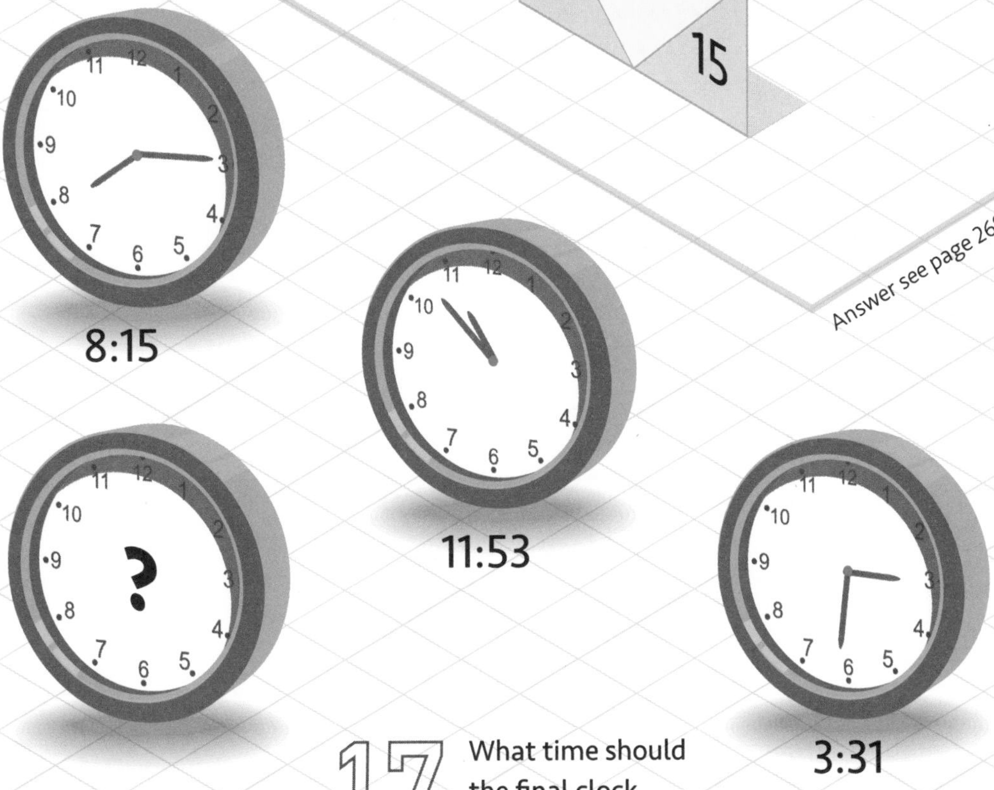

8:15

11:53

3:31

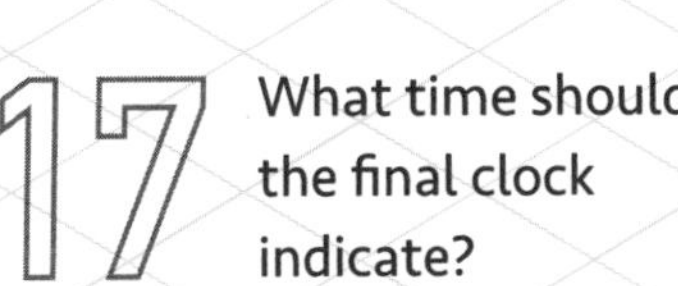

17

What time should the final clock indicate?

Answer see page 269

Combine the segments below to find the names of ten celebrities.

KATE	VE	WILL	ME
JAKE	ED	WAY	MI
DAN	GAN	HAAL	BU
CUM	ANNE	BILL	SLET
HA	BEN	ICT	RAY
CLI	BER	KE	SCE
WIN	MUR	BIN	CEY
STE	FOX	IAMS	RAD
GYLL	EN	BATCH	FFE
VIN	SPA	IEL	RO
			THA

Answer see page 269

Answer see page 269

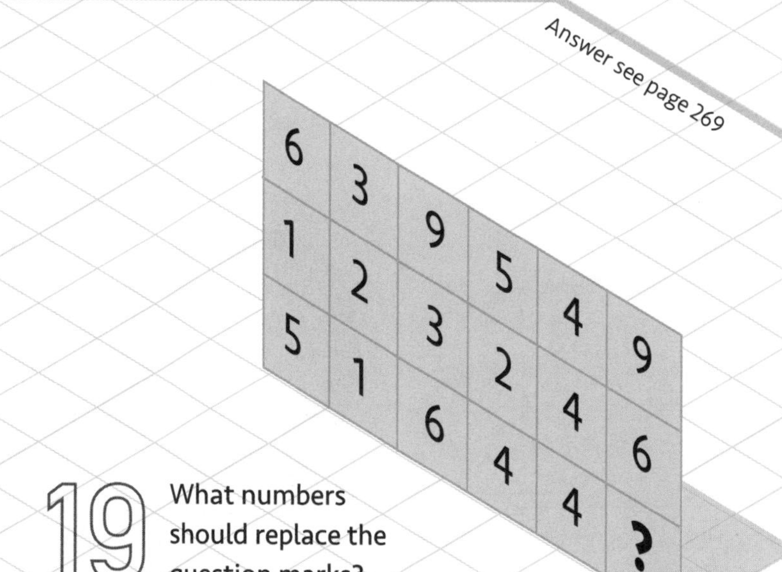

19 What numbers should replace the question marks?

20

Which symbols are missing from the grid below?

Answer see page 269

Test 9

01

Which of the pentagons at the bottom should replace the question mark?

Answer see page 269

?

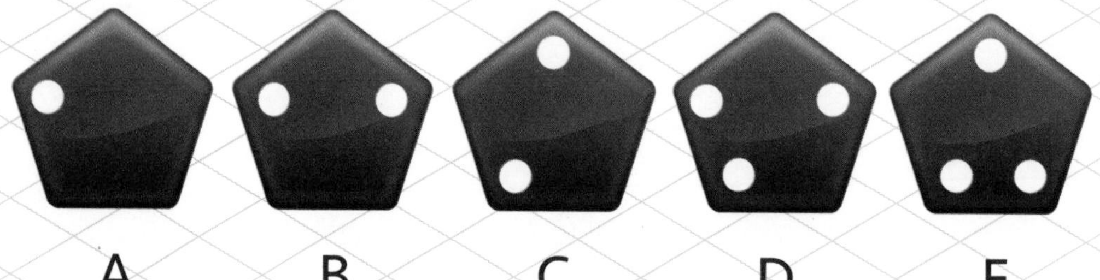

A B C D E

02

Scales 1 and 2 are in perfect balance. How many triangles are needed to balance scale 3?

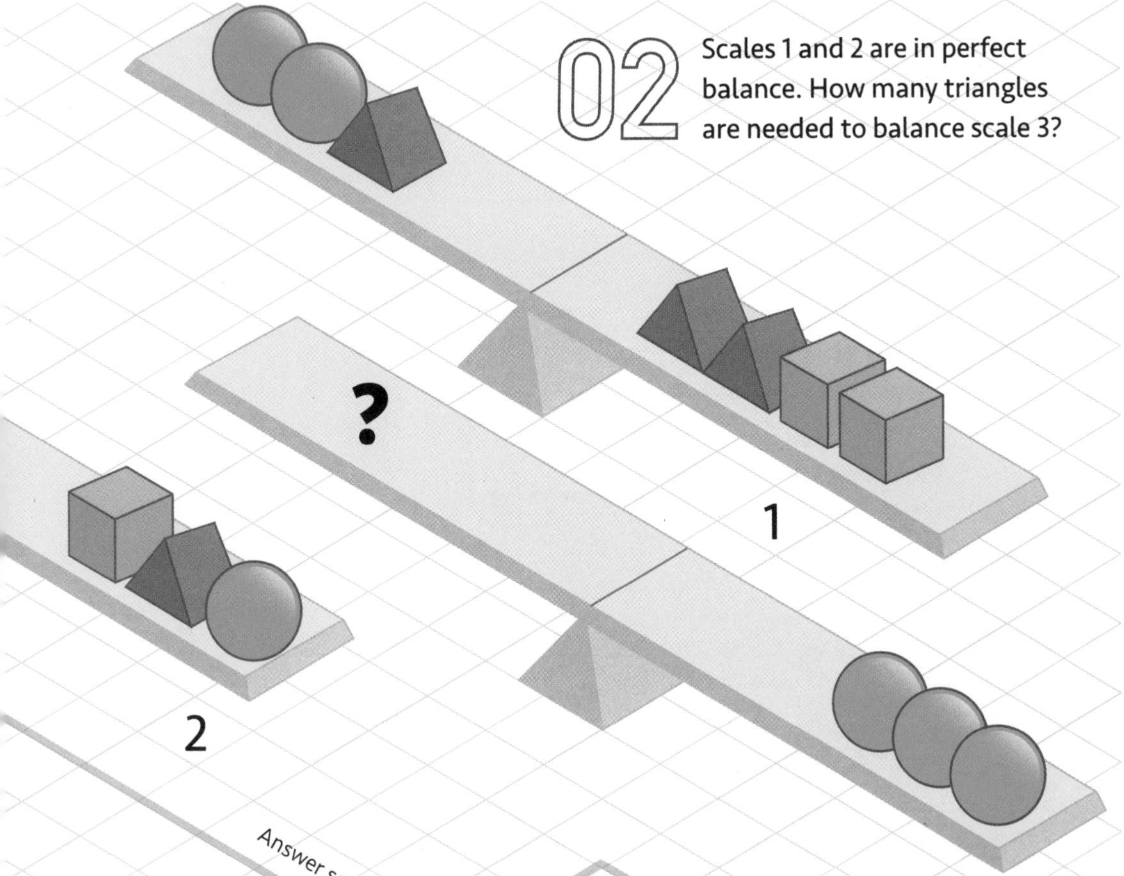

?

1

2

3

Answer see page 270

03

If 2/5 is 6, how much is 3?

Answer see page 270

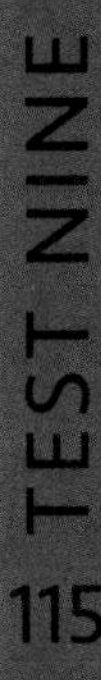

Which shape below can be put with the one above to form a perfect square?

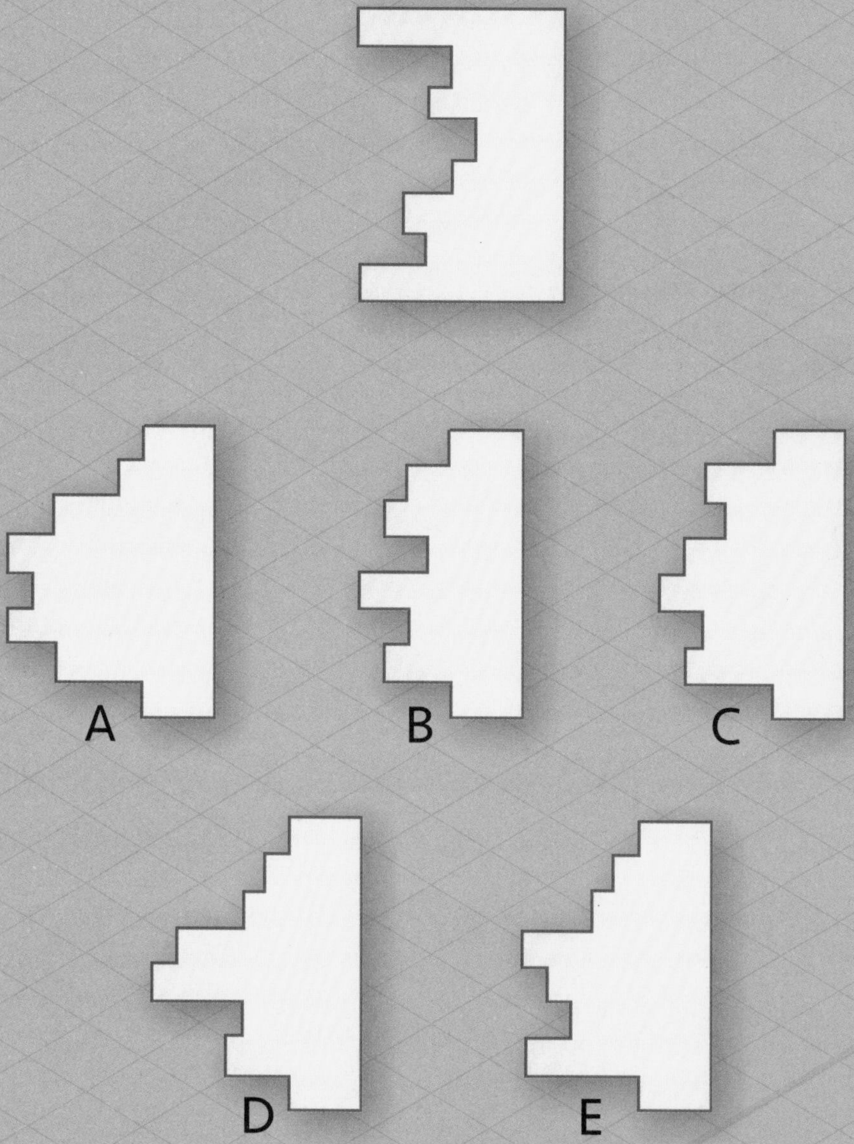

A

B

C

D

E

Answer see page 270

Select the correct figure from the numbered ones below, to replace the question mark.

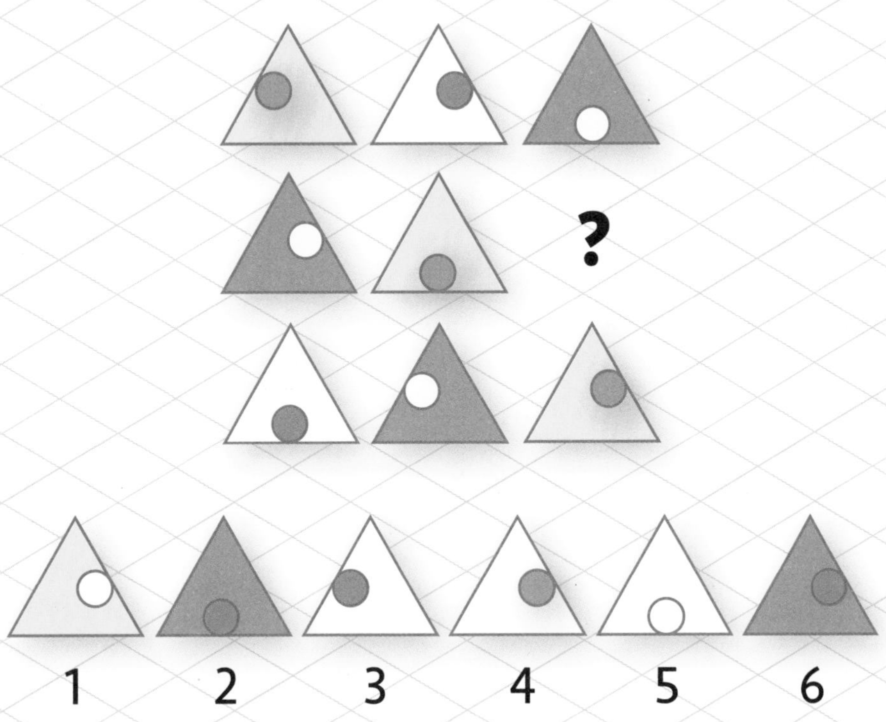

Answer see page 270

Answer see page 270

Complete the square using nine consecutive numbers, so that all rows, columns, and large diagonals add up to the same total.

07

Each of the nine squares in the grid marked 1A to 3C should incorporate all of the items which are shown in the squares of the same letter and number, at left and top. For example, square 2A should incorporate all of the items in squares 2 and A. One square however, is incorrect. Which is it?

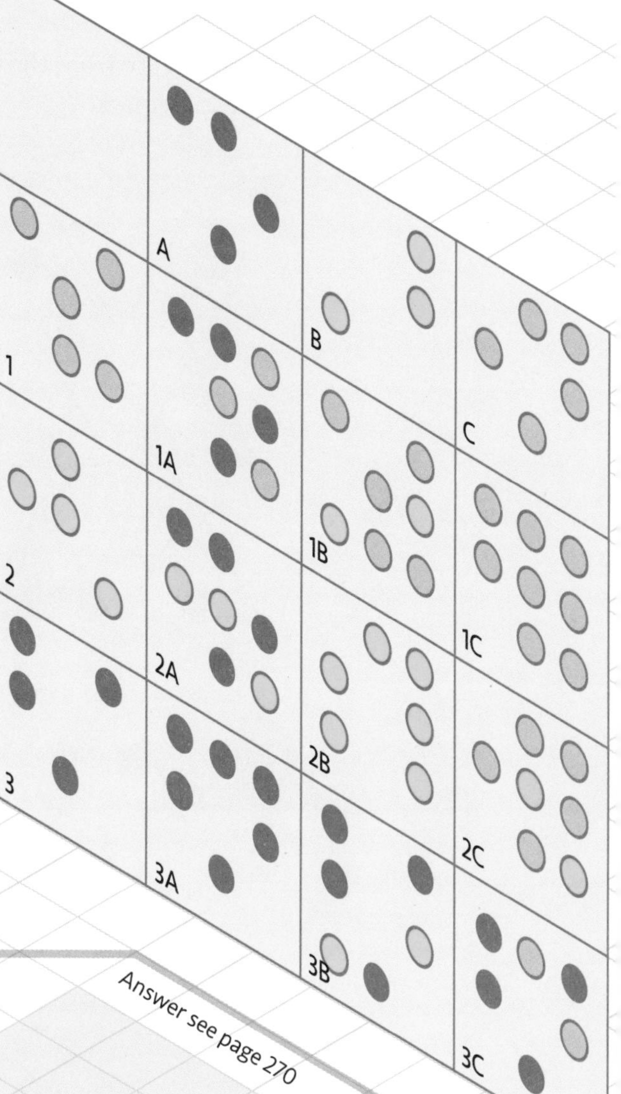

Answer see page 270

08

Which is the odd one out?

Answer see page 270

09 Which is the odd one out?

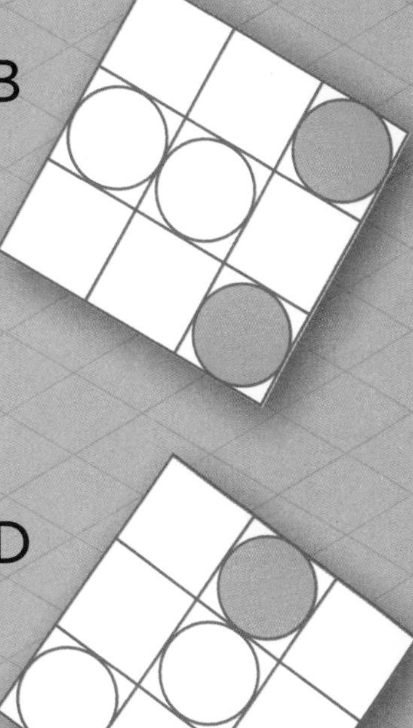

B

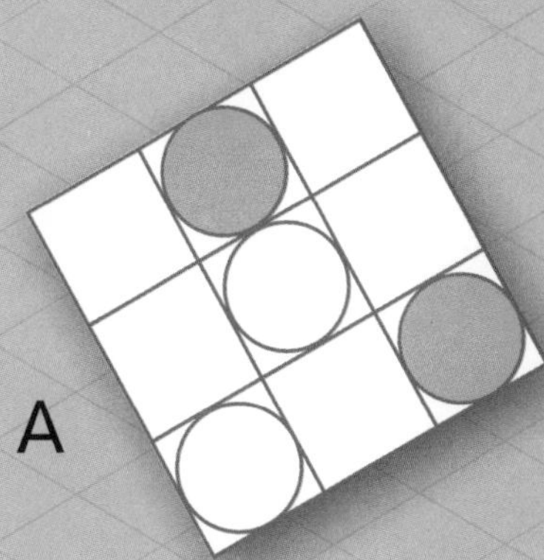

A

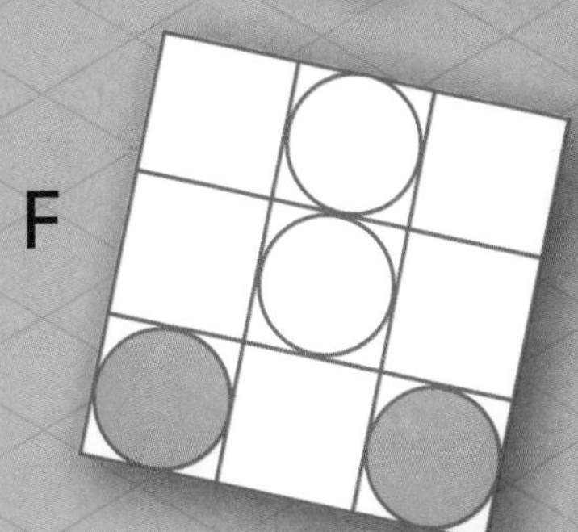

D

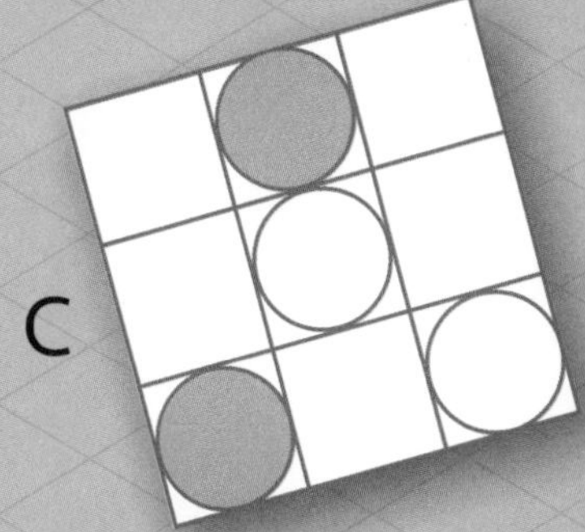

C

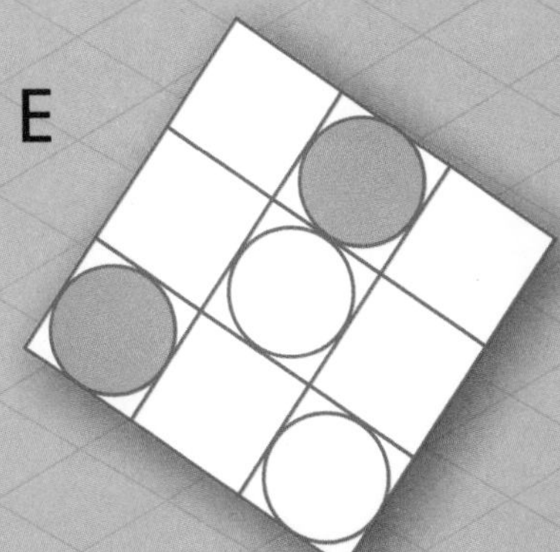

E

F

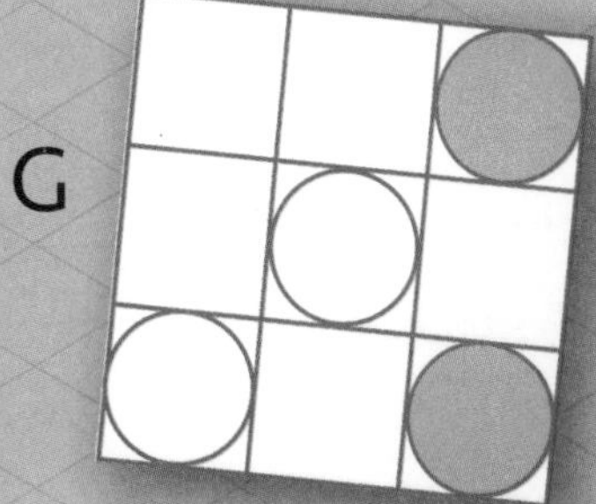

G

Answer see page 270

10

What is the value of a square?

Answer see page 270

11

Insert the missing number.

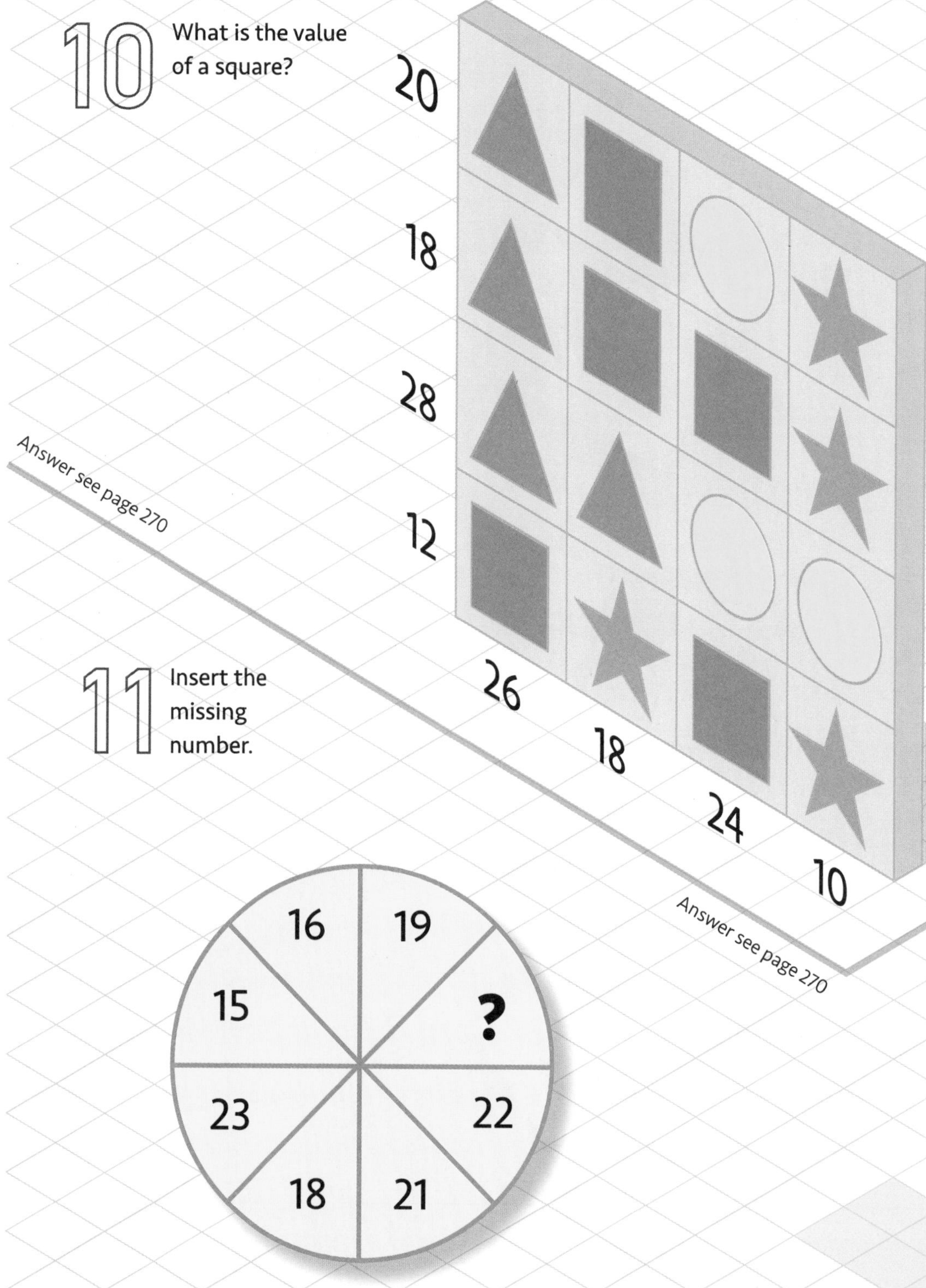

Answer see page 270

12

Which of the constructed boxes below cannot be made from the given shape?

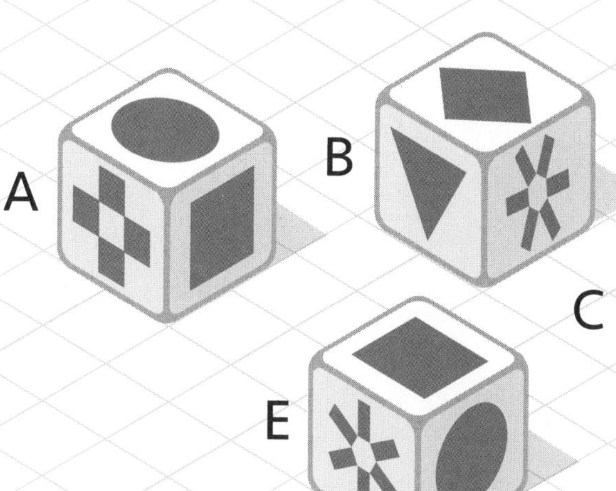

Answer see page 270

13

Which number is the odd one out?

A	3	1	7	5	3	9
B	6	5	7	2	8	9
C	8	2	6	4	6	7
D	4	6	4	9	8	3

Answer see page 270

14

When complete, this 6 x 6 x 6 cube contains 216 individual blocks. How many blocks are required to complete the cube?

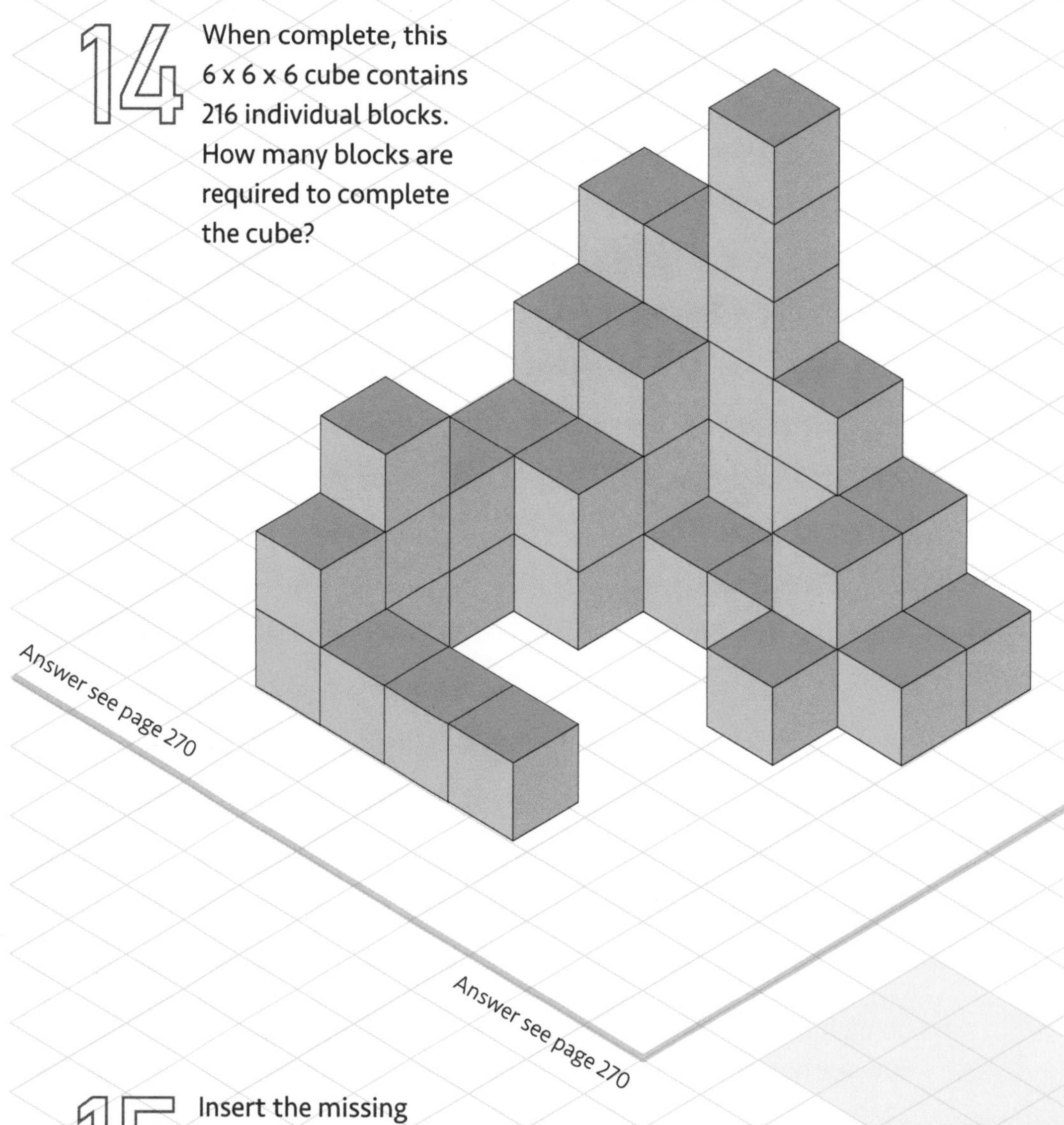

Answer see page 270

Answer see page 270

15

Insert the missing numbers.

2 5 10 17 26 ? ?

16

Tokyo is 12 hours ahead of Buenos Aires, which is 7½ hours behind Kabul. It is 2:15 a.m. on Friday in Kabul, what time is it in the other two cities?

KABUL

TOKYO

BUENOS AIRES

Answer see page 270

17

What number should replace the question mark?

7
11
27
3
6

Answer see page 270

18

Which of these dice is not like the others?

A B C D E F

Answer see page 270

19

Which line of two numbers below has the same relationship as the two above?

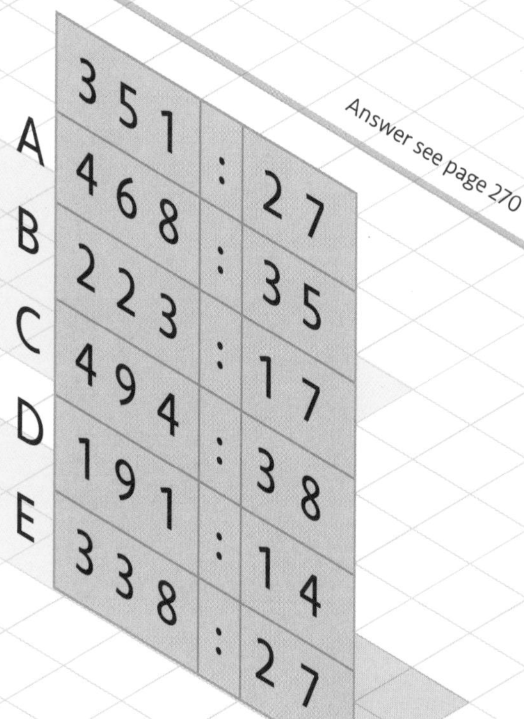

Answer see page 270

20

Which of the lettered clocks below continues the numbered series?

1 2 3

4 5

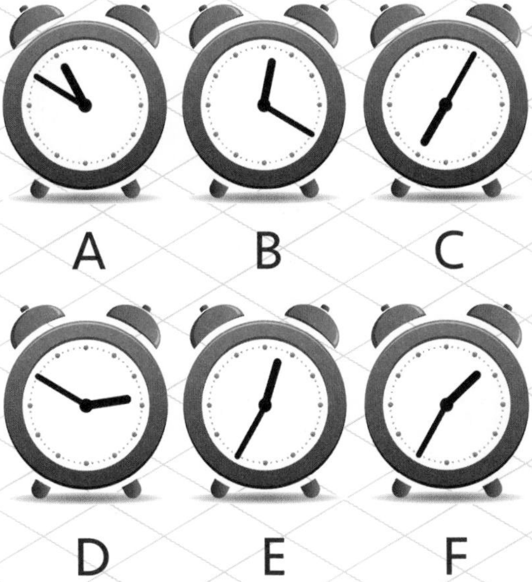

A B C

D E F

Answer see page 270

Test 10

01

Which of the four shapes A to D fits to complete the square?

Answer see page 271

A

B

C

D

02

How many [pyramid] are required to balance the final scale?

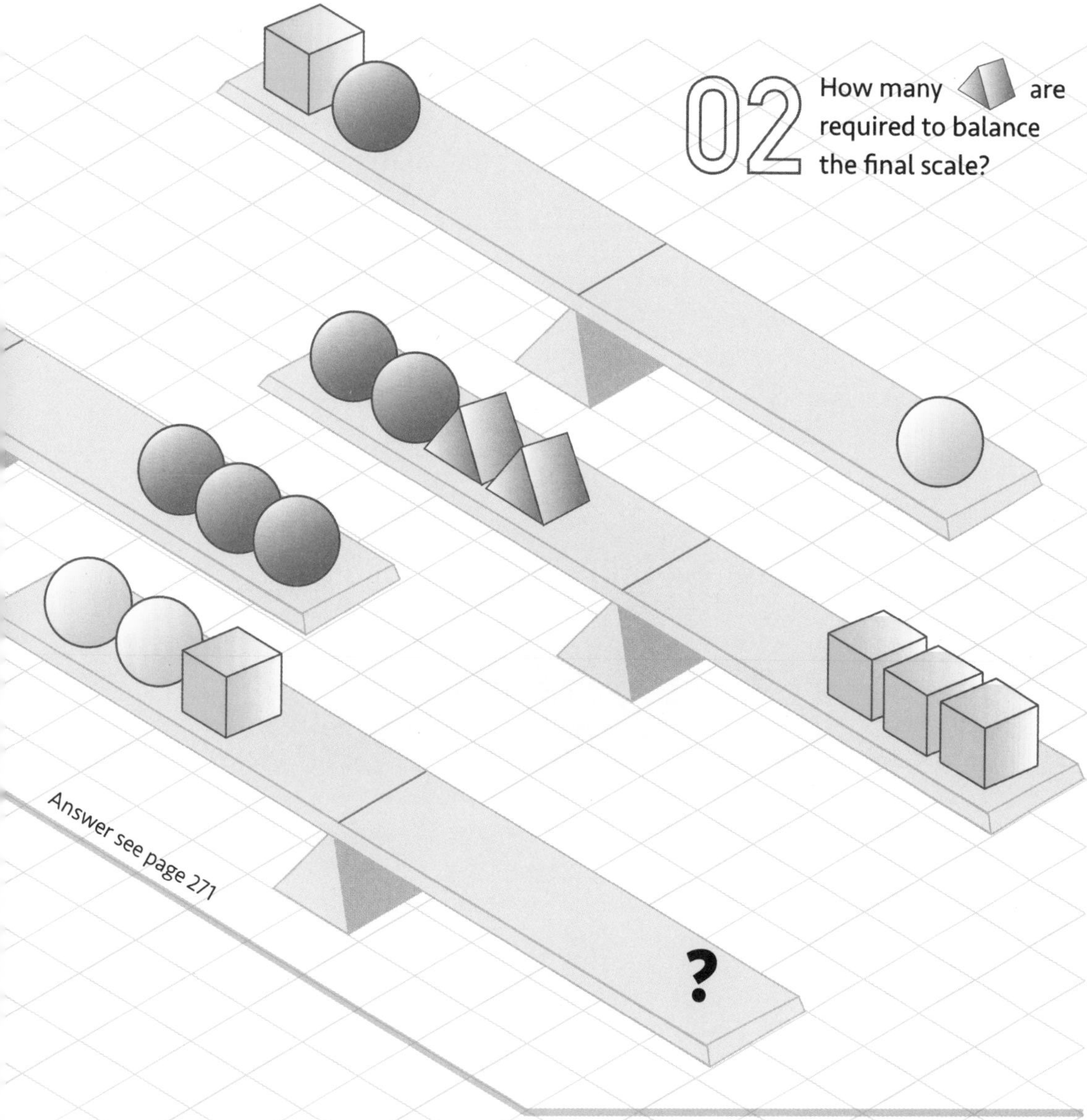

?

Answer see page 271

Answer see page 271

03

Fill in the missing plus, minus, multiplication, and division signs to make the equation below correct, performing all calculations strictly in the order they appear on the page.

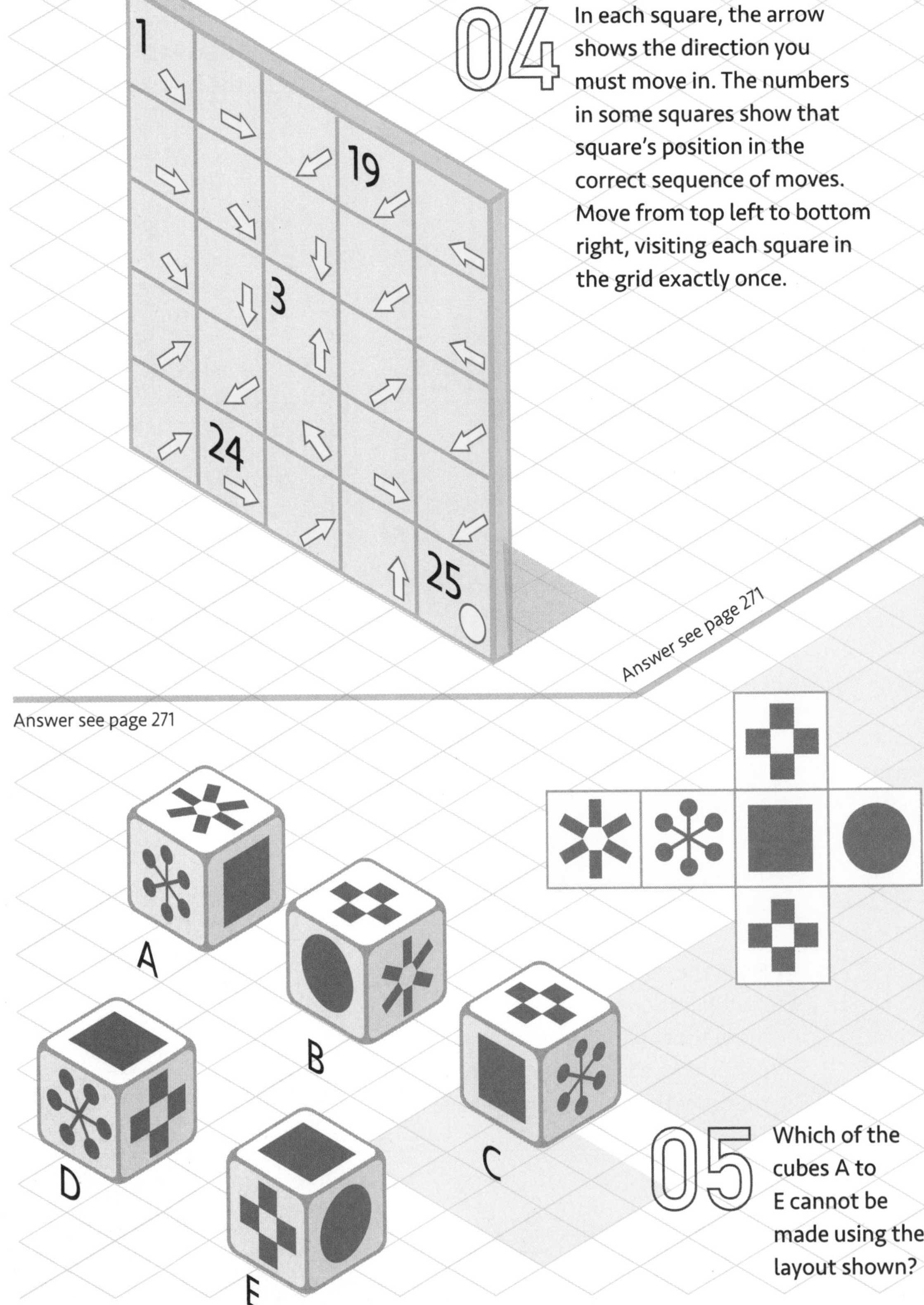

04

In each square, the arrow shows the direction you must move in. The numbers in some squares show that square's position in the correct sequence of moves. Move from top left to bottom right, visiting each square in the grid exactly once.

Answer see page 271

Answer see page 271

05

Which of the cubes A to E cannot be made using the layout shown?

06

Which of the options A to E most accurately continues the sequence?

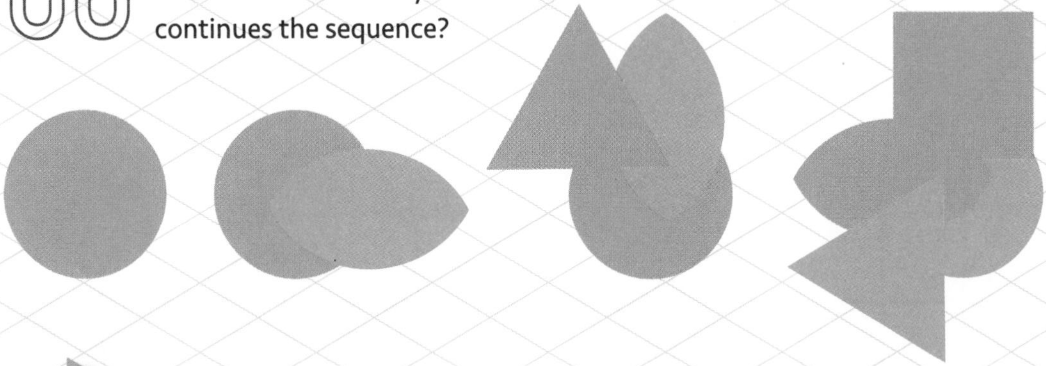

A B C D E

Answer see page 271

Answer see page 271

07

What number should replace the question mark?

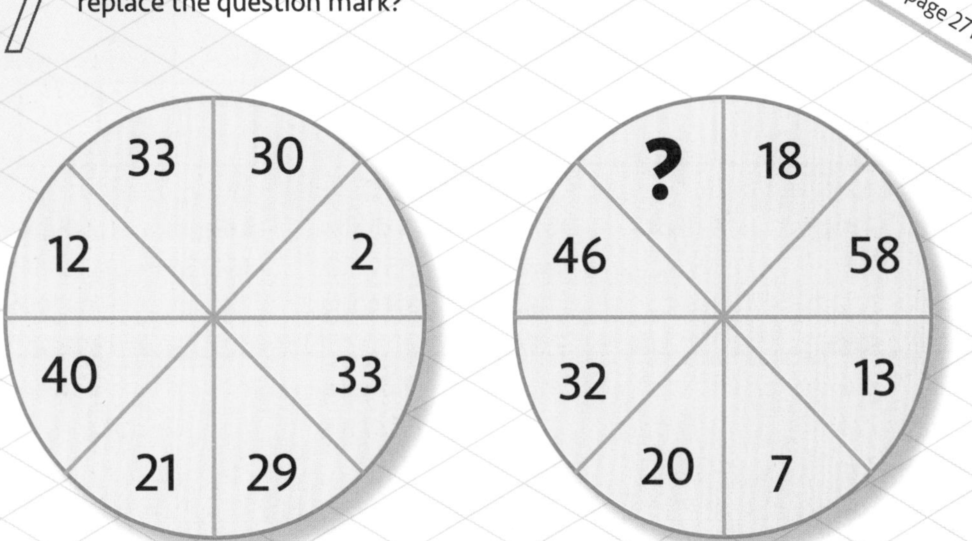

Fit the numbers shown into the design to complete the grid.

Answer see page 271

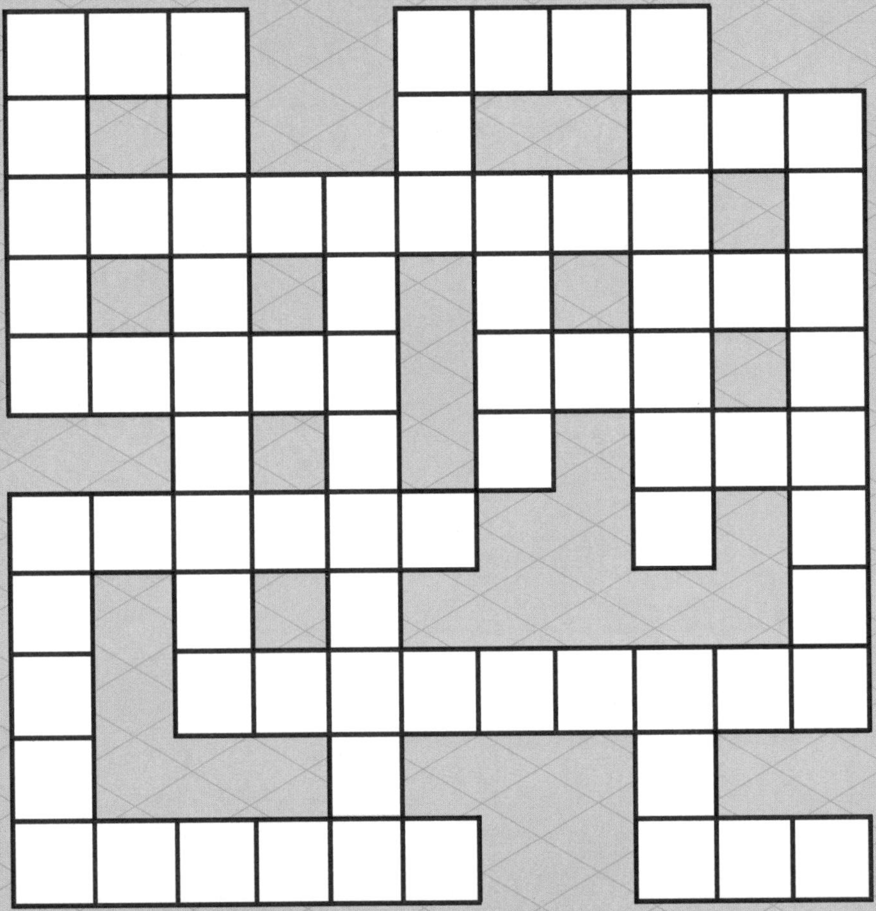

3 digits	4 digits	5 digits	6 digits	8 digits	9 digits
106	3276	44836	455790	86433649	134584575
228	5505	48843	644004		413799160
576		91874			531196179
610			**7 digits**		874246384
723			5247178		
751					
754					
911					

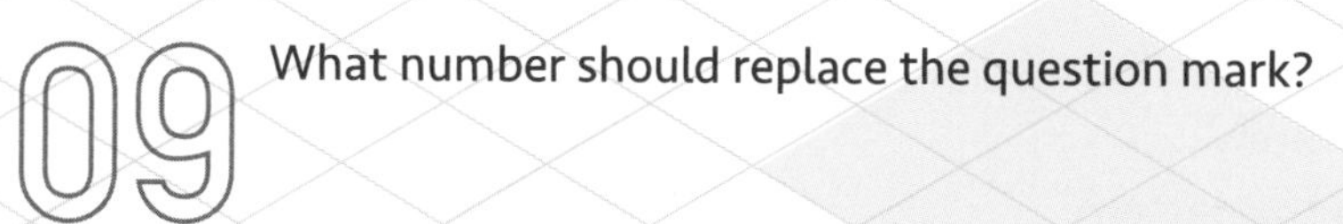

09

What number should replace the question mark?

Answer see page 271

Answer see page 271

10

Which of the designs A to E is the odd one out?

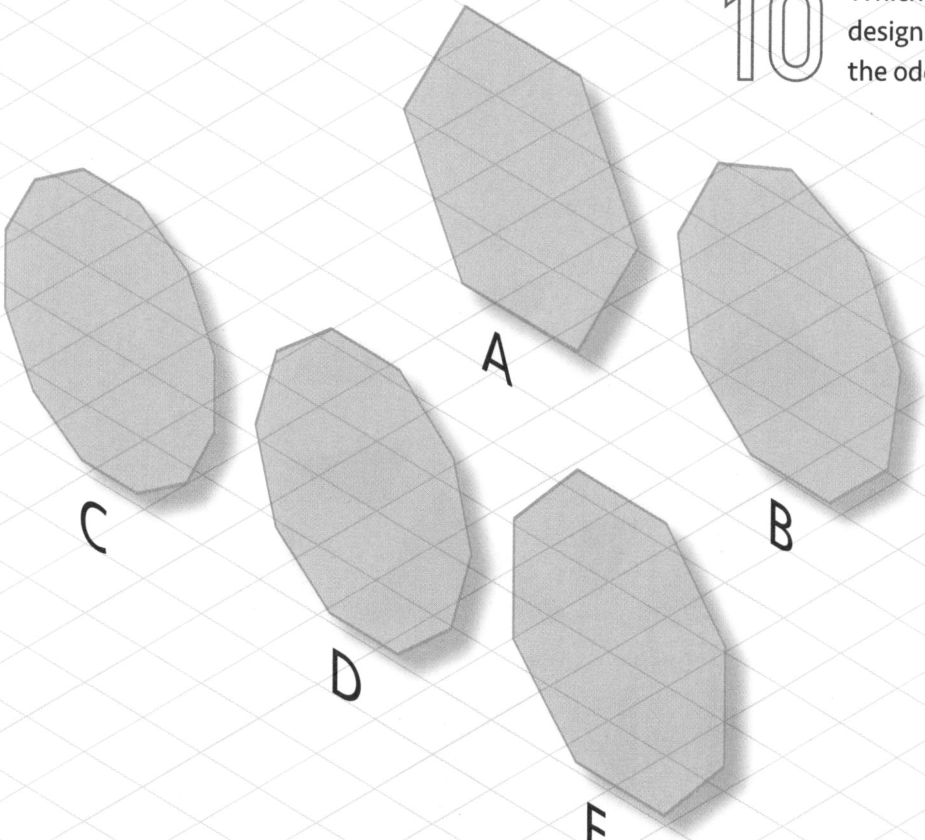

A

B

C

D

E

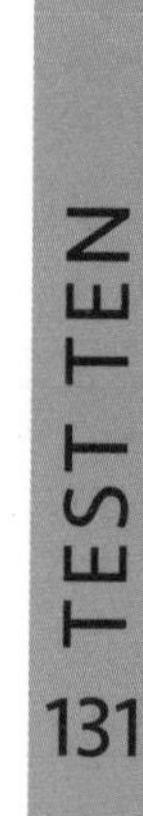

11

Which option A to E most accurately completes the pattern?

is to

as

is to:

A

B

C

D

E

Answer see page 271

12

The pieces can be assembled into a regular geometric shape. What is it?

Answer see page 271

13

Use four straight lines to divide the field below into eight identically-sized sections, each containing eleven balls.

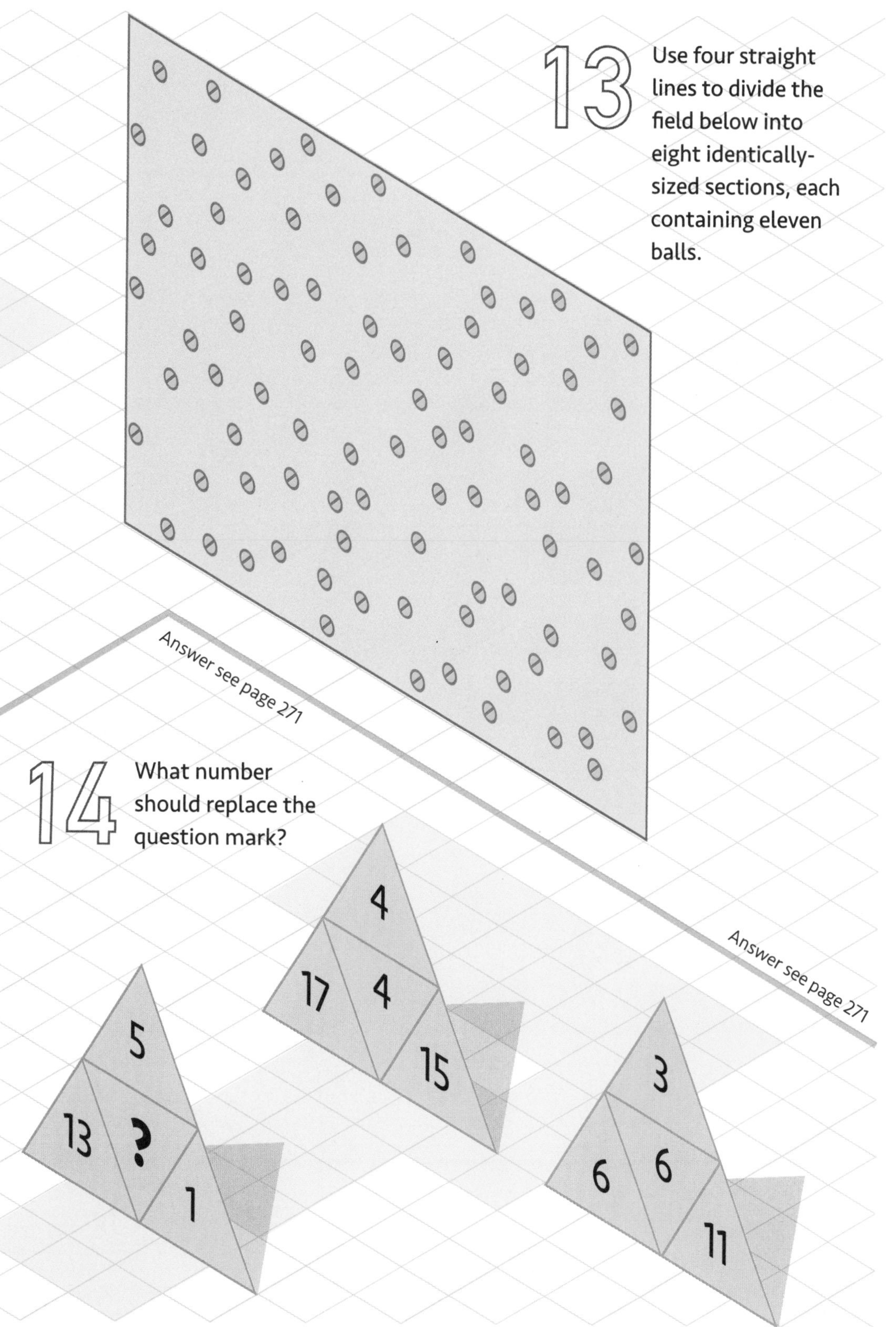

Answer see page 271

14

What number should replace the question mark?

Answer see page 271

15

In the grid below, how much is each symbol worth?

Answer see page 271

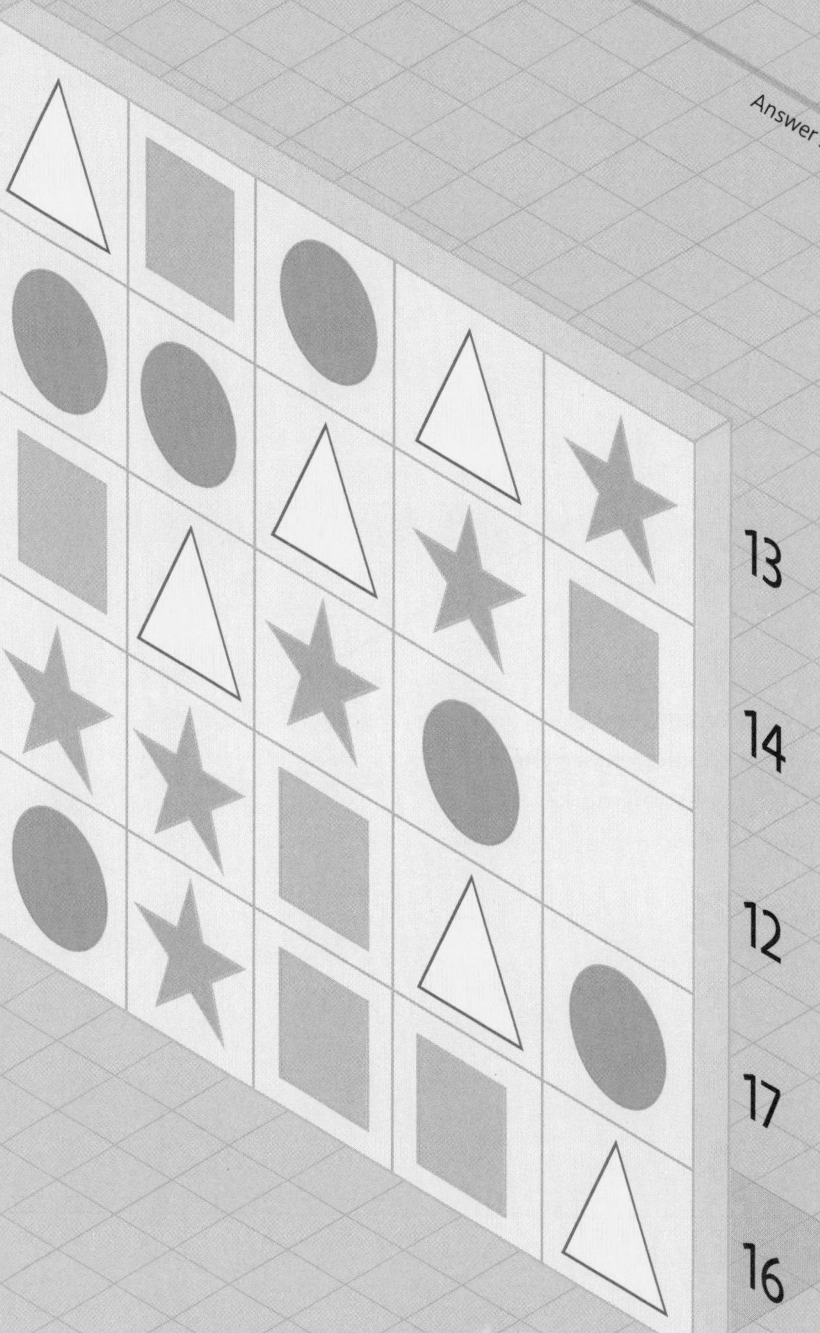

16

What number should replace the question mark?

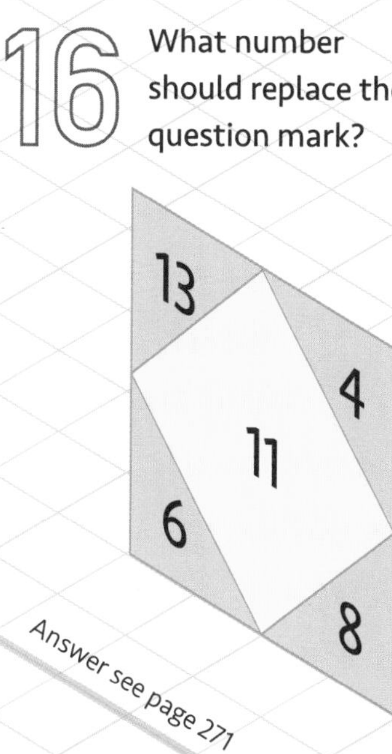

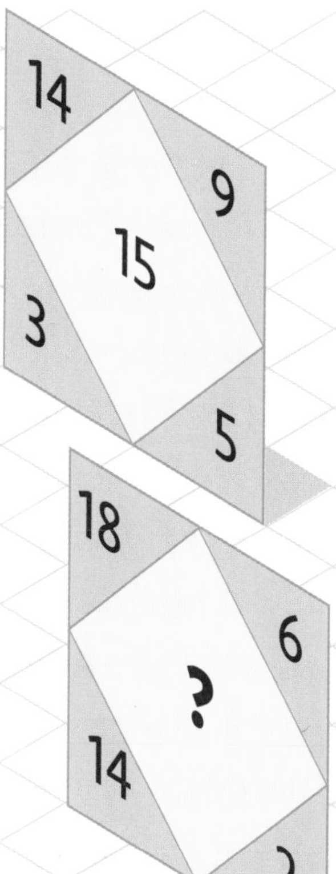

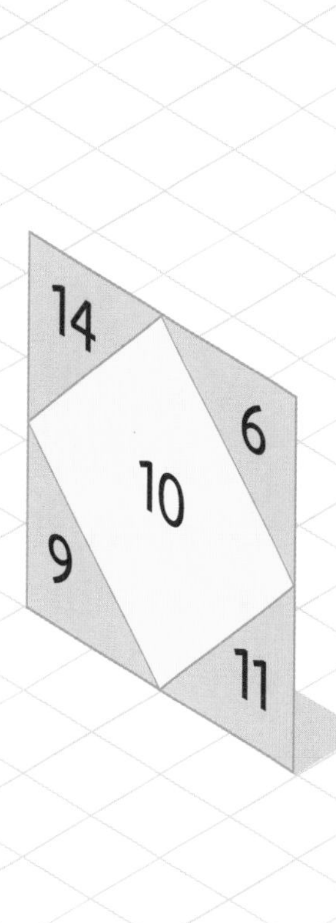

Answer see page 271

12:35

1:45

7:35

17

What time would the next clock indicate?

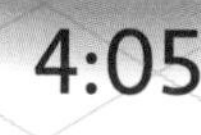

4:05

Answer see page 272

18

Combine the segments below to find the names of ten celebrities.

IS	AS	PORT	AR
RIO	LIE	ES	AN
MAN	ON	TA	DO
FERR	SON	STA	JAM
JA	DER	TO	CAP
CO	GRINT	ELL	CHAN
WILL	THAM	ON	LE
BAN	CKIE	JA	FRAN
SON	NIO	DI	RU
HARR	JACK	NICH	NA
OL	PERT	FORD	

Answer see page 272

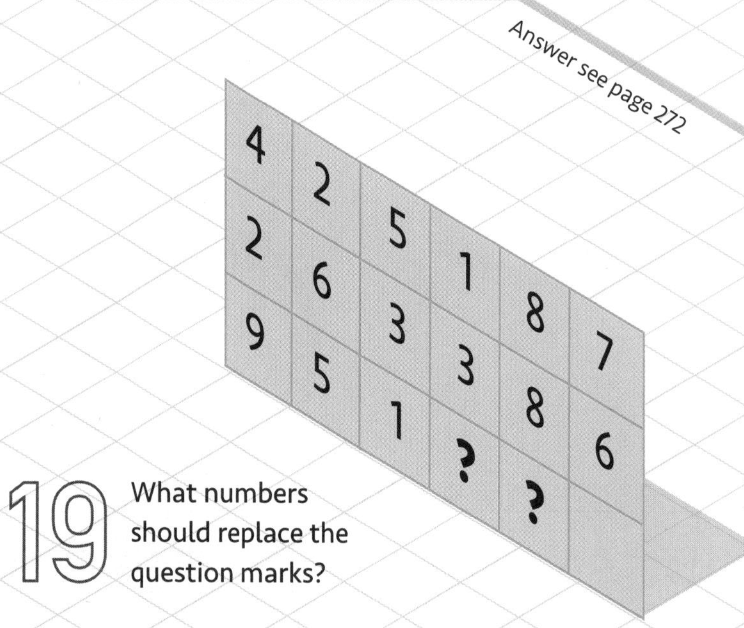

Answer see page 272

19

What numbers should replace the question marks?

20

Which symbols are missing from the grid below?

●	○	△	●	△	■	○	■	■	❑	❑	●	△	●	○
■	■	❑	❑	●	△	●	○	△	●	△	■	○	■	■
○	△	●	△	■	○	■	■	❑	❑	●	△	●	○	△
■	❑	❑	●	△	●	○	△	●	△	■	○	■	■	❑
△	●	△	■	○	■	■	❑	❑	●	△	●	○	△	●
❑	❑	●	△	●	○	△	●	△	■	○	■	■	❑	❑
●	△	■	○	■	■				●	●	○	△	●	△
❑	●	△	●	○	△				○	■	■	❑	❑	●
△	■	○	■	■	❑				●	○	△	●	△	■
●	△	●	○	△	●	△	■	○	■	■	❑	❑	●	△
■	○	■	■	❑	❑	●	△	●	○	△	●	△	■	○
△	●	○	△	●	△	■	○	■	■	❑	❑	●	△	●
○	■	■	❑	❑	●	△	●	○	△	●	△	■	○	■
●	○	△	●	△	■	○	■	■	❑	❑	●	△	●	○
■	■	❑	❑	●	△	●	○	△	●	△	■	○	■	■

Answer see page 272

Test 11

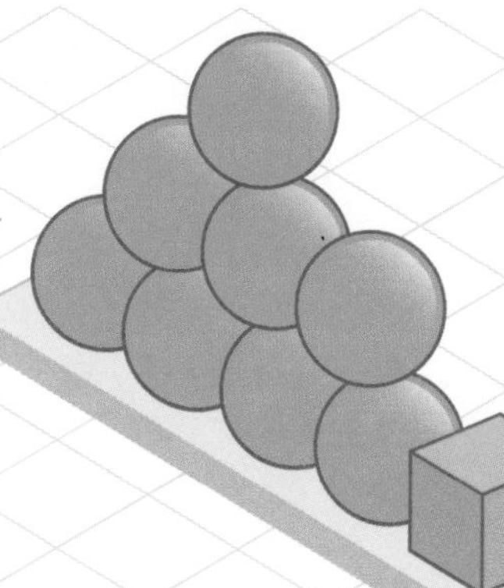

01

Which of the pentagons at the bottom should replace the question mark?

Answer see page 272

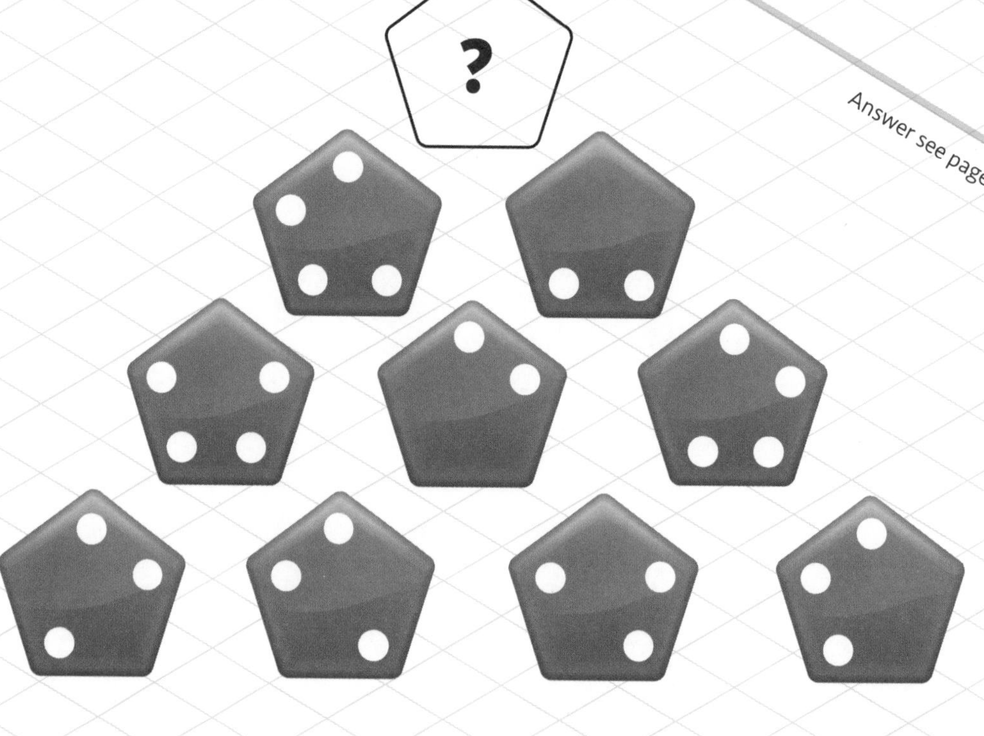

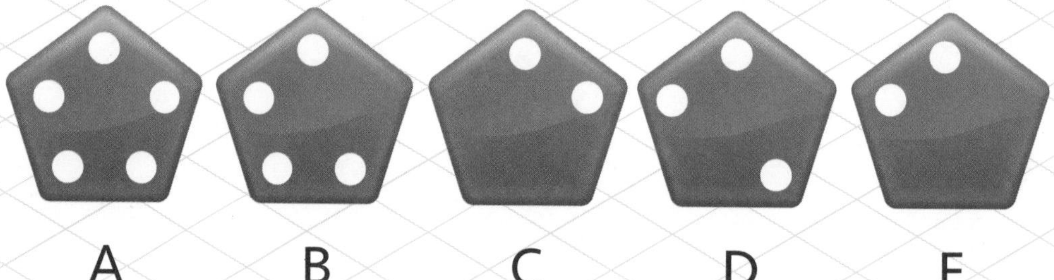

A B C D E

02

Scales 1 and 2 are in perfect balance. How many circles are needed to balance scale 3?

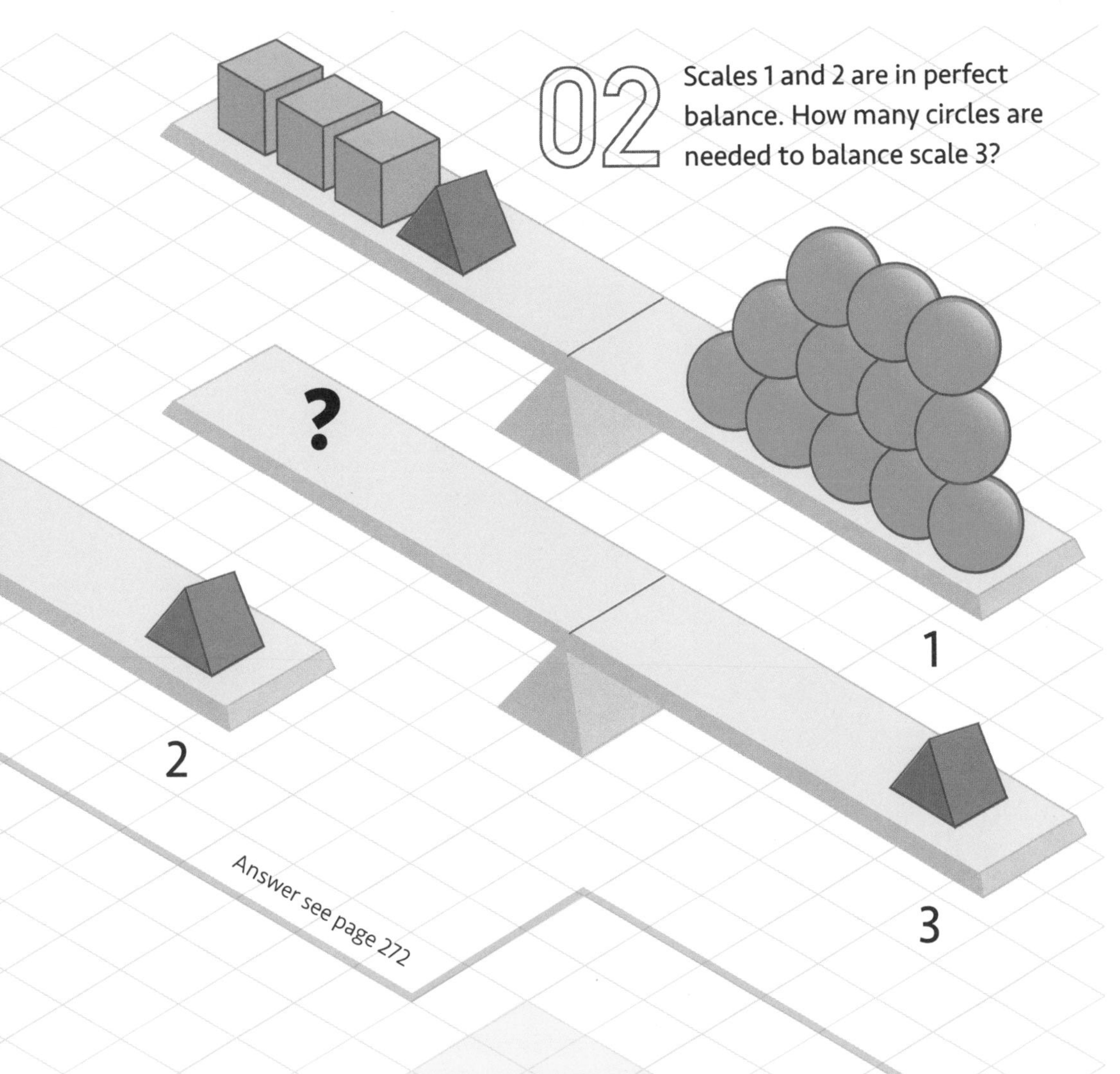

Answer see page 272

Answer see page 272

03

If ⅔ is 4, how much is 5?

Which shape below can be put with the one above to form a perfect square?

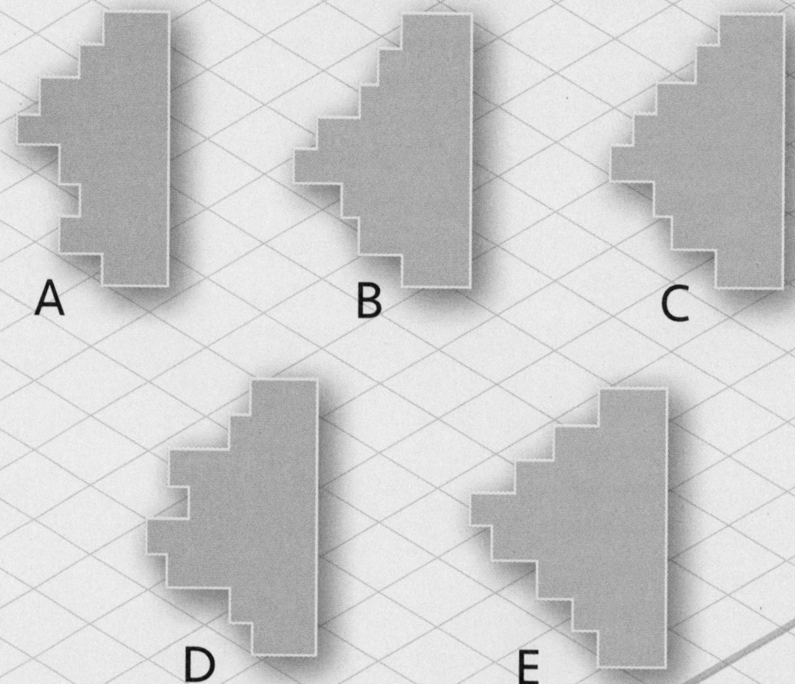

A

B

C

D

E

Answer see page 272

Select the correct figure from the numbered ones below, to replace the question mark.

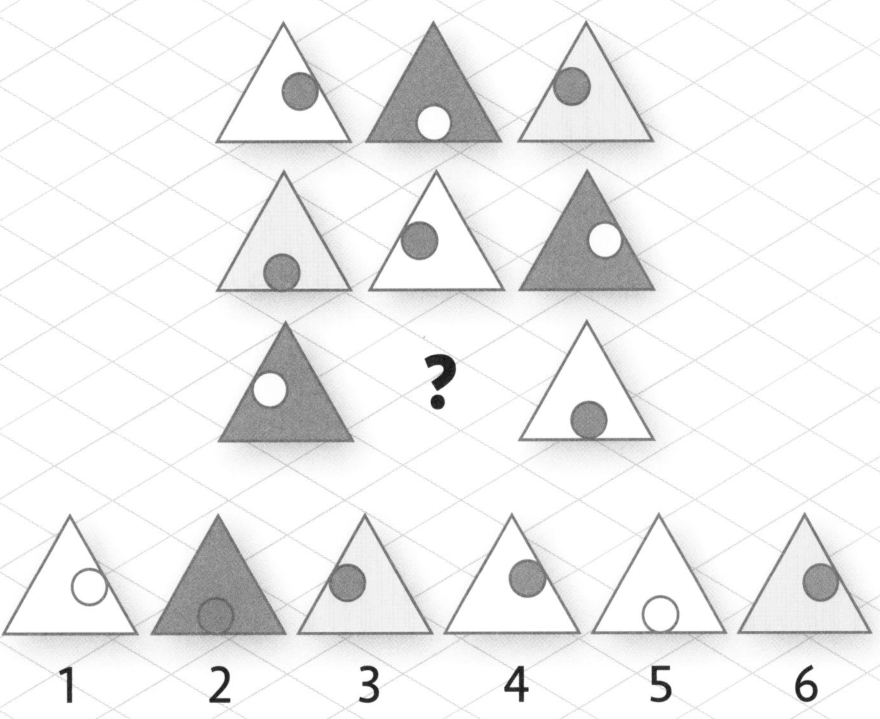

Answer see page 272

Answer see page 272

Complete the square using nine consecutive numbers, so that all rows, columns, and large diagonals add up to the same total.

07

Each of the nine squares in the grid marked 1A to 3C should incorporate all of the items which are shown in the squares of the same letter and number, at left and top. For example, square 2A should incorporate all of the items in squares 2 and A. One square however, is incorrect. Which is it?

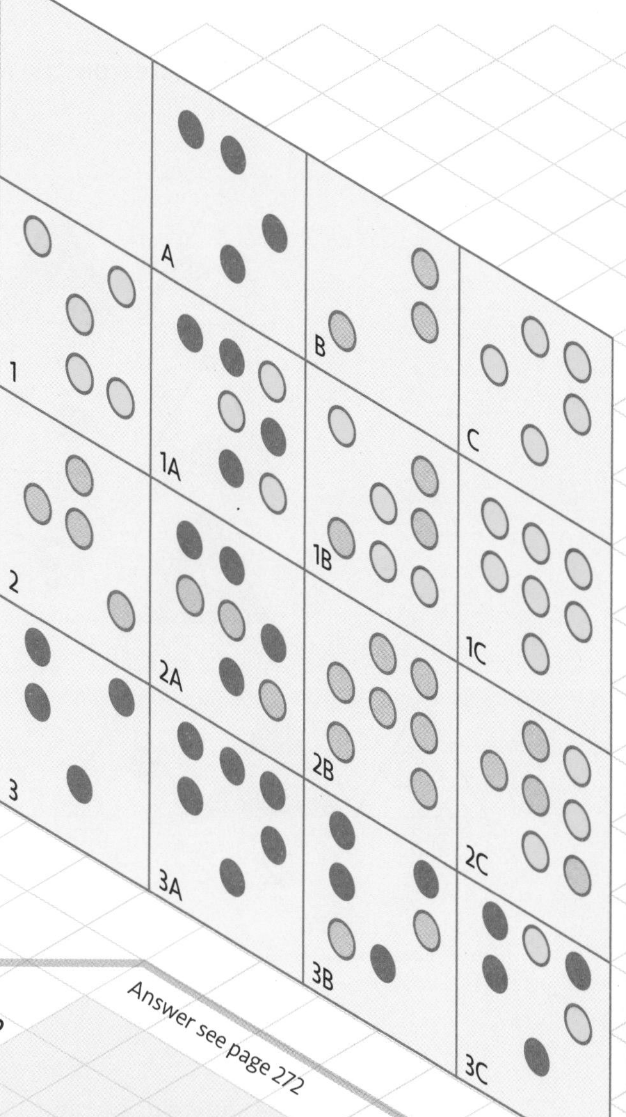

Answer see page 272

08

Which is the odd one out?

Answer see page 272

Which is the odd one out?

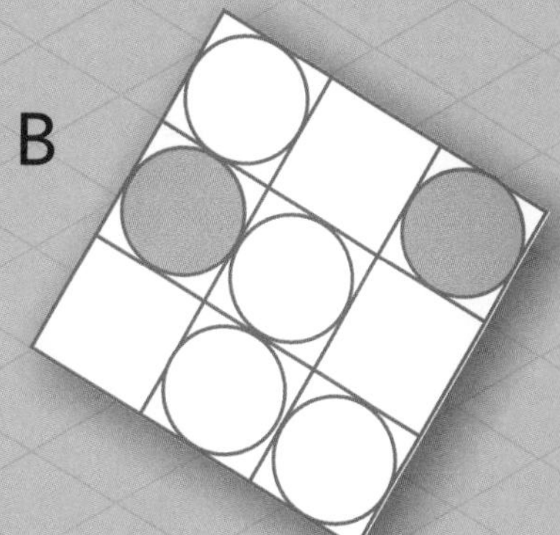

B

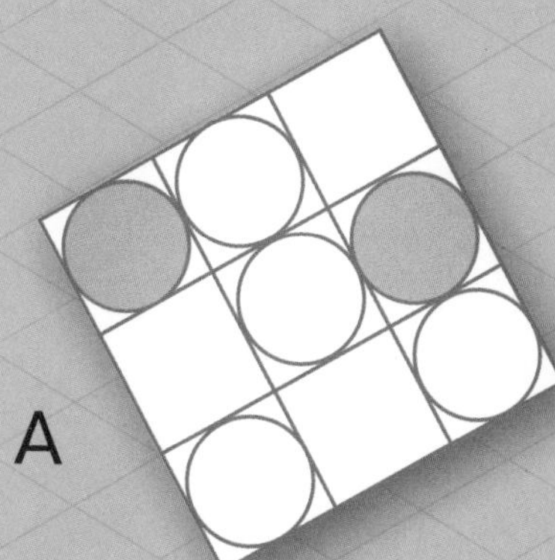

A

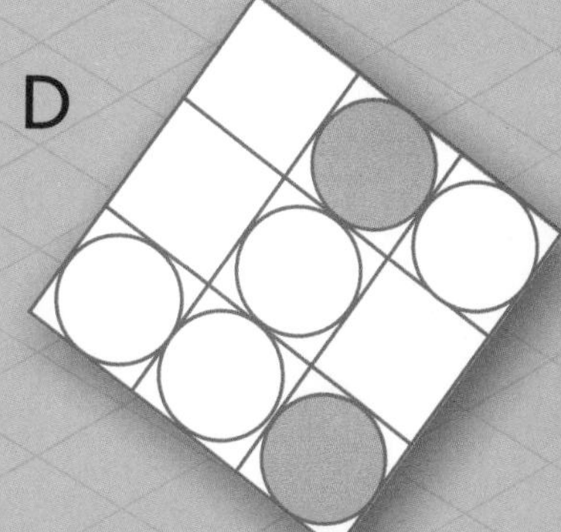

D

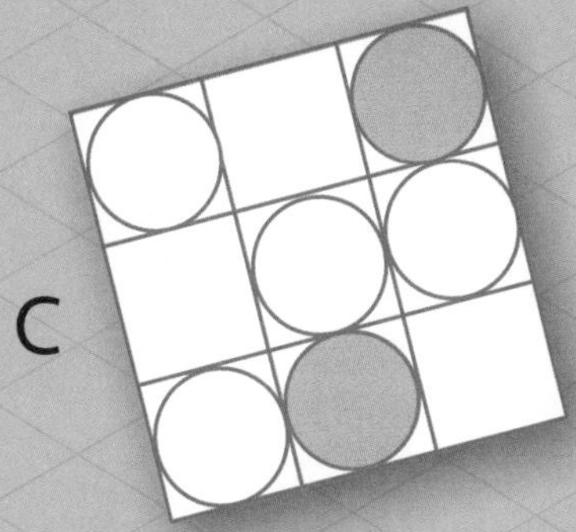

C

F

E

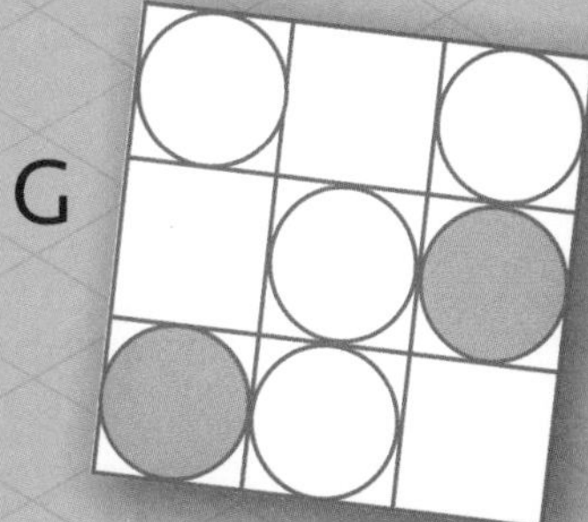

G

Answer see page 272

10

What is the value of a square?

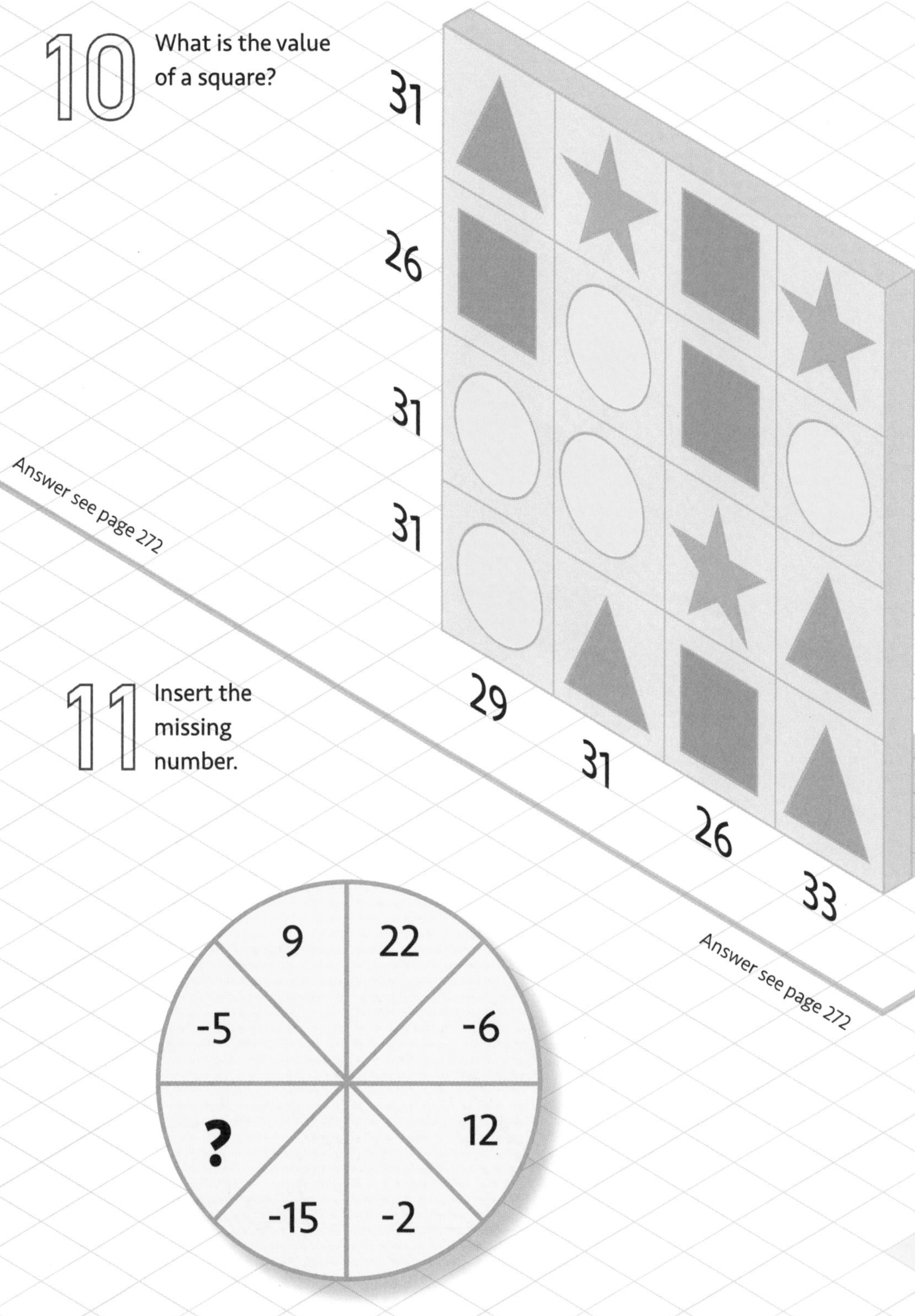

Answer see page 272

11

Insert the missing number.

Answer see page 272

12

Which of the constructed boxes below cannot be made from the given shape?

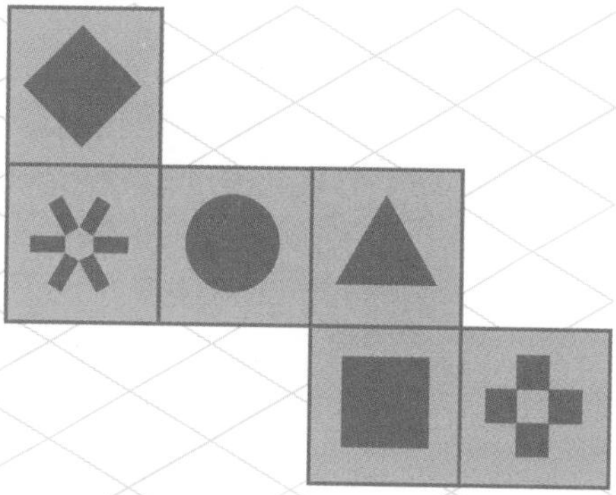

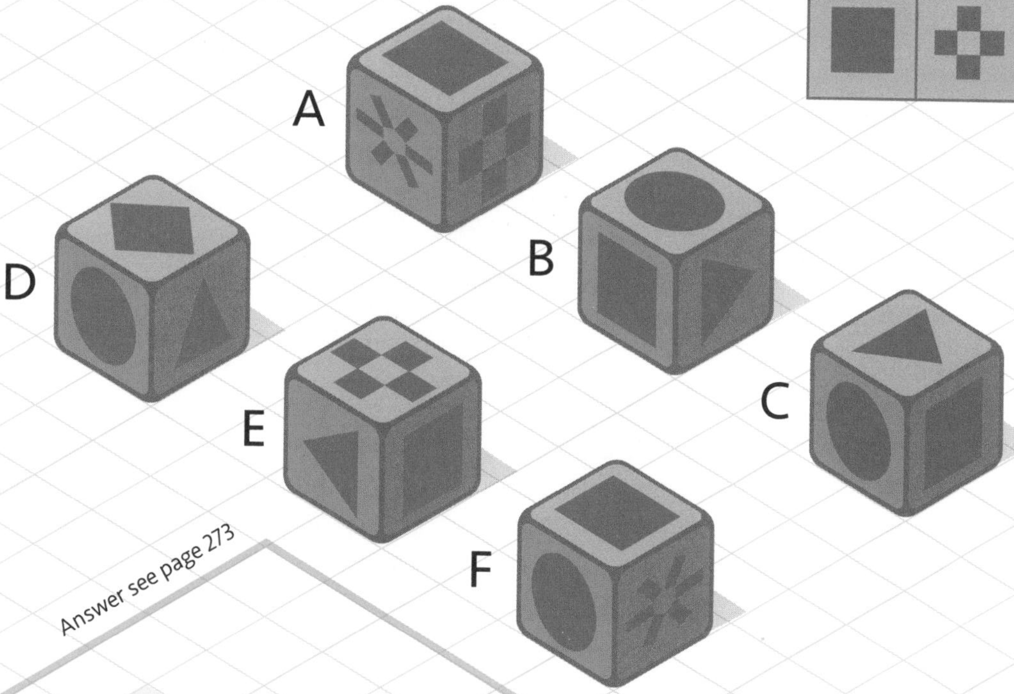

A

B

C

D

E

F

Answer see page 273

13

Which number is the odd one out?

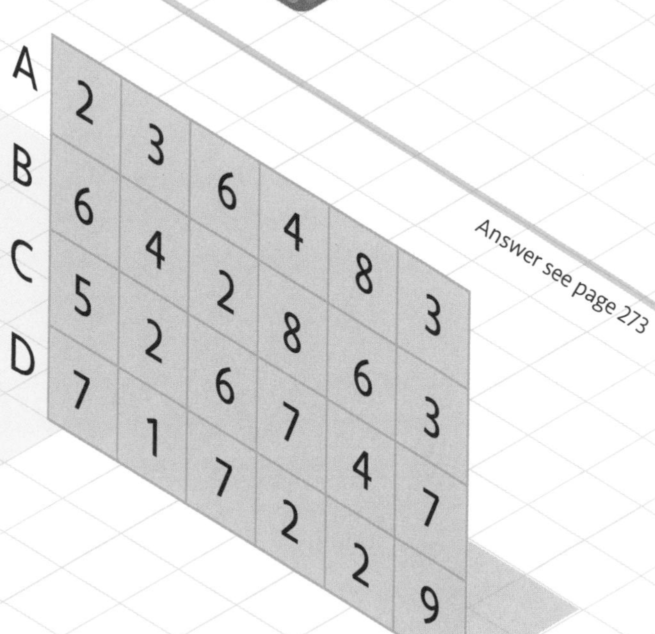

Answer see page 273

14

When complete, this 7 x 7 x 7 cube contains 343 individual blocks. How many blocks are required to complete the cube?

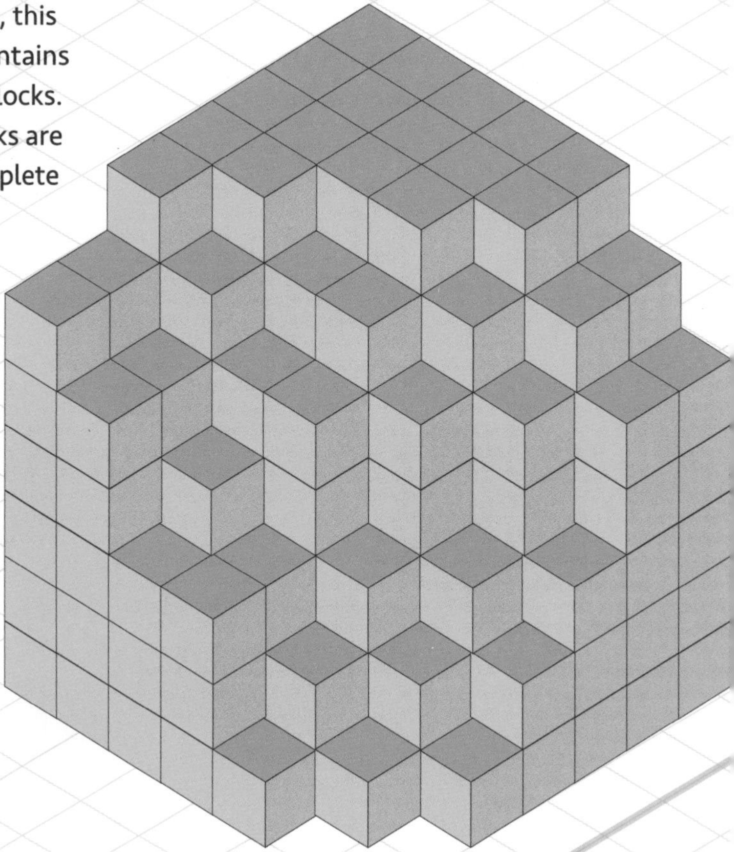

Answer see page 273

Answer see page 273

15

Insert the missing number.

1 16 36 ? 81 100 144

16

Dubai is 1 hour ahead of Moscow, which is 1 hour ahead of Cairo. It is 11:15 a.m. on Wednesday in Dubai, what time is it in the other two cities?

DUBAI

MOSCOW

CAIRO

Answer see page 273

17

What number should replace the question mark?

Answer see page 273

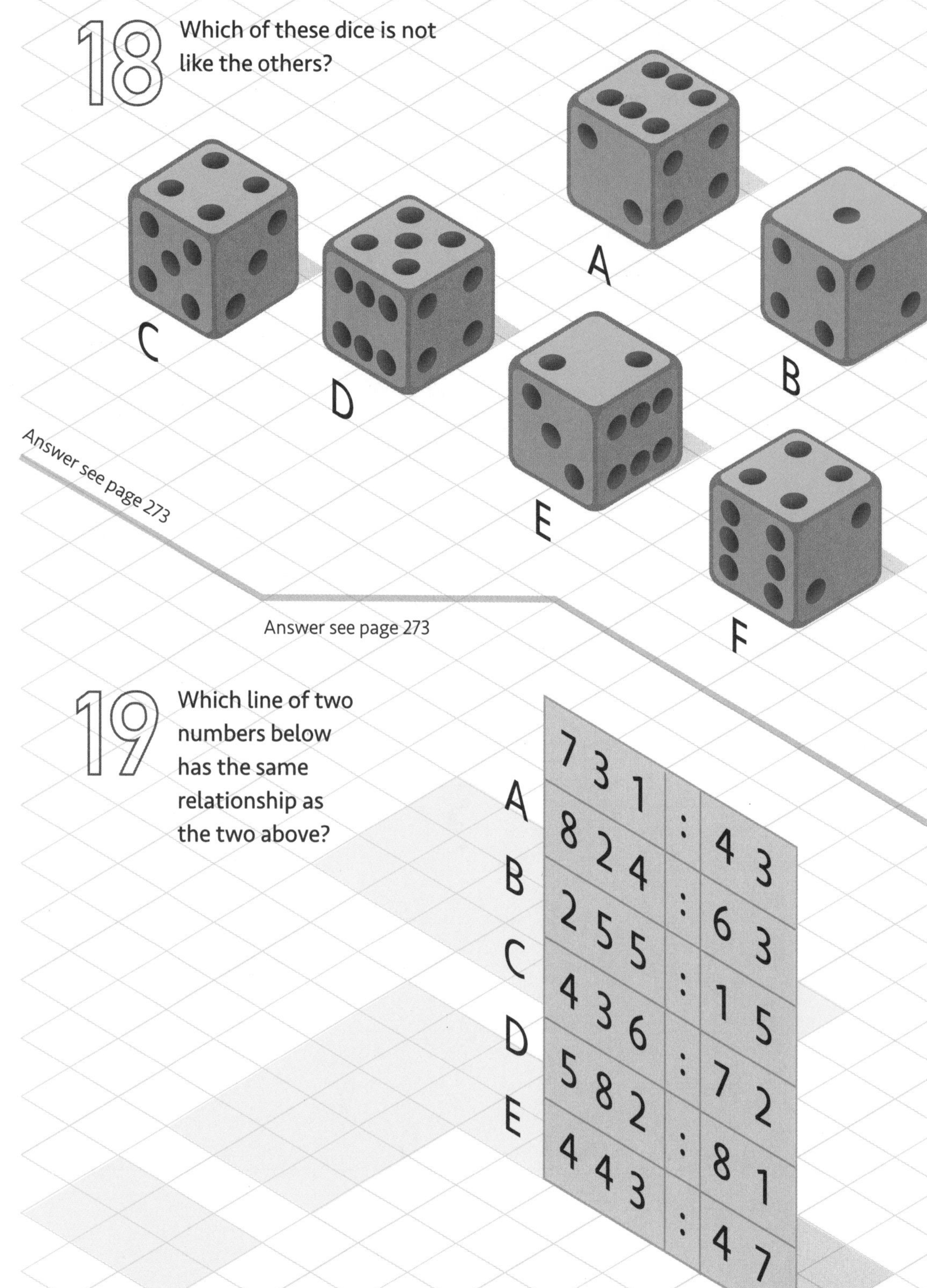

18

Which of these dice is not like the others?

Answer see page 273

Answer see page 273

19

Which line of two numbers below has the same relationship as the two above?

	7 3 1	:	4 3
A	8 2 4	:	6 3
B	2 5 5	:	1 5
C	4 3 6	:	7 2
D	5 8 2	:	8 1
E	4 4 3	:	4 7

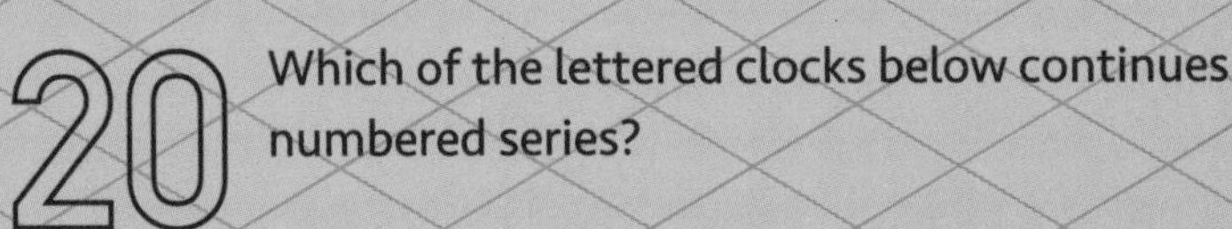

20

Which of the lettered clocks below continues the numbered series?

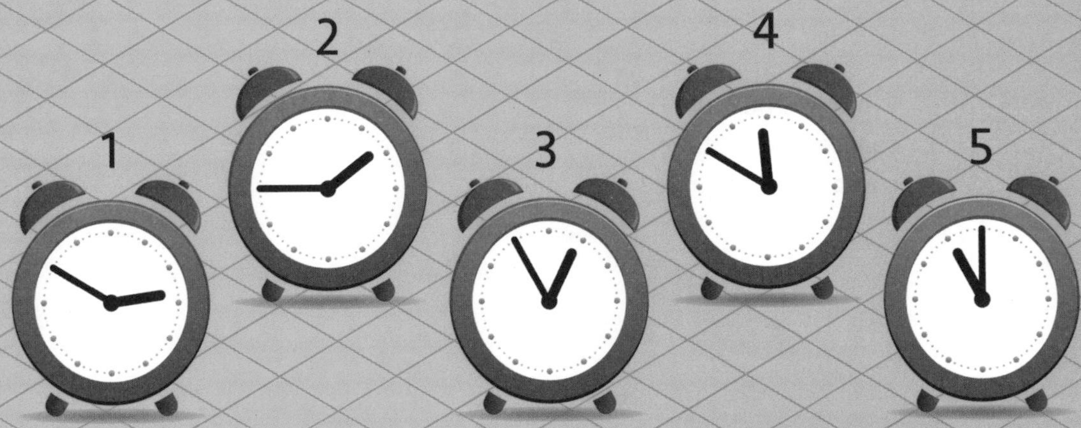

Answer see page 273

Test 12

01

Which of the four shapes A to D fits to complete the square?

A

B

C

D

Answer see page 273

02

How many [ball] are required to balance the final scale?

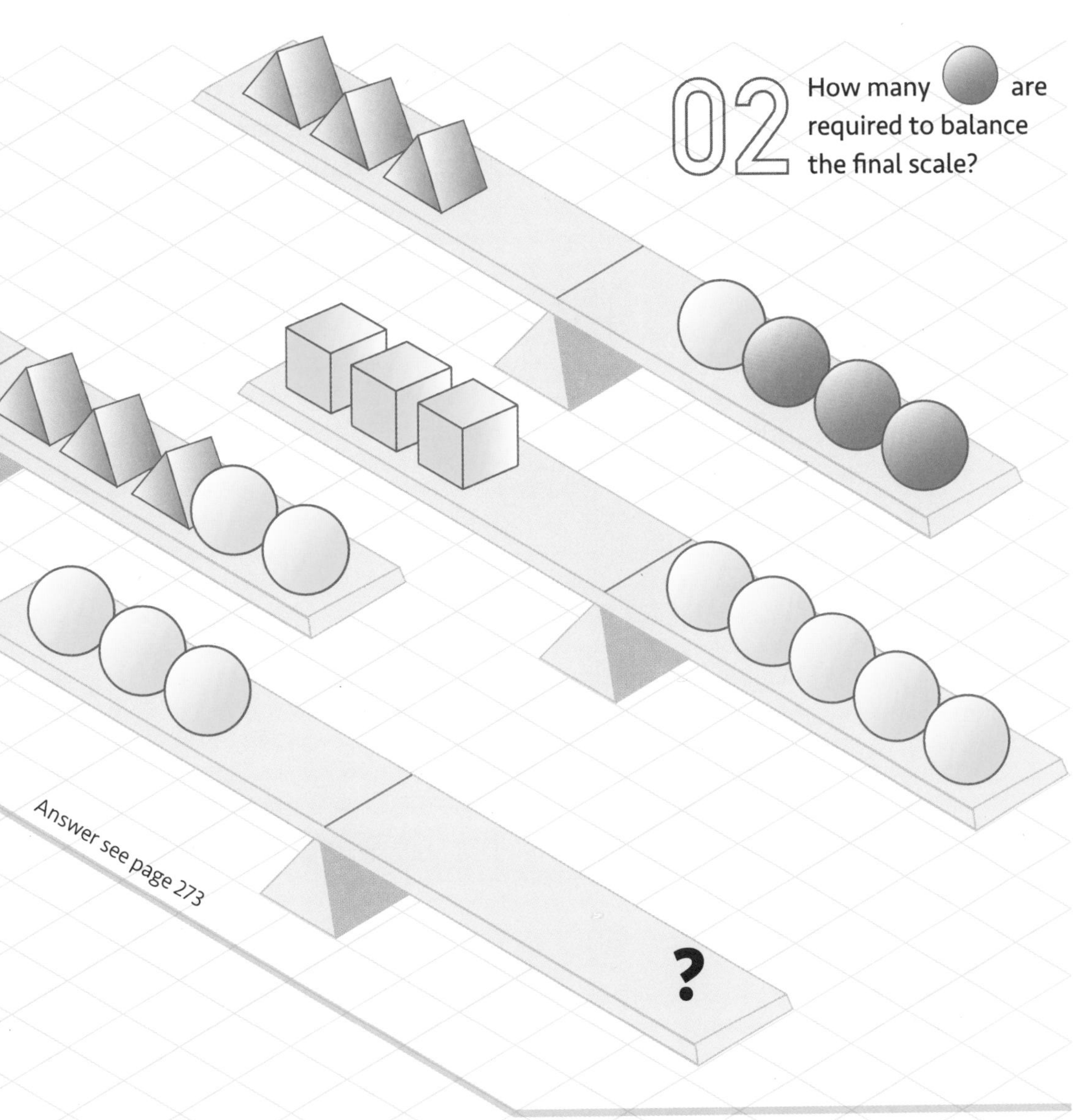

Answer see page 273

Answer see page 273

03

Fill in the missing plus, minus, multiplication, and division signs to make the equation below correct, performing all calculations strictly in the order they appear on the page.

25 11 9 35 19 28 = 93

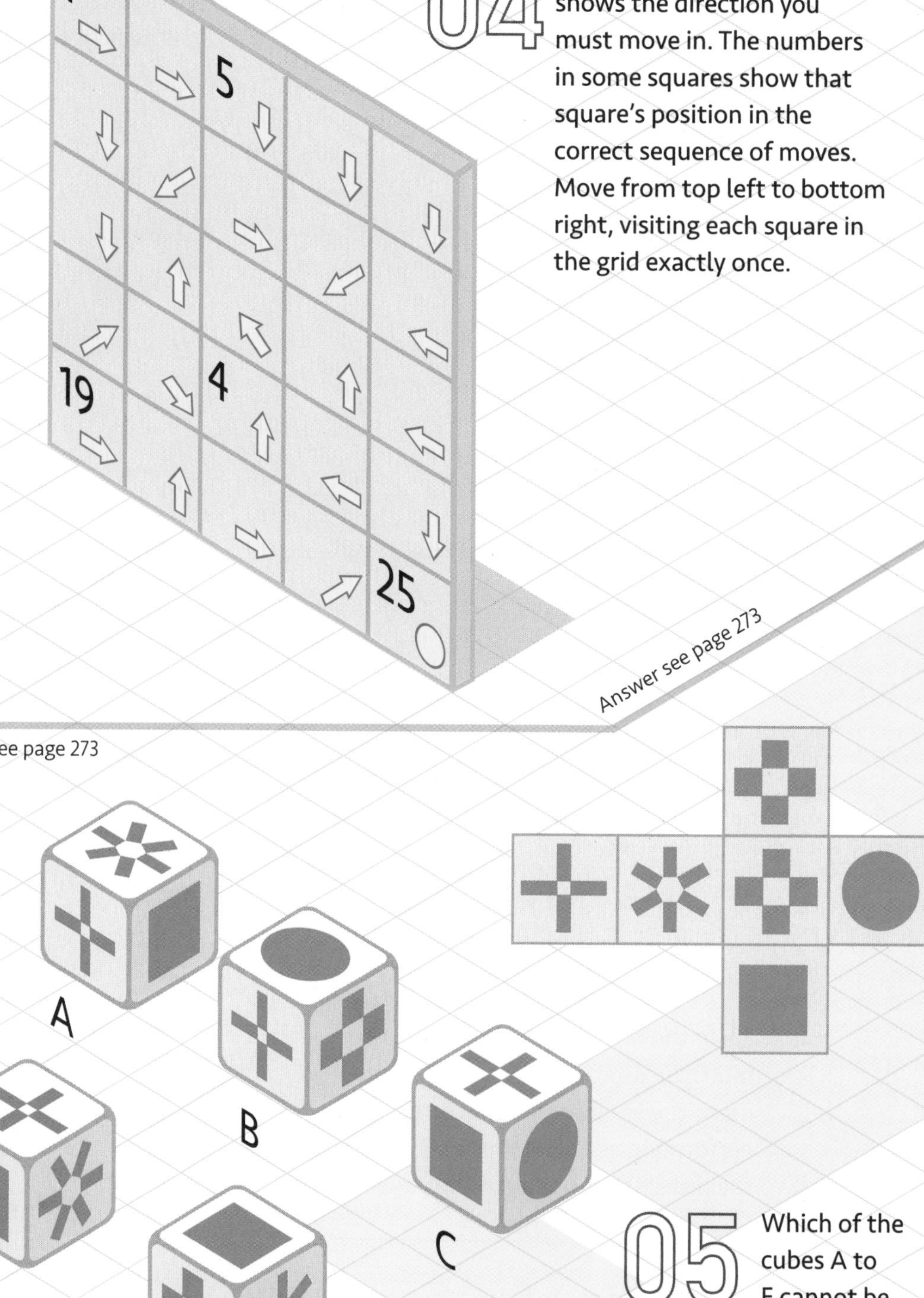

04

In each square, the arrow shows the direction you must move in. The numbers in some squares show that square's position in the correct sequence of moves. Move from top left to bottom right, visiting each square in the grid exactly once.

Answer see page 273

Answer see page 273

05

Which of the cubes A to E cannot be made using the layout shown?

Which of the options A to E most accurately continues the sequence?

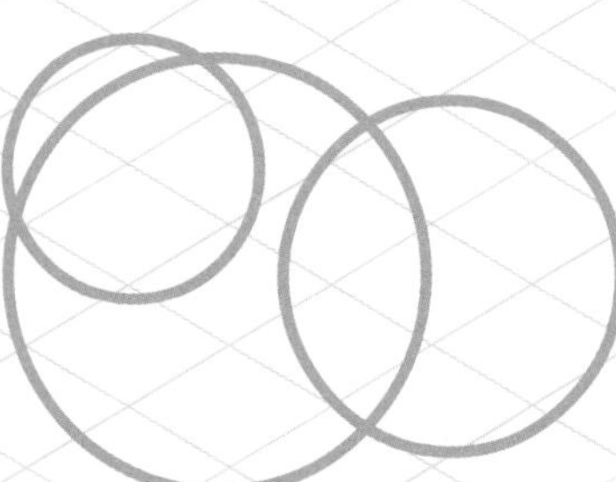

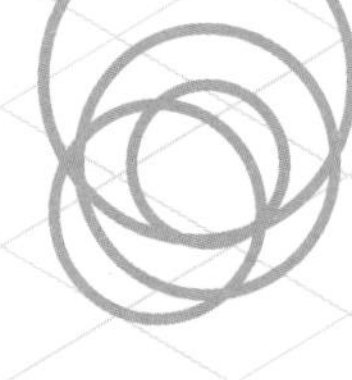

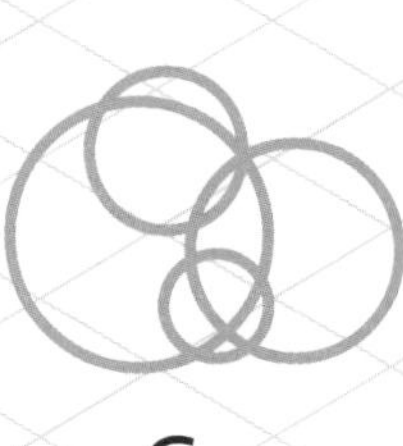

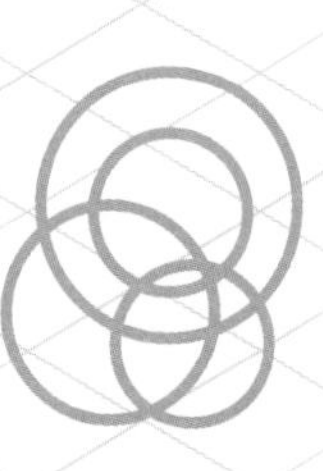

A B C D E

Answer see page 273

Answer see page 273

What number should replace the question mark?

28 60
42 7
59 24
6 38

? 21
15 43
23 51
45 37

Fit the numbers shown into the design to complete the grid.

Answer see page 273

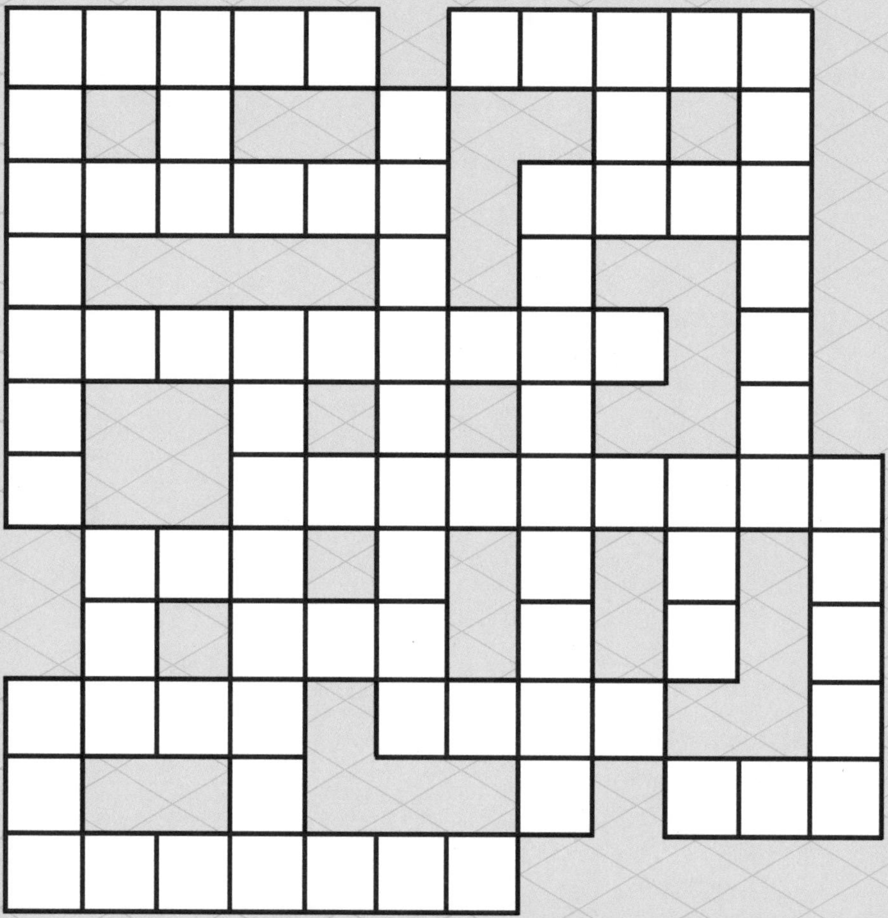

3 digits	4 digits	5 digits	6 digits	7 digits	8 digits	9 digits
260	4496	10591	431552	1941759	62346342	328706289
507	4599	97837		7566228		433101594
571	7783	98326		8952561		521928774
584						775679238
617						
768						
816						
844						

09

What number should replace the question mark?

Answer see page 274

Answer see page 274

10

Which of the designs A to E is the odd one out?

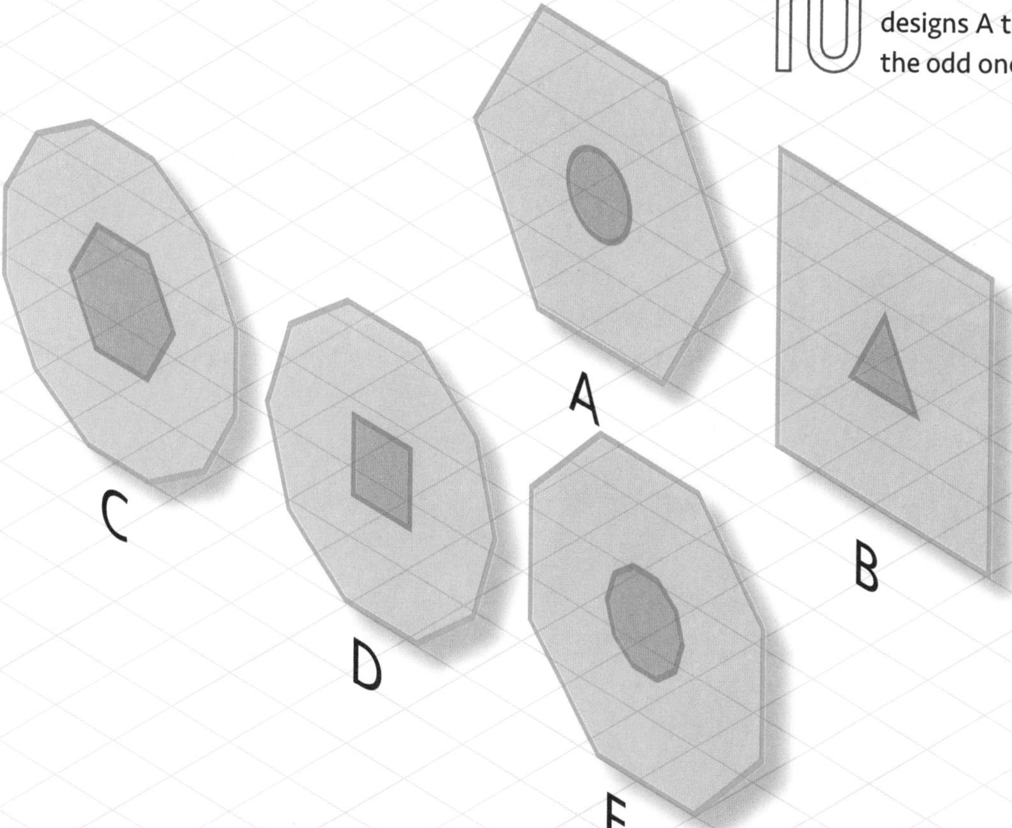

A

B

C

D

E

11

Which option A to E most accurately completes the pattern?

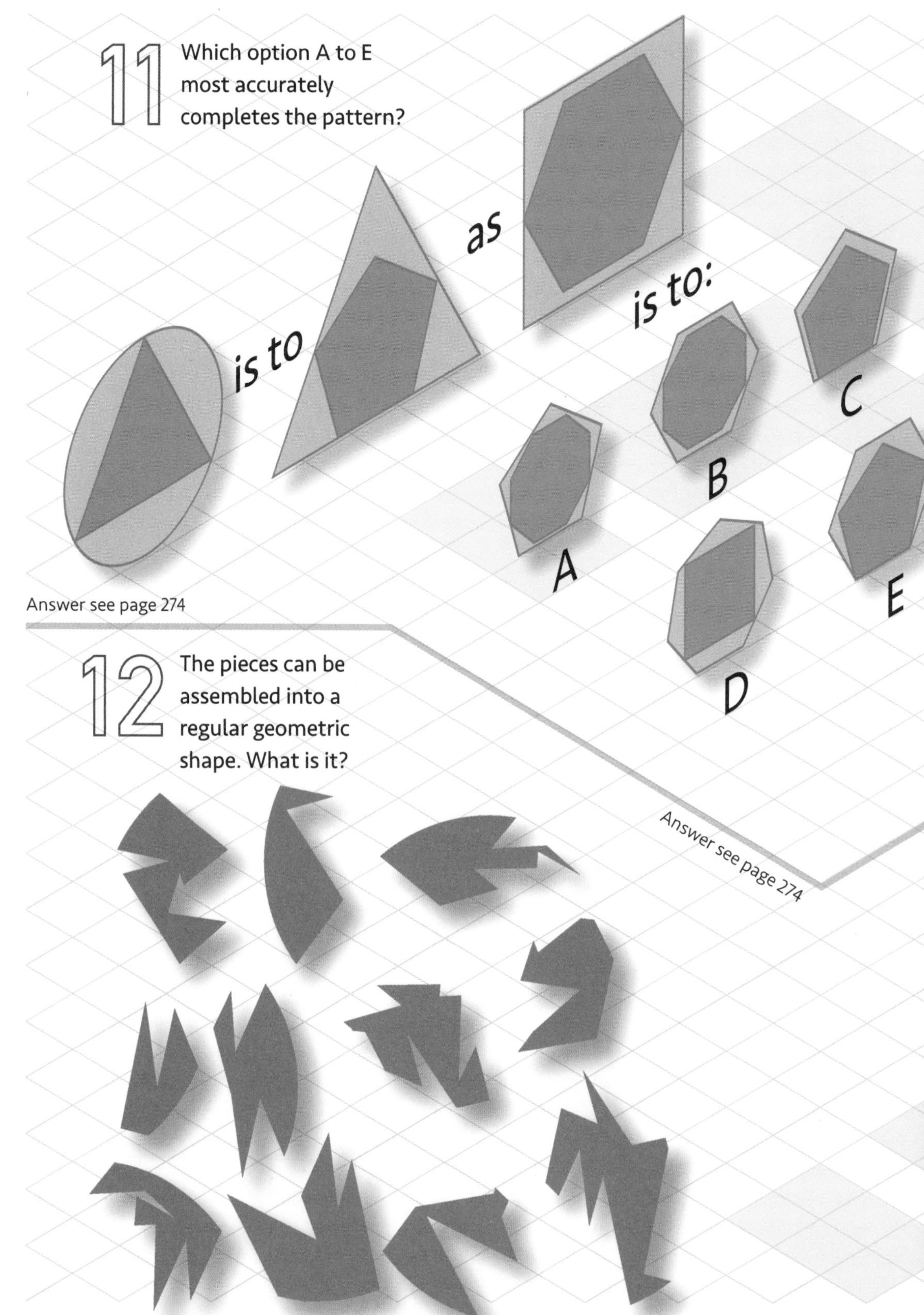

Answer see page 274

12

The pieces can be assembled into a regular geometric shape. What is it?

Answer see page 274

13

Use six straight lines to divide the field below into eight identically-sized sections, each containing eight pentagons.

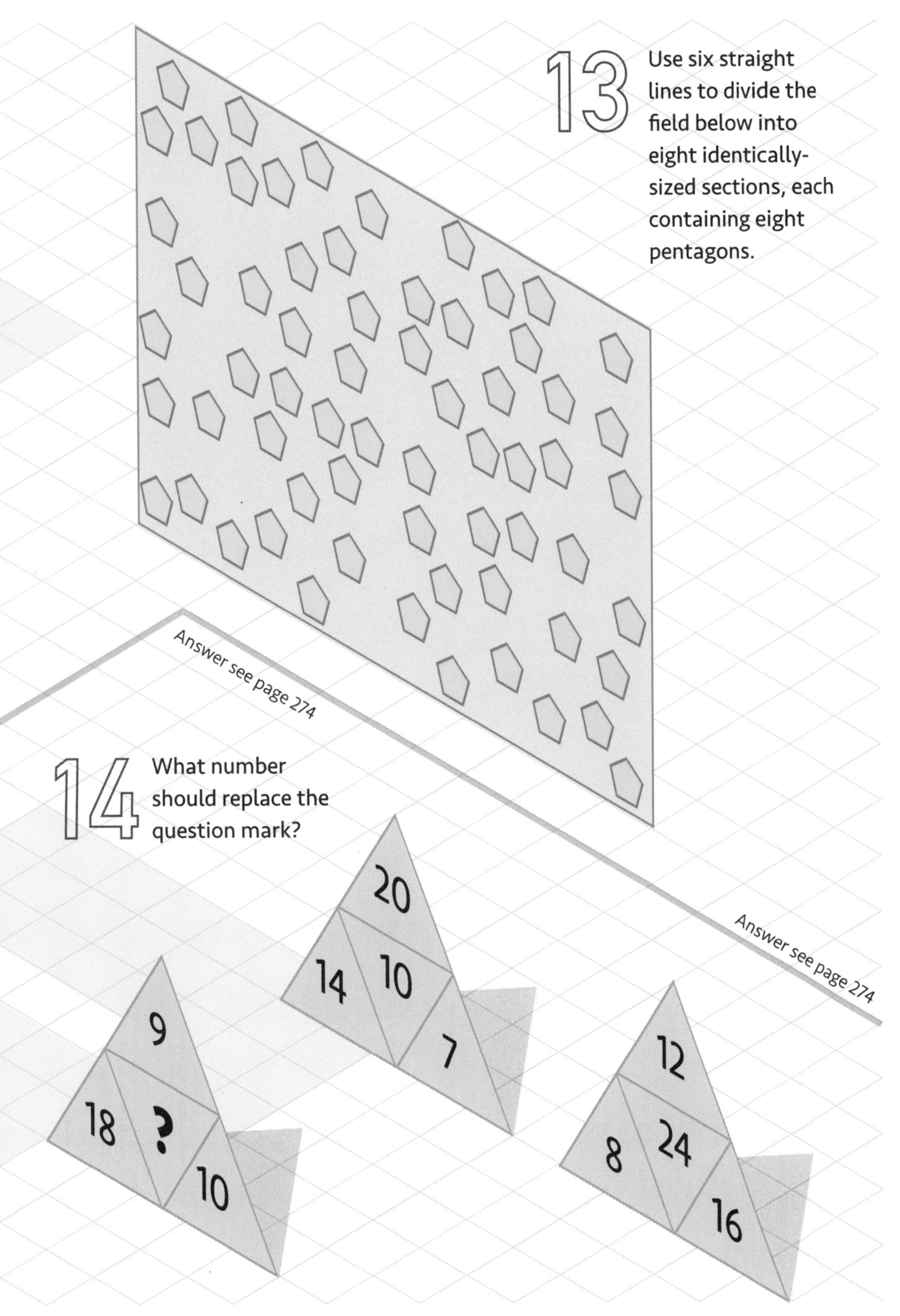

Answer see page 274

14

What number should replace the question mark?

Answer see page 274

15

In the grid below, how much is each symbol worth?

Answer see page 274

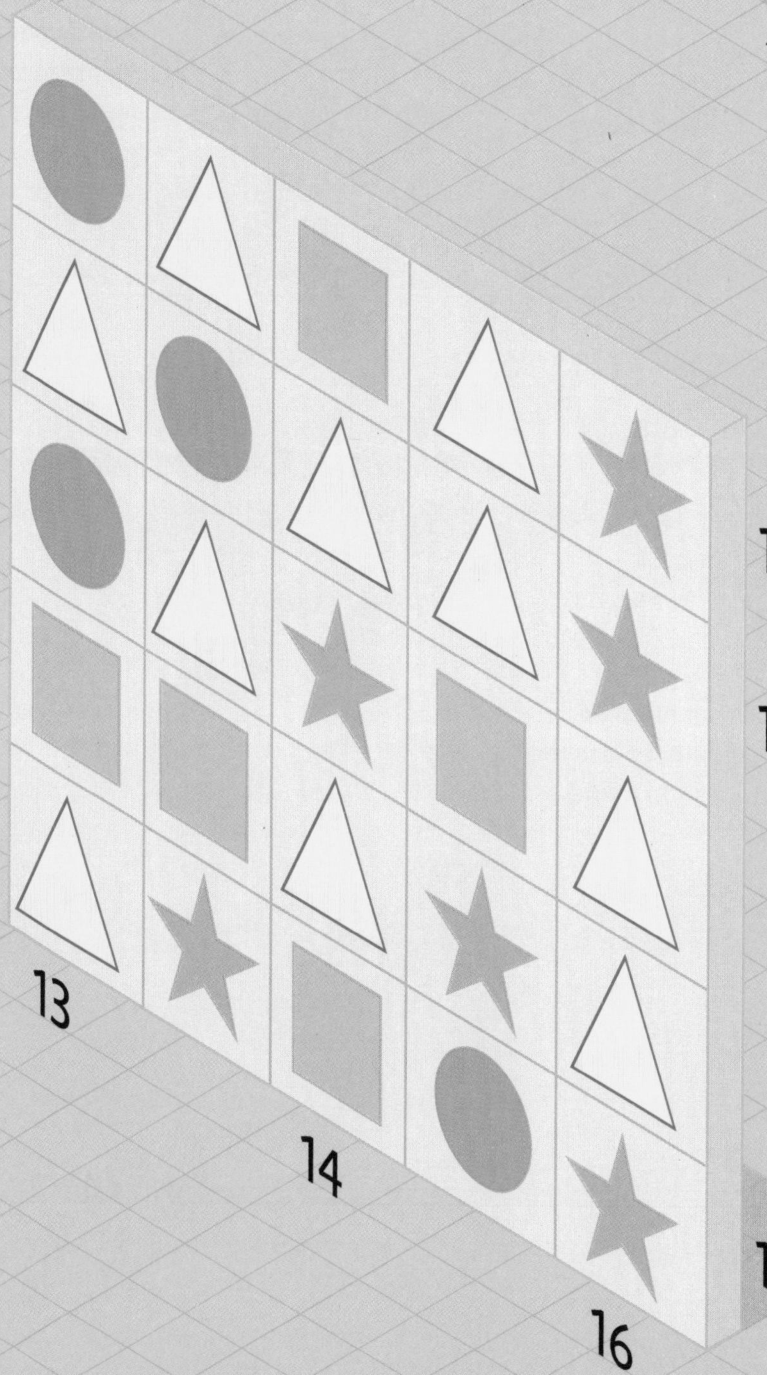

16

What number should replace the question mark?

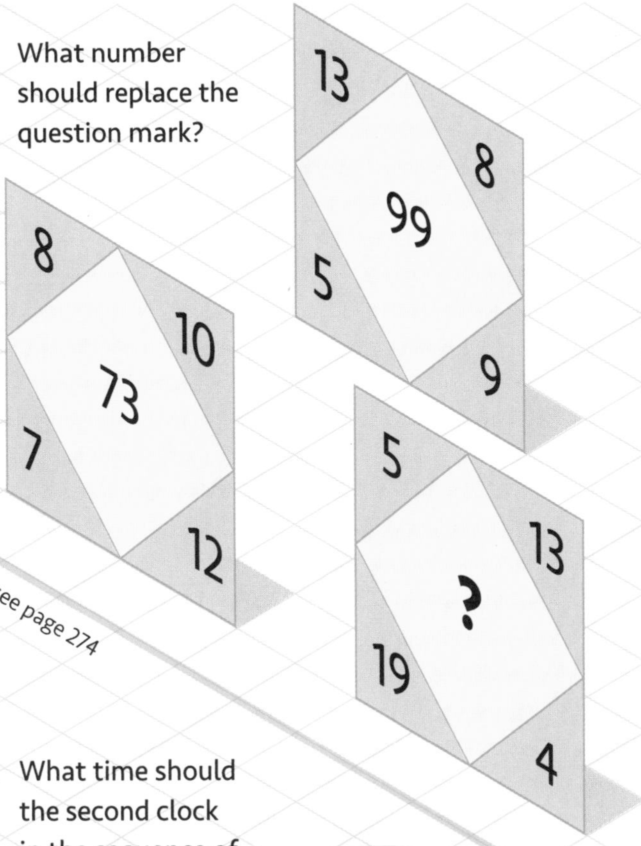

8, 10, 73, 7, 12

13, 8, 99, 5, 9

4, 16, 56, 8, 1

5, 13, ?, 19, 4

Answer see page 274

17

What time should the second clock in the sequence of four indicate?

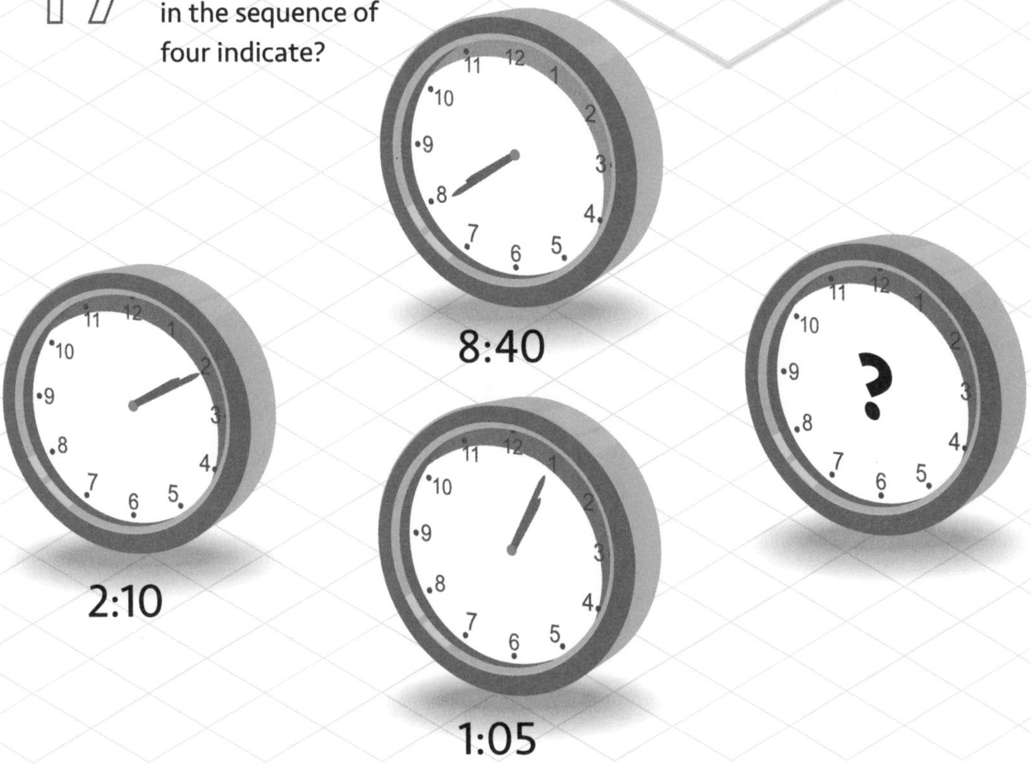

2:10

8:40

1:05

Answer see page 274

18

Combine the segments below to find the names of ten celebrities.

EL	ING	IES	YWEA
GGS	NBI	BRU	ILLIS
EMM	ENN	UISE	TO
IDT	JIMC	VIND	AR
ZELW	URNE	DEN	TSON
WIL	DAV	SIGO	CEW
AWA	JASO	TON	ANT
VER	ASH	MCR	
LSM	REY	ITH	

Answer see page 274

Answer see page 274

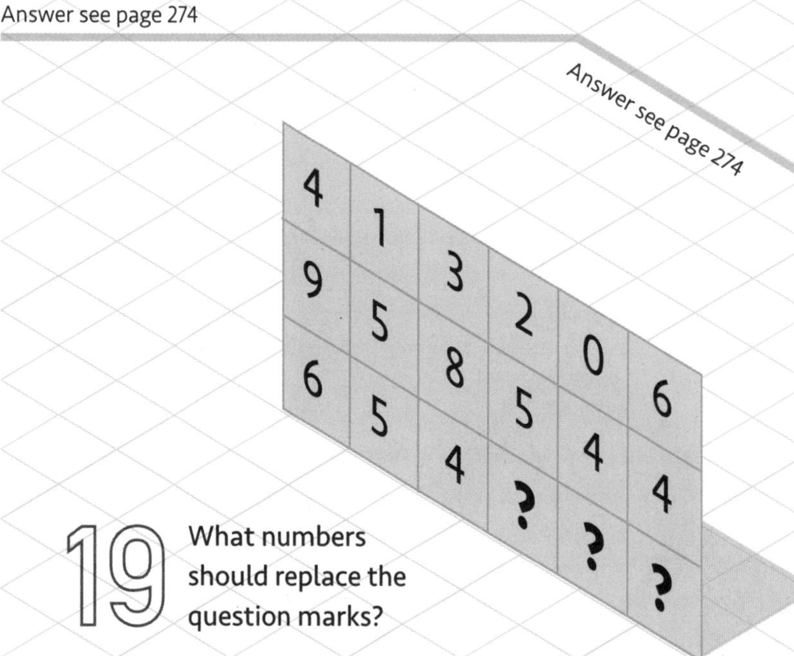

19

What numbers should replace the question marks?

20

Which symbols are missing from the grid below?

Answer see page 274

Test 13

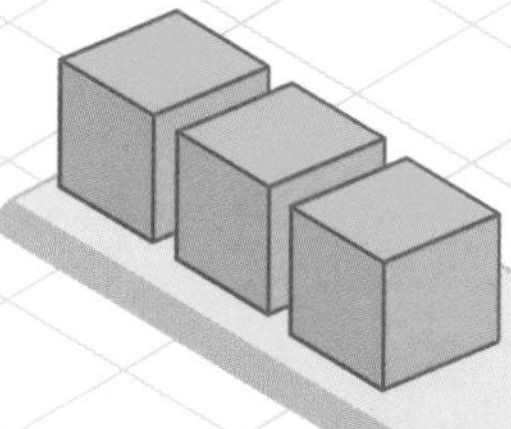

01

Which of the pentagons at the bottom should replace the question mark?

?

Answer see page 274

A B C D E

02

Scales 1 and 2 are in perfect balance. How many circles are needed to balance scale 3?

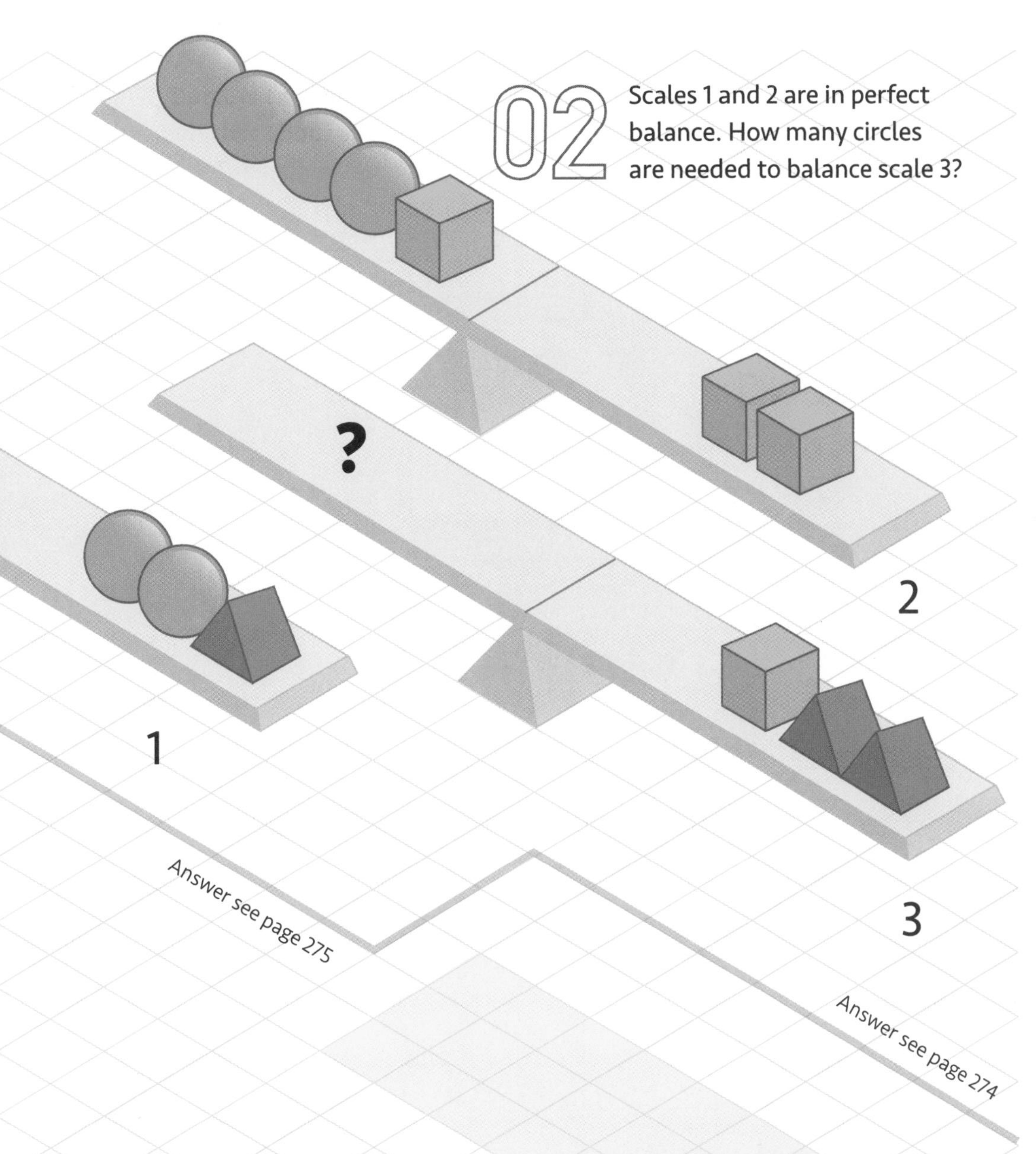

Answer see page 275

Answer see page 274

03

If ¾ is 6, how much is 4?

Which shape below can be put with the one above to form a perfect square?

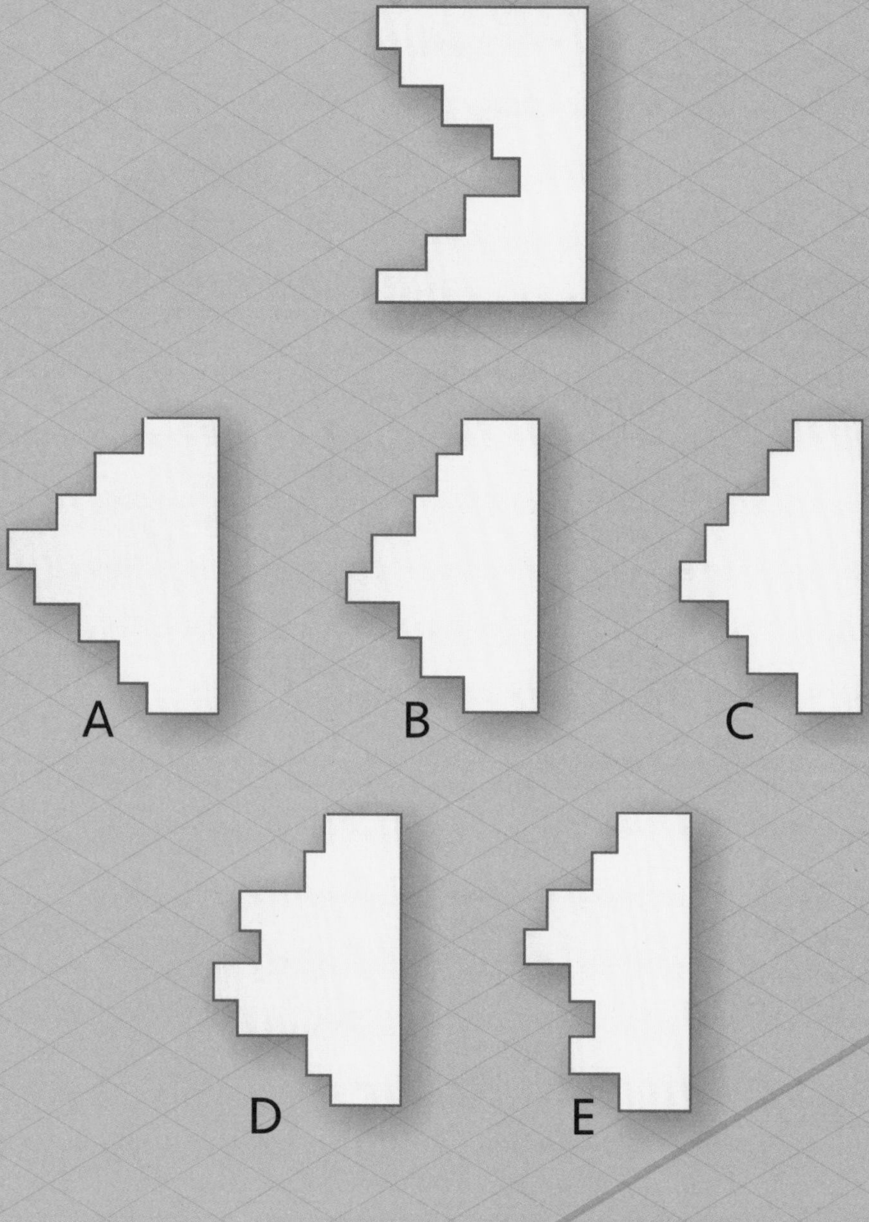

A

B

C

D

E

Answer see page 275

Select the correct figure from the numbered ones below, to replace the question mark.

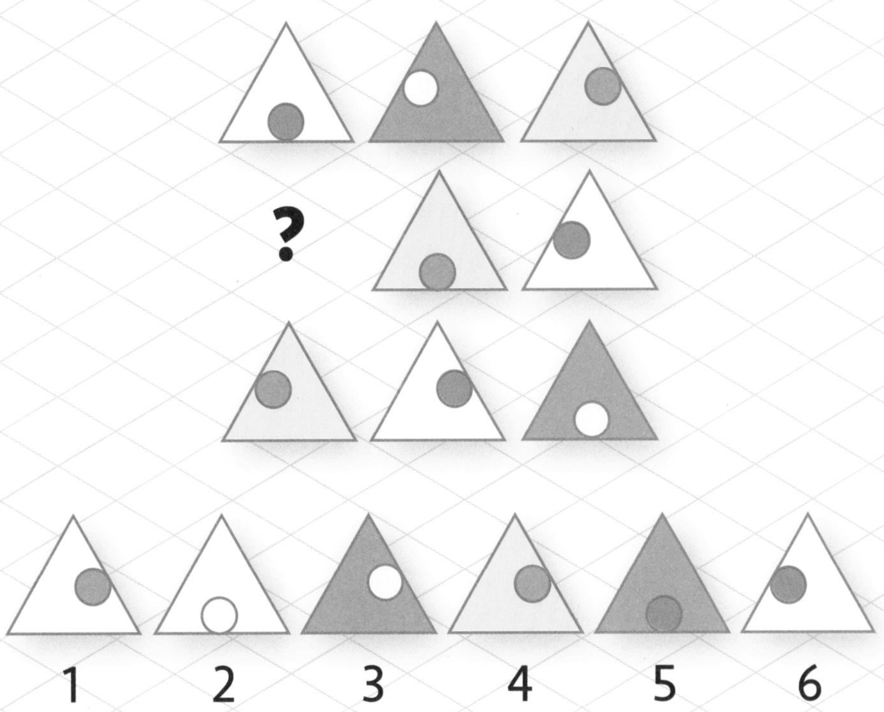

Answer see page 275

Answer see page 275

Complete the square using nine consecutive numbers, so that all rows, columns, and large diagonals add up to the same total.

07

Each of the nine squares in the grid marked 1A to 3C should incorporate all of the items which are shown in the squares of the same letter and number, at left and top. For example, square 2A should incorporate all of the items in squares 2 and A. One square however, is incorrect. Which is it?

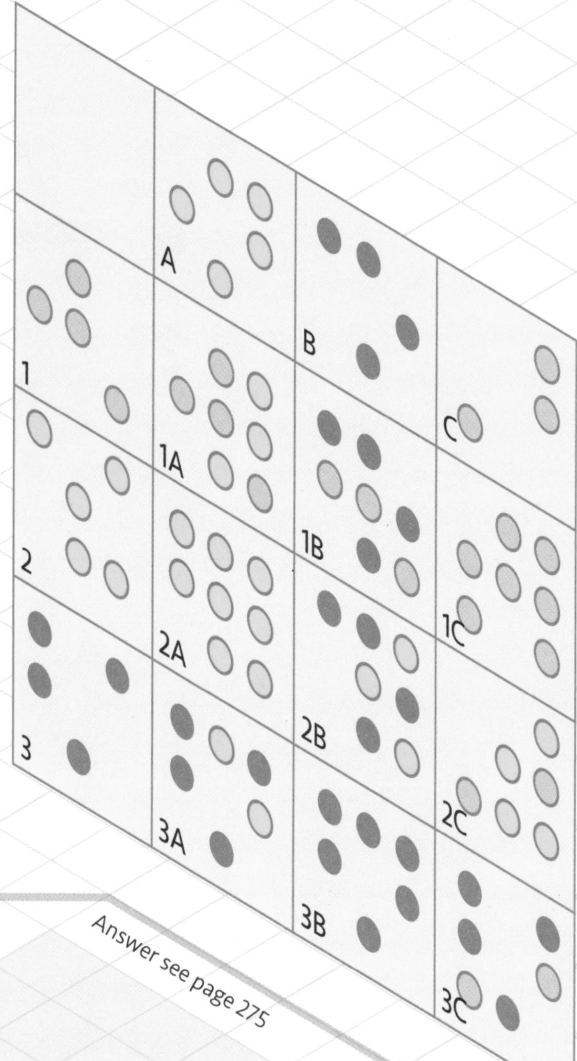

Answer see page 275

08

Which is the odd one out?

Answer see page 275

09

Which is the odd one out?

B

A

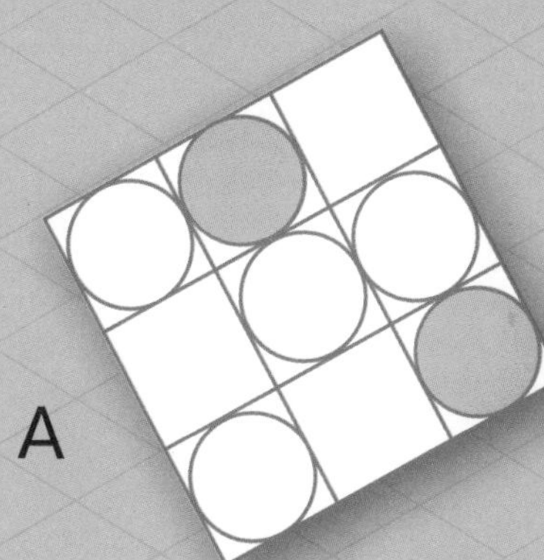

D

C

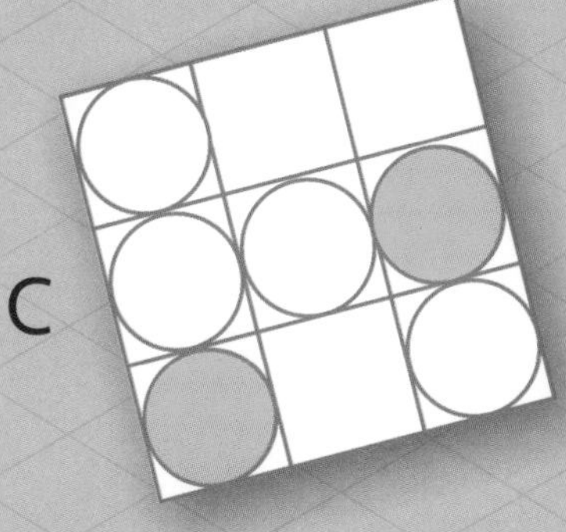

F

E

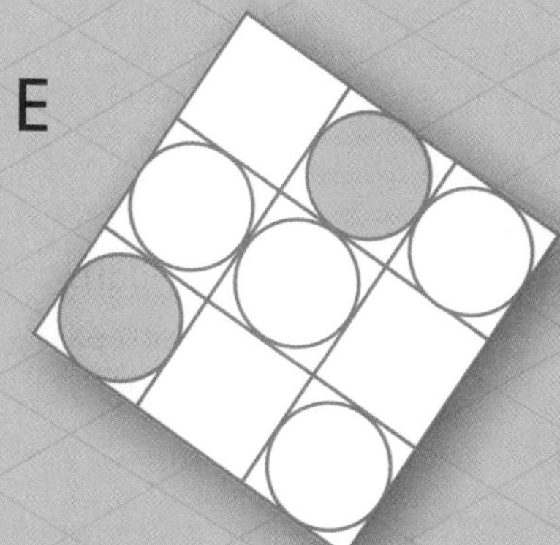

G

Answer see page 275

10

What is the value of a star?

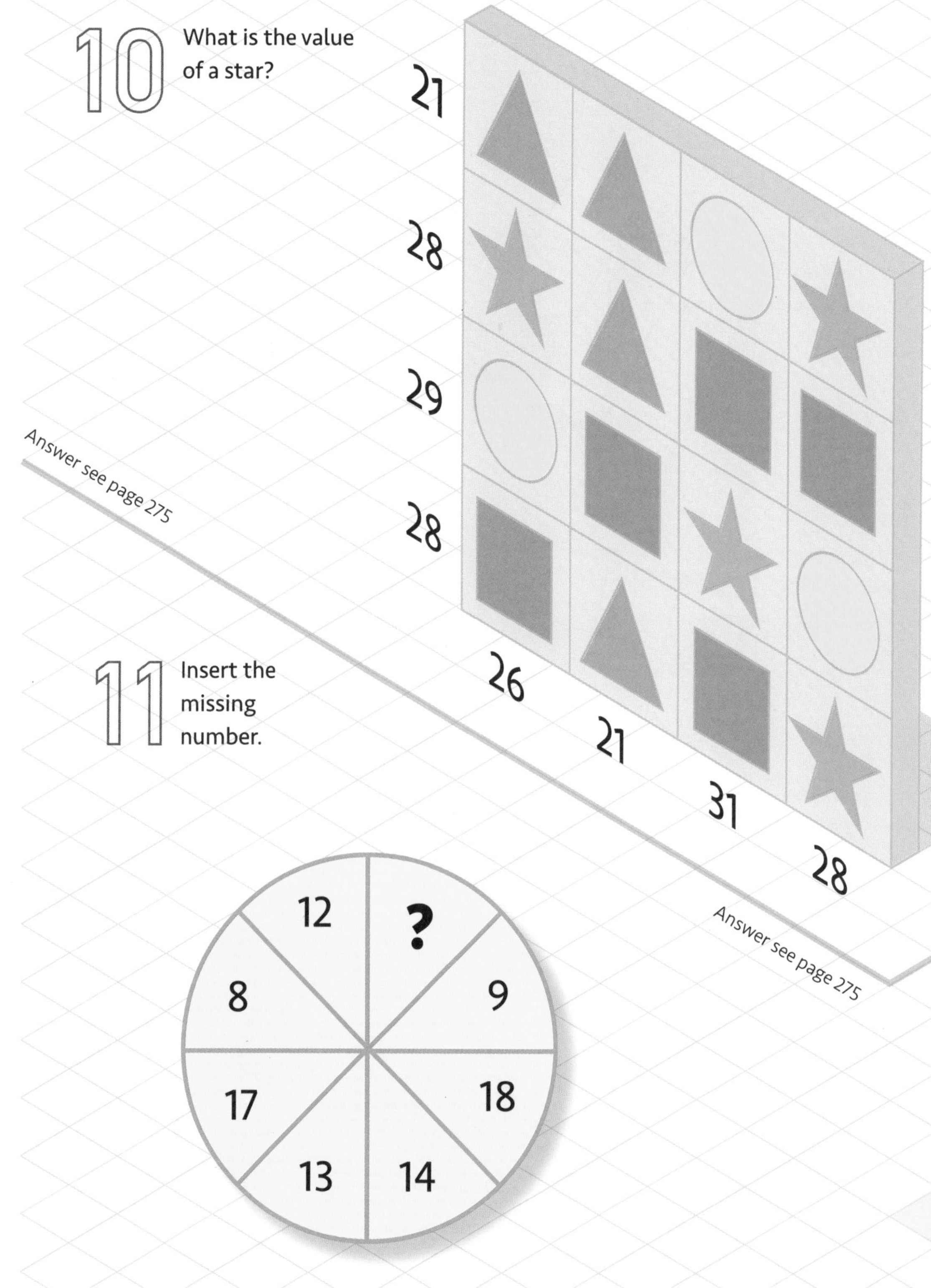

Answer see page 275

11

Insert the missing number.

Answer see page 275

12

Which of the constructed boxes below cannot be made from the given shape?

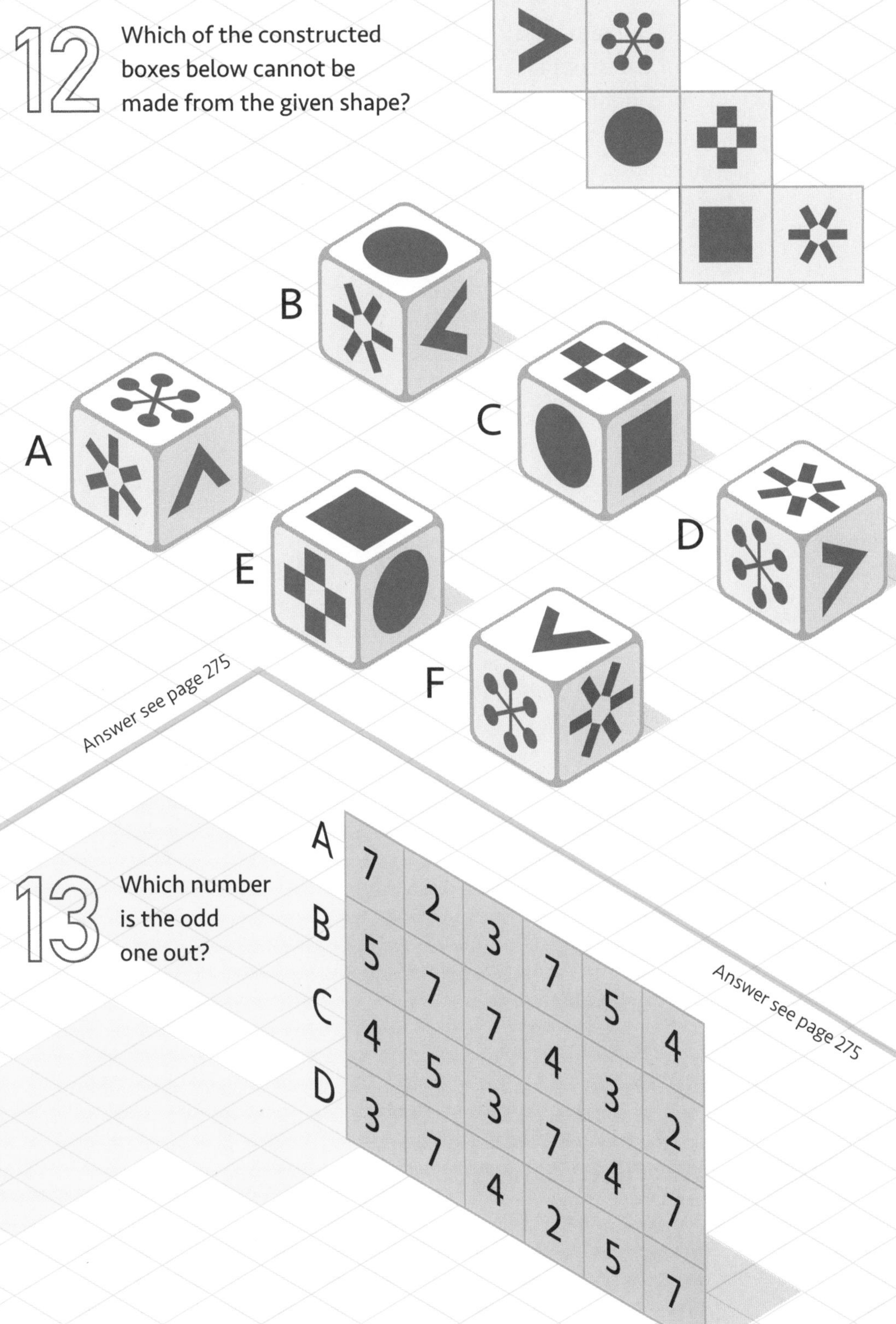

Answer see page 275

13

Which number is the odd one out?

A	7	2	3	7	5	4
B	5	7	7	4	3	2
C	4	5	3	7	4	7
D	3	7	4	2	5	7

Answer see page 275

14

When complete, this 7 x 7 x 7 cube contains 343 individual blocks. How many blocks are required to complete the cube?

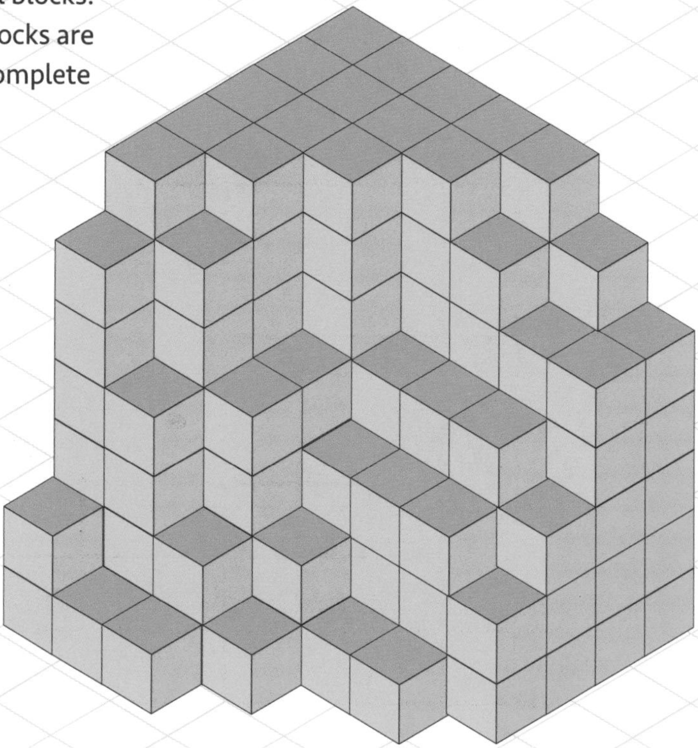

Answer see page 275

Answer see page 275

15

Insert the missing numbers.

1 2 6 15 31 ? ?

16

Dublin is 1 hour behind London, and 4 hours ahead of New York. It is 11:15 a.m. on Wednesday in London. What time is it in the other two cities?

Answer see page 275

17

What number should replace the question mark?

Answer see page 275

18

Which of these dice is not like the other three?

B

C

Answer see page 275

Answer see page 275

19

Which line of two numbers below has the same relationship as the two above?

	743	:	84
A	824	:	63
B	259	:	89
C	436	:	72
D	582	:	81
E	443	:	47

Which of the lettered clocks below continues the numbered series?

1

2

3

4

5

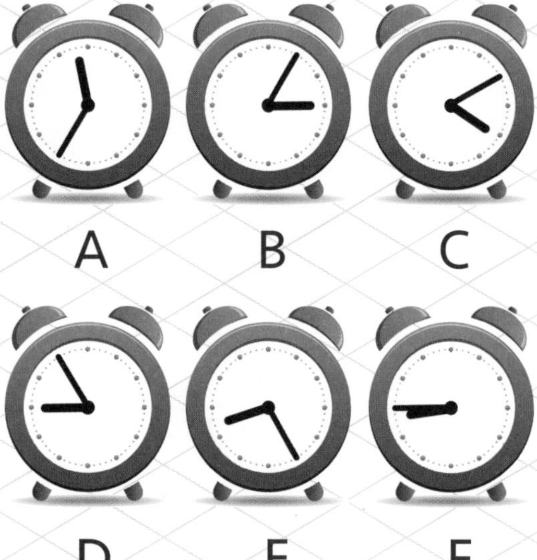

A B C

D E F

Answer see page 276

Test 14

01

The pieces can be assembled into a regular geometric shape. What is it?

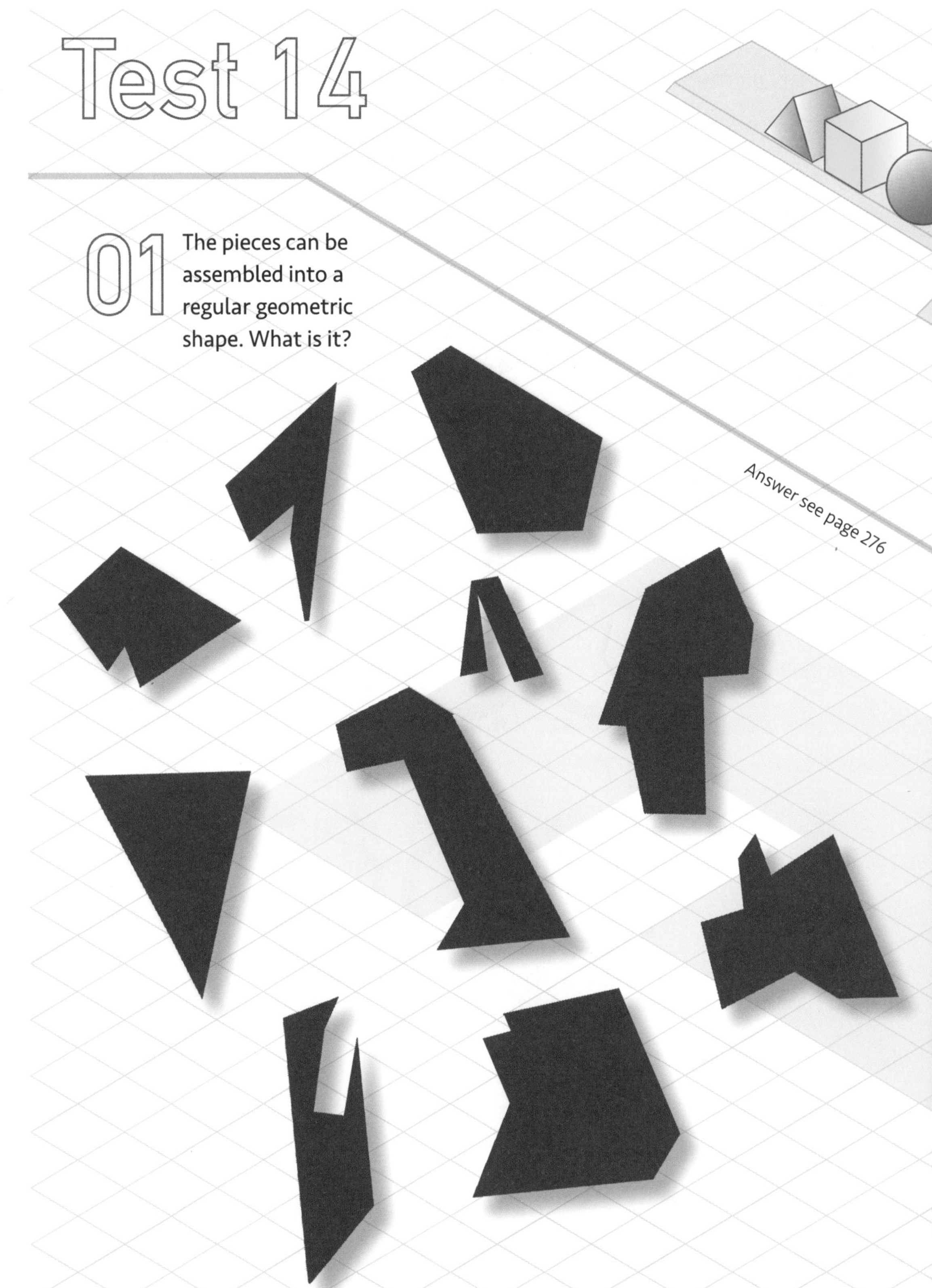

Answer see page 276

02

How many [pyramid shape] are required to balance the final scale?

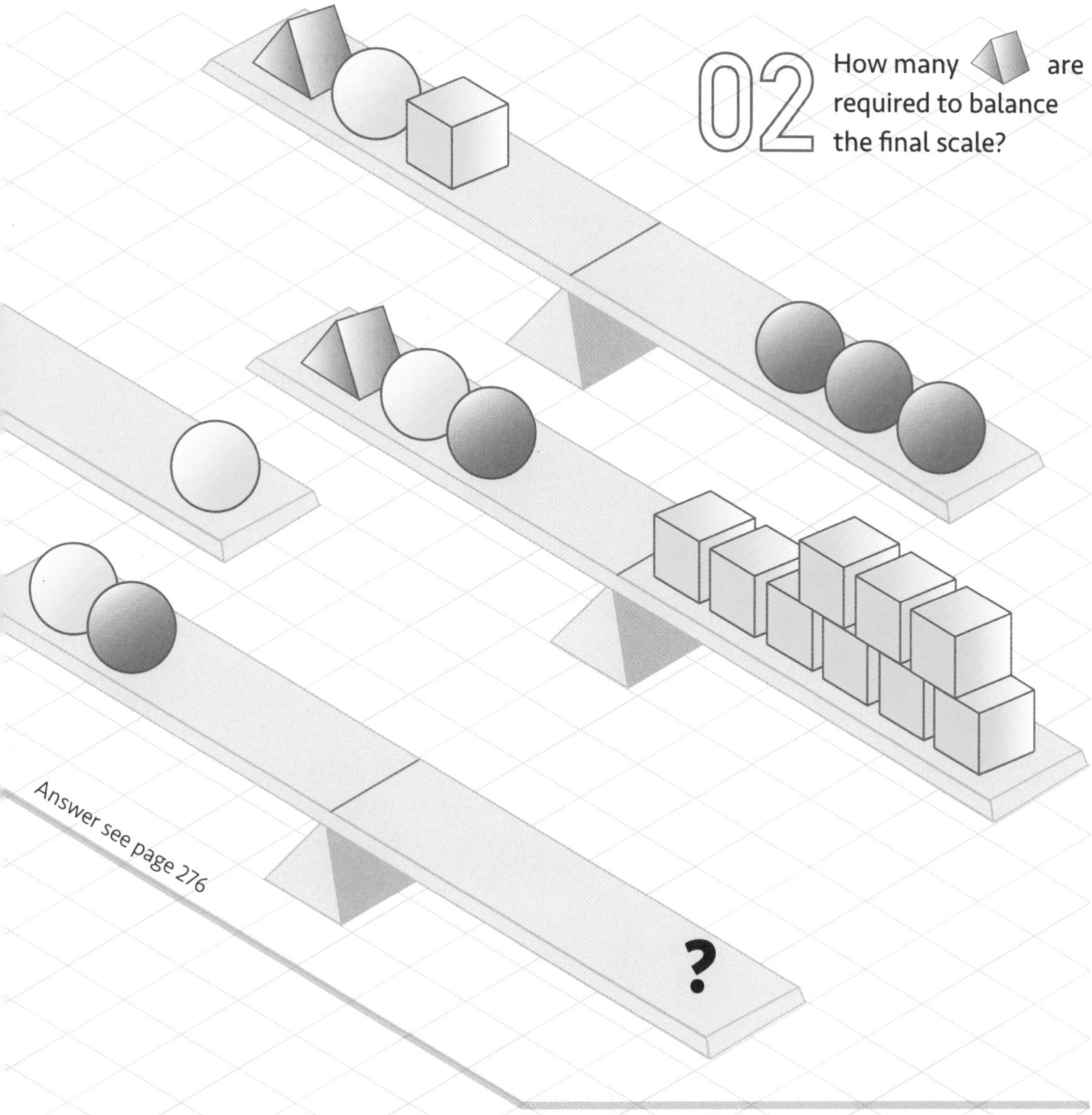

?

Answer see page 276

Answer see page 276

03

Fill in the missing plus, minus, multiplication, and division signs to make the equation below correct, performing all calculations strictly in the order they appear on the page.

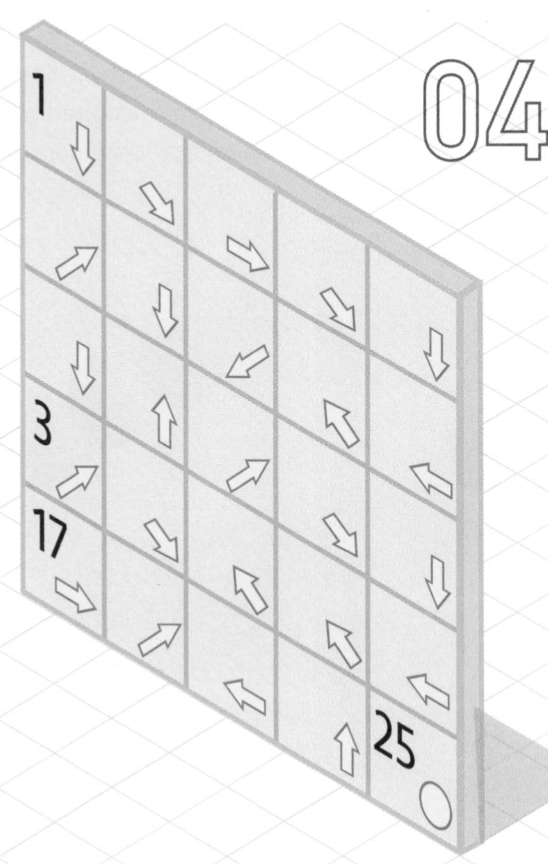

04

In each square, the arrow shows the direction you must move in. The numbers in some squares show that square's position in the correct sequence of moves. Move from top left to bottom right, visiting each square in the grid exactly once.

Answer see page 276

Answer see page 276

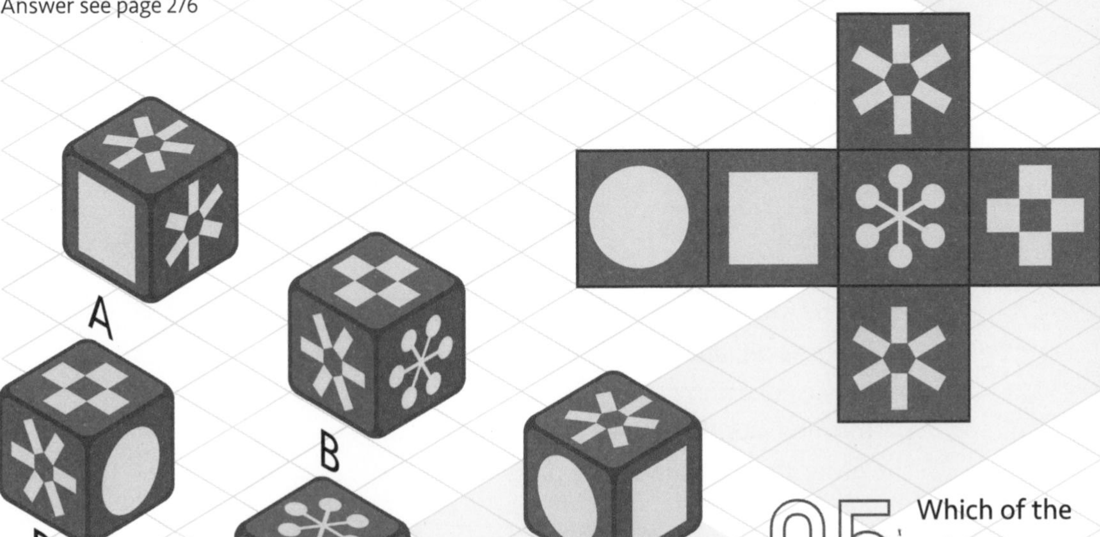

05

Which of the cubes A to E cannot be made using the layout shown?

06

Which of the options A to E most accurately continues the sequence?

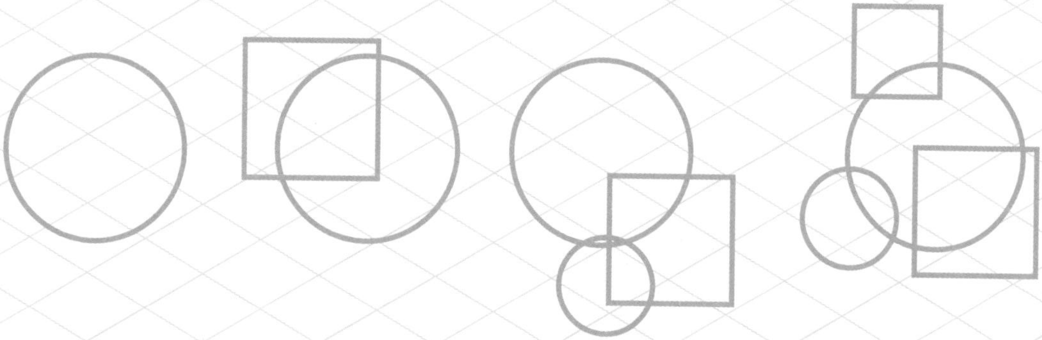

A B C D E

Answer see page 276

Answer see page 276

07

What number should replace the question mark?

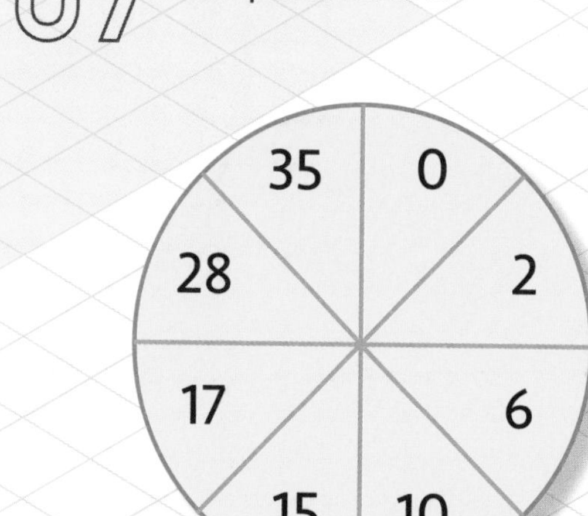

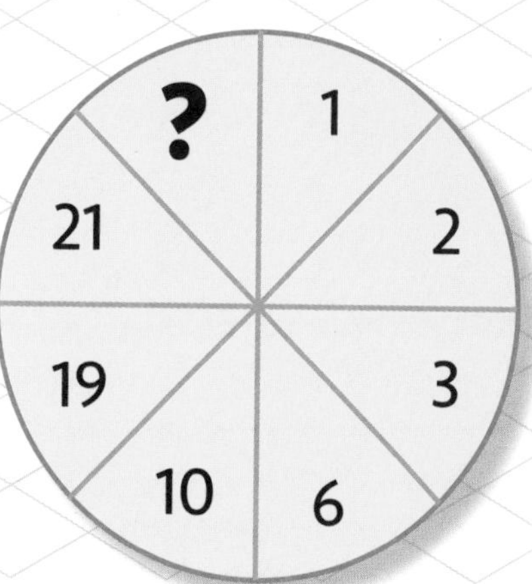

Fit the numbers shown into the design to complete the grid.

Answer see page 276

3 digits	4 digits	5 digits	6 digits	7 digits	8 digits	9 digits
151	3053	11508	597819	2095532	59109445	115526629
400	5012	73551	727739	7945014	71562111	251331299
468	5394	91157		9064917		527354421
560	8840	99124				709627724
603	9970					
759						
841						
897						
921						

What number should replace the question mark?

Answer see page 276

Answer see page 276

10

Which of the designs A to E is the odd one out?

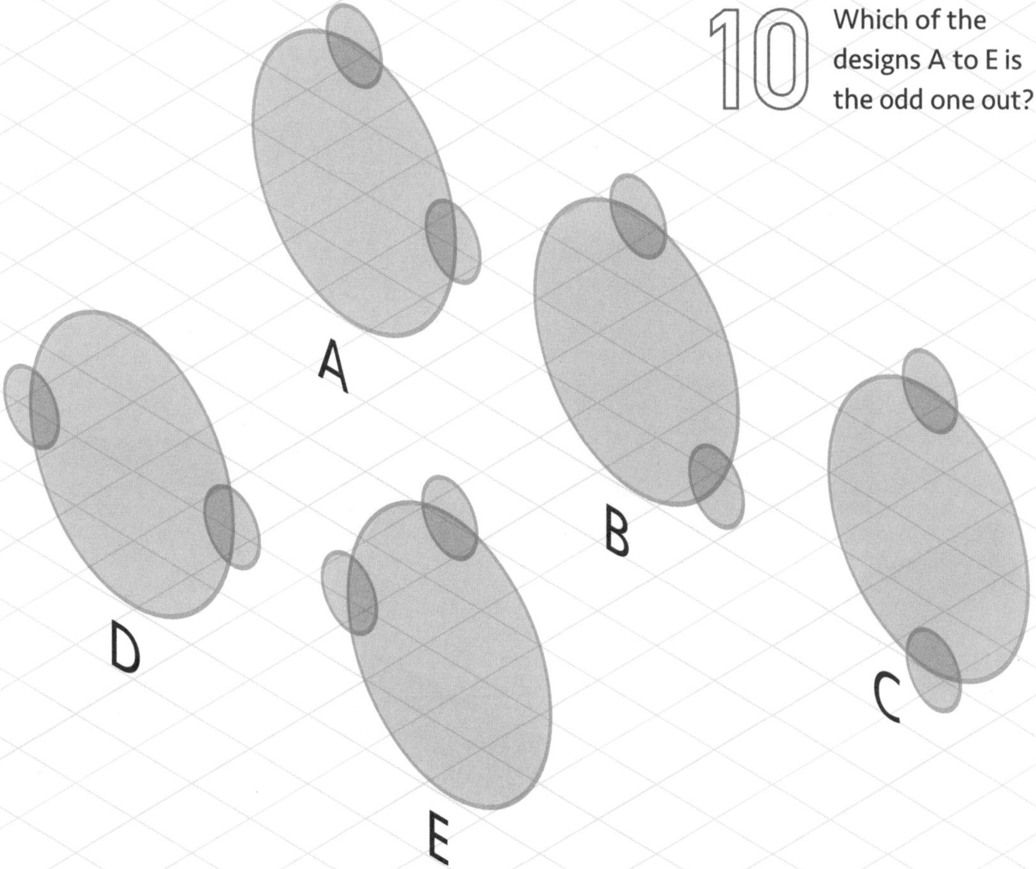

11 Which option A to E most accurately completes the pattern?

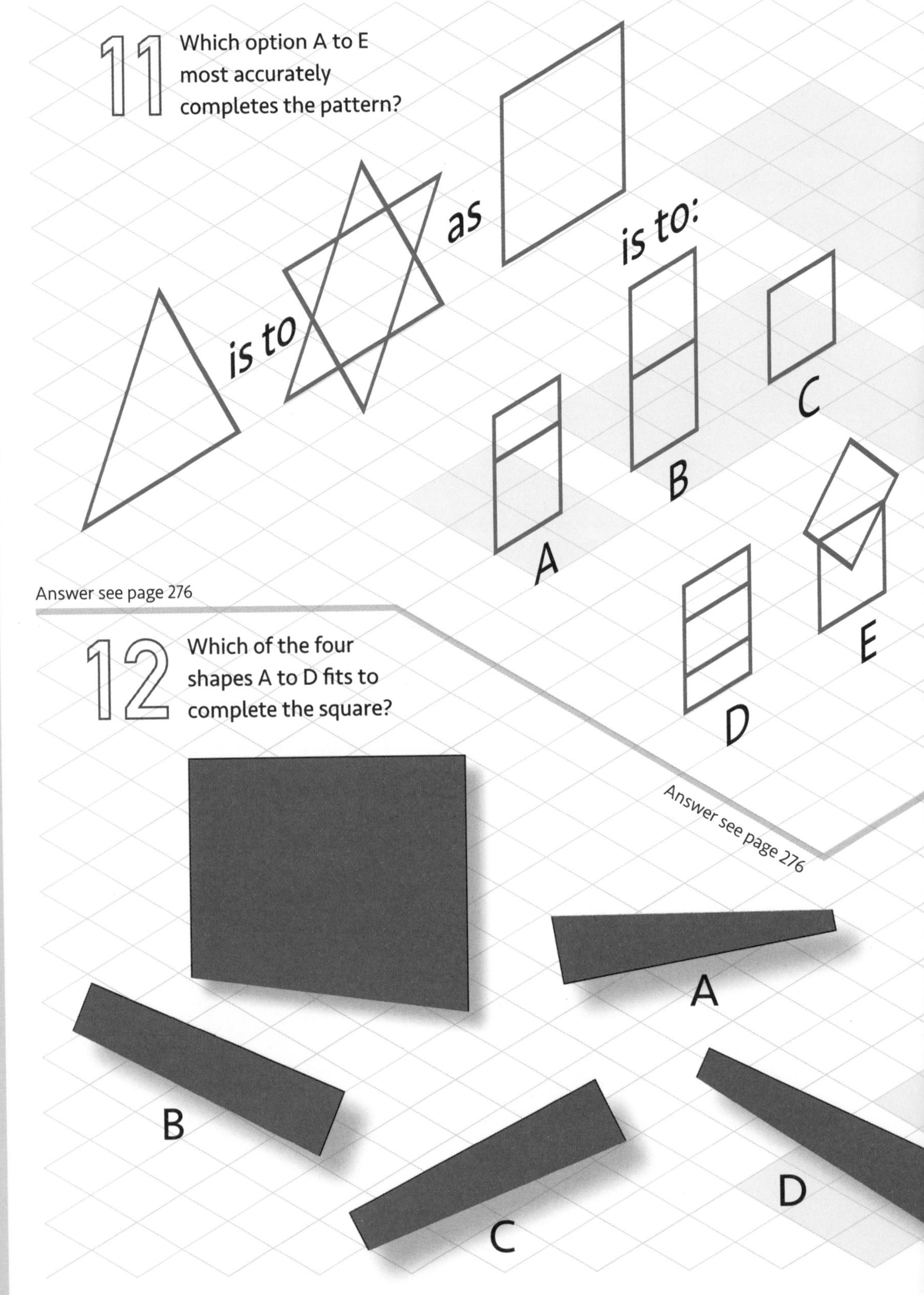

Answer see page 276

12 Which of the four shapes A to D fits to complete the square?

Answer see page 276

13

Use five straight lines to divide the field below into seven sections containing 12, 14, 16, 18, 20, 22 and 24 hexagons.

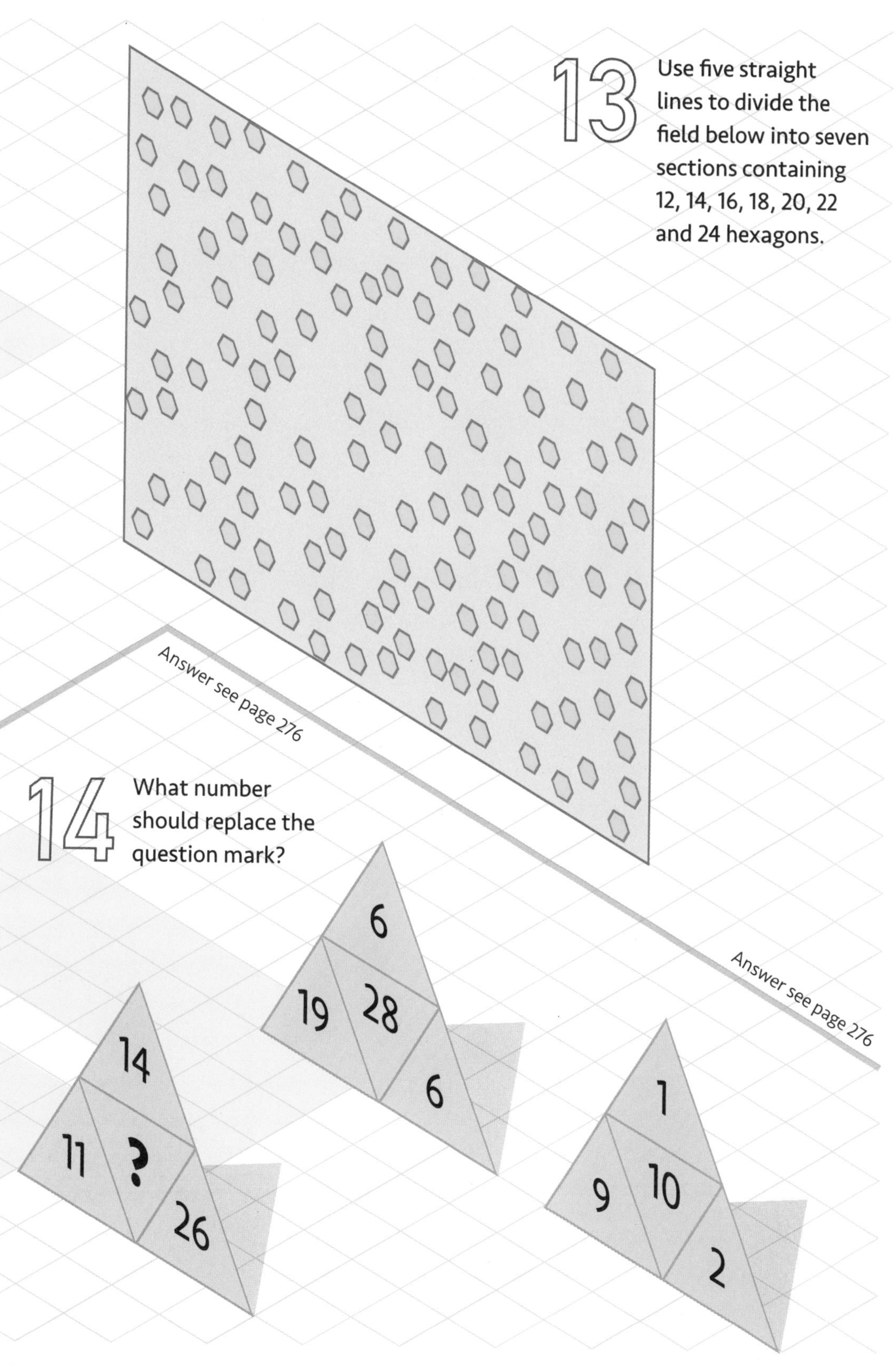

Answer see page 276

14

What number should replace the question mark?

Answer see page 276

15

In the grid below, how much is each symbol worth?

Answer see page 277

16

What number should replace the question mark?

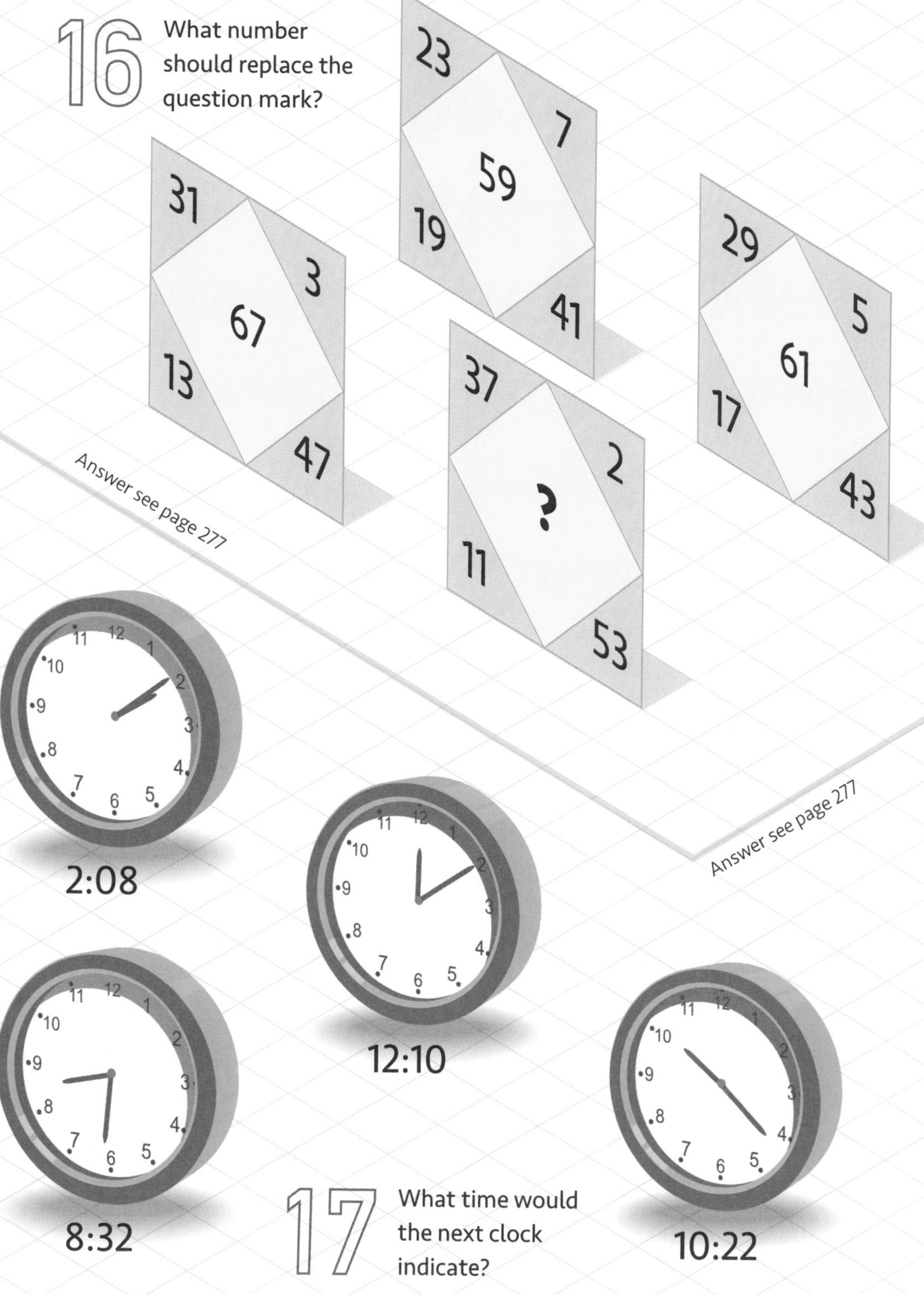

Answer see page 277

17

What time would the next clock indicate?

Answer see page 277

18

Combine the segments below to find the names of ten celebrities.

ATH	VOY	EN	CHR	MCA
LIF	JAM	GER	TOM	BR
CKI	NSA	KIN	NDI	IAN
SON	EEJ	SWO	SER	HE
FRA	KAT	ON	AK	CAM
EBE	AZ	HGA	ZAC	WA
ES	LE	IS	EM	
ERO	DAN	RO	NAT	
NKS	ES	HA	TOM	
MYL	LED	ISH	RTH	

Answer see page 277

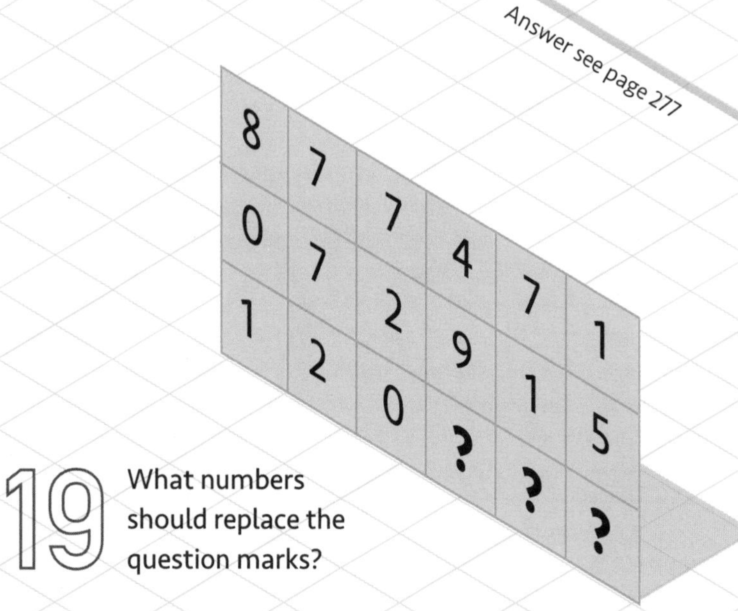

19

What numbers should replace the question marks?

20

Which symbols are missing from the blue squares in the grid below?

Answer see page 277

Test 15

01

Which of the pentagons at the bottom should replace the question mark?

Answer see page 277

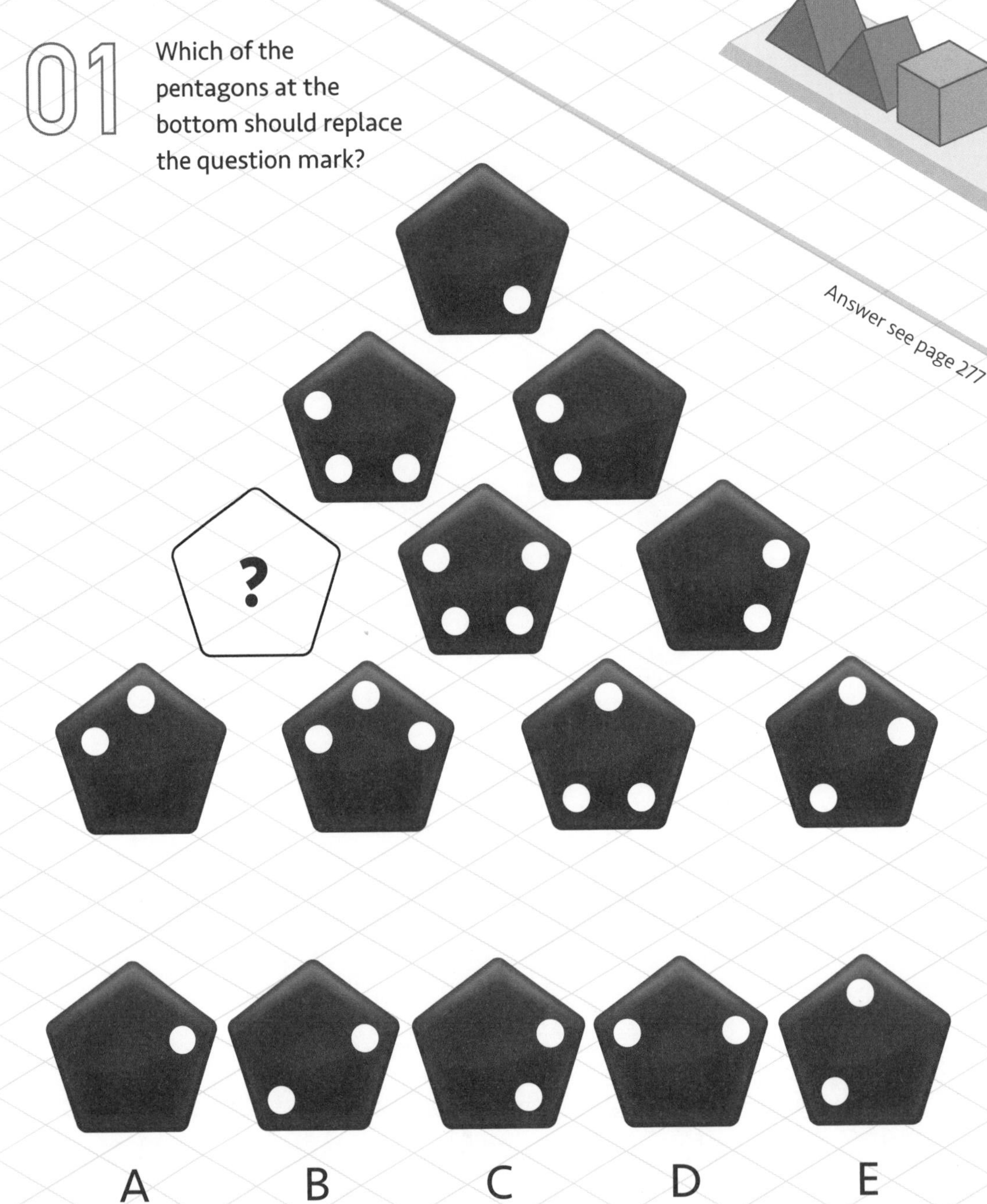

02

Scales 1 and 2 are in perfect balance. How many triangles are needed to balance scale 3?

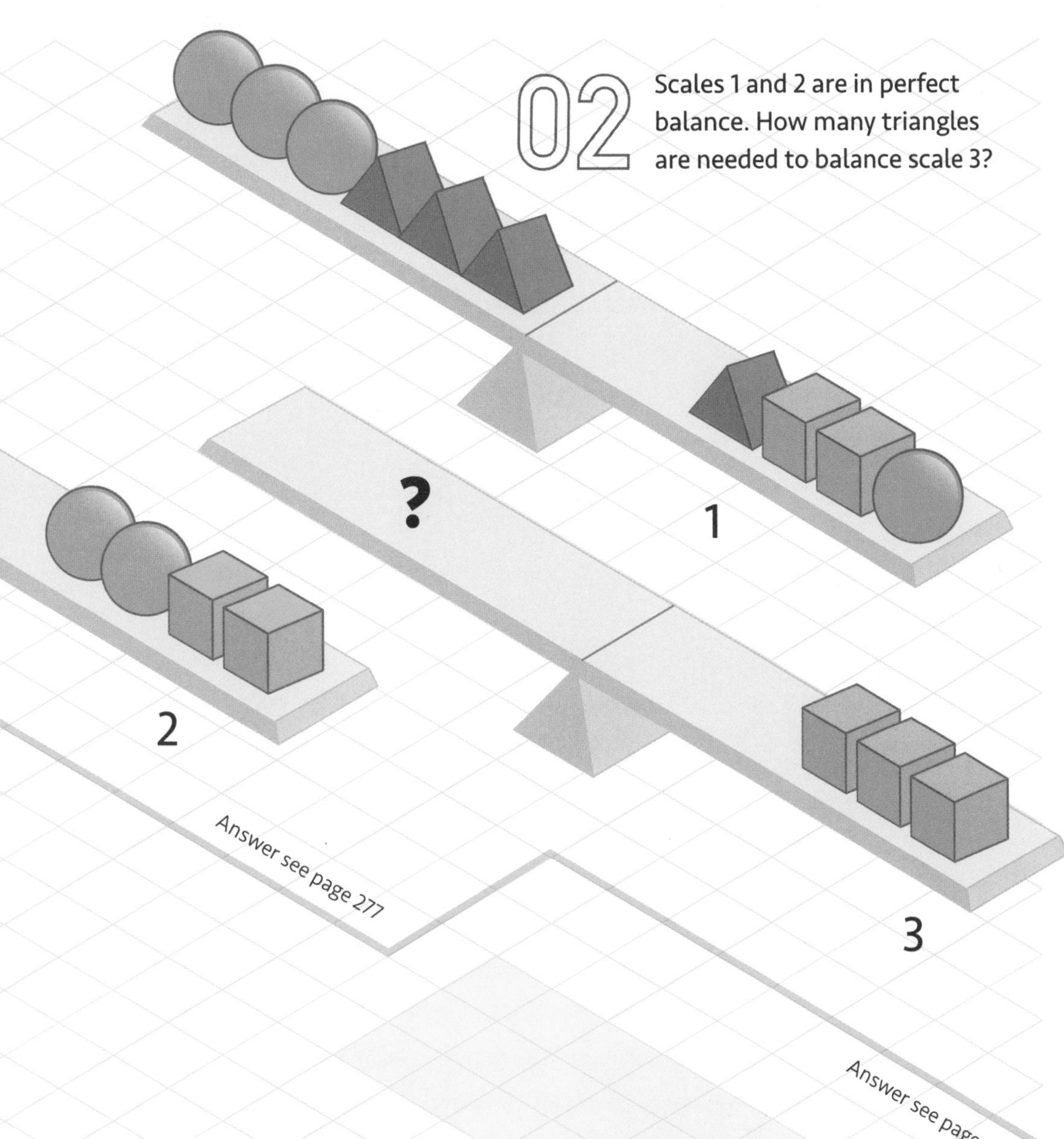

Answer see page 277

Answer see page 277

03

If $^{4}/_{5}$ is 8, how much is 6?

Which shape below can be put with the one above to form a perfect square?

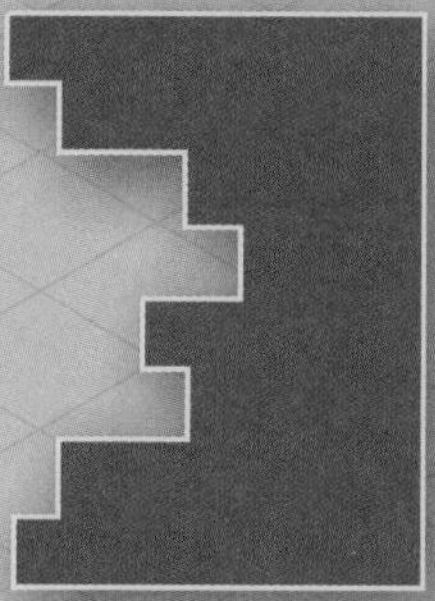

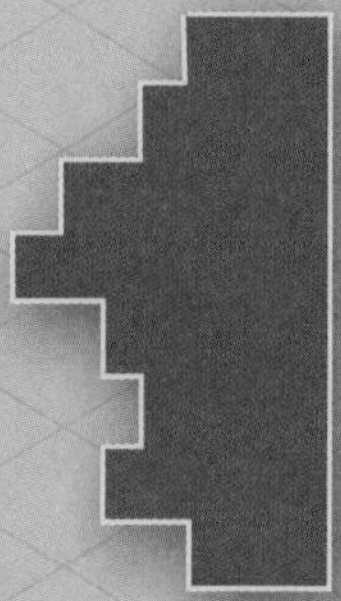

A

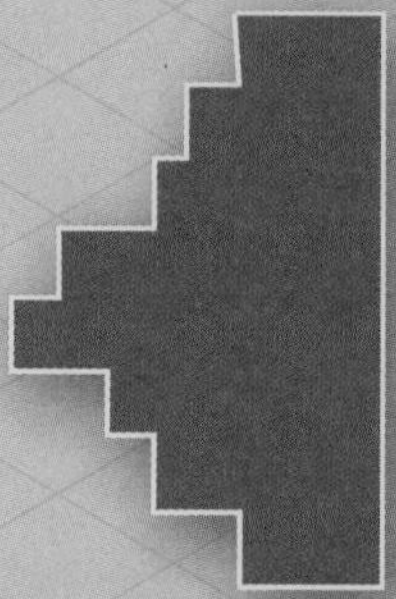

B

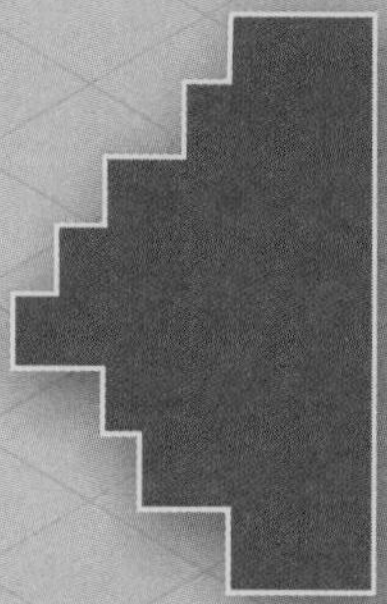

C

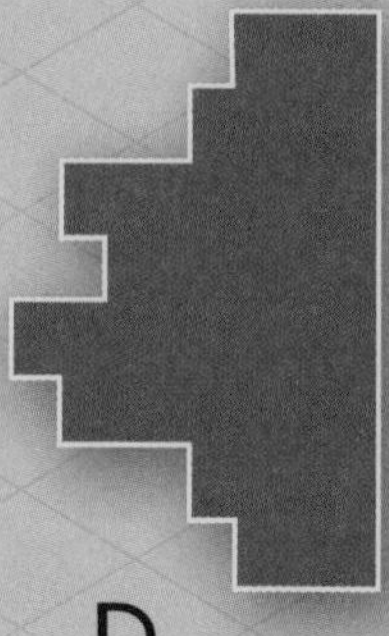

D

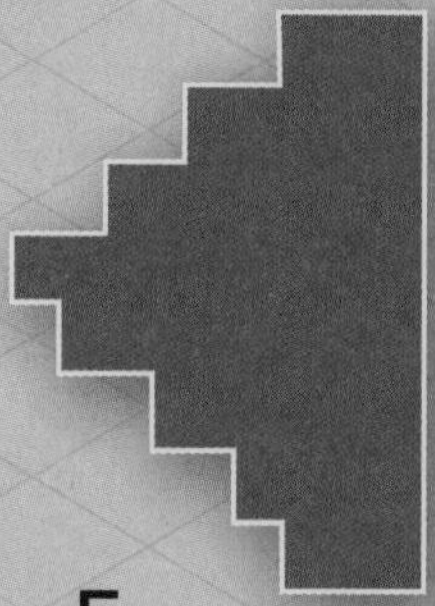

E

Answer see page 277

Select the correct figure from the numbered ones below, to replace the question mark.

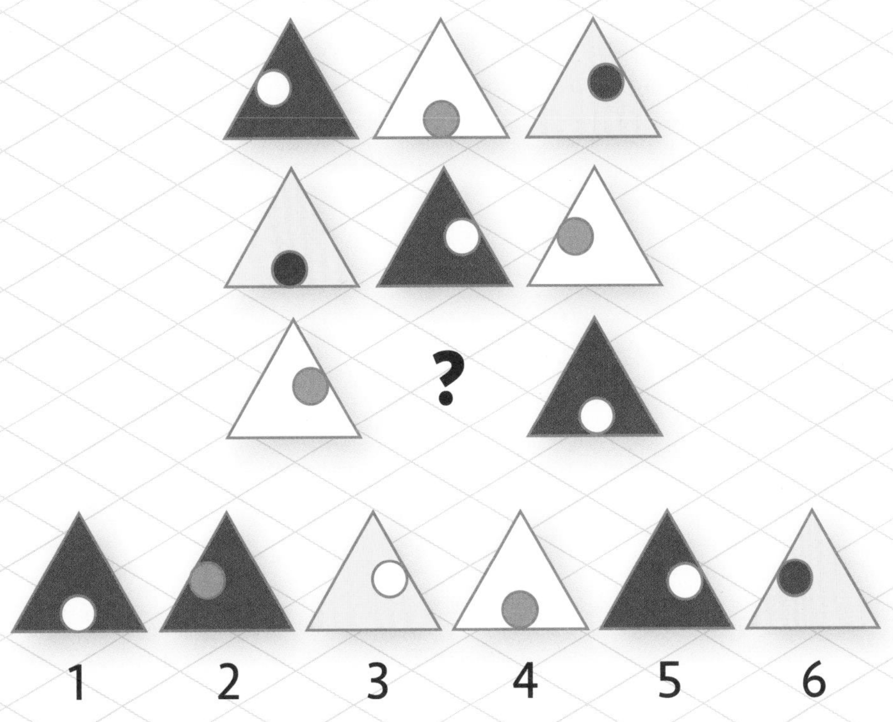

Answer see page 277

Answer see page 277

Complete the square using nine consecutive numbers, so that all rows, columns, and large diagonals add up to the same total.

07

Each of the nine squares in the grid marked 1A to 3C should incorporate all of the items that are shown in the squares of the same letter and number, at left and top. For example, square 2A should incorporate all of the items in squares 2 and A. One square however, is incorrect. Which is it?

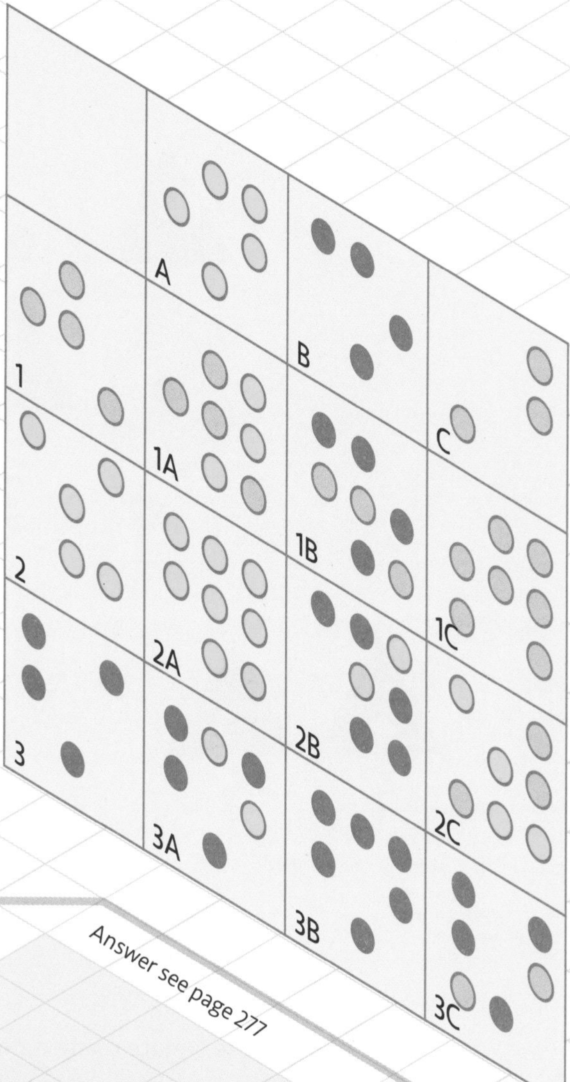

Answer see page 277

08

Which is the odd one out?

63 44 27

81 36 72

Answer see page 277

Which are the odd ones out?

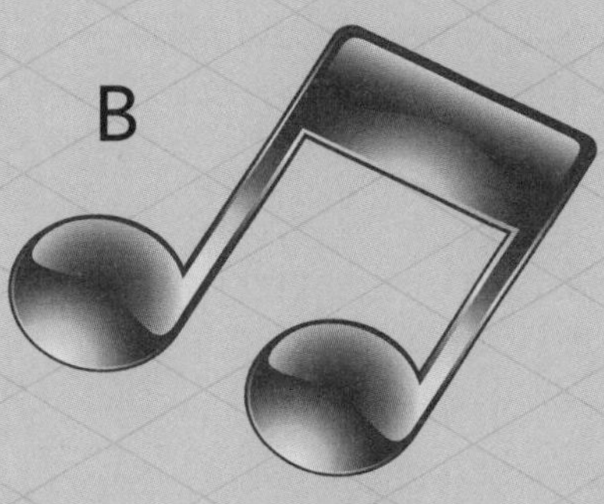

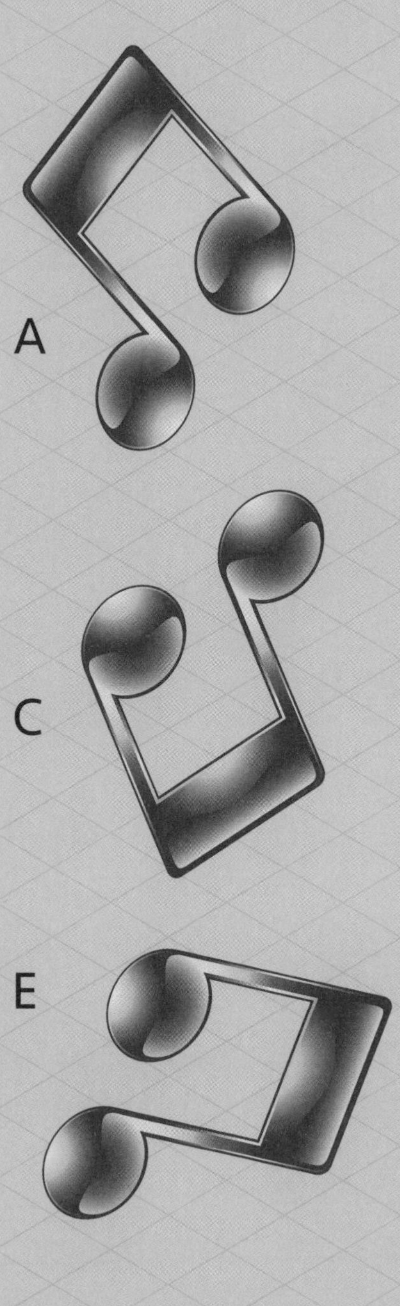

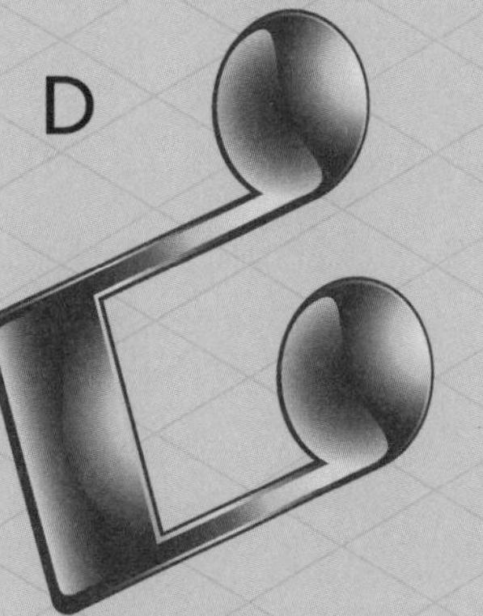

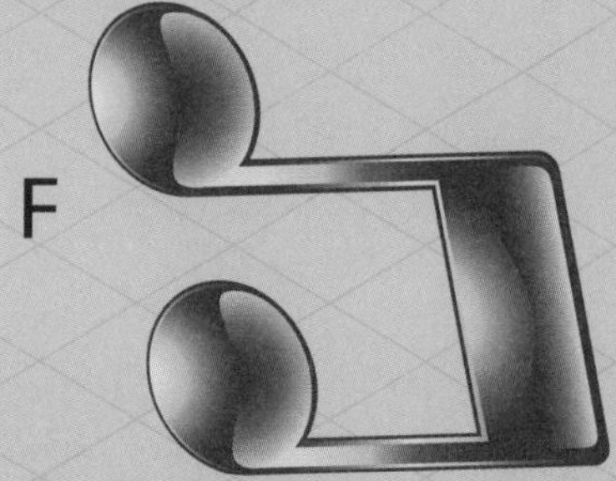

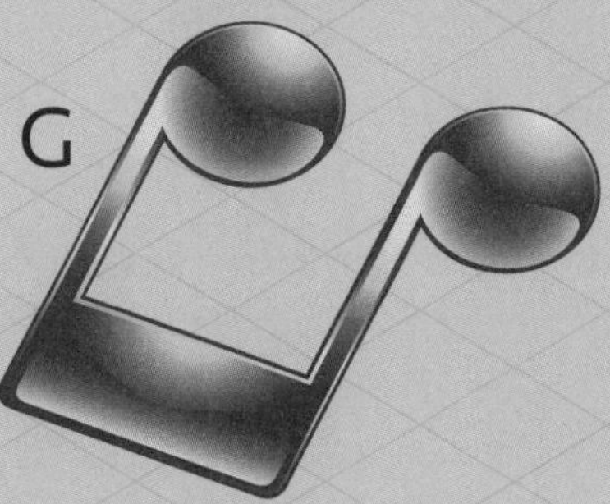

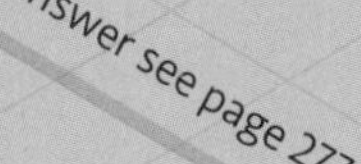
Answer see page 277

10 What is the value of a circle?

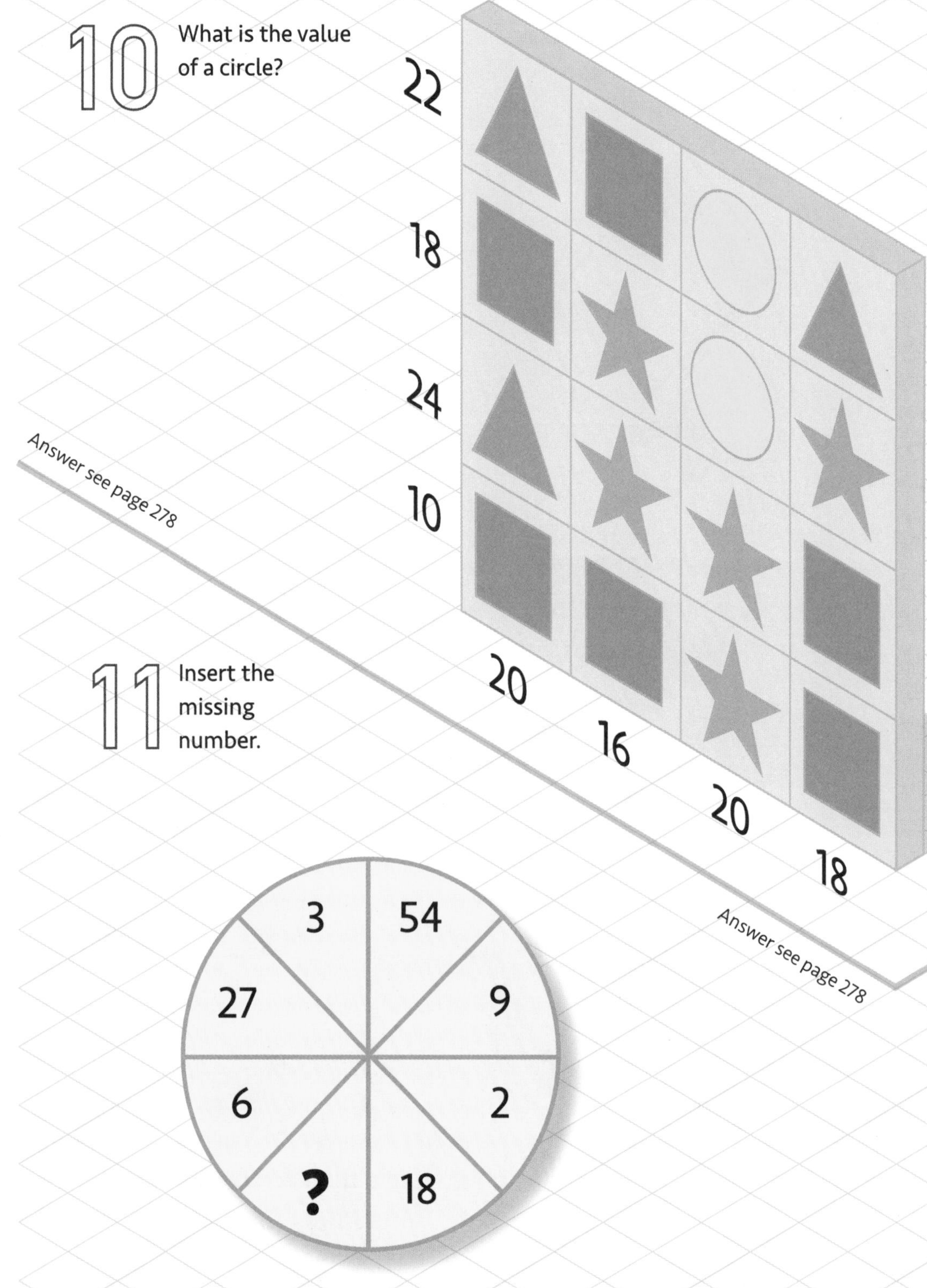

Answer see page 278

11 Insert the missing number.

Answer see page 278

12

Which of the constructed boxes below cannot be made from the given shape?

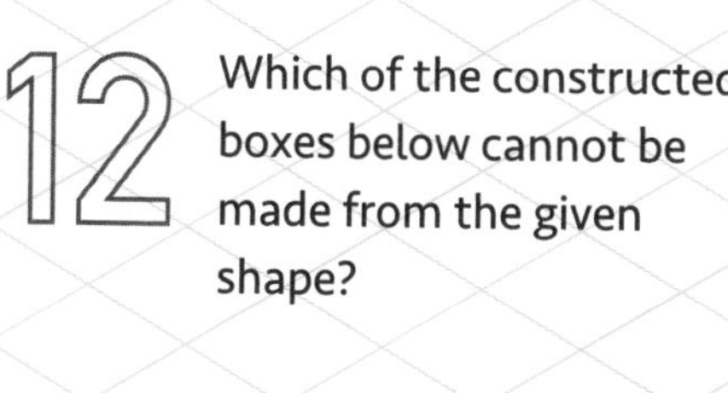

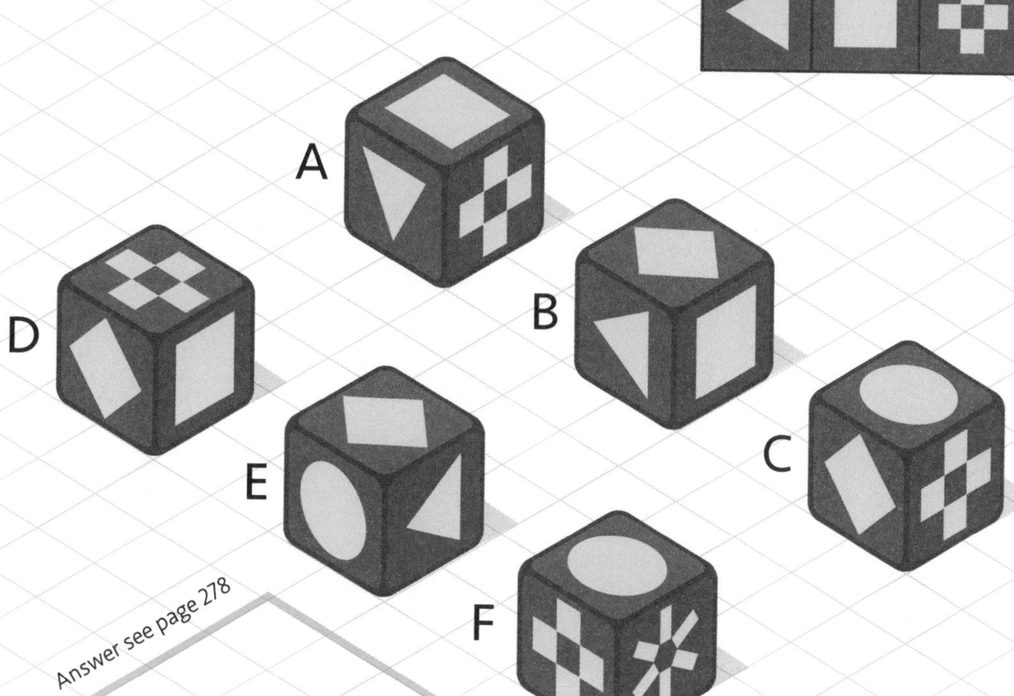

Answer see page 278

13

Which number is the odd one out?

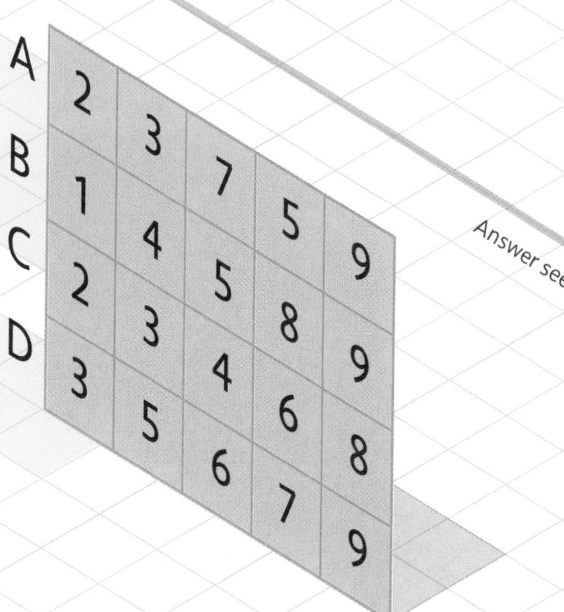

Answer see page 278

14

When complete, this 6 x 6 x 6 cube contains 216 individual blocks. How many blocks are required to complete the cube?

Answer see page 278

Answer see page 278

15

Insert the missing numbers.

5 9 19 37 75 149 ? ?

Havana is 9 hours behind Islamabad, which is 2 hours ahead of Moscow. It is 11:35 p.m. on Thursday in Moscow, what time is it in the other two cities?

MOSCOW

ISLAMABAD

HAVANA

Answer see page 278

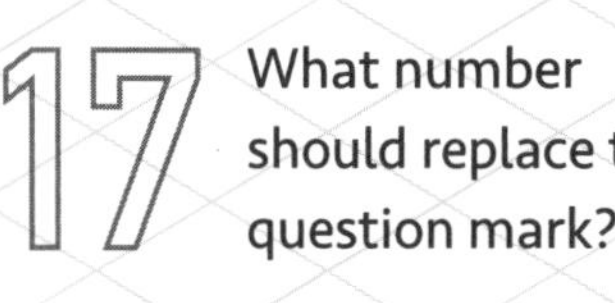

What number should replace the question mark?

21
15 16 12

9
7 7 5

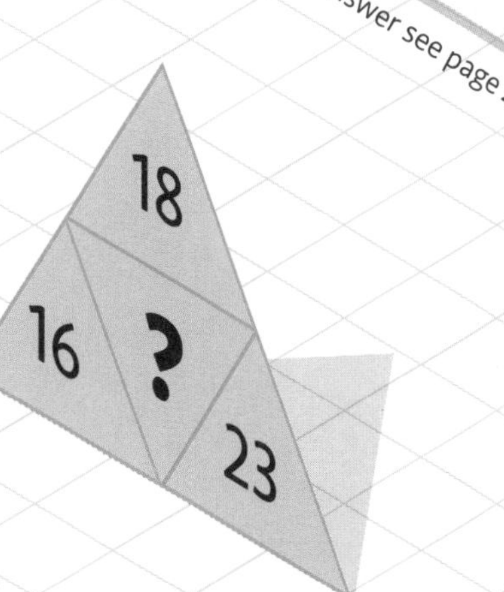

Answer see page 278

18

Which of these dice is not like the other three?

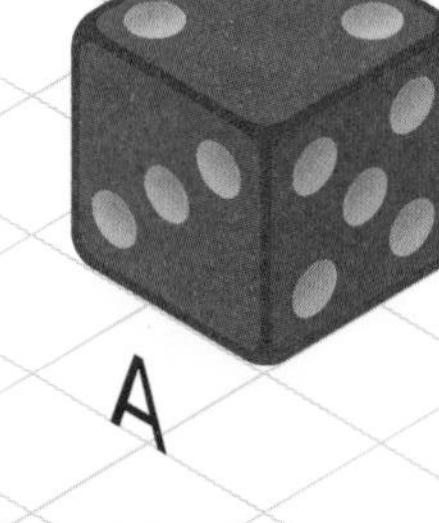

A

B

C

D

Answer see page 278

Answer see page 278

19

Which line of two numbers below has the same relationship as the two above?

	6 3 2	:	3 6
A	2 3 4	:	2 7
B	3 8 2	:	4 3
C	5 6 3	:	9 1
D	9 2 4	:	7 2
E	8 1 5	:	3 8

Which of the lettered clocks below continues the numbered series?

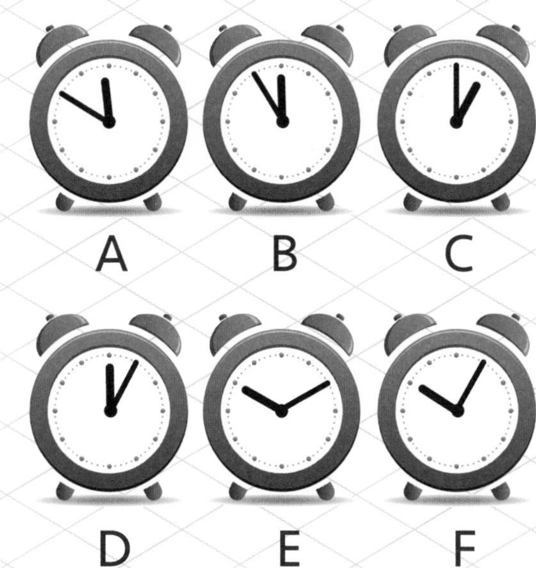

Answer see page 278

Test 16

01

Which of the designs A to E is the odd one out?

Answer see page 278

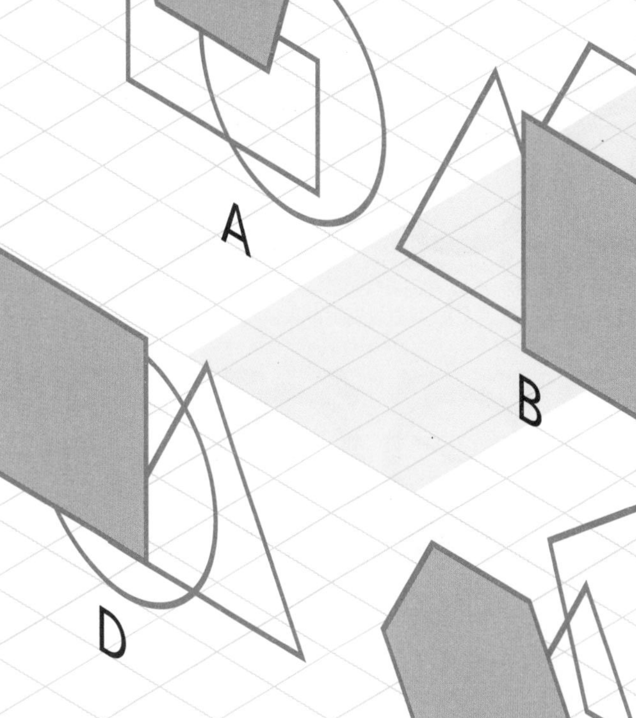

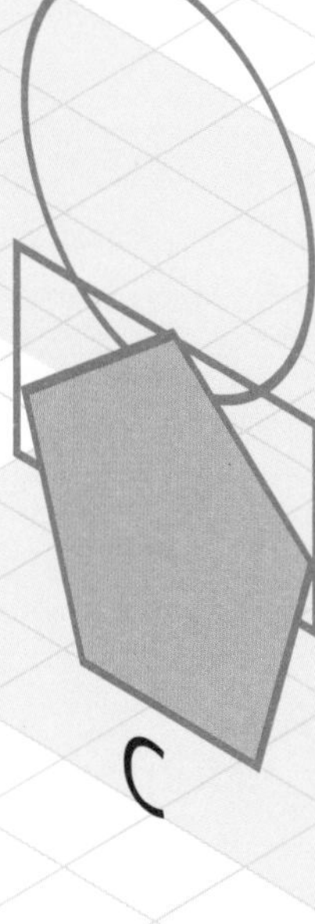

198

02

How many [cube] are required to balance the final scale?

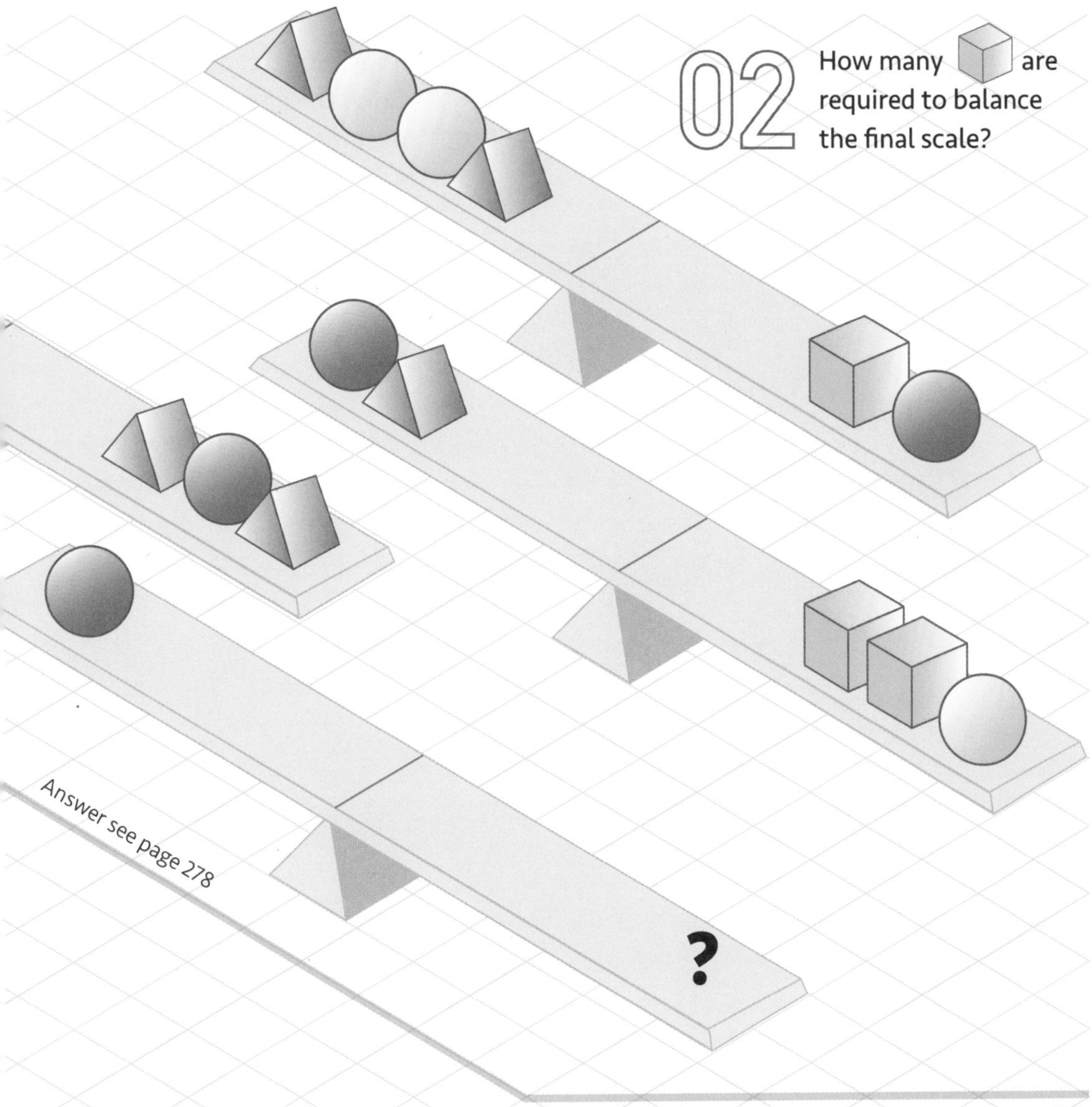

?

Answer see page 278

Answer see page 278

03

Fill in the missing plus, minus, multiplication, division, and factorial signs to make the equation below correct, performing all calculations strictly in the order they appear on the page.

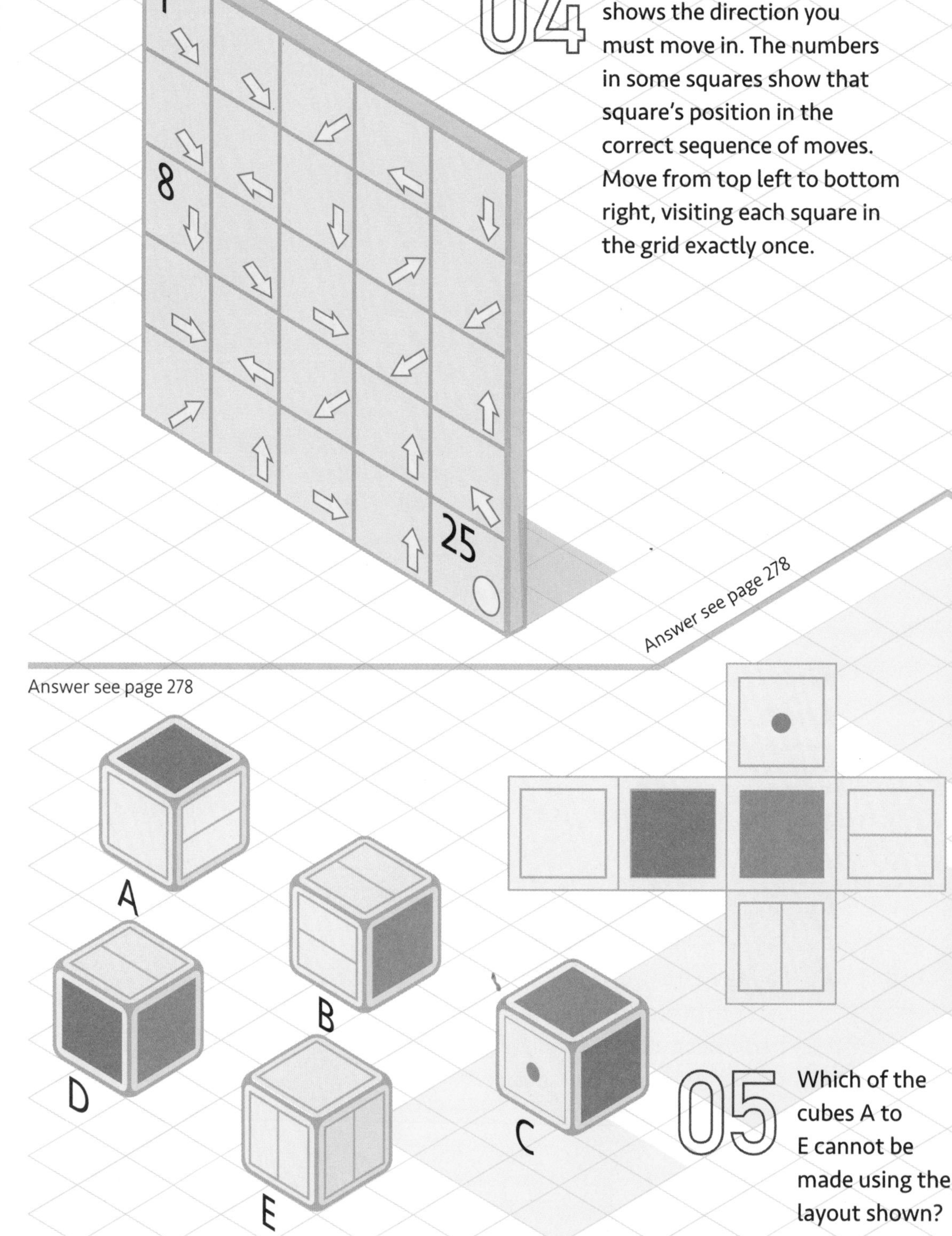

04

In each square, the arrow shows the direction you must move in. The numbers in some squares show that square's position in the correct sequence of moves. Move from top left to bottom right, visiting each square in the grid exactly once.

Answer see page 278

Answer see page 278

05

Which of the cubes A to E cannot be made using the layout shown?

A B C D E

Which of the options A to E most accurately continues the sequence?

Answer see page 278

What number should replace the question mark?

Answer see page 279

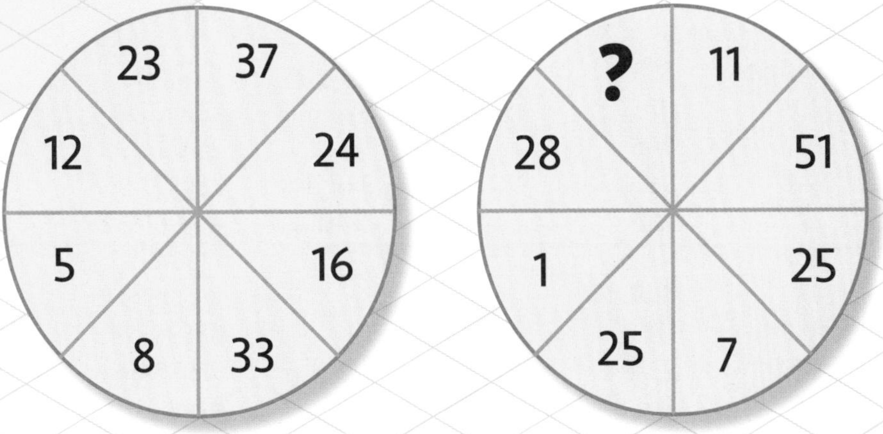

23 37
12 24
5 16
8 33

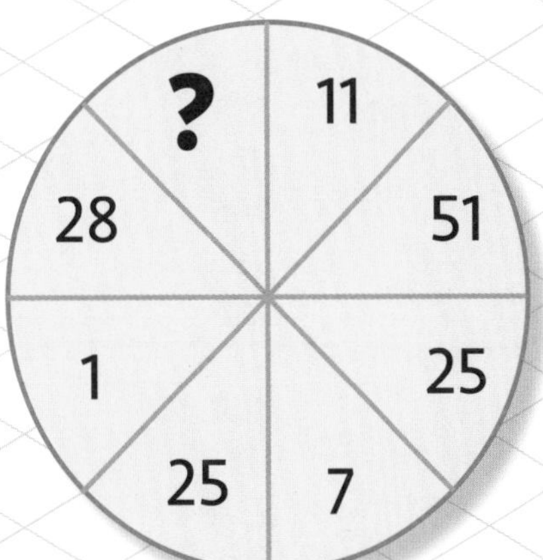

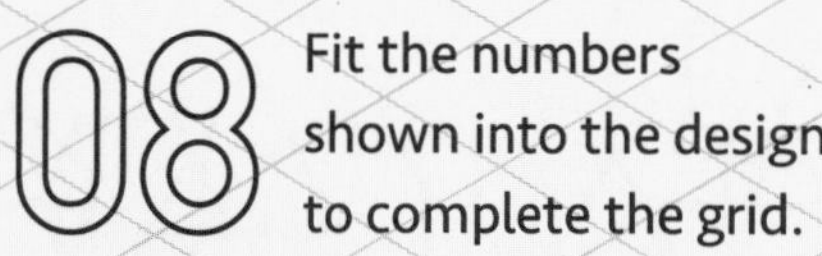

Fit the numbers shown into the design to complete the grid.

Answer see page 279

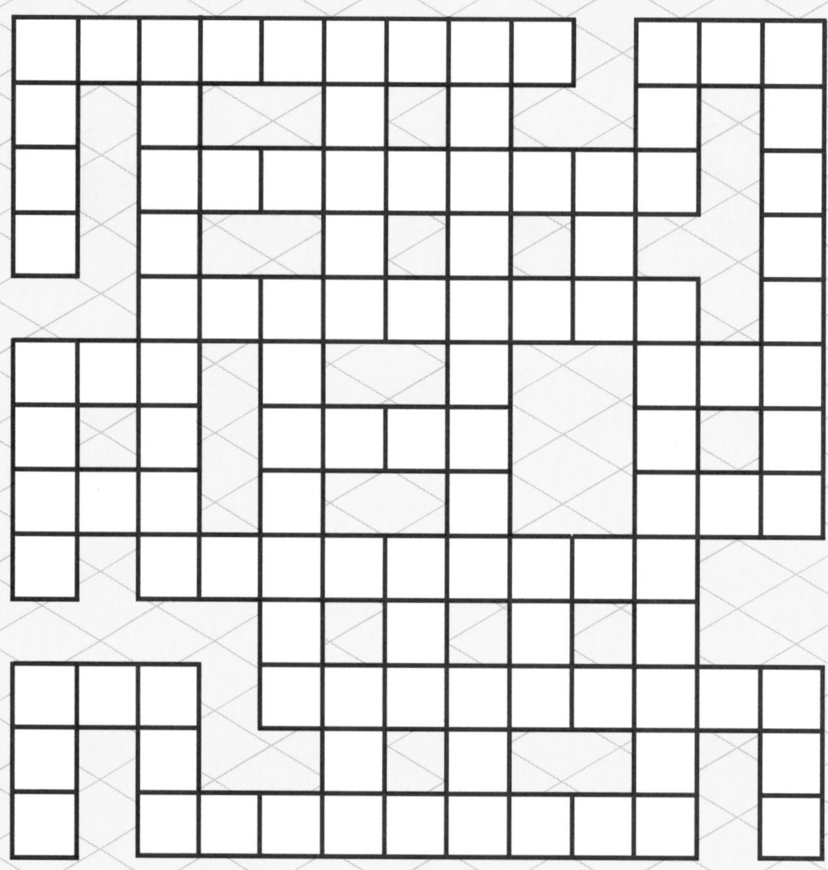

3 digits
204
321
348
379
432
439
450
453
645
727
859
876
946
961
977

4 digits
1780
2378
9088

5 digits
19756

7 digits
6123608

8 digits
72400224

9 digits
173651241
244217290
389371169
464161852
716616412
840969570
885307247
929704936
976362411

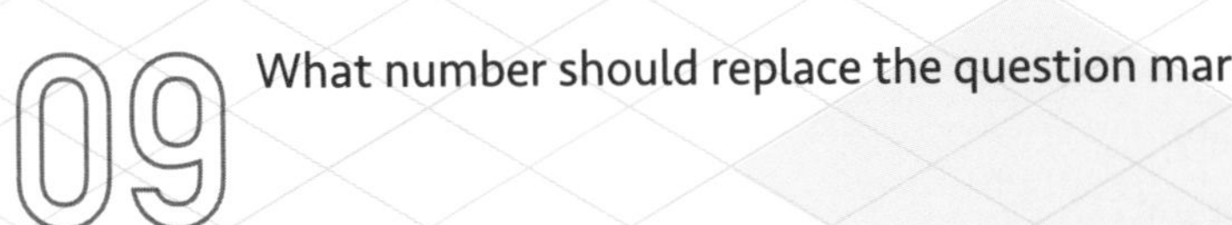

09

What number should replace the question mark?

4 6 12 18 30 42 ?

Answer see page 279

Answer see page 279

10

The pieces can be assembled into a regular geometric shape. What is it?

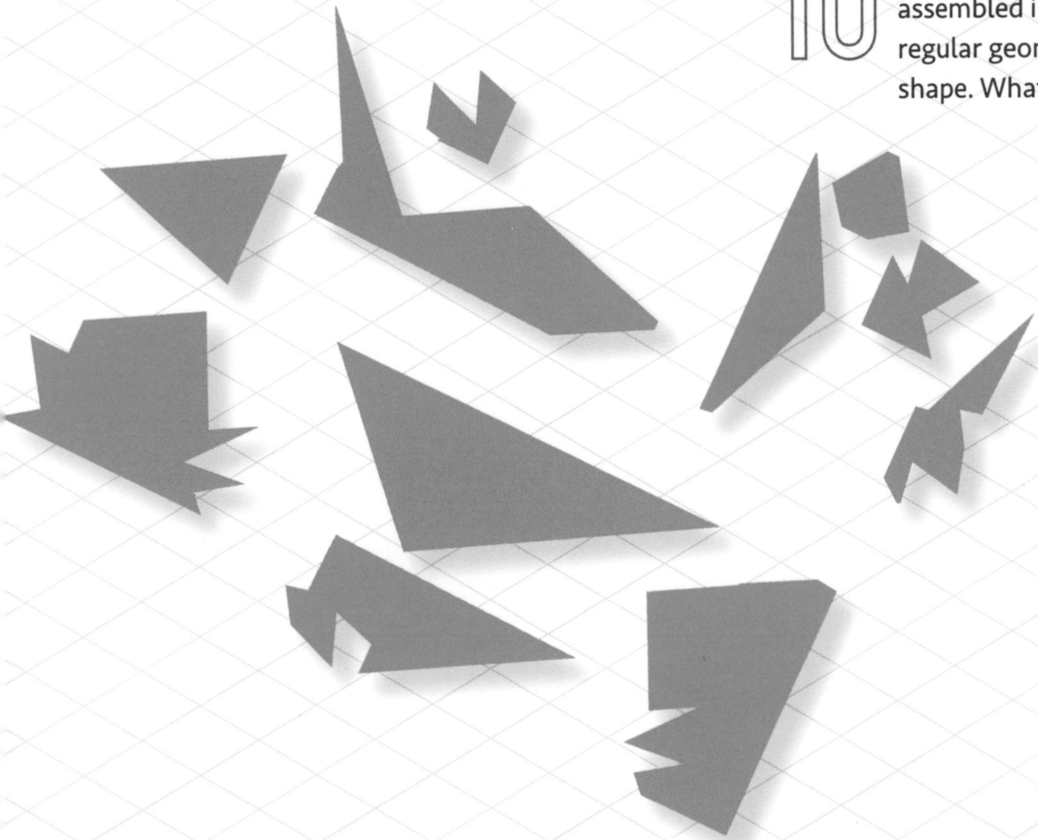

11

Which option A to E most accurately completes the pattern?

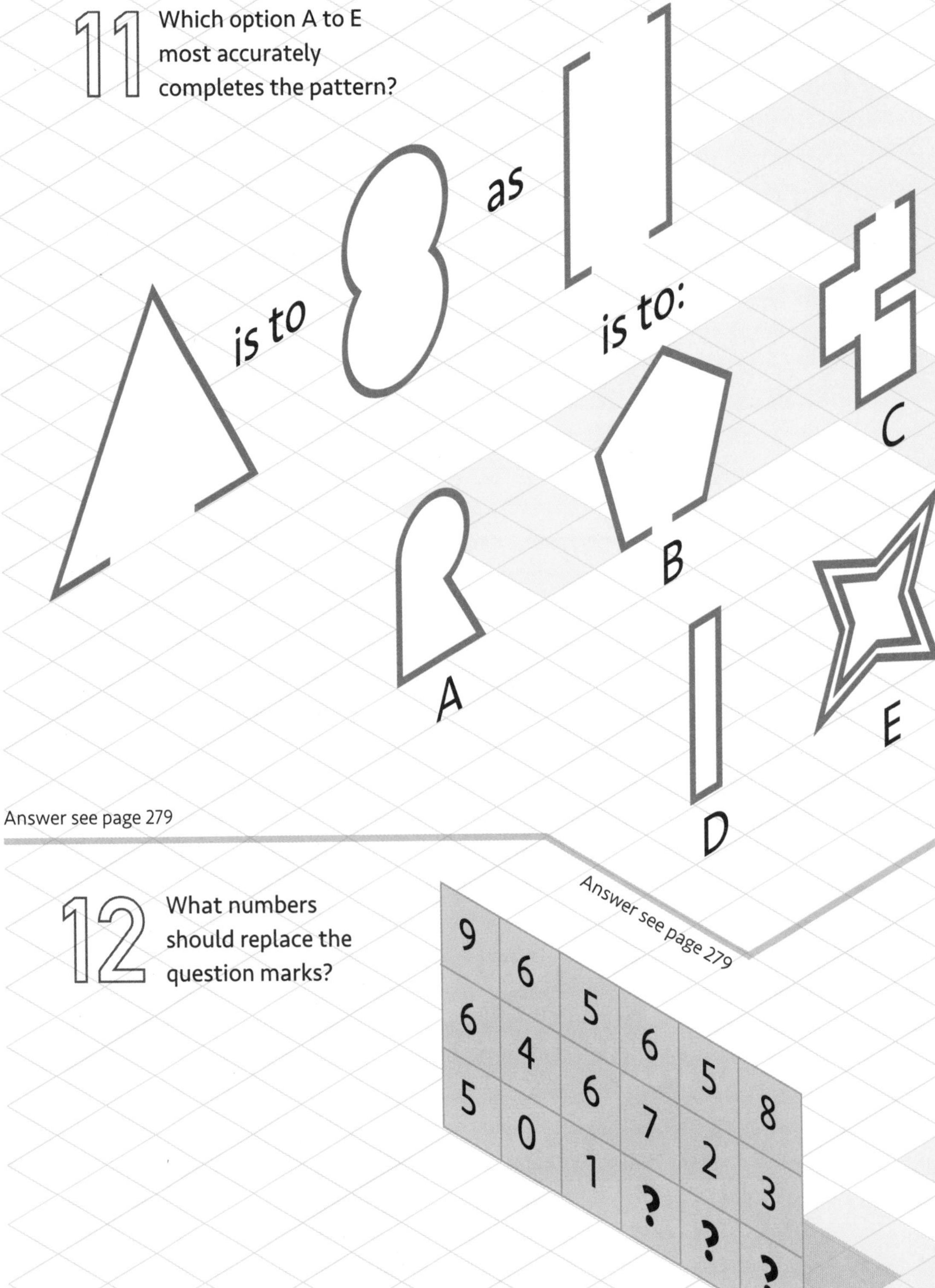

Answer see page 279

12

What numbers should replace the question marks?

9	6	5	6	5	8
6	4	6	7	2	3
5	0	1	?	?	?

Answer see page 279

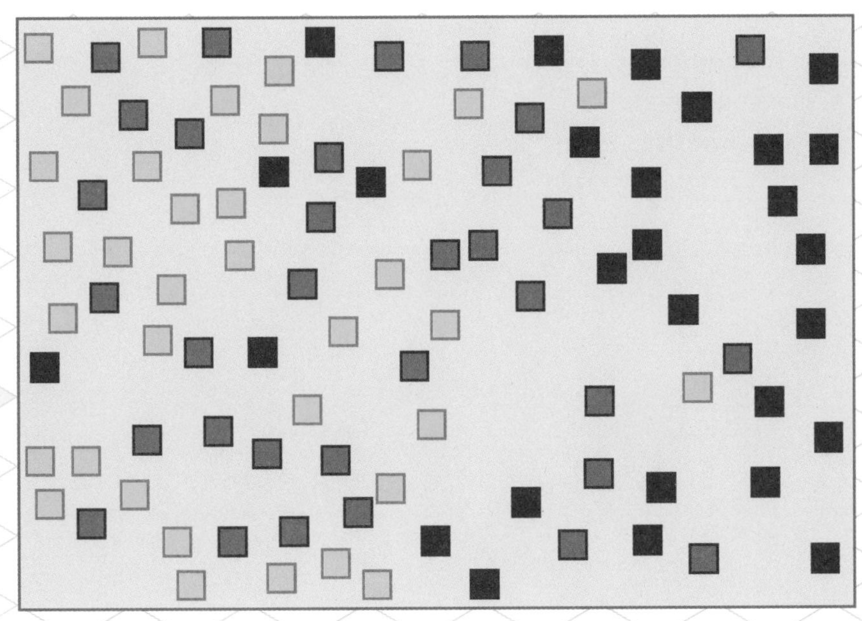

13

Use four straight lines to divide the field above into six sections each containing 16 squares, at least one of which must be of each color.

Answer see page 279

14

What number should replace the question mark?

Answer see page 279

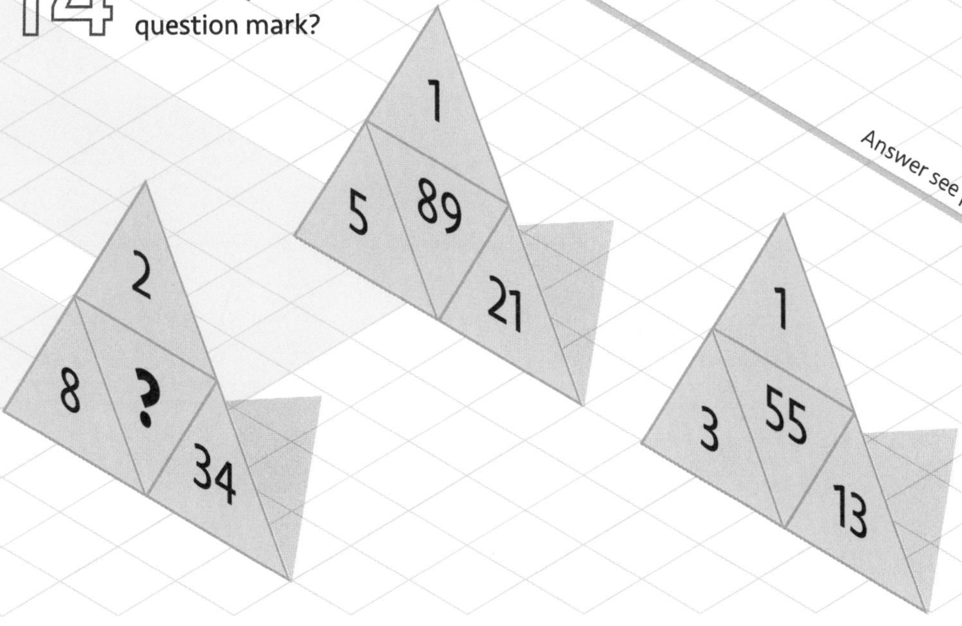

15 In the grid below, how much is each symbol worth?

Answer see page 279

16

What number should replace the question mark?

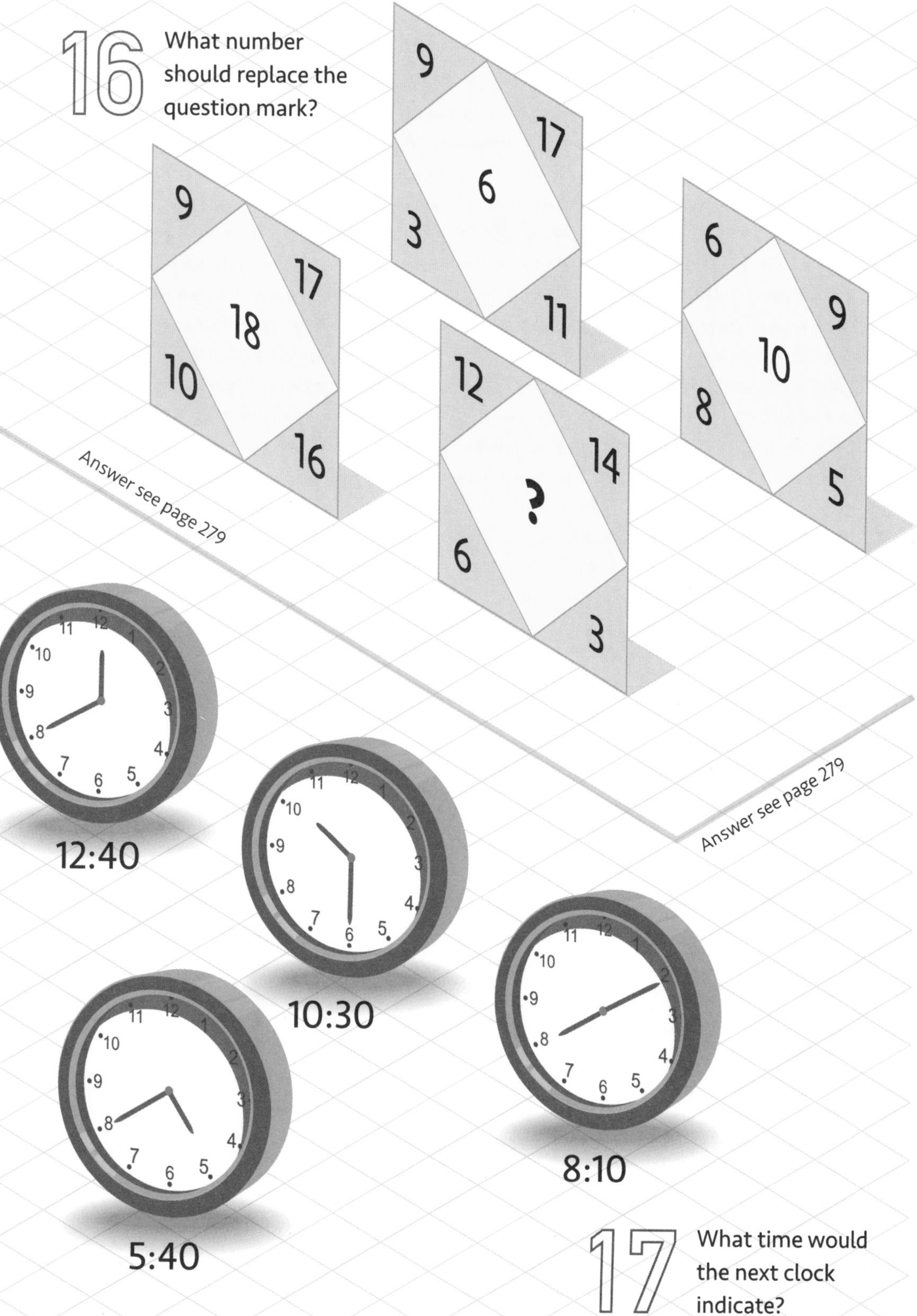

Answer see page 279

Answer see page 279

17

What time would the next clock indicate?

18

Combine the segments below to find the names of ten celebrities.

AD	ANB	CKS	INO	ON
SAM	AND	LJA	MC	ROB
AL	IS	CLI	IRO	SON
OOM	AST	DEN	OWE	UEL
PAC	NTE	ORL	LS	SSI
ALE	CAA	ERT	MEL	TI
JE	RAC	GIB	NWI	
LBA	CHR	HEL	OD	
AMS	ON	OBL	WO	

Answer see page 279

19

Which of the four shapes A to D fits to complete the triangle?

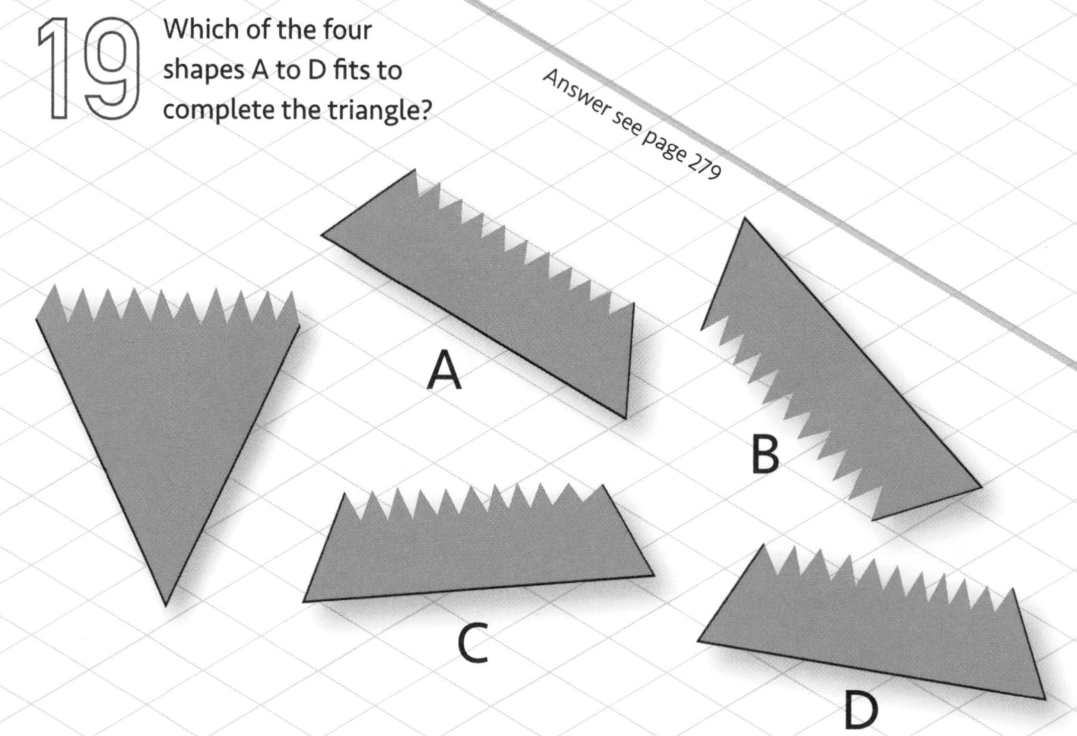

20

Which symbols are missing from the blue squares in the grid below?

●	●	■	●	○		❑	●	△	■	✻	○		❑	✻
△	○	✻	△		●	✻	○	△	●		●	○		△
■			✻	○	■	△		●	○	○	△	●	●	●
●	○	○	❑	●	△	●	✻			●	✻	■	■	○
	●	●		■	●	○	■	❑	○	△	❑	✻	△	
❑	△	△	●	✻	○		●	✻	●	■			●	○
✻	✻	■	■			○	○	△	△	●	●	○	○	●
△	❑	●				●		●	✻		■	●		■
●						■	○	○	❑	❑	△	△	✻	✻
○	●	❑				✻	●			✻	●	■	■	
		✻		■	○		△	○	●	△	○	●	●	○
○	△	△	✻	●		○	✻	●	■	●			○	●
●	●	●	■		○	●	❑	■	△	○	✻	❑		△
■	○	○	●	❑	●	△		✻	●		■	✻	○	■
✻			○	✻	△	■	●		○	○	●	△	●	●

Answer see page 280

Test 17

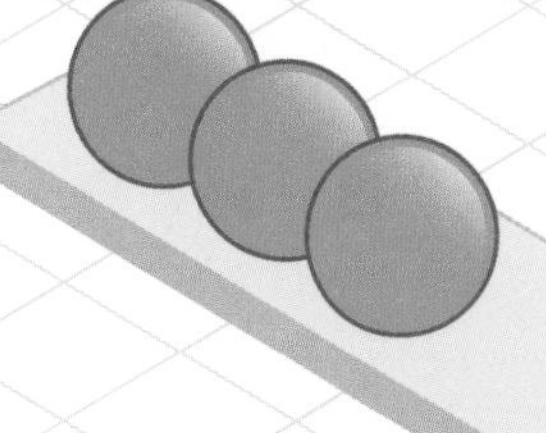

01

Which of the pentagons below should replace the question mark?

Answer see page 280

A B C D E

02

Scales 1 and 2 are in perfect balance. How many squares are needed to balance scale 3?

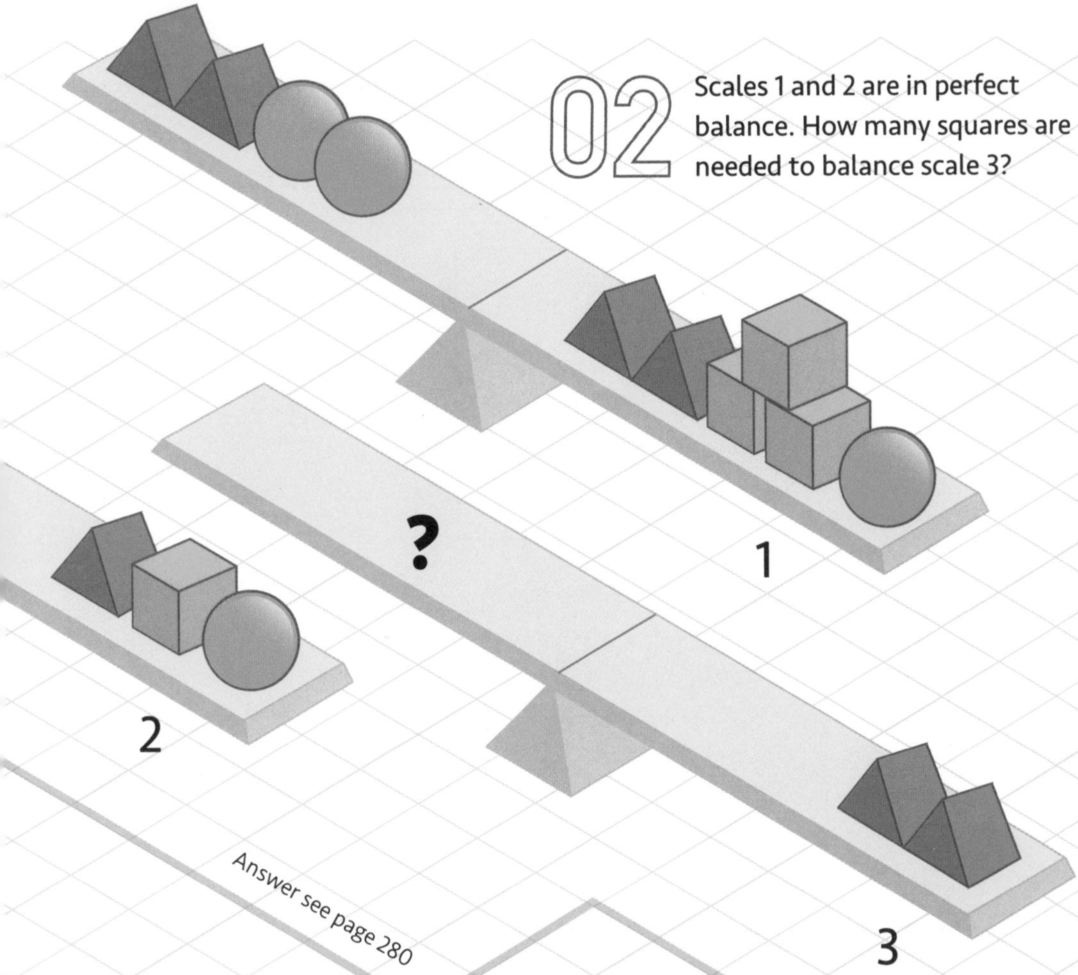

?

1

2

3

Answer see page 280

Answer see page 280

03

If ⅔ is 5⅓, how much is ½?

Which shape below can be put with the one above to form a perfect square?

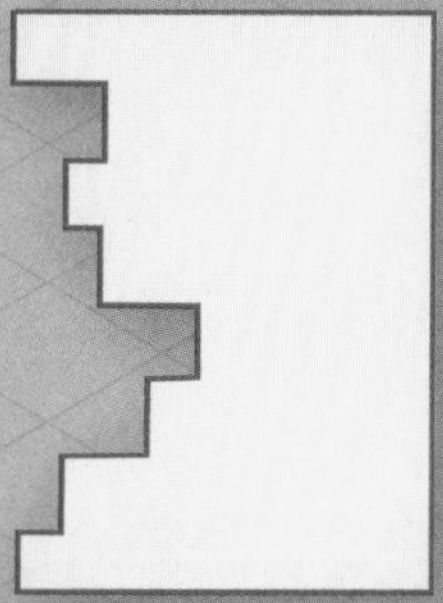

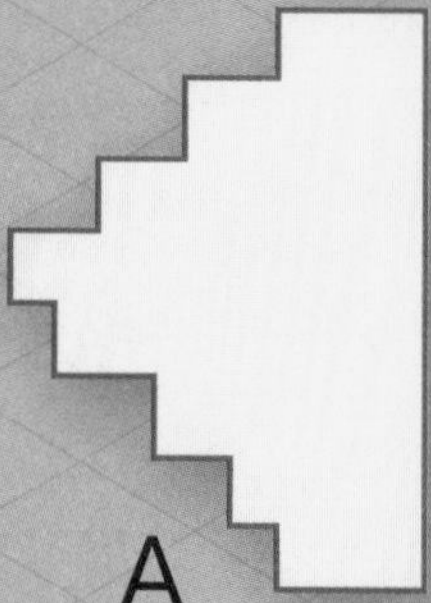

A

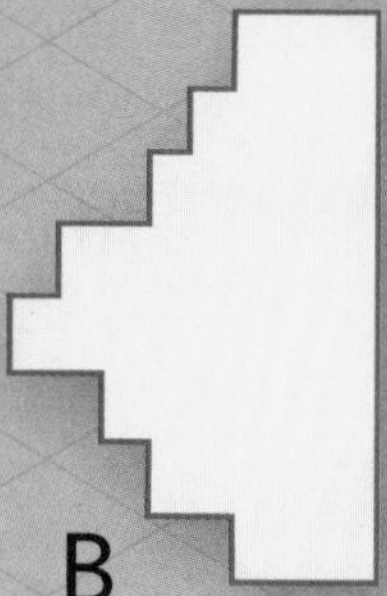

B

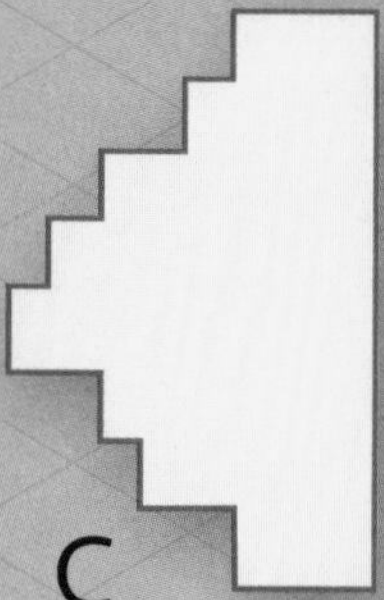

C

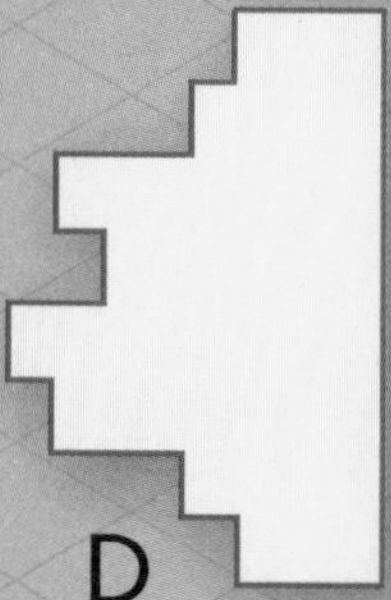

D

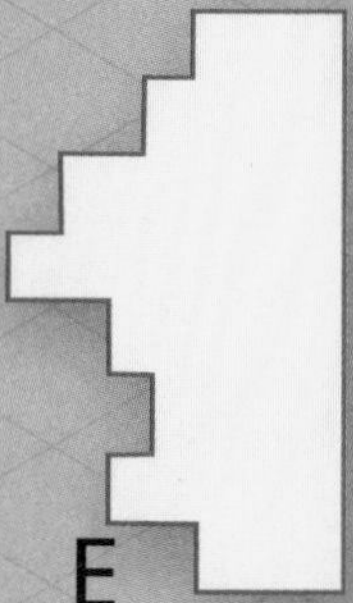

E

Answer see page 280

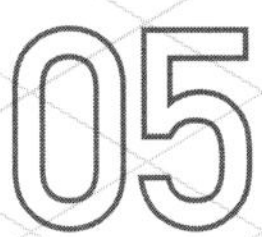

Select the correct figure from the numbered ones below, to replace the question mark.

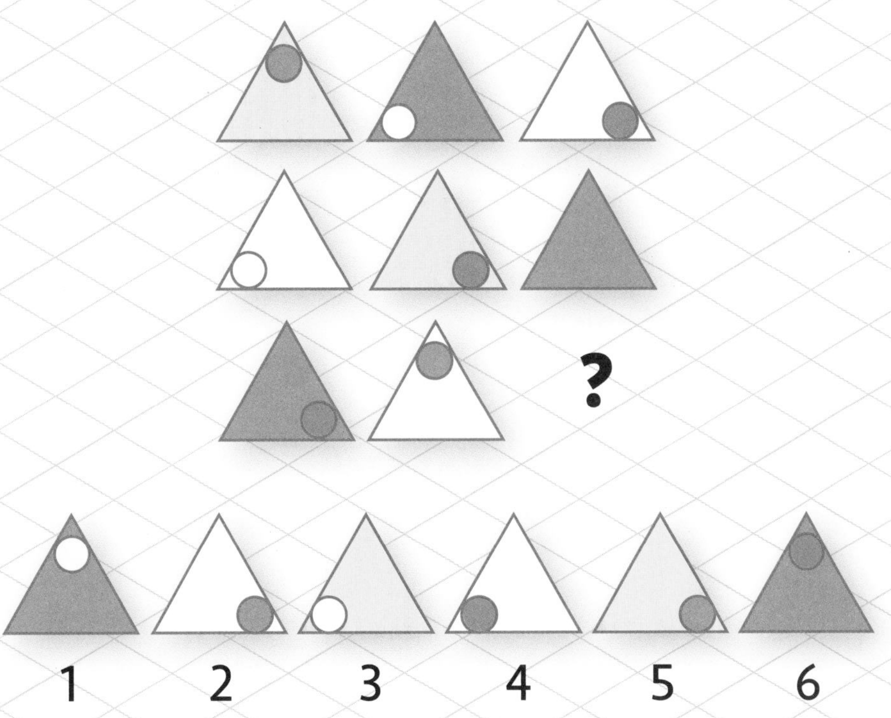

Answer see page 280

Answer see page 280

Complete the square using nine consecutive numbers, so that all rows, columns, and large diagonals add up to the same total.

07

Each of the nine squares in the grid marked 1A to 3C should incorporate all of the items that are shown in the squares of the same letter and number, at left and top. For example, square 2A should incorporate all of the items in squares 2 and A. One square however, is incorrect. Which is it?

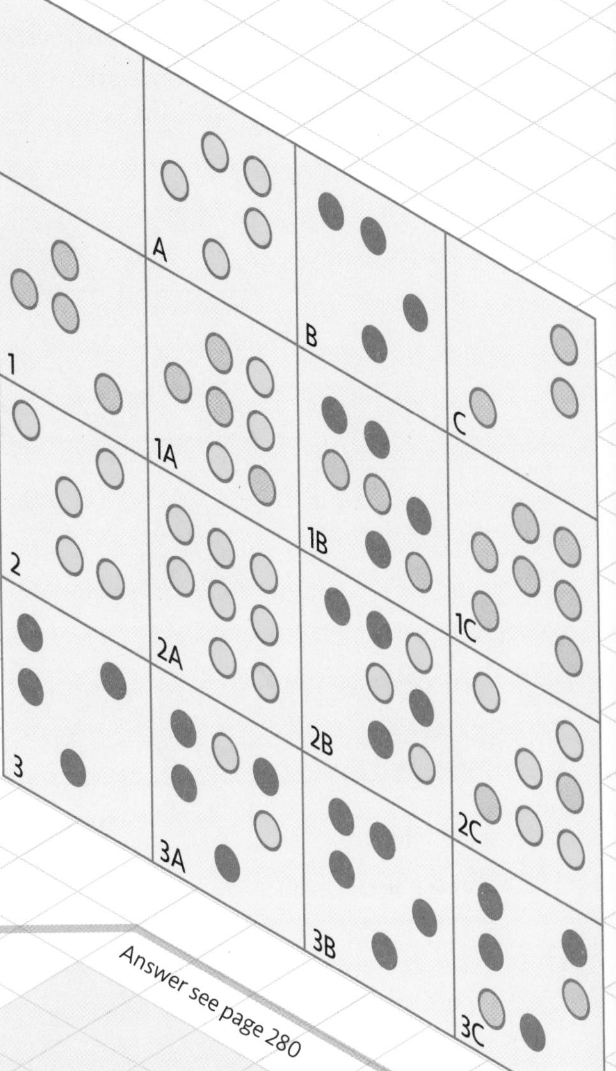

Answer see page 280

08

Which is the odd one out?

Answer see page 280

09

Which is the odd one out?

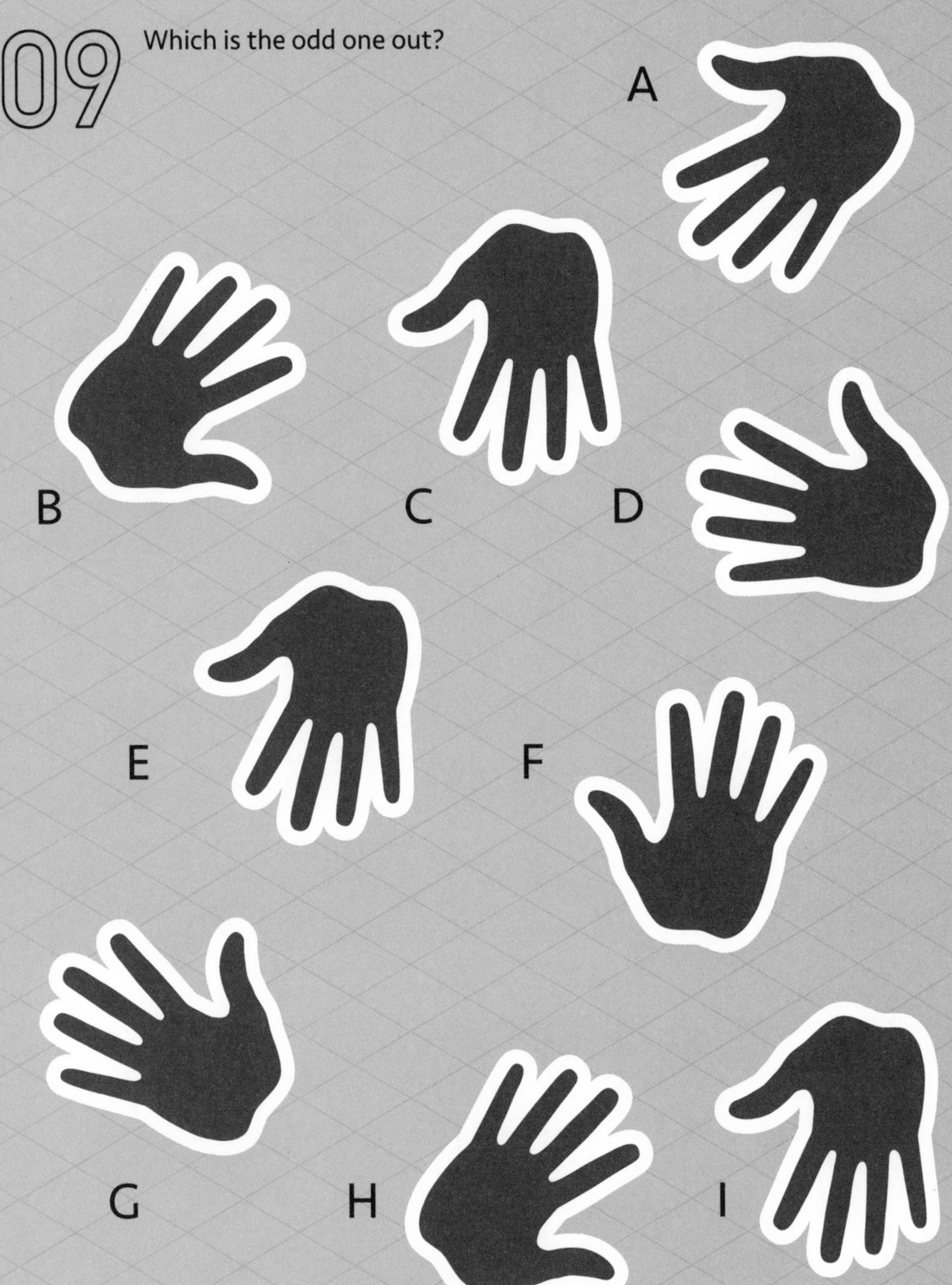

Answer see page 280

10

What is the value of a square?

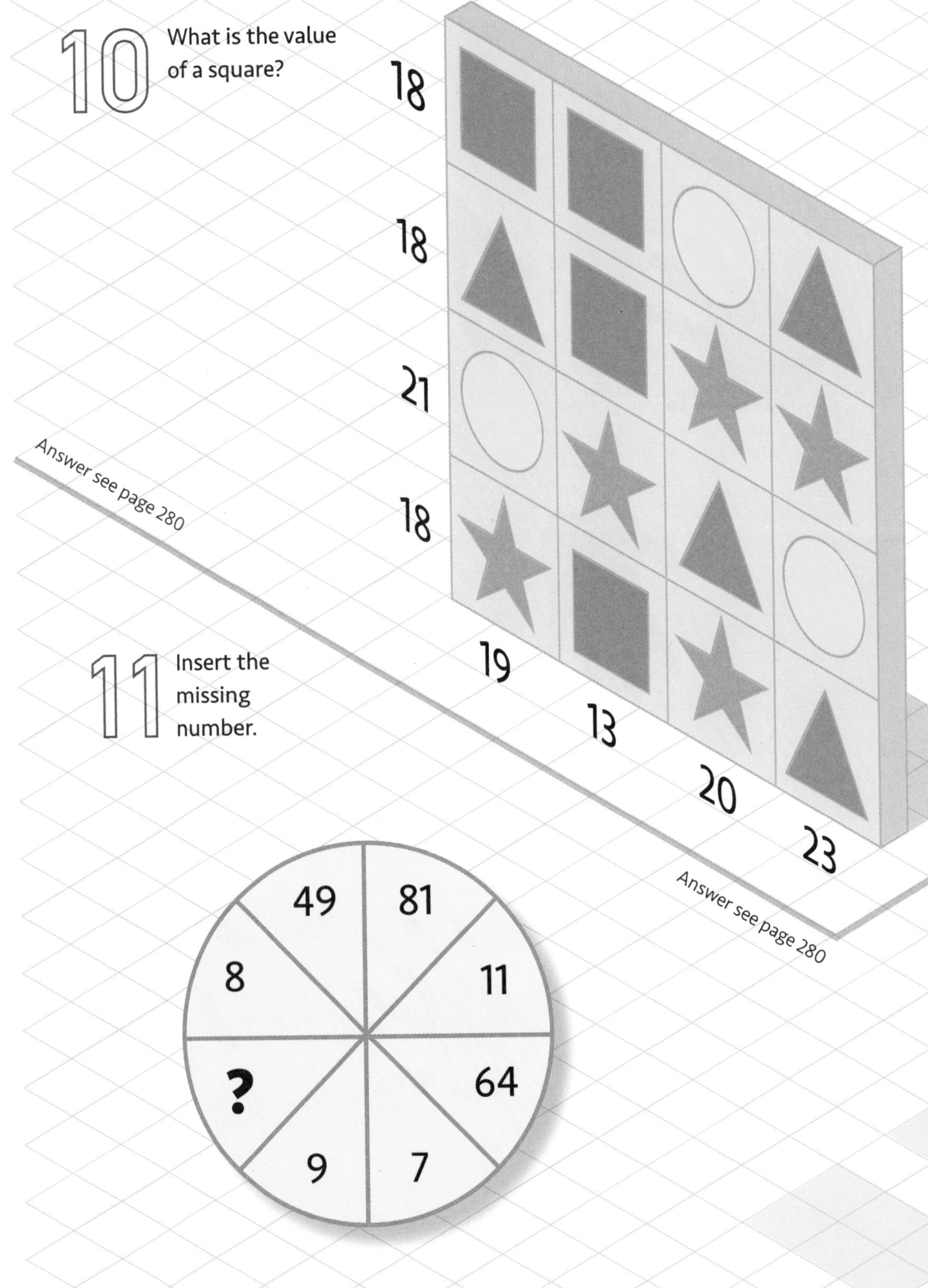

Answer see page 280

11

Insert the missing number.

Answer see page 280

12

Which of the constructed boxes below cannot be made from the given shape?

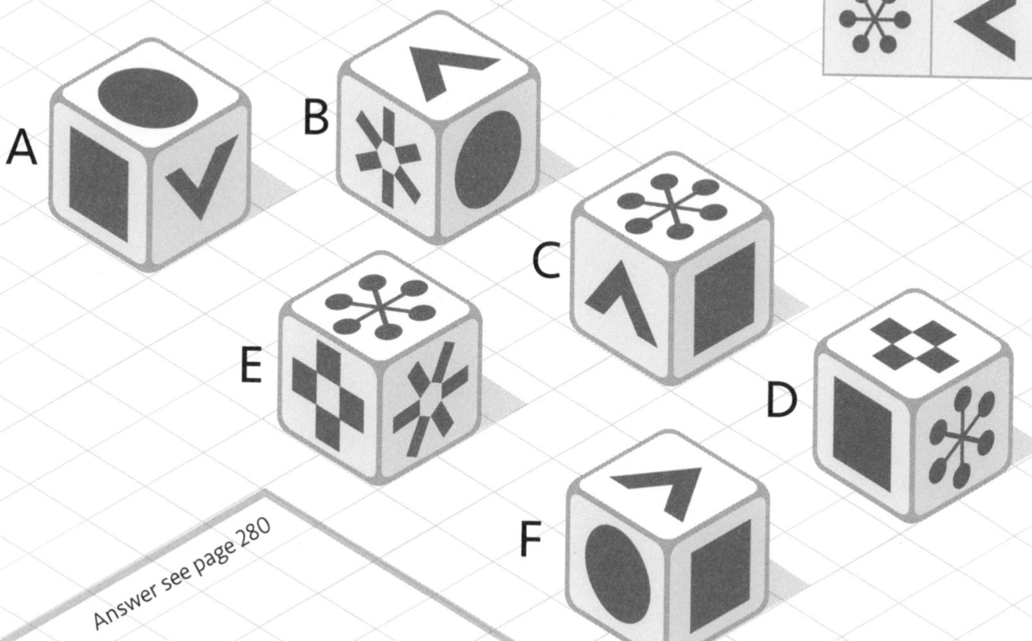

Answer see page 280

13

Which number is the odd one out?

A	2	3	6	8	5	5
B	3	1	2	7	6	7
C	5	4	3	6	7	4
D	8	2	4	7	3	5

Answer see page 280

14

When complete, this 6 x 6 x 6 cube contains 216 individual blocks. How many blocks are required to complete the cube?

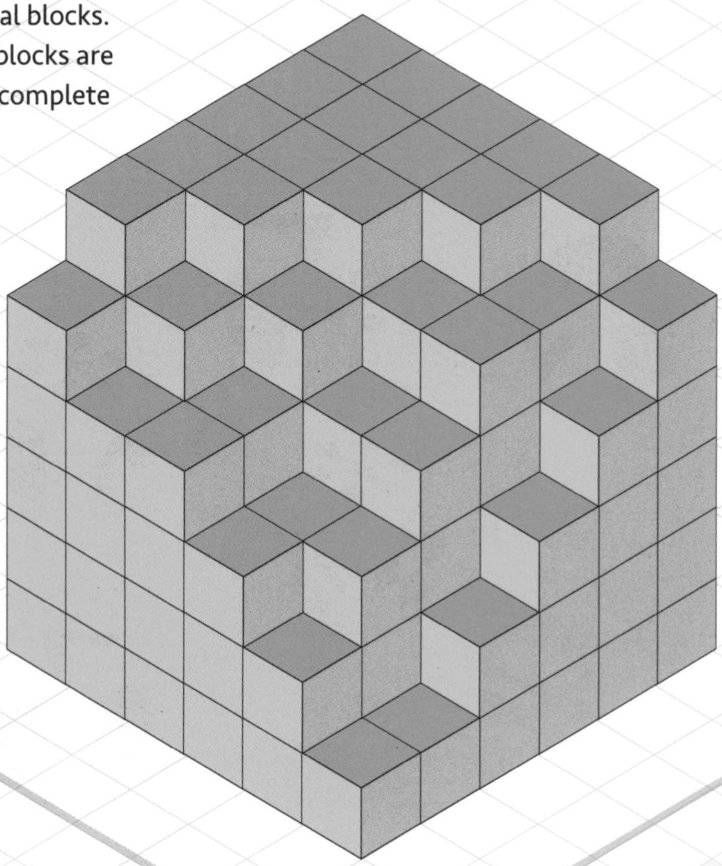

Answer see page 280

15

Insert the missing numbers.

1 4 9 18 35 ? ?

Answer see page 280

16

Cairo is 5 hours ahead of Buenos Aires, which is 10 hours behind Hanoi. It is 7:15 a.m. on Thursday in Cairo, what time is it in the other two cities?

CAIRO

HANOI

Answer see page 281

BUENOS AIRES

17

What number should replace the question mark?

3
4 33 4

2
1 15 2

3
3 24 2

Answer see page 281

18

Which of these dice is not like the other three?

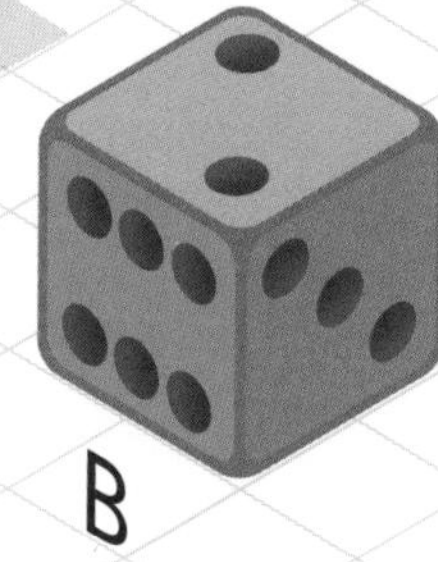

D

Answer see page 281

Answer see page 281

19

Which line of two numbers below has the same relationship as the two above?

	634	:	36
A	726	:	53
B	835	:	56
C	574	:	47
D	937	:	84
E	483	:	35

Which of the lettered clocks below continues the numbered series?

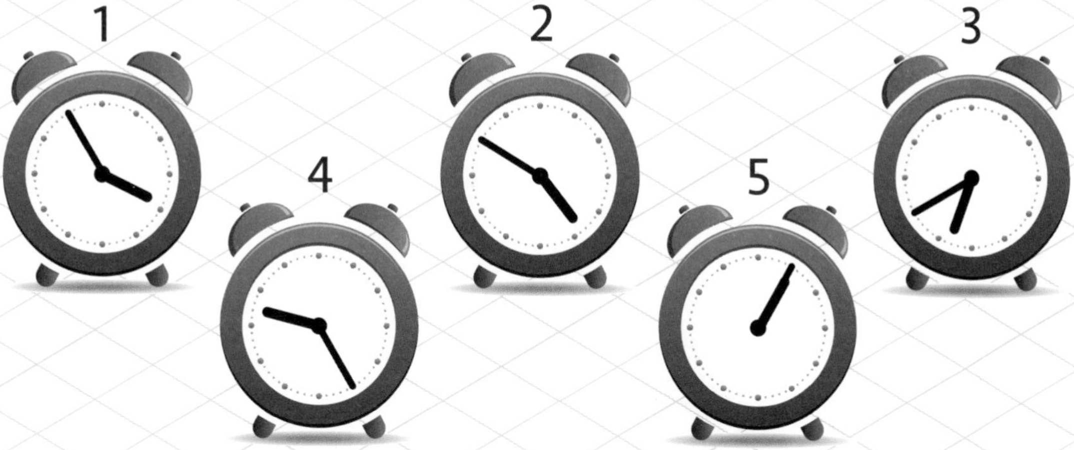

1 2 3

4 5

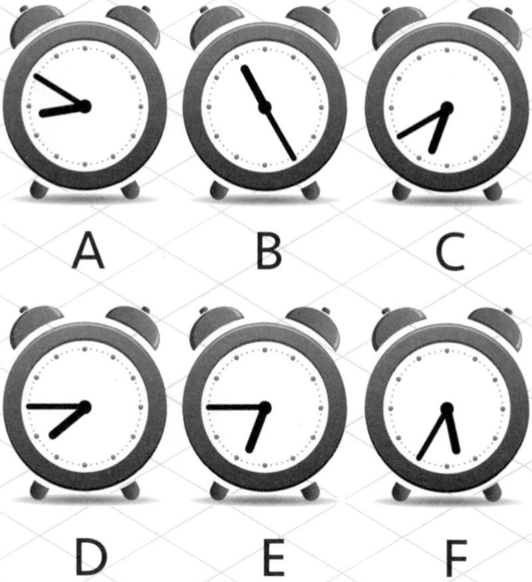

A B C

D E F

Answer see page 281

Test 18

01

The pieces can be assembled into a regular geometric shape. What is it?

Answer see page 281

02

How many ◯ are required to balance the final scale?

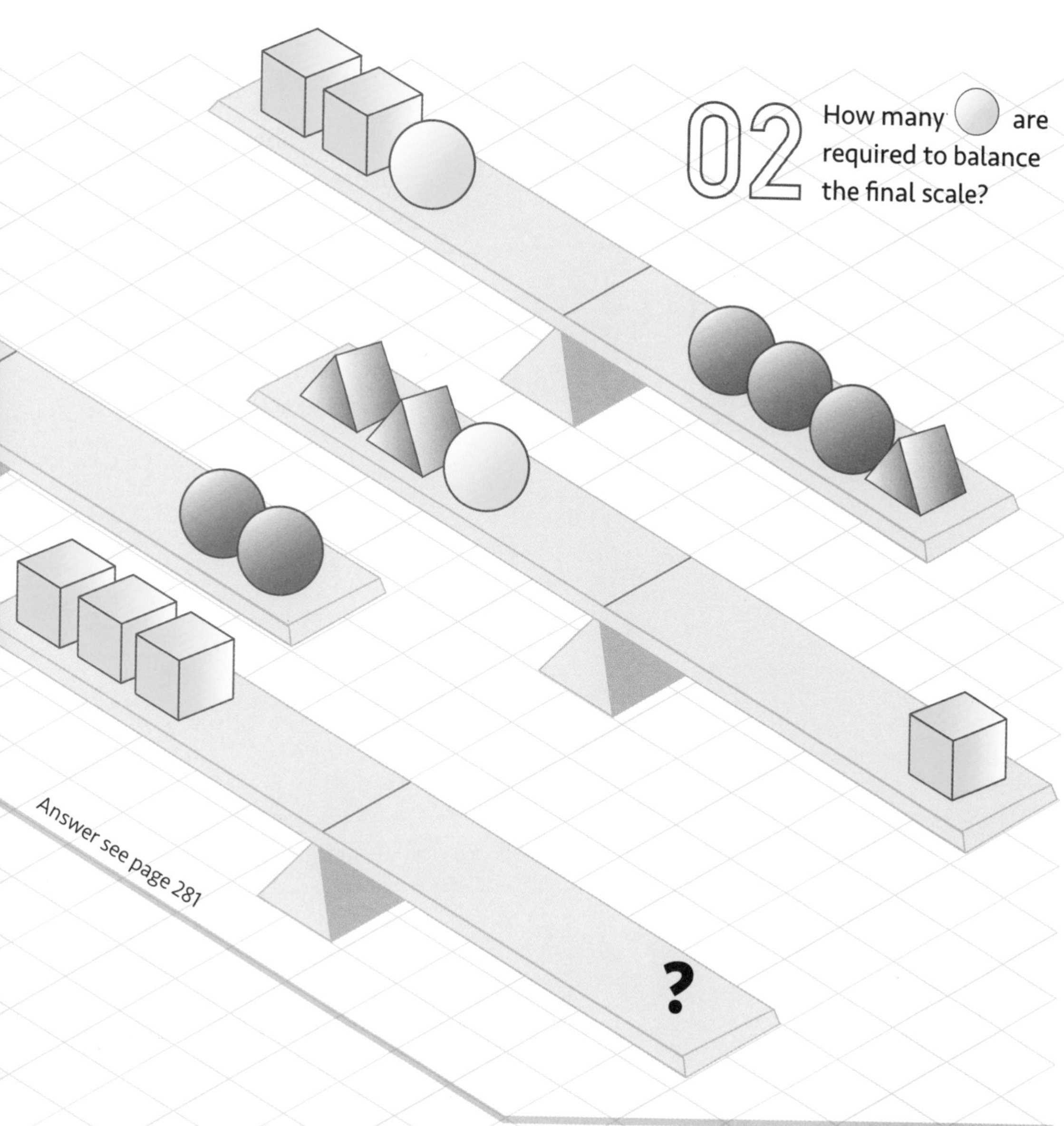

Answer see page 281

Answer see page 281

03

Fill in the missing plus, minus, multiplication, division, and factorial signs to make the equation below correct, performing all calculations strictly in the order they appear on the page.

16 10 11 3 9 15 = 25

04

In each square, the arrow shows the direction you must move in. The numbers in some squares show that square's position in the correct sequence of moves. Move from top left to bottom right, visiting each square in the grid exactly once.

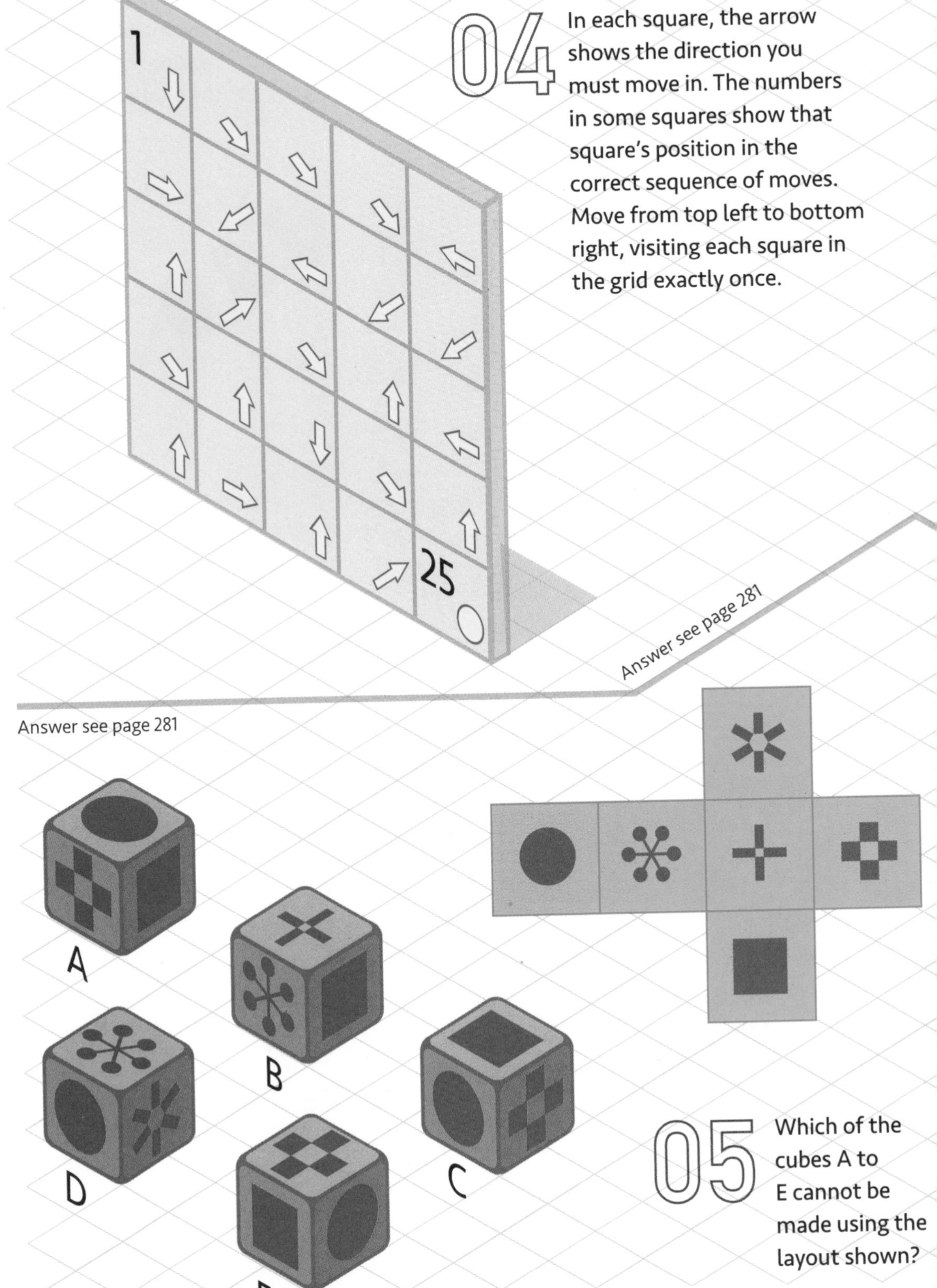

Answer see page 281

Answer see page 281

05

Which of the cubes A to E cannot be made using the layout shown?

06

Which of the options A to E most accurately continues the sequence?

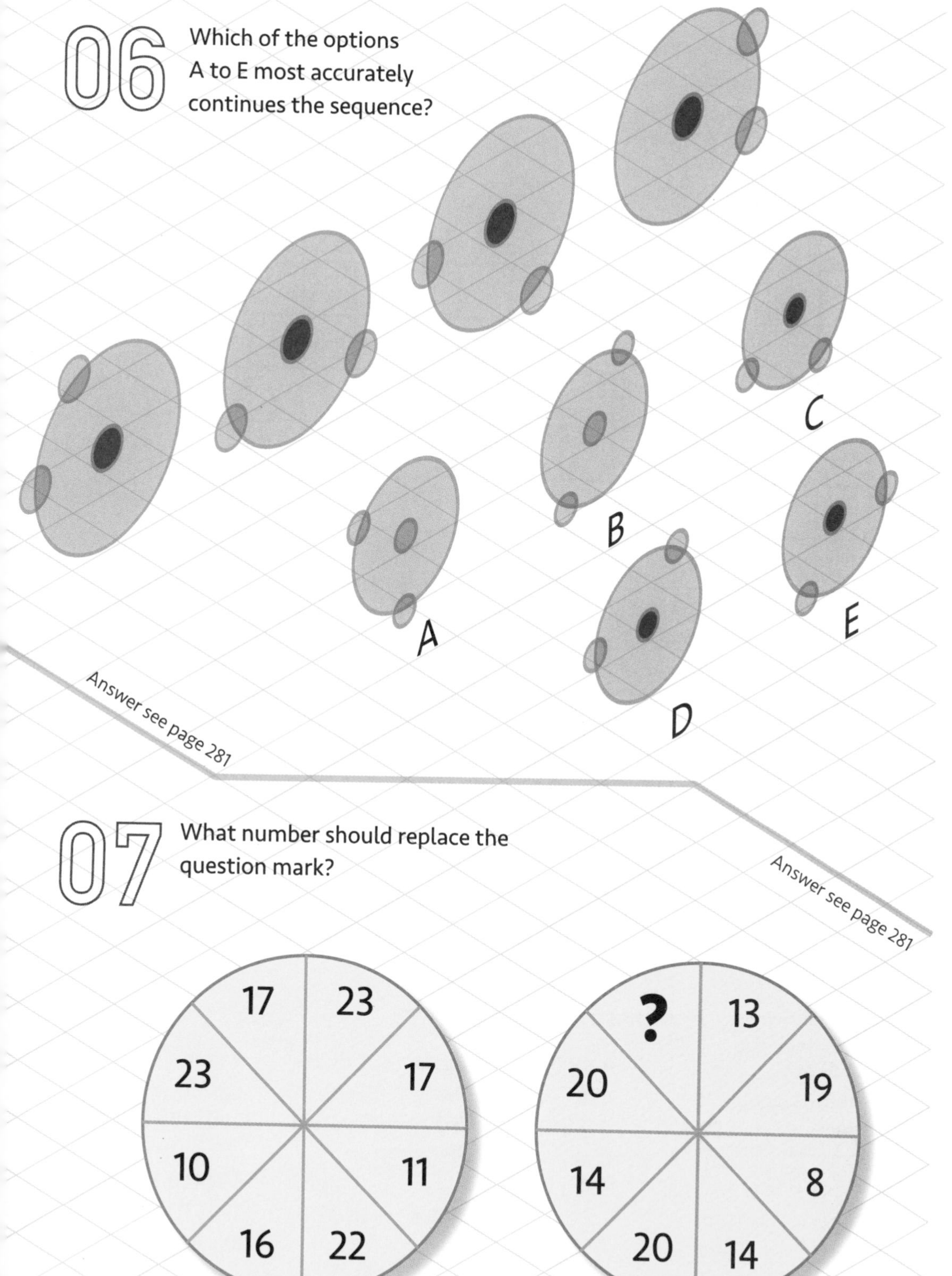

Answer see page 281

07

What number should replace the question mark?

Answer see page 281

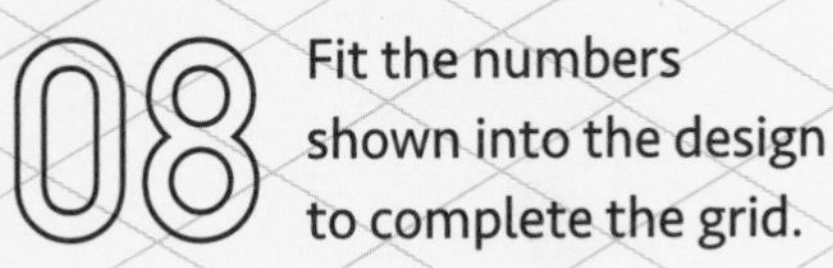

Fit the numbers shown into the design to complete the grid.

Answer see page 282

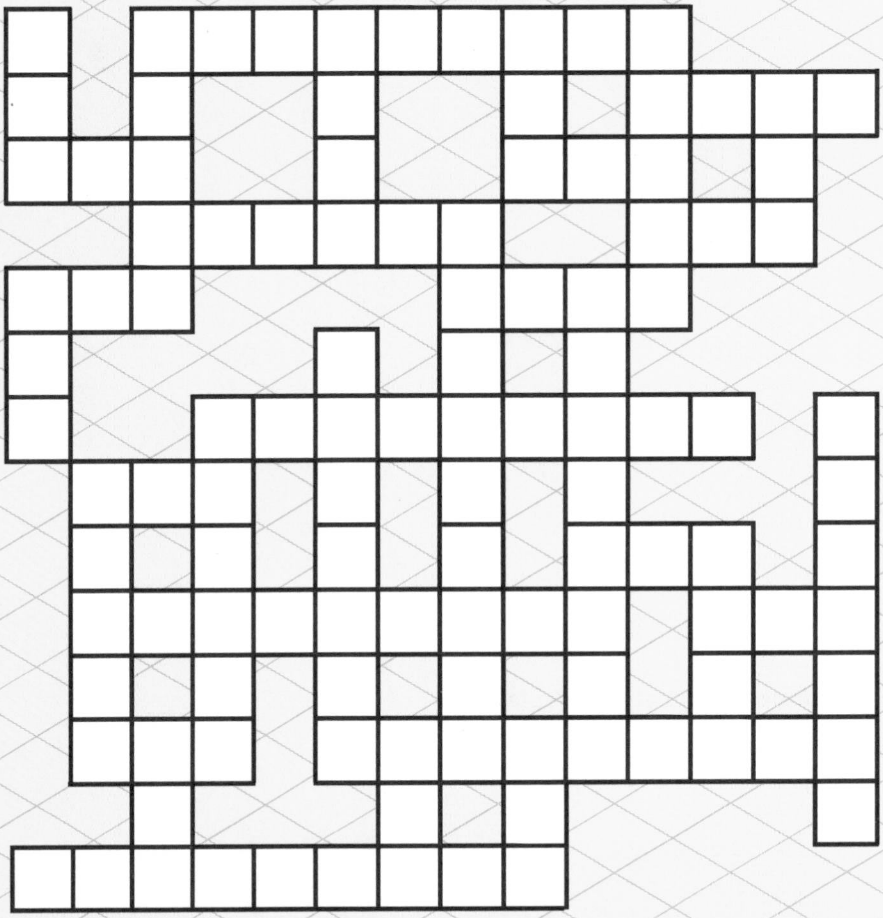

3 digits		4 digits	5 digits	7 digits	9 digits
168	510	4210	42932	1979731	108855380
190	559	6488	77702	7801348	280588703
230	589	8580	94050		411646199
325	701	8980		**8 digits**	504413875
338	800		**6 digits**	80388100	794531721
343	808		119480		833301083
362	955		328882		
374					

What number should replace the question mark?

Answer see page 282

Answer see page 282

Which option A to E most accurately completes the pattern?

is to:

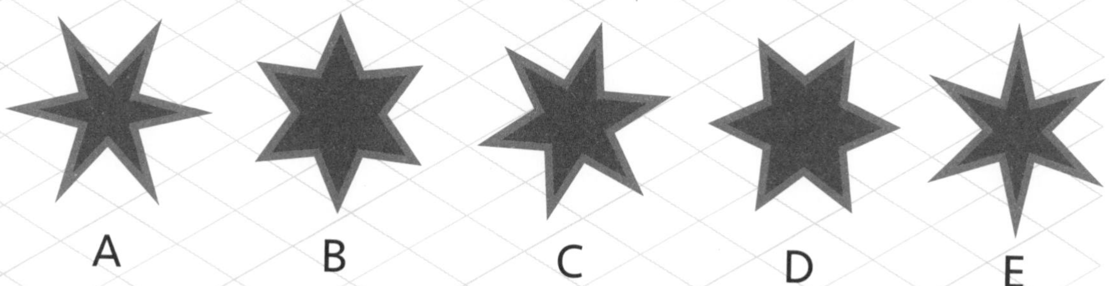

11

Which of the designs A to E is the odd one out?

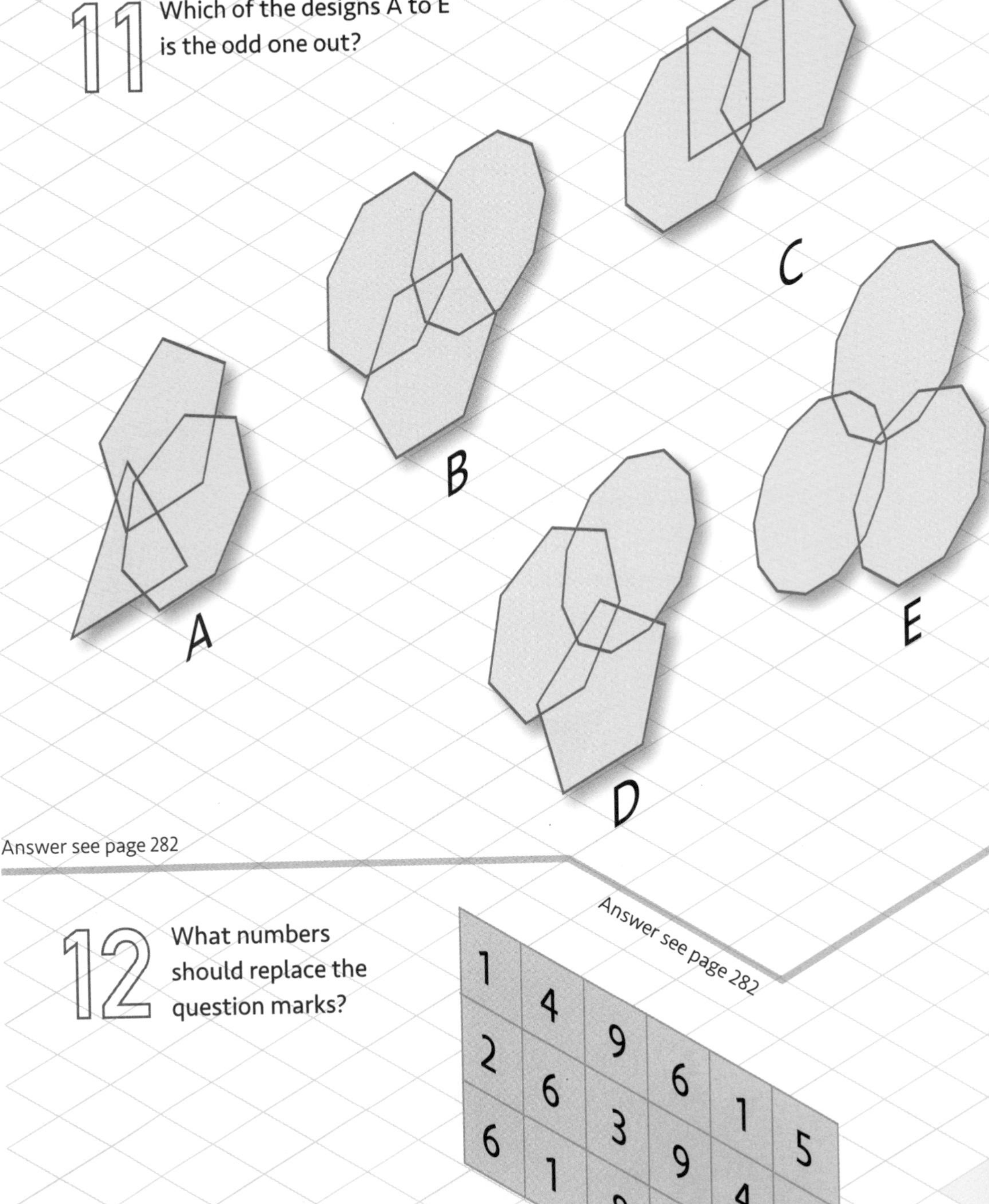

Answer see page 282

12

What numbers should replace the question marks?

1	4	9	6	1	5
2	6	3	9	4	4
6	1	8	?	?	?

Answer see page 282

13 Use seven straight lines, each touching a maximum of one side of the border, to divide the field above into eight sections, each containing an equal number of each of the five shapes.

Answer see page 282

14 What number should replace the question mark?

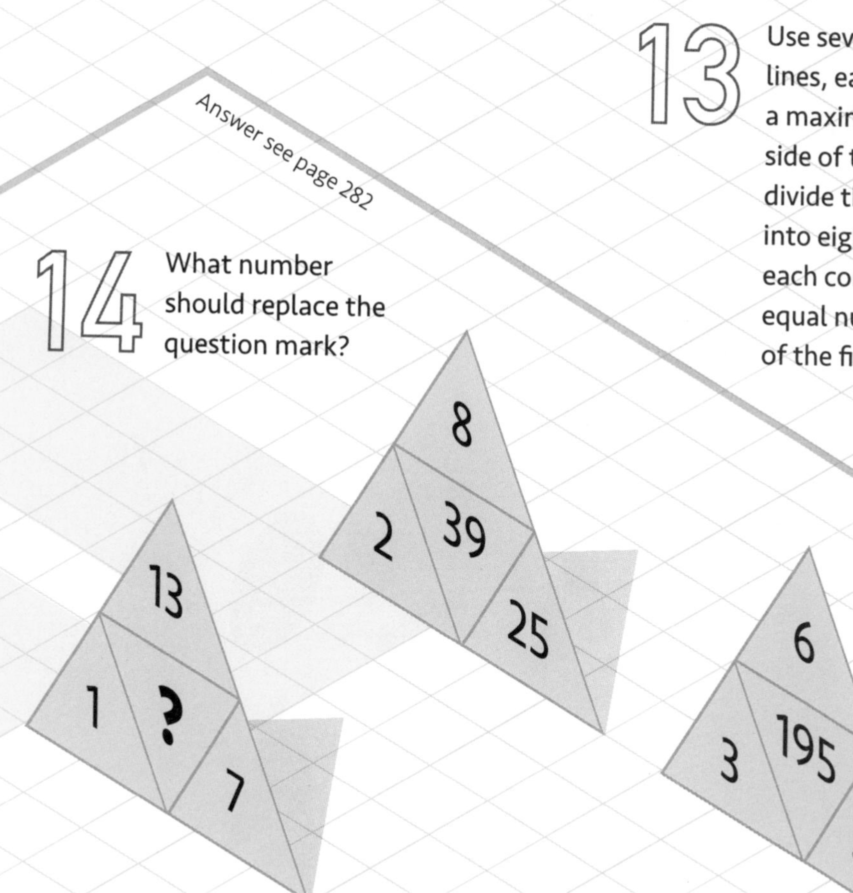

Answer see page 282

15

In the grid below, how much is each symbol worth?

Answer see page 282

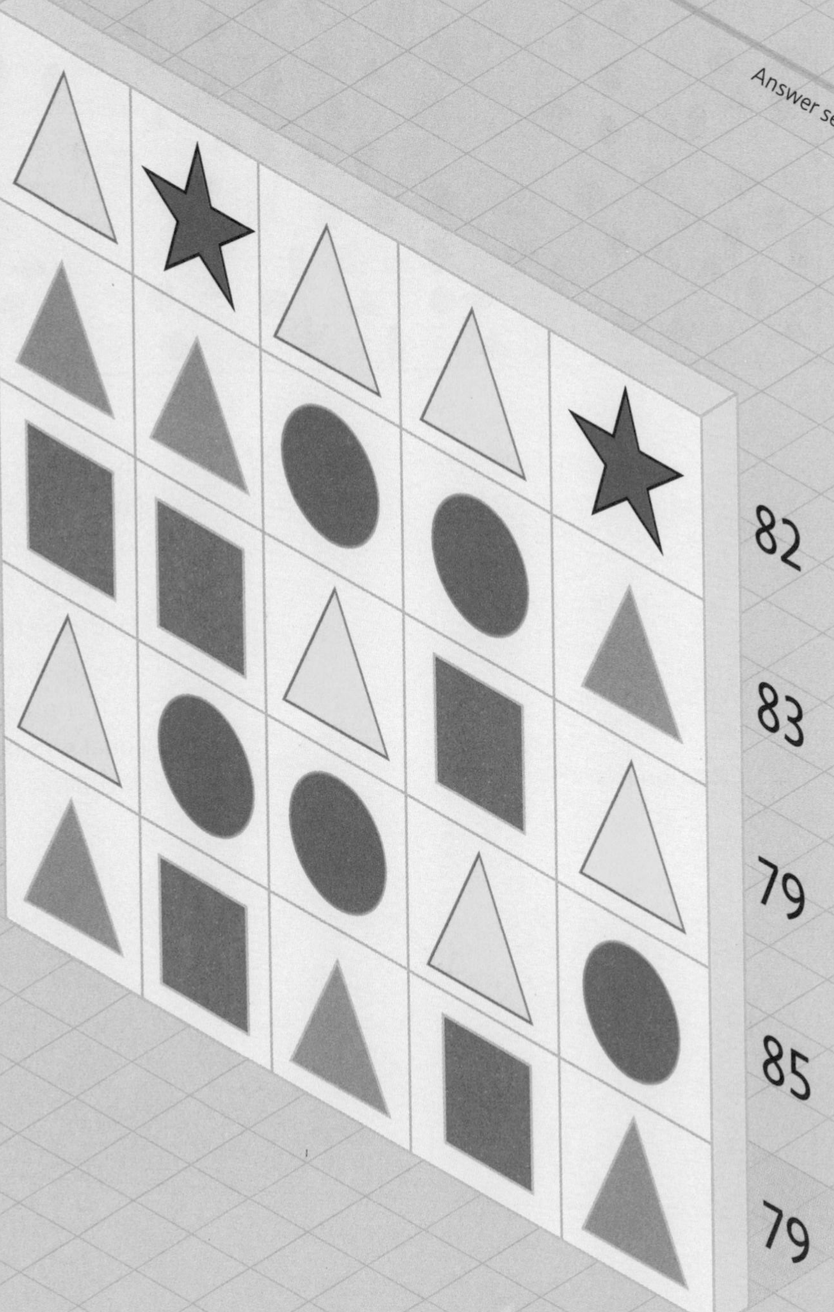

16

What number should replace the question mark?

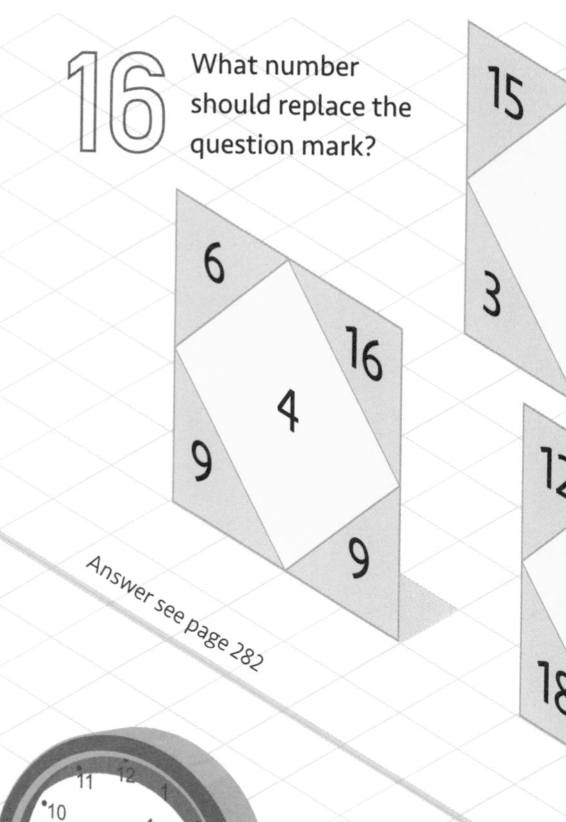

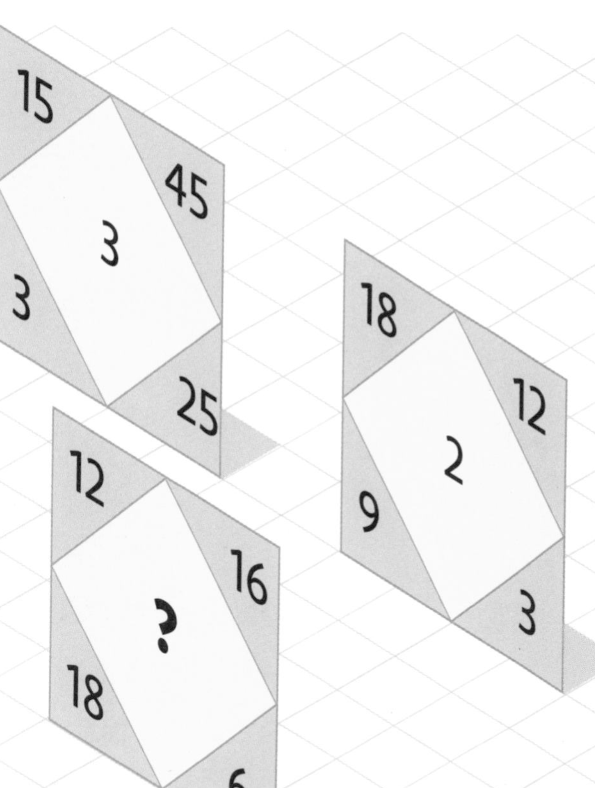

Answer see page 282

Answer see page 282

17

What time would the next clock indicate?

18

Combine the segments below to find the names of ten celebrities.

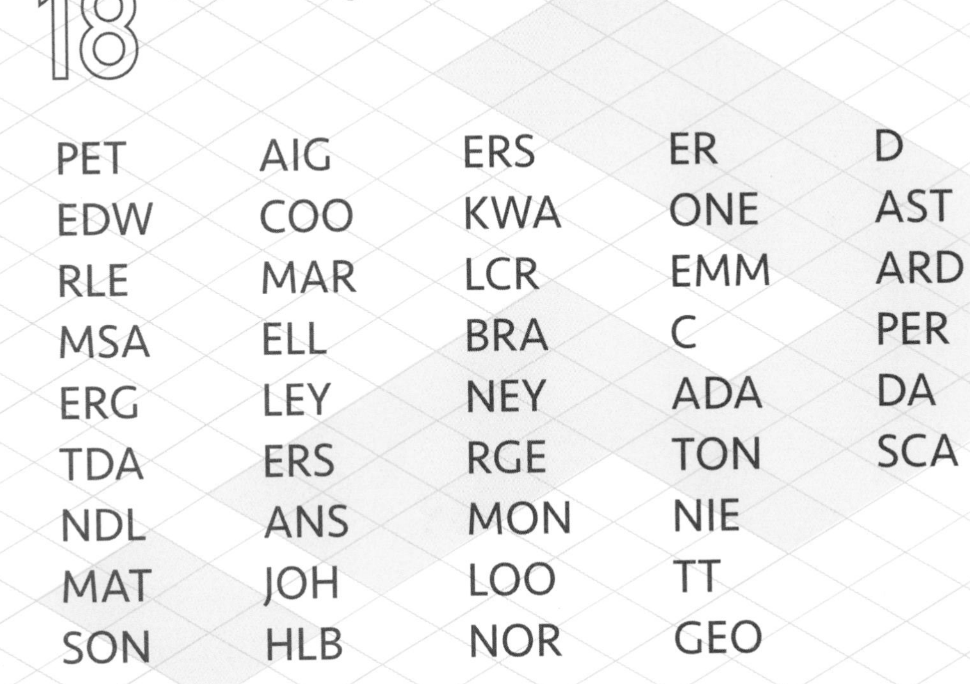

PET	AIG	ERS	ER	D
EDW	COO	KWA	ONE	AST
RLE	MAR	LCR	EMM	ARD
MSA	ELL	BRA	C	PER
ERG	LEY	NEY	ADA	DA
TDA	ERS	RGE	TON	SCA
NDL	ANS	MON	NIE	
MAT	JOH	LOO	TT	
SON	HLB	NOR	GEO	

Answer see page 282

Answer see page 282

19

Which of the four shapes A to D fits to complete the triangle?

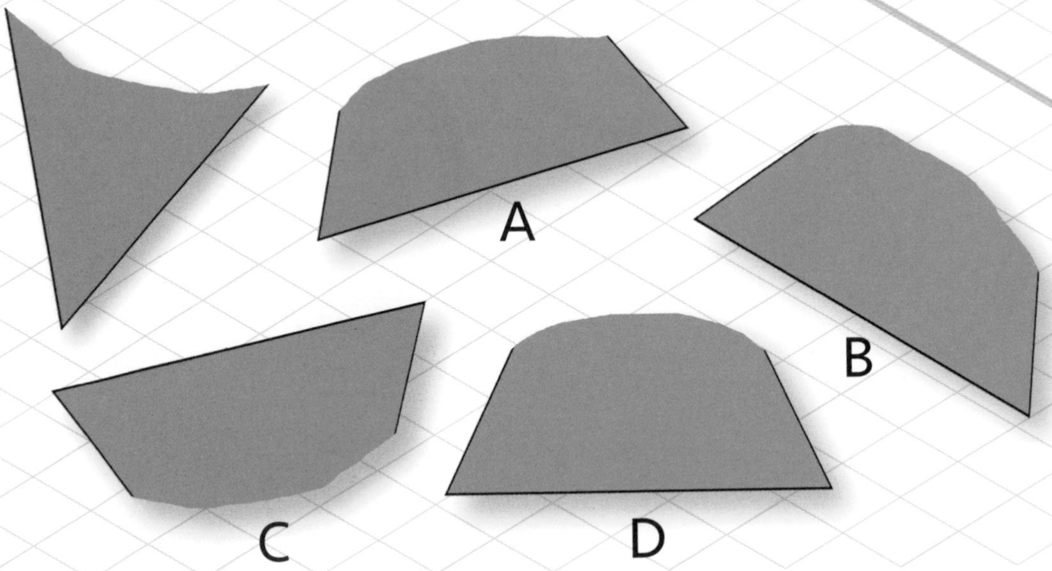

A

B

C

D

20

Which symbols are missing from the blue squares in the grid below?

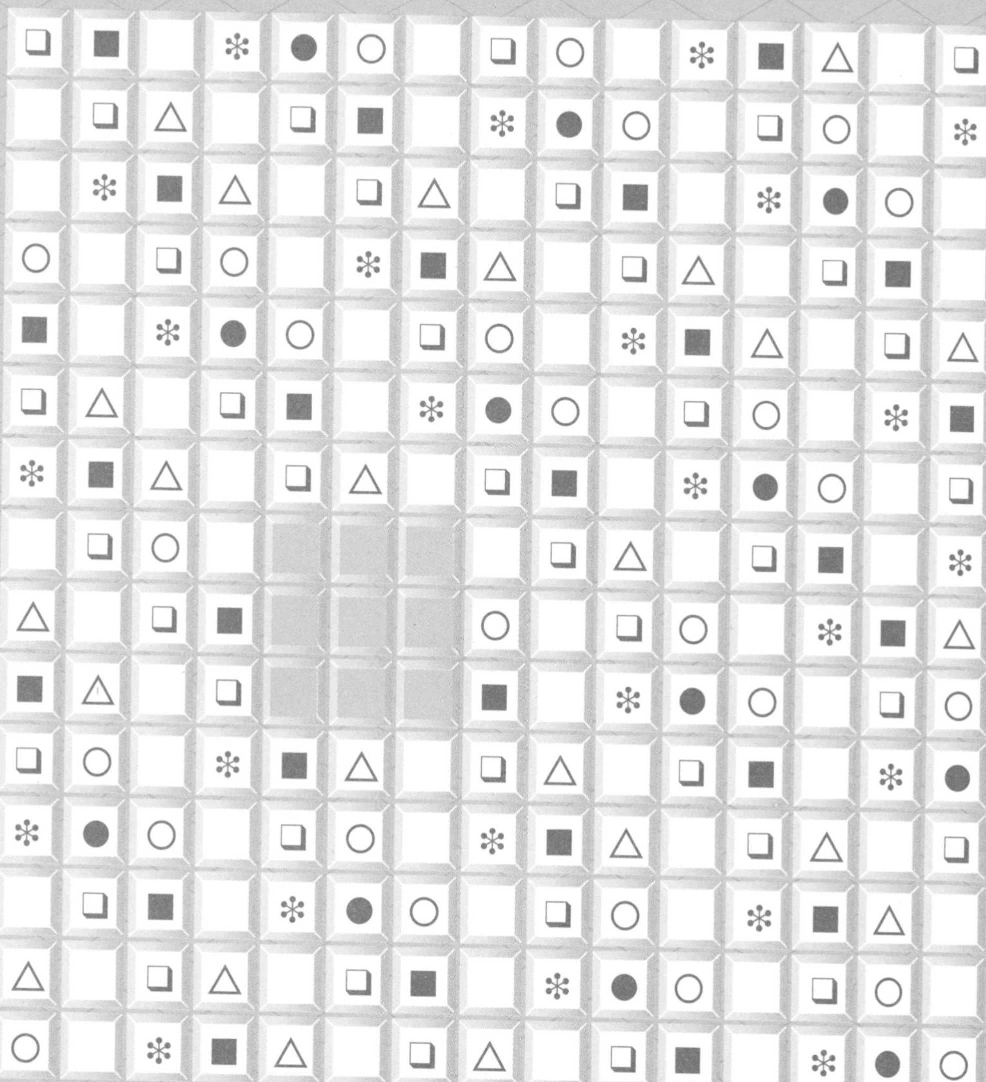

Answer see page 282

Test 19

01

Which of the pentagons at the bottom should replace the question mark?

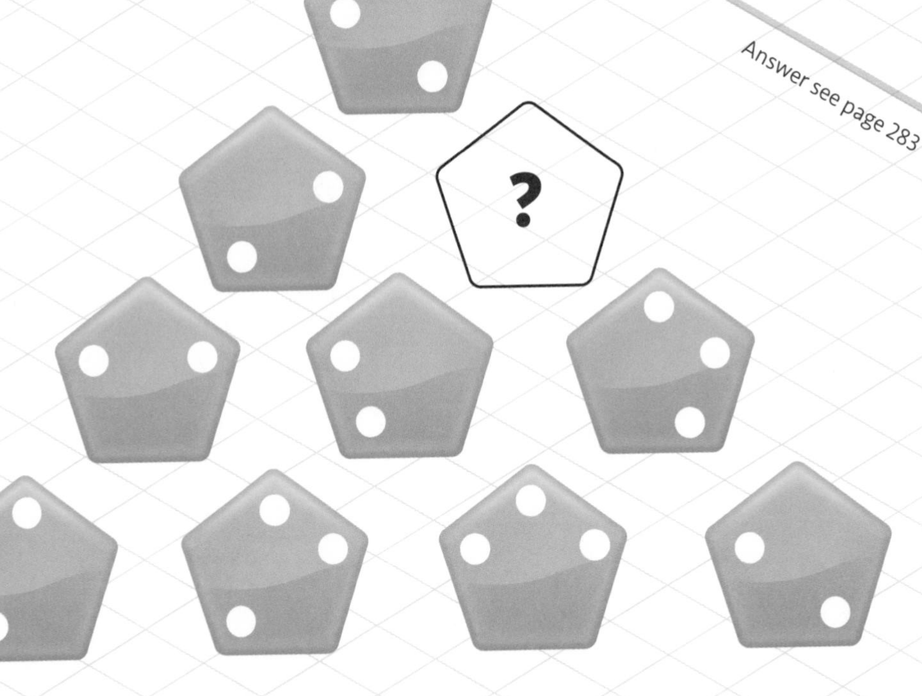

Answer see page 283

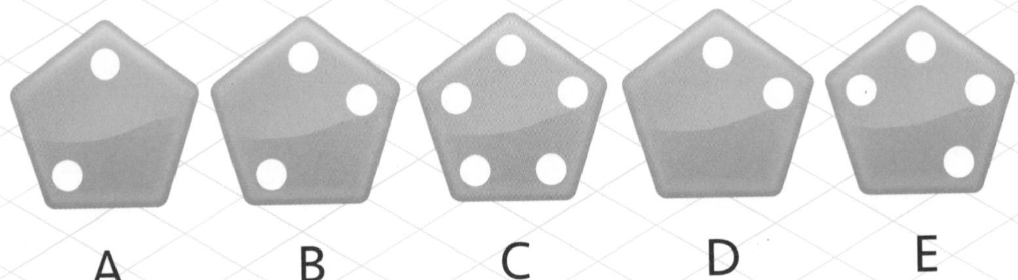

A B C D E

02

Scales 1 and 2 are in perfect balance. How many triangles are needed to balance scale 3?

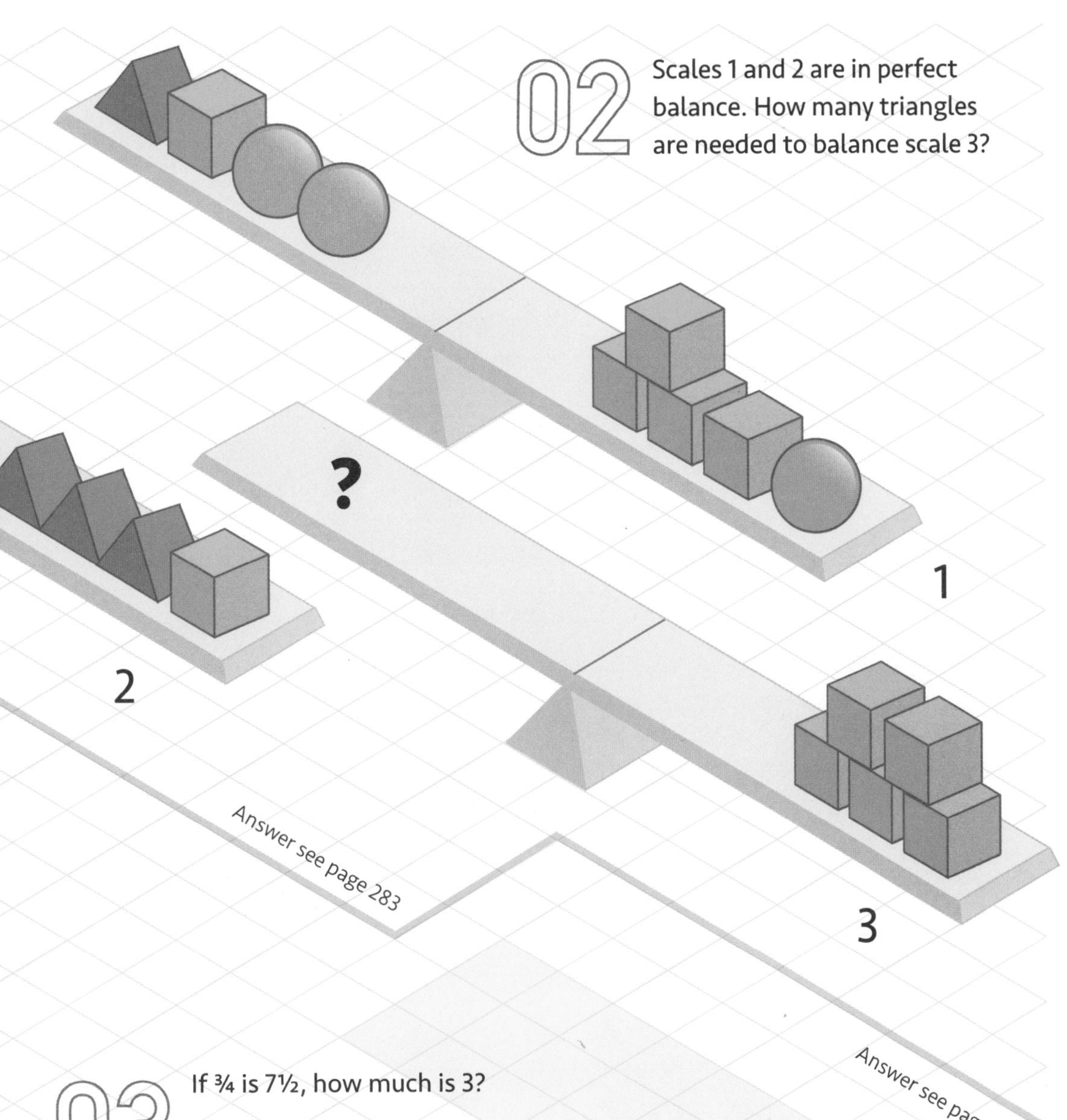

Answer see page 283

03

If ¾ is 7½, how much is 3?

Answer see page 283

04

Which shape below can be put with the one above to form a perfect square?

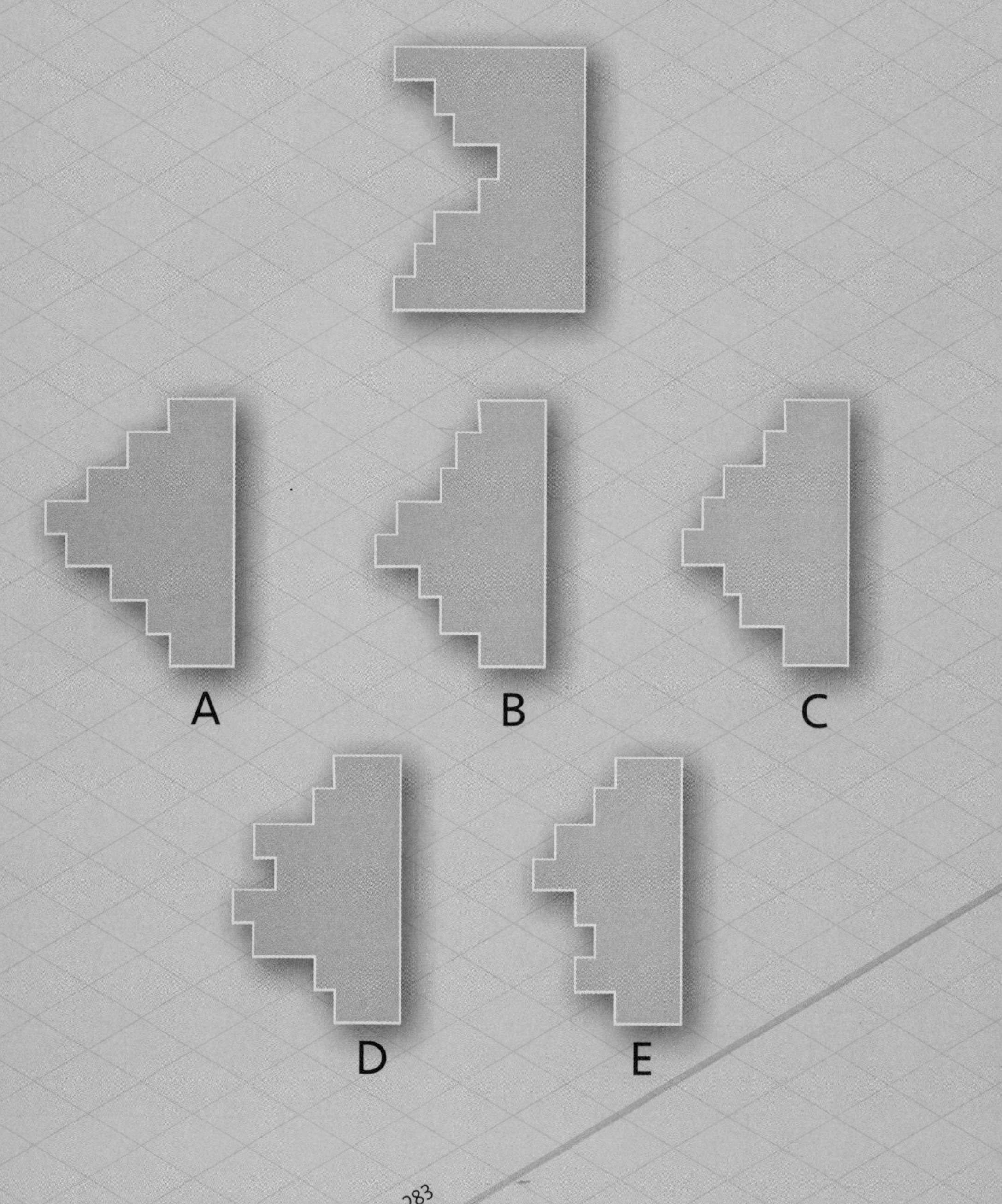

Answer see page 283

Select the correct figure from the numbered ones below, to replace the question mark.

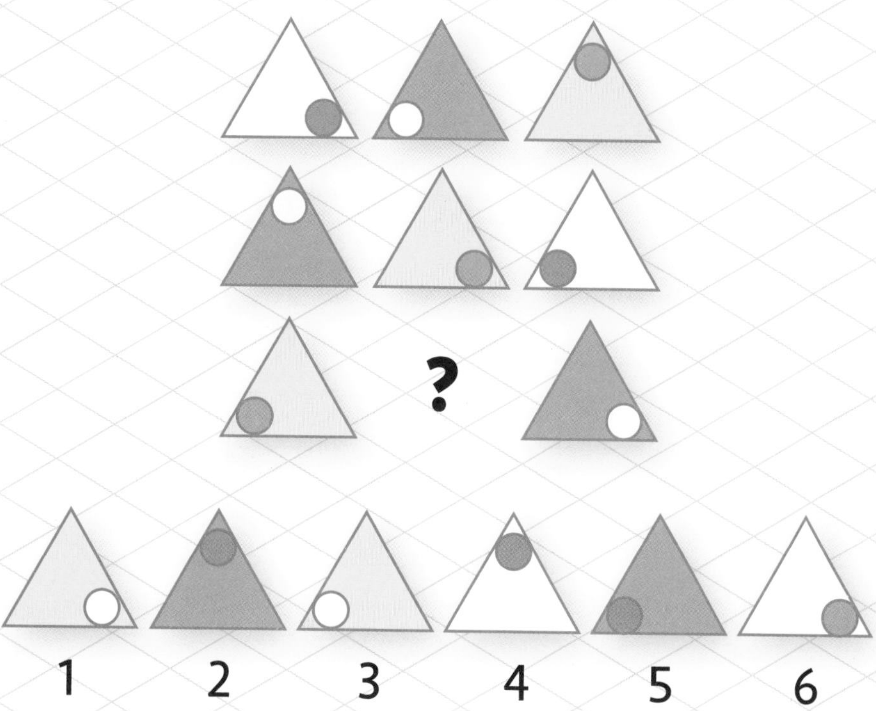

Answer see page 283

Which is the odd one out?

Answer see page 283

07

Each of the nine squares in the grid marked 1A to 3C should incorporate all of the items that are shown in the squares of the same letter and number, at left and top. For example, square 2A should incorporate all of the items in squares 2 and A. One square however, is incorrect. Which is it?

	A	B	C
1	1A	1B	1C
2	2A	2B	2C
3	3A	3B	3C

Answer see page 283

Answer see page 283

08

Complete the square using nine consecutive numbers, so that all rows, columns, and large diagonals add up to the same total.

09 Which is the odd one out?

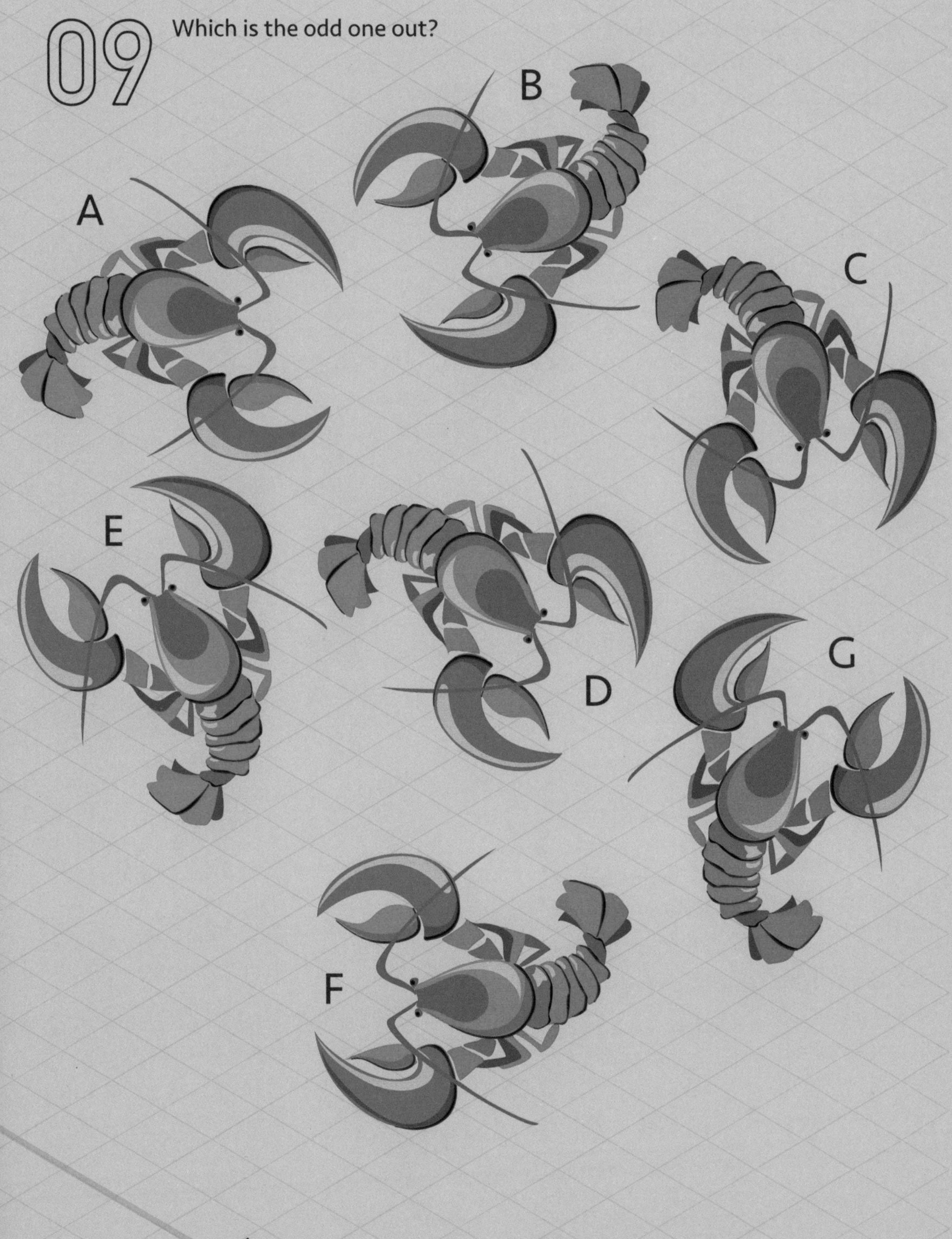

Answer see page 283

10 What is the value of a triangle?

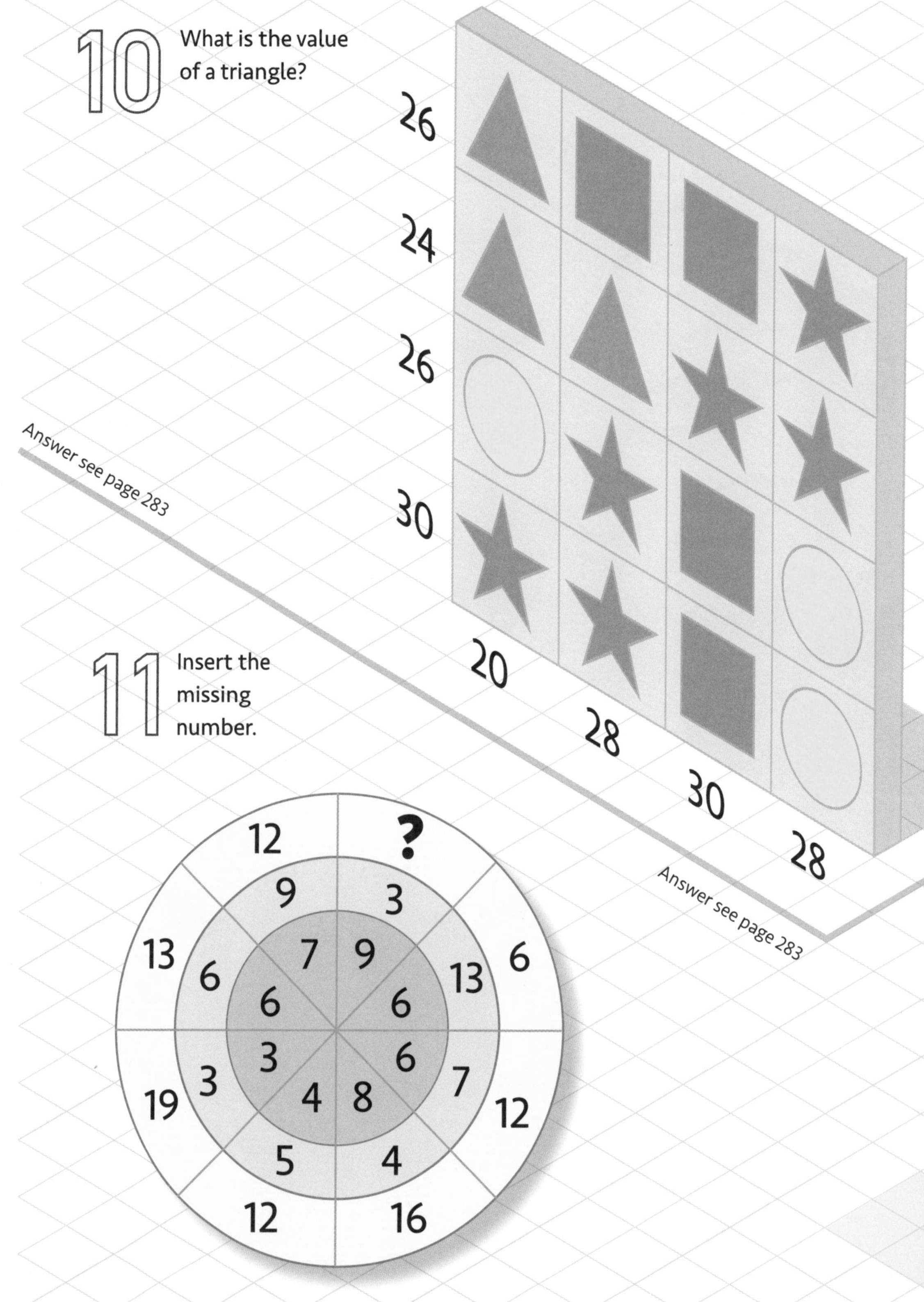

Answer see page 283

11 Insert the missing number.

Answer see page 283

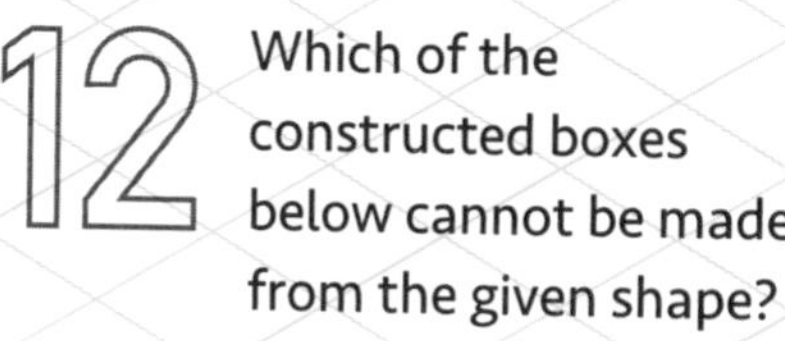

12 Which of the constructed boxes below cannot be made from the given shape?

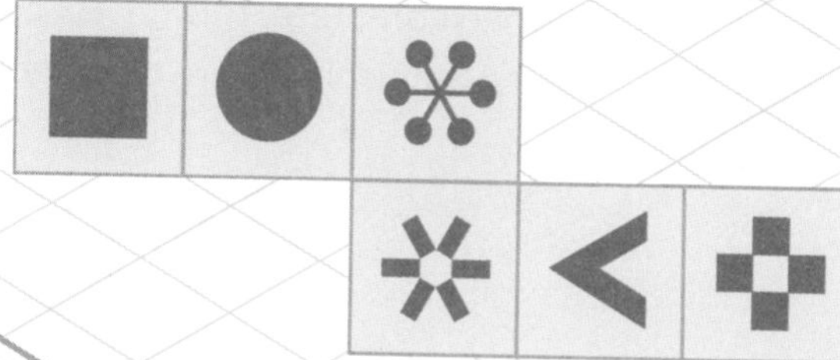

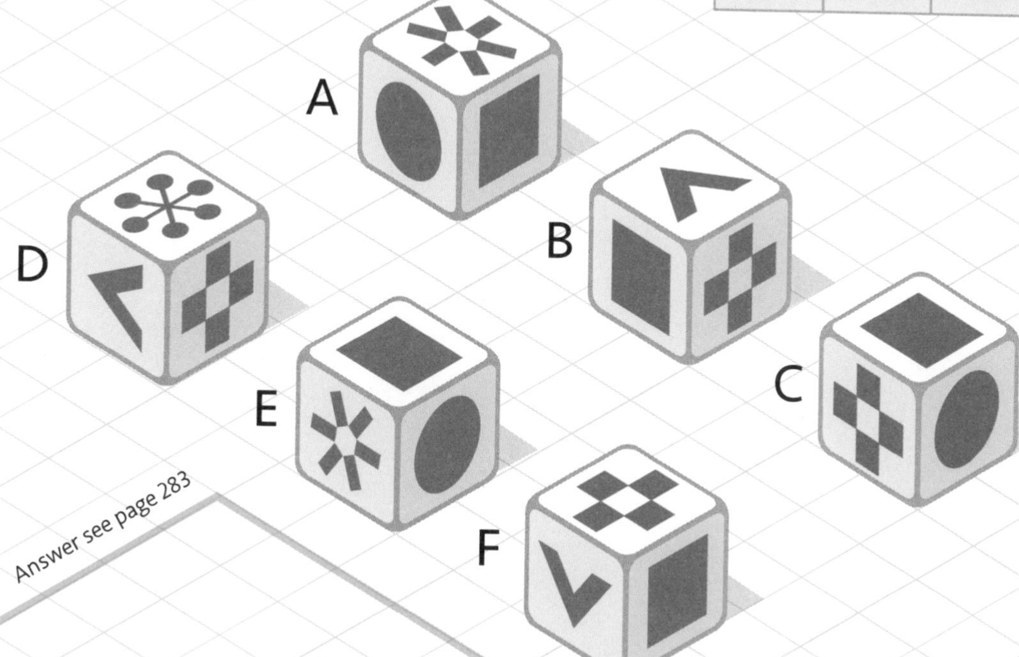

Answer see page 283

3 Which number is the odd one out?

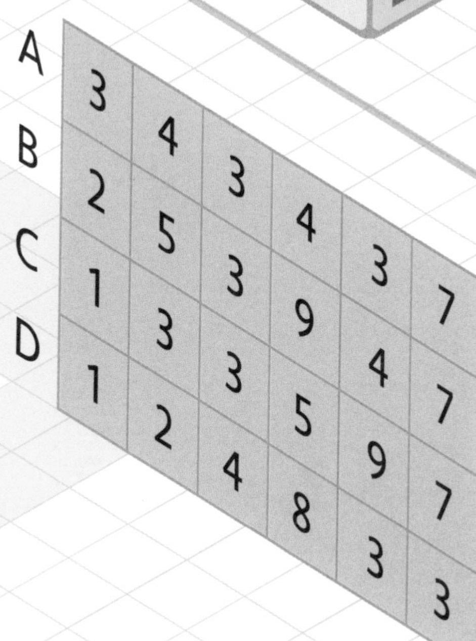

A	3	4	3	4	3	7
B	2	5	3	9	4	7
C	1	3	3	5	9	7
D	1	2	4	8	3	3

Answer see page 283

14

When complete, this 6 x 6 x 6 cube contains 216 individual blocks. How many blocks are required to complete the cube?

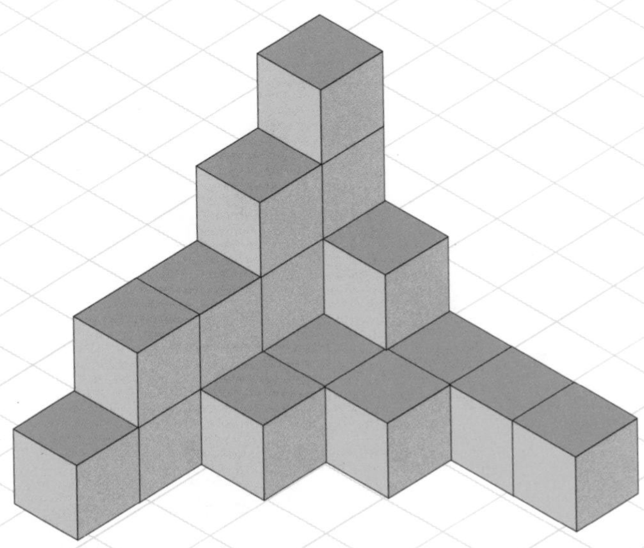

Answer see page 283

Answer see page 283

15

Insert the missing numbers.

17 33 65 ? 257 ?

16 Moscow is 1 hour ahead of Cairo, which is 5 hours behind Hanoi. It is 9:25 p.m. on Saturday in Moscow, what time is it in the other two cities?

Answer see page 283

17 What number should replace the question mark?

Answer see page 283

18

Which of the lettered clocks below continues the numbered series?

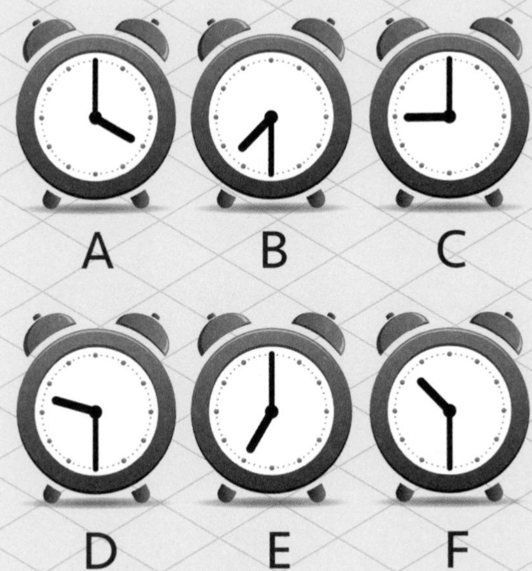

Answer see page 284

19

Which of these dice is not like the other three?

Answer see page 284

20

Which line of two numbers A, B, C, D or E has the same relationship as the top line?

	642	:	36
A	584	:	59
B	378	:	45
C	763	:	62
D	927	:	83
E	645	:	57

Answer see page 284

Test 20

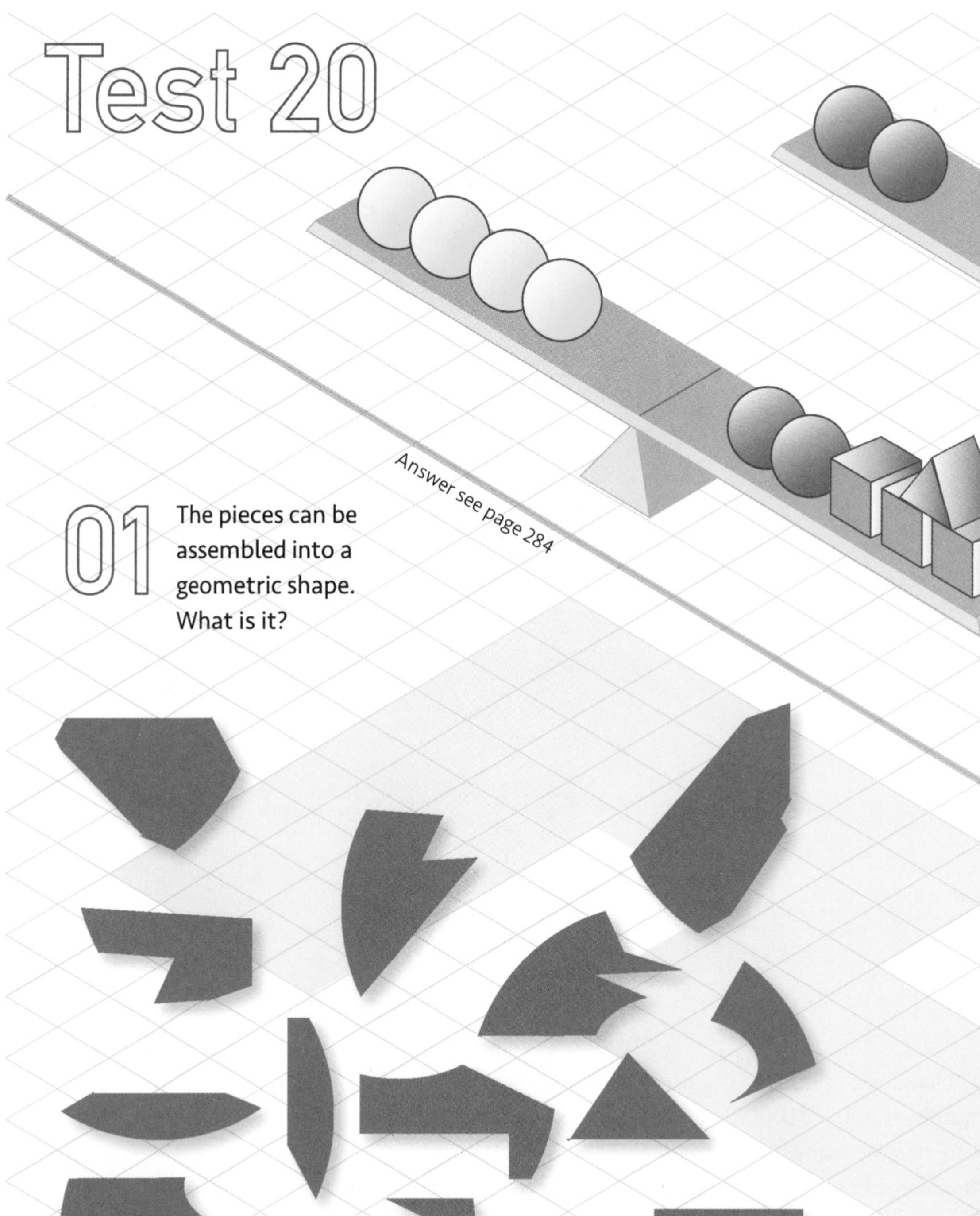

Answer see page 284

01

The pieces can be assembled into a geometric shape. What is it?

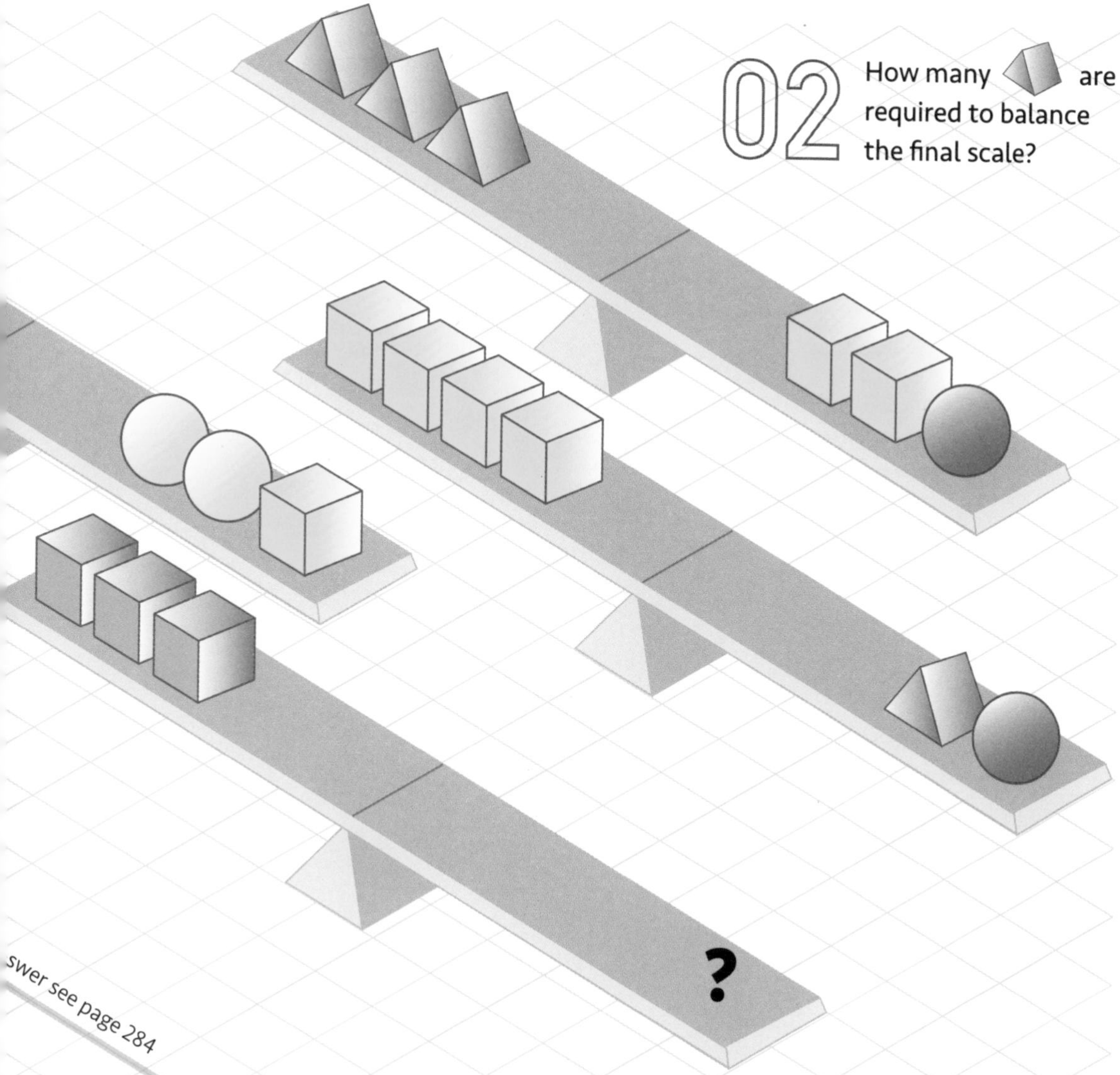

02

How many [pyramid] are required to balance the final scale?

?

swer see page 284

Answer see page 284

03

Fill in the missing plus, minus, multiplication, division, and factorial signs to make the equation below correct, performing all calculations strictly in the order they appear on the page.

30 6 5 27 16 4 1 = 80

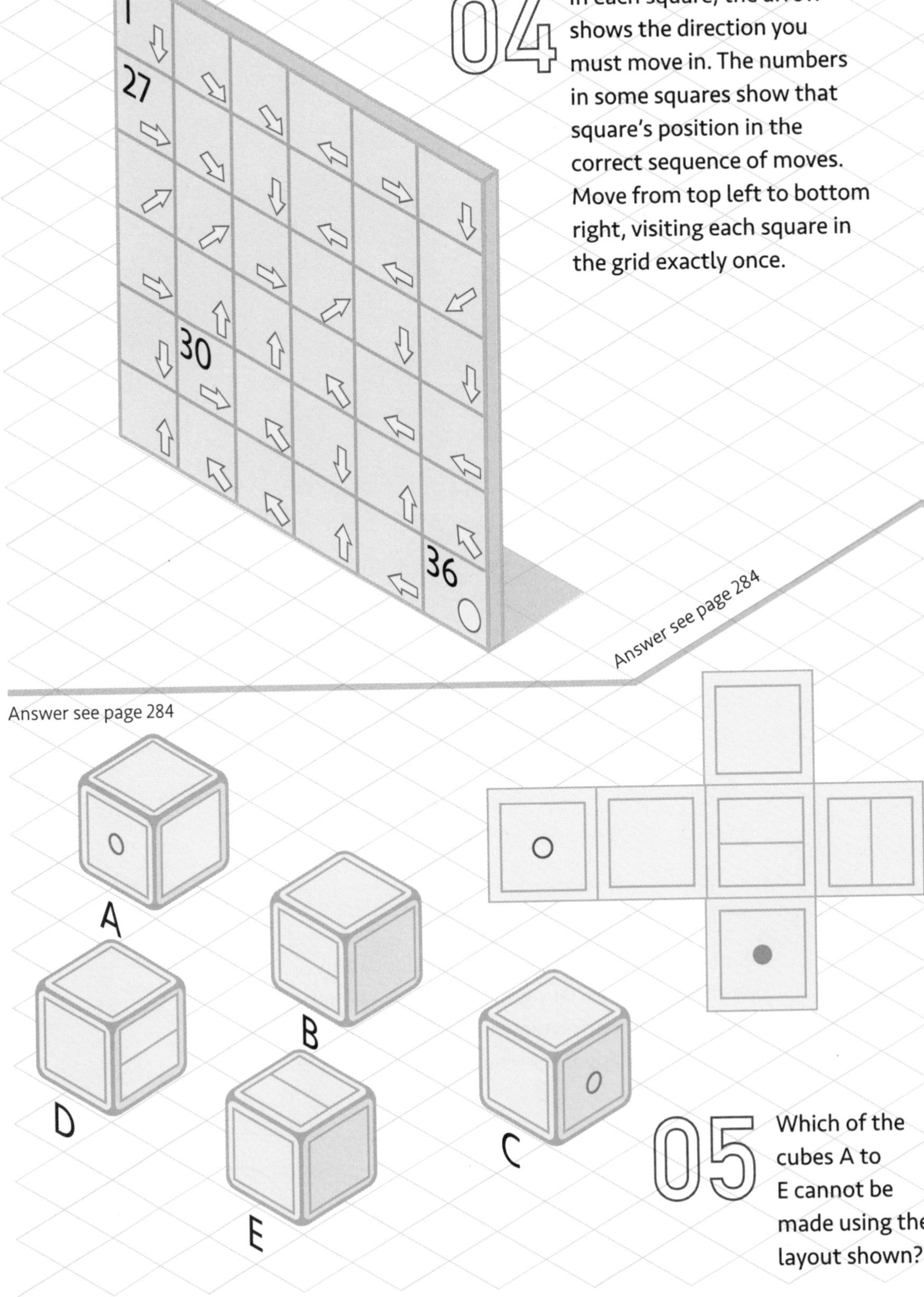

04

In each square, the arrow shows the direction you must move in. The numbers in some squares show that square's position in the correct sequence of moves. Move from top left to bottom right, visiting each square in the grid exactly once.

Answer see page 284

Answer see page 284

05

Which of the cubes A to E cannot be made using the layout shown?

Which of the options A to E most accurately continues the sequence?

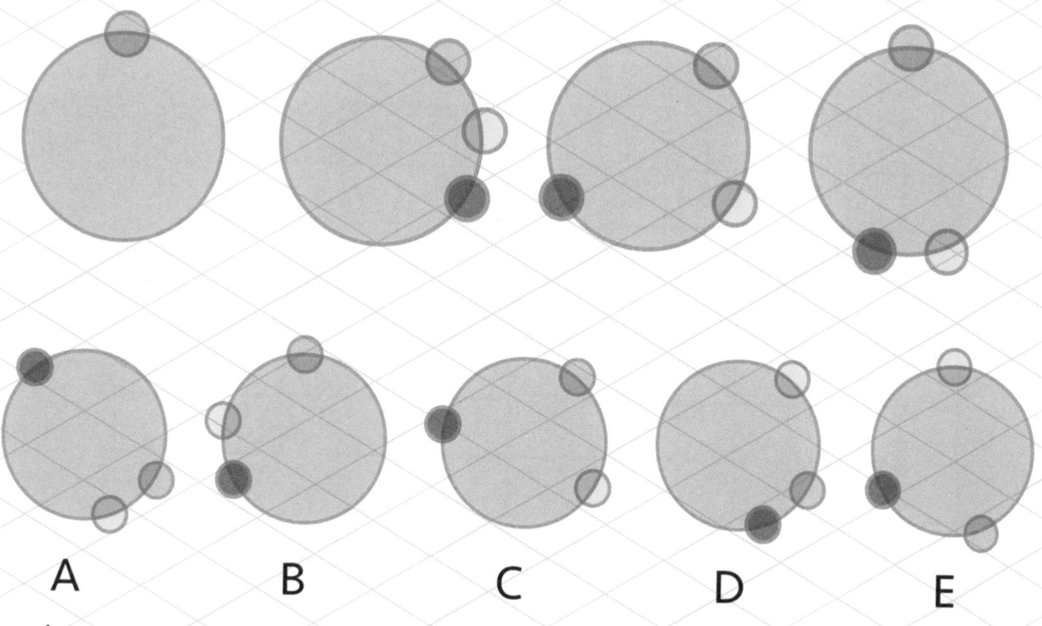

Answer see page 284

What number should replace the question mark?

Answer see page 284

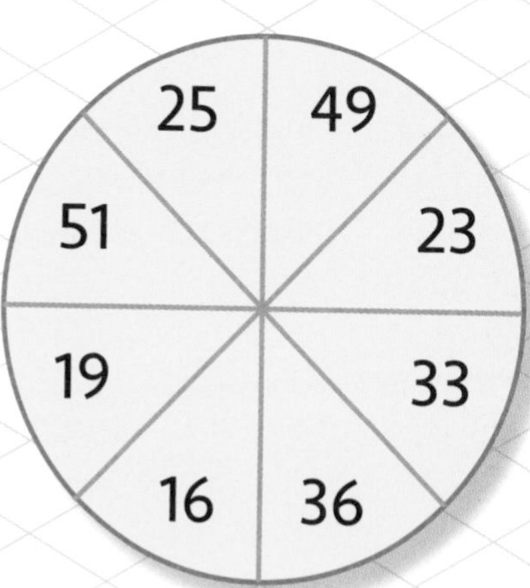

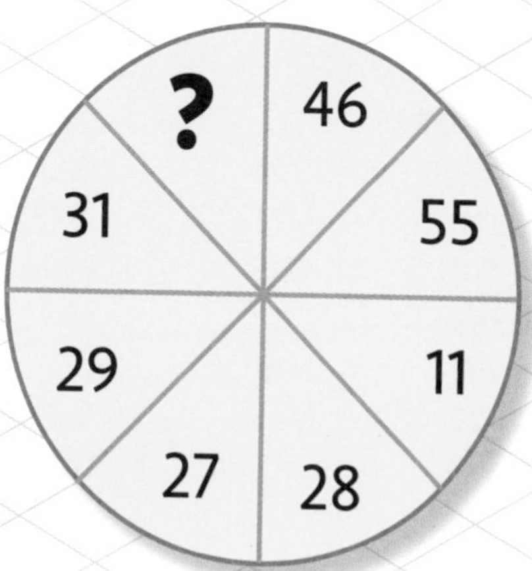

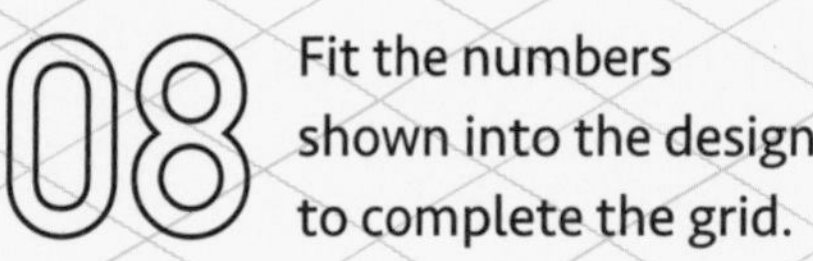

08 Fit the numbers shown into the design to complete the grid.

Answer see page 284

3 digits
229
347
350
388
399
429
497
626
701
717
744
912
933

4 digits
7654
9050
9241

5 digits
18395
19450
49421
79035

6 digits
123070
332724

7 digits
1240638
3794619
4506853
5942083
7206506
9883783

8 digits
30220820
94987216

9 digits
153089939
336603290
523469923
574036838
873077538
992739533

What number should replace the question mark?

Answer see page 285

Answer see page 285

10 Which option A to E most accurately completes the pattern?

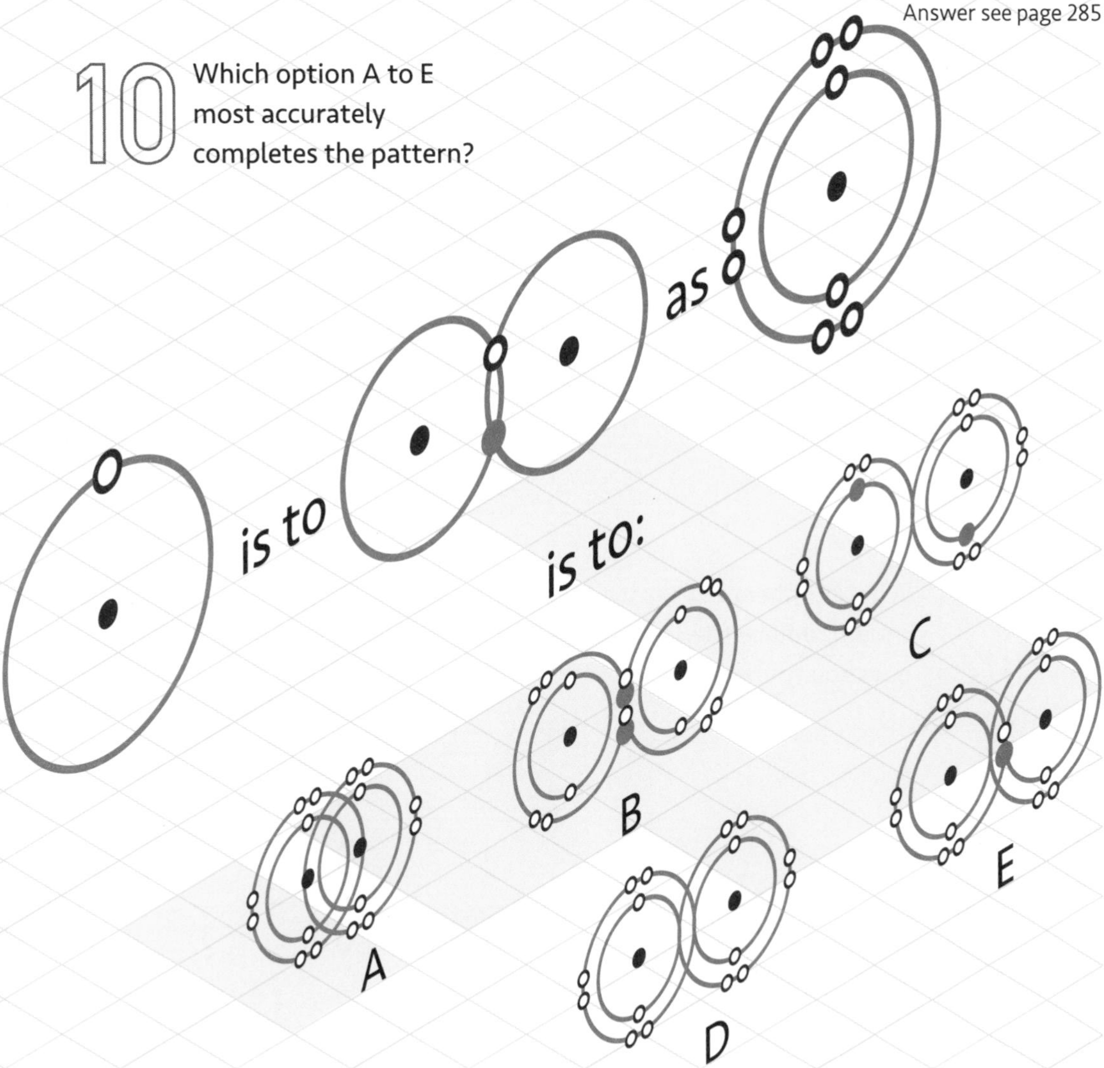

is to

as

is to:

A

B

C

D

E

11

Which of the designs A to E is the odd one out?

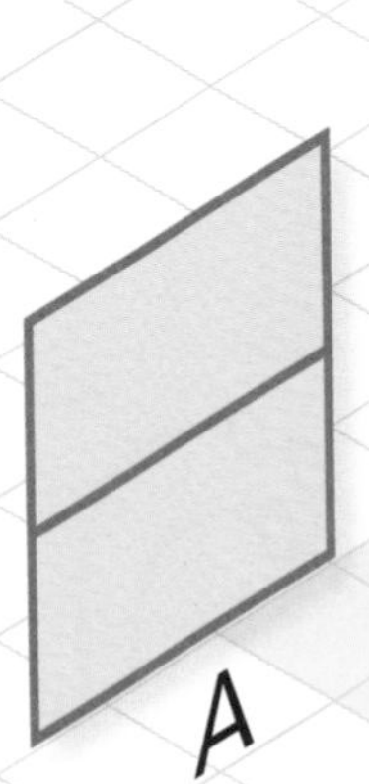

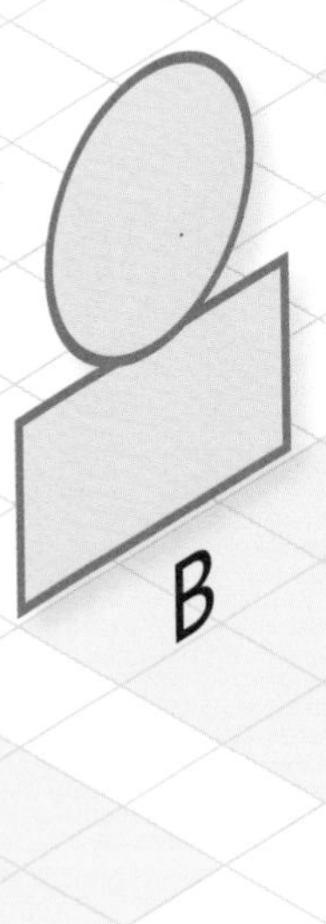

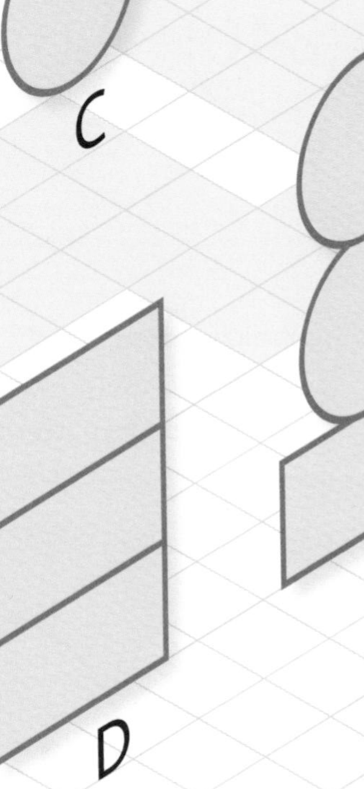

Answer see page 285

12

What numbers should replace the question marks?

8	6	8	6	3	7
0	1	4	9	5	2
3	4	3	?	?	?

Answer see page 285

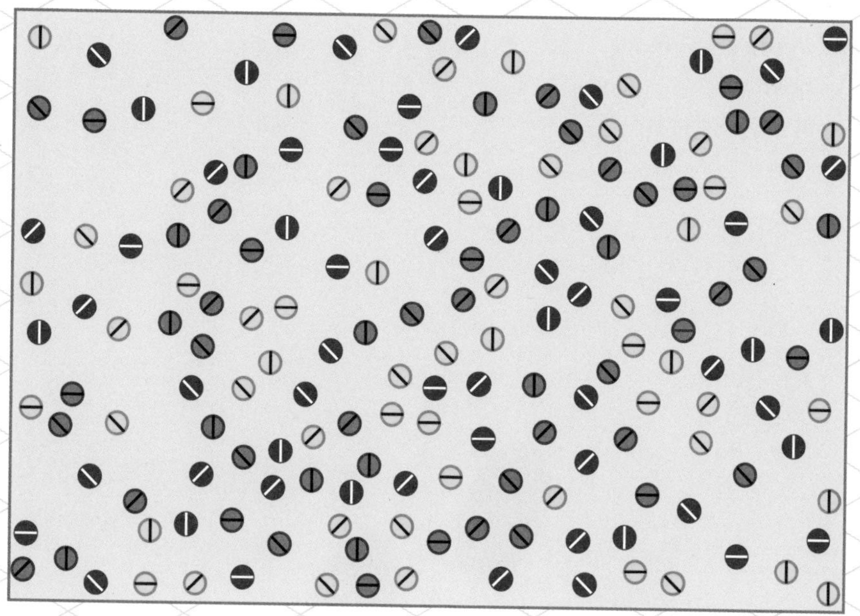

13

Use thirteen straight lines to divide the field above into twelve sections, each containing an equal number of each of the three different styles of ball.

Answer see page 285

14

What number should replace the question mark?

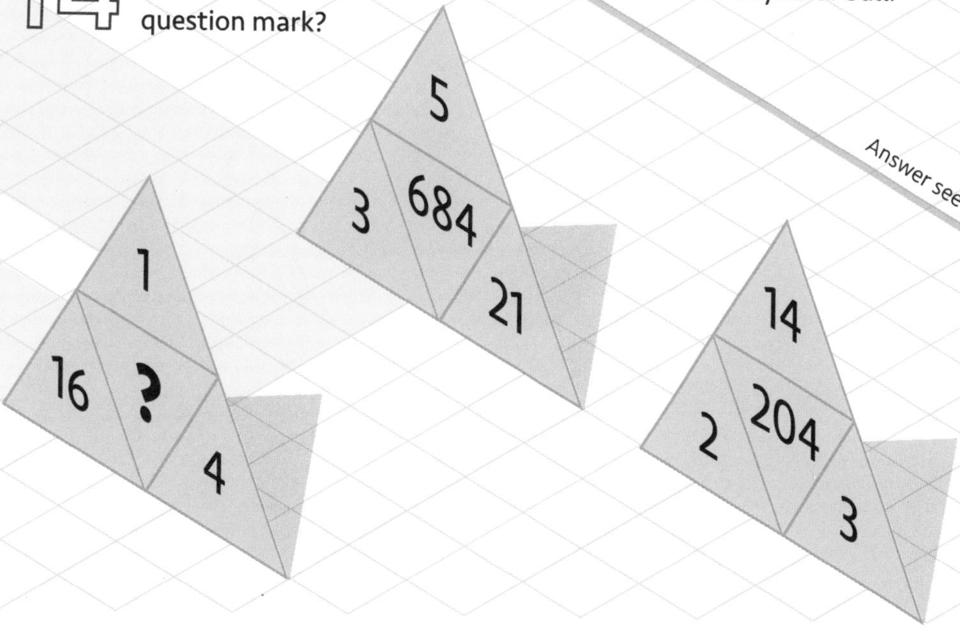

5
3 684 21

14
2 204 3

1
16 ? 4

Answer see page 285

15

In the grid below, how much is each symbol worth?

Answer see page 285

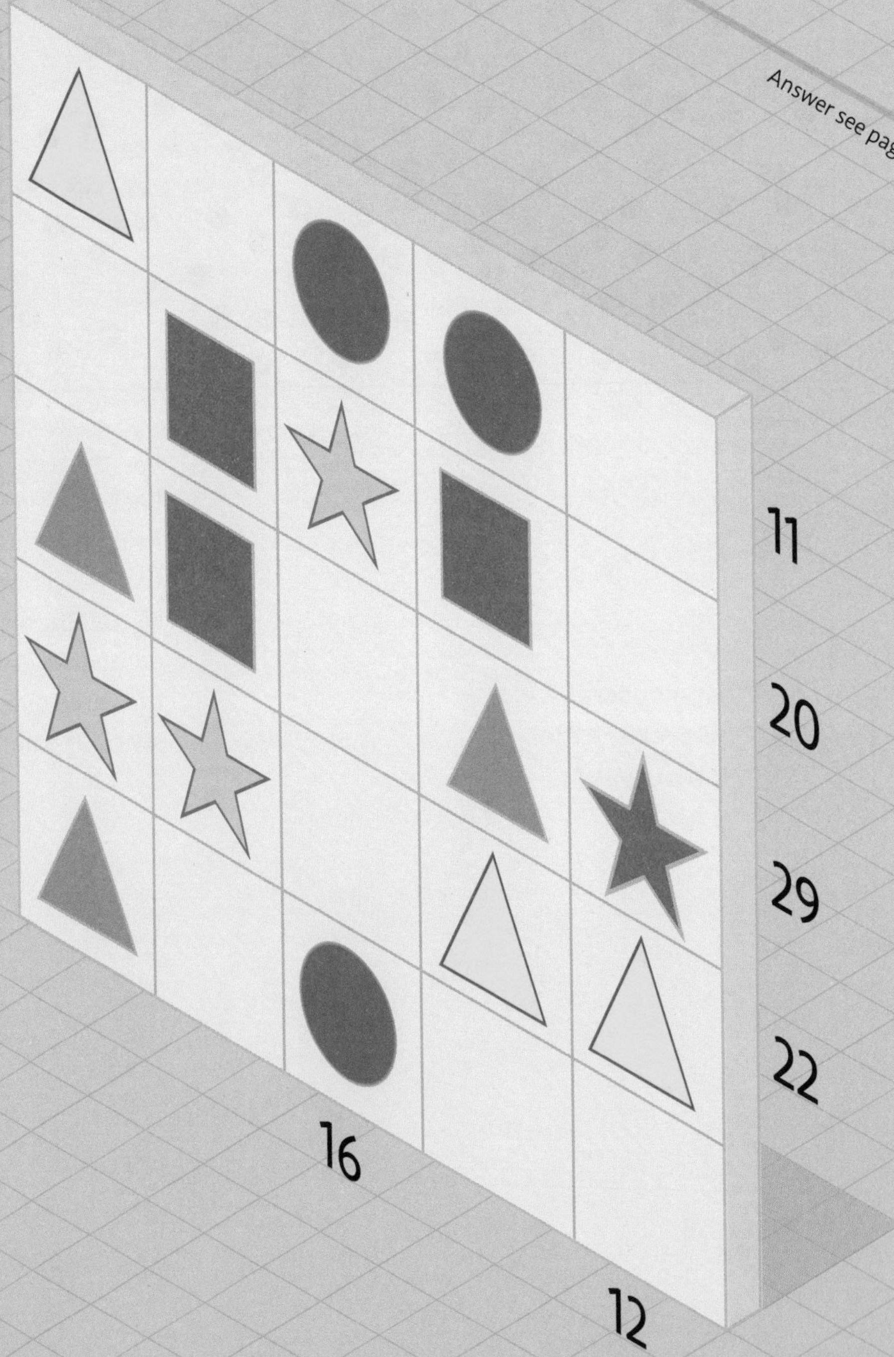

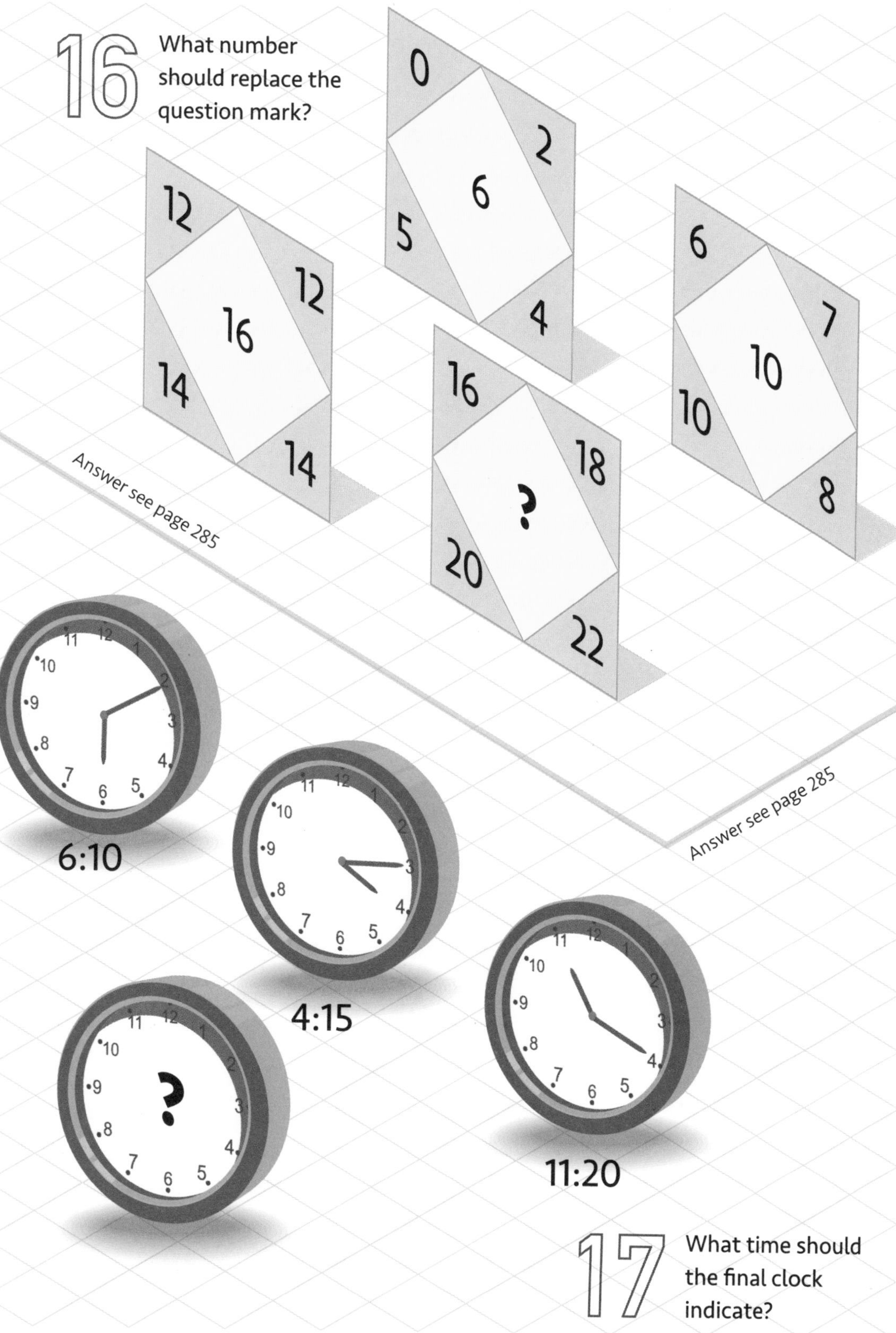
16
What number should replace the question mark?
0
2
6
5
4
12
12
16
14
14
6
7
10
10
8
16
18
?
20
22
Answer see page 285
6:10
4:15
11:20
?
Answer see page 285
17
What time should the final clock indicate?

18

Combine the segments below to find the names of ten celebrities.

AC	AN	OB	RO	AN	TE
AD	SN	ER	LI	ON	TI
BR	AR	KS	ON	ES	C
NI	BE	EY	LI	PE	TS
NM	ER	CO	PI	PI	N
AK	CK	GU	NE	RJ	L
LL	TL	IA	IR	RY	T
AL	EB	IN	NE	SE	EC
AM	NE	JU	T	EN	EL
GH	ER	KE	NS	SS	

Answer see page 285

19

Which of the four shapes A to D fits to complete the triangle?

Answer see page 285

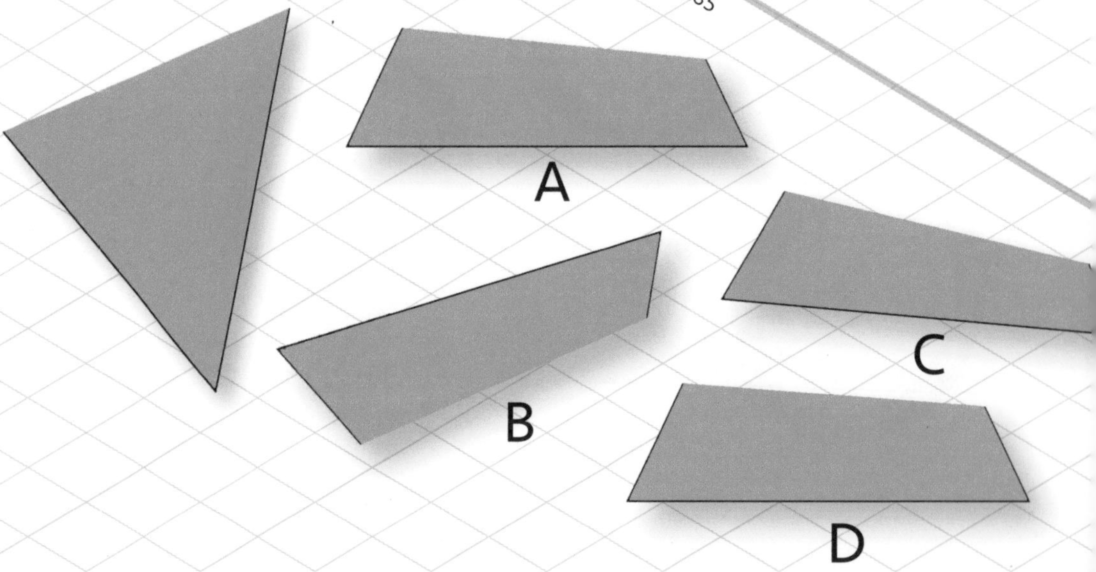

A

B

C

D

20

Which symbols are missing from the blue squares in the grid below?

	●	○	●	○		○	○	●	○		○	●	●	○
	○	●	●	○		●	○	●	○		○	○	●	
○	●	○		●					○	○	●	○	○	●
●	●	●	○					○		●	○			○
○	○	○		○					●	○	●	○	○	●
○		○	○	○		○	○	●	○	●	○	●	●	○
	○		●	●		○	○	●		○		●	●	
○	●	○	○	○	○	●	○	○	○		○	○	○	○
●	○	●	○	●	●	●	○		●	○	○			○
○	○	○			○	●		○	●	○	●	●	●	●
●		●	○	○	●	●	○		○	●	○	○	○	○
	○		●	○	●		○	●	●	○		●	●	
○	●	○	●	●	○		○	●	○	○		○	○	○
●	○	●		○	●	●	○		○	●	○	○		●
●	○		○	●	○	○		○	●	○	●		○	●

Answer see page 285

ANSWERS

Test 1

01

B. Different positioned circles in adjoining pentagons on the same row are carried into the pentagon between them on the row above. Similarly positioned circles are omitted.

02

15 ▲. ▲ = 2 ■ = 5 ● = 6
Subtract ●■ from both sides of scale2: ▲▲▲ = ●[1]. Substitute result[1] for ● in scale 1: 11▲■ = 6▲3■[2]. Subtract common elements (6▲■) from both sides of result[2].
5▲ = 2■[3]. Scale 3 has 6 ■ and requires 3 x 5 = 15▲ to maintain a balance.

03

14. $4\frac{1}{2} = \frac{18}{4}$ which is $6 \times \frac{3}{4}$, therefore $2\frac{1}{3}$ (x 6) = 14.

04

C.

05

5.

06

11	**4**	**9**
6	**8**	**10**
7	**12**	**5**

07

1A.

08

42. The others are multiples of 8.

09

B, **D** and **E**, being the reflected versions of the majority shape. Consider the longest side to be the base, as fig. A. The steepest side is on the left, as is figs. C, F, and G.

10

17. ● = 3, ▲ = 4, ■ = 5.

11

26. The sum of the inner and diagonally opposite outer segments total 37, i.e., (22 + 15) = 37, (11 + 26) = 37.

12

E.

13

C. Break down the larger (left) number:
(2nd digit x 3rd digit) + 1st digit to produce the smaller (right) number.

14

94.

15

6 and 5.

This series does not at first make any sense as it is a combination of two sequences merged alternately.

6		8		11		15		20	
	19		14		10		7		5

Examining the differences reveals that the upper sequence is increasing +2, +3, +4, etc., while the lower sequence is decreasing −5, −4, −3, etc.

16

12:15 a.m. on Saturday in Kabul.
2:45 a.m. on Saturday in Hanoi.

17

2. (Top left - bottom left) - (top right - bottom right) = the middle number, i.e., (14 – 4) – (8 – 6) = 8.

18

B.

19

D. The sum of the individual digits of 832566 = 30, for the others it's a total of 31.

20

F. The minute hand moves back 10 minutes on each clock and the hour hand moves forward 4, 5, 6, 7 hours, etc.

Test 2

01

A square.

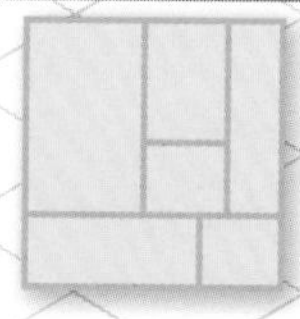

02

The scale is balanced by eight:

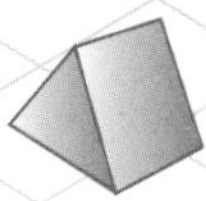

03

14 + 9 - 5 + 7 + 2 + 8 = 35.

04

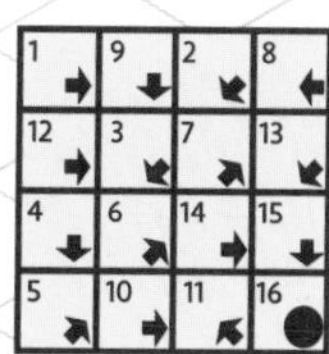

05

D.

06

A.

07

15 x 3 = 45. Second circle alternates being x 2 and x 3 of the equivalent sector of the first circle.

08

09

8 + 13 = 21. (Sum of two previous numbers.)

10

E. (All other designs have each object intersecting the others.)

11

A.

12

C.

13

(One possible solution.)

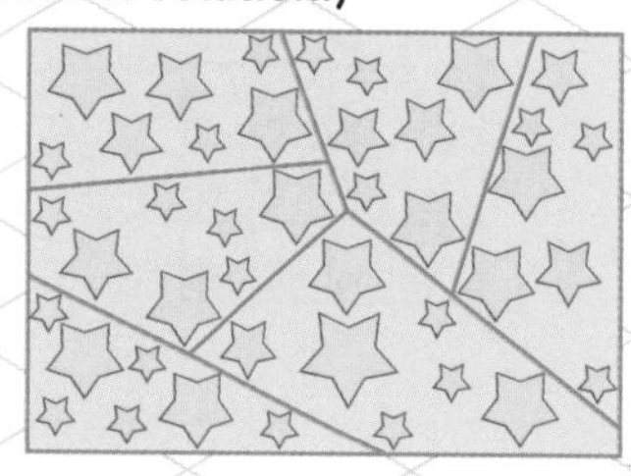

14

(7 + 8) x 9 = 135.

15

▲ = 1, ■ = 2, ● = 3.

16

1 + 4 + 0 - 9 = -4.

17

12:00.

18

Angelina Jolie, Britney Spears, Bruce Springsteen, James Cameron, Jennifer Aniston, Kobe Bryant, Oprah Winfrey, Sandra Bullock, Steven Spielberg, Tiger Woods.

19

740 - 346 = 394.

20

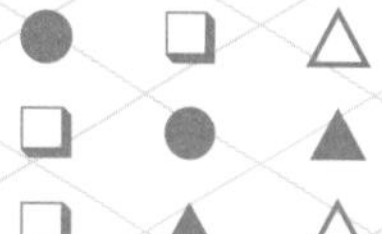

Test 3

01

E. Different positioned circles in adjoining pentagons on the same row are carried into the pentagon between them on the row above. Similarly positioned circles are omitted.

02

12●. ● = 2, ▲ = 5, ■ = 6

Subtract 2■● from both sides of scale 2: ■●● = ▲▲[1]. Subtract ●▲ from both sides of scale 1: ■■ = ●▲▲[2]. Using (result[1]), substitute for 2▲ in result[2]: 2■ = ■ 3●[3]. Subtract common items from both sides of result[3]. ■ = 3●.

03

105. $7 = {}^{21}/_{3}$ which is $21 \times {}^{1}/_{3}$, therefore 5 (x 21) = 105.

04

E.

05

4.

06

267. The sum of the individual digits is 14 for all the other numbers i.e., (2 + 3 + 9) = 14, (7 + 7) = 14, etc.

07

2A.

08

10	**3**	**8**
5	**7**	**9**
6	**11**	**4**

09

C, **D,** and **F** being the reflected versions of the majority shape.

10

48. ■ = 6, ● = 15, ▲ = 21.

11

45. The inner number of each segment is the product of the outer two numbers multiplied, less the sum of the outer two numbers in the opposite segment, ie., (9 x 3) – (6 + 7) = 14.

12

B.

13

A. Break down the larger (left) number :
(1st digit + 3rd digit) x 2nd digit to produce the smaller (right) number.

14

65.

15

720, 5040.
Each term is multiplied by an increasing amount to get the following term, so a x 2 = b, b x 3 = c, c x 4 = d, etc.

16

3:45 a.m. on Wednesday in Cairo.
10:45 a.m. on Wednesday in Tokyo.

17

15. Multiply the bottom two numbers, then subtract the top number to get the center number for each triangle, i.e., (2 x 9) – 3 = 15.

18

B. The minute hand moves forward 10 minutes and the hour hand moves back 1 hour each time.

19

C.

20

B. The digits of the other numbers are arranged from highest (left) to lowest (right).

Test 4

01

E.

02

The scale is balanced by four

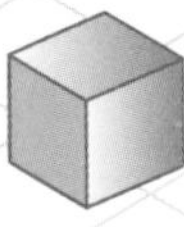

03

32. (Adding equivalent sectors in both circles totals 40, i.e., 8 + 32 = 40.)

04

A triangle.

05

40 - 9 - 5 + 14 + 12 - 32 = 20.

06

D.

07

B.

08

4	7	6	4	6	7				
7		7				9	0	6	6
5	9	7		2	6	5		6	
3		9		2		0		2	
2	6	1	6	5	3	1	6		
7			7			9			
1			2			9			
6	5	5	1	3		7	3	1	
1		0		9		3		0	
		3	0	4	4	9	5	7	

09

98.

10

1 ↘	10 →	11 ↙	5 ↓
7 →	12 ↓	8 ↘	6 ←
3 ↓	13 ↓	2 ←	9 ↖
4 ↗	14 →	15 →	16 ●

11

C. (The only design without a circle inside.)

12

C.

13

(One possible solution.)

14

11 + 10 - 8 = 13.

15

▲ = 1, ■ = 2, ● = 5.

16

(15 + 9 - 18) x 12 = 72.

17

4:10 + 0:35 = 4:45. 50 minutes was added, then 45, then 40, then 35.

18

Shia LaBeouf, Halle Berry, Macaulay Culkin, Johnny Depp, James Earl Jones, John Travolta, Charlie Chaplin, Marlon Brando, Hugh Jackman, Morgan Freeman

19

992 - 439 = 553.

20

A 13-symbol sequence runs horizontally, switching back and forth at end of line, starting from top left.

Test 5

01

A. Different positioned circles in adjoining pentagons on the same row are carried into the pentagon between them on the row above. Similarly positioned circles are omitted.

02

1. Subtract scale 2 from scale 1: ● = ■■.

03

14. 1½ = ³/₂, 3 = ⁶/₂ which is 2 x ³/₂, therefore 7 (x 2) = 14.

04

E.

05

3.

06

4 3 8
9 5 1
2 7 6

07

1C.

08

57. The sum of the individual digits is 13 for all the other numbers, ie., (2 + 5 + 6) = 13, (7 + 6) = 13, etc.

09

B, E and F. With the large double white triangle as the base, the top orange triangle is pointing to the left in the other 4.

10

16. ● = 2, ▲ = 3, ★ = 4, ■ = 5

11

7. The inner number of each segment is the product of the outer two numbers, less the sum of the outer two numbers in the opposite segment. ie.,
(2 x 5) – (3 + 4) = 3.

12

A.

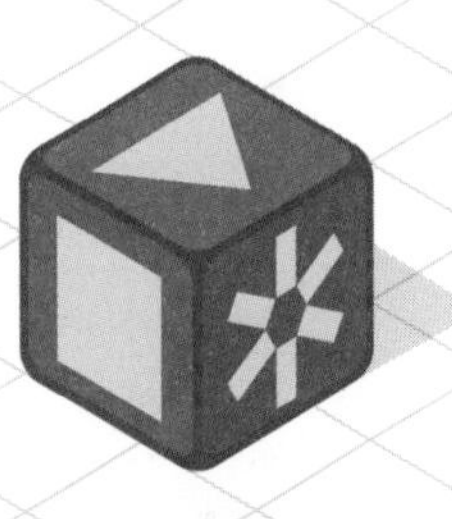

13

A. 246731 is a prime number.
The others are all divisible by 7.

14

124.

15

8 and 13.
Not a single series, but a combination of two running alternately:

7 9 11 13 15
12 10 8 6 4

The rules are easy to spot once you have separated the series ... (+2) for the top one, (-2) for the bottom one.

16

2:45 a.m. on Wednesday in Havana.
8:45 a.m. on Wednesday in Cairo.

17

70. Add the bottom two numbers and multiply by the top number to get the center number for each triangle, ie., (5 + 9) x 5 = 70.

18

D. The minute hand moves forward 5, 10, 15, 20 minutes, etc. The hour hand moves forward 4 hours on each clock.

19

B. Break down the larger (left) number: (1st digit x 2nd digit) + 3rd digit to produce the smaller (right) number.

20

E.

Test 6

01

A.

02

The scale is balanced by five:

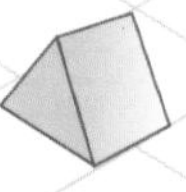

03

32 - 28 x 4 - 21 + 7 x 18 = 36.

04

A square.

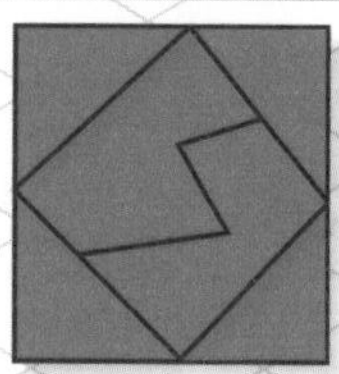

05

E.

06

B. (Group rotates 90 degrees clockwise, then triangle rotates 180 degrees).

07

32. (Adding equivalent sectors in both circles totals 46, 49, 52, etc., up to 67. 35 + 32 = 67.)

08

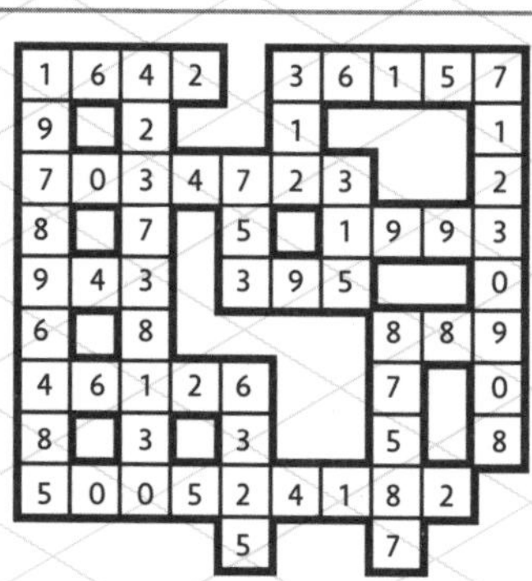

09

18. (Square numbers starting with 16, with the order of the digits reversed.)

10

11

D. (All three shapes overlap).

12

B.

13

(One possible solution.)

14

1 - 14 - 9 = -22 x -1 = 22.

15

▲ = 3, ■ = 5, ● = 8.

16

(18 x 19) + (3 x 12) = 342 + 36 = 378.

17

4:30 + 1:40 = 6:10.

18

Tim Allen, Sylvester Stallone, Nicolas Cage, Drew Barrymore, Tom Hiddleston, Channing Tatum, Keanu Reeves, Ben Affleck, Dwayne Johnson, Russell Crowe.

19

174. 747174 – 173784 = 573390.

20

A 13-symbol sequence runs vertically, starting from top left.

Test 7

01

E. The central balance shows ♥ = ♦♠. Thus balance 3♥ = 3♦ 3♠.

02

D. Different positioned circles in adjoining pentagons on the same row are carried into the pentagon between them on the row above. Similarly positioned circles are omitted.

03

D.

04

4.

05

84. The others are all square numbers.

06

3B.

07

18	**11**	**16**
13	**15**	**17**
14	**19**	**12**

08

B. These are all reflected numbers, but B is the only number with the "reflection" on the right.

09

23. ★ = 5, ▲ = 6, ● = 7.

10

8. The inner number is the sum of the numbers in the outer opposite segment.

11

F.

12

D. 220057 is a prime number.
The others are all divisible by 23.

13

149.

14

81 and 131.
5 7 12 19 31 50 81 131
Examine the differences:
2 5 7 12 19 31 50
Examine the second differences:
3 2 5 7 12 19
It can be seen that the pattern starts to repeat in the differences. The rule here is (a + b = c), (b + c = d), (c + d = e), etc., or, (5 + 7 = 12), (7 + 12 = 19), (12 + 19 = 31), etc.

15

12:45 a.m. on Thursday in Beijing.
11:45 p.m. on Wednesday in Hanoi.

16

42. Add the outer numbers and multiply by two for each triangle.

17

D. The minute hand moves forward 30 minutes on each clock. The hour hand moves forward 2 hours, then 3, then 4, etc.

18

84. 9 is $^{63}/_{7}$, which is 21 x $^{3}/_{7}$, therefore 4 (x 21) = 84.

19

D.

20

E. The larger (left) number is the square of the smaller (right) number.

Test 8

01

A circle.

02

The scale is balanced by two:

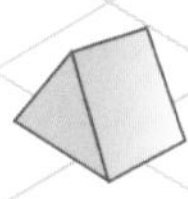

03

28 + 38 - 41 / 5 + 6 5 = 55.

04

05

C.

D. (Group rotates 90 degrees clockwise and the smaller balls switch color).

07

21. (Reverse the digits in the first circle sector and then subtract 1 to get the equivalent second circle sector.)

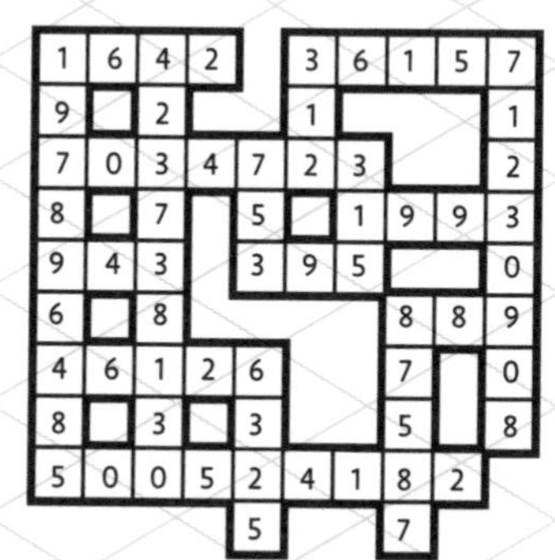

09

30. (Numerical sequence of numbers divisible by 6 or containing the digit 6.)

10

A. (Same shape inside).

11

C.

12

C.

13

(One possible solution.)

14

(23 - 17) x 12 = 72.

15

▲ = 2, ● = 3, ■ = 5, ★ = 6.

16

(8 x 15) - (9 x 4) = 120 - 36 = 84.

17

3:31 + 3:38 = 7:09.

18

Jake Gyllenhaal, Kate Winslet, Megan Fox, Benedict Cumberbatch, Kevin Spacey, Bill Murray, Steve Buscemi, Anne Hathaway, Daniel Radcliffe, Robin Williams.

19

4 + 4 = 8. (col 1 + col 2 = col 3; col 4 + col 5 = col 6)

20

A 10-symbol sequence spirals in clockwise, starting from top left.

Test 9

01

B. Different positioned circles in adjoining pentagons on the same row are carried into the pentagon between them on the row above. Similarly positioned circles are omitted.

02

6. ▲ = 2 ■ = 3 ● = 4.

Remove ■ from both sides of scale 2: ▲● = ■■[1]. Comparing scale1 and result[1] reveals that 4■ 8● = 12 ●[2]. Subtract result[1] from scale 1: ● = 2▲ or, 3● = 6▲.

03

45. 6 is $^{30}/_{5}$ which is 15 x $^{2}/_{5}$, therefore 3 (x 15) = 45.

04

C.

05

3.

06

15 8 13
10 12 14
11 16 9

07

2B.

08

45. The sum of the individual digits is 11 for each of the others.

09

G. A + D, B + F and C + E are pairs.

10

5. ★ = 1, ● = 7, ■ = 5, ▲ = 7.

11

14. The sum of opposite numbers is 37.

12

D.

13

C. 826467 is divisible by 3.
The others are all prime numbers.

14

170.

15

37 and 50.

2 5 10 17 26 37 50
Examine the differences:
3 5 7 9 11 13
You may also spot that the sequence is a series of (square numbers +1) (1^2 +1), (2^2 + 1), (3^2 + 1) etc.

16

6:45 a.m. on Friday in Tokyo
6:45 p.m. on Thursday in Buenos Aires

17

8. For each square the center number is the sum of the outer numbers.

18

B.

19

C. The larger (left) number is 13 x the smaller (right) number.

20

F. The minute hand moves back 15 minutes on each clock. The hour hand moves back 2 hours on each clock.

Test 10

01

C.

02

The scale is balanced by ten:

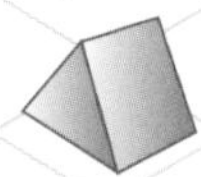

03

23 + 25 / 2 / 8 x 38 / 6 = 19.

04

1 ↘	18 →	4 ↙	19 ↙	17 ←
13 →	2 ↘	21 ↓	14 ↙	12 ←
5 ↘	23 ↓	3 ↑	11 ↗	7 ↙
20 ↗	15 ↙	22 ↖	8 →	9 ↙
16 ↗	24 →	6 ↗	10 ↑	25 ●

05

A.

06

C. (Group rotates 90 degrees anticlockwise then a shape is added with one side more than the previous added shape. Every other shape is solid.)

07

6. (The numbers in each circle sum to a total of 200.)

08

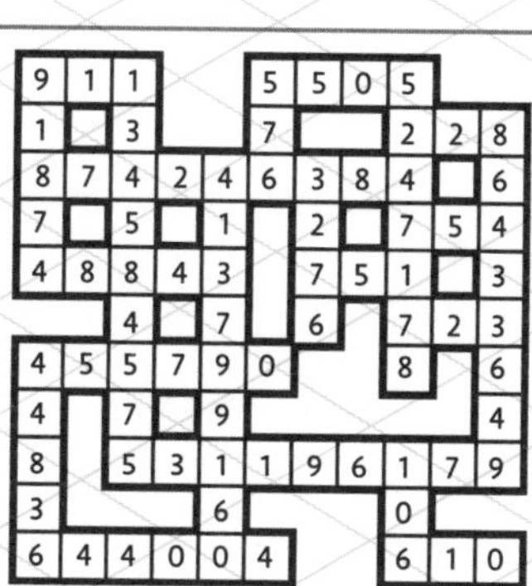

09

372. (Each term = (previous term - 5) x 3).

10

B. (Odd number of sides.)

11

C.

12

A triangle.

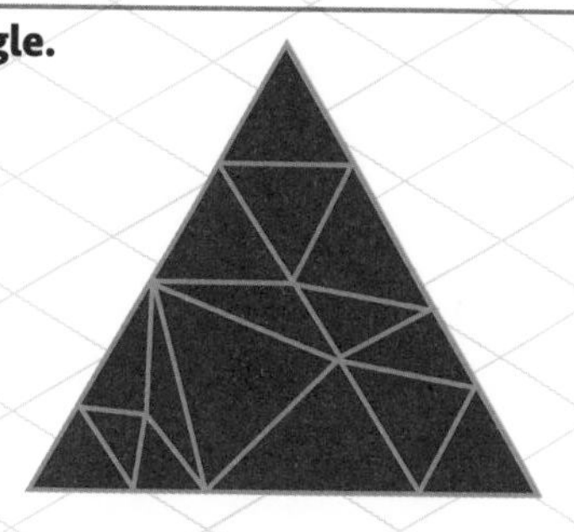

13

(One possible solution.)

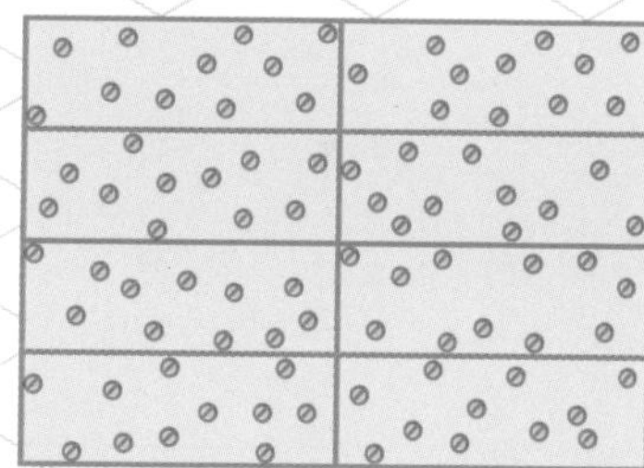

14

1. (first triangle, middle = top, second triangle, middle = bottom left, third triangle, middle = bottom right)

15

▲ = 1, ● = 2, ■ = 4, ★ = 5

16

(Sum of two largest numbers) - (sum of two smallest numbers) = 32 - 8 = 24

17

7:35 + 280m = 12:15. 70 minutes were added, then 140, then 210, then 280 (multiples of 7).

18

Jason Statham, Harrison Ford, Natalie Portman, Jackie Chan, Will Ferrell, Leonardo DiCaprio, Rupert Grint, Antonio Banderas, James Franco, Jack Nicholson.

19

187 + (2 x 386) = 959.

20

A 13-symbol sequence runs vertically from bottom right, getting closer to the left edge.

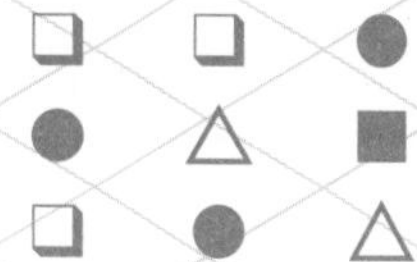

Test 11

01

E. Different positioned circles in adjoining pentagons on the same row are carried into the pentagon between them on the row above. Similarly positioned circles are omitted.

02

9. ● = 1 ■ = 1 ▲ = 9.
Add 3■ to both sides of scale 2:
4■ 8● = ▲ 3■[1].Comparing scale 1 and result[1] reveals that 4■ 8● = 12●[2]. Subtract common elements (8●) from both sides of result[2]:
4■ = 4● or, ■ = ●[3]. Substitute as result[3] for the ■ in scale 2: 9● = ▲.

03

30. 4 is $\frac{12}{3}$, which is 6 times $\frac{2}{3}$, therefore 5 (x 6) = 30.

04

D.

05

6.

06

13	**14**	**9**
8	**12**	**16**
15	**10**	**11**

07

1C.

08

49. The others are all cube numbers.

09

D. A + C, B + F and E + G are pairs.

10

6. ■ = 6, ● = 7, ★ = 8, ▲ = 9.

11

13. The sum of opposite numbers is 7.

12

C.

13

D. The others all divisible by 13.
(717229 is a prime number.)

14

105.

15

64. You will hopefully have noticed that these are all square numbers:

1 16 36 64 81 100 144

But there are squares missing as this is the sequence of "nonprime" squares.
The prime numbers 2, 3, 5, 7 and 11 have been omitted, leaving 8 as the only other nonprime number in the range.

16

10:15 a.m. on Wednesday in Moscow.
9:15 a.m. on Wednesday in Cairo.

17

10. For each square (top left – bottom right) + (top right – bottom left), i.e., (14 - 8) + (6 – 2) = 10.

18

C.

19

B. The larger (left) number is 17 x the smaller (right) number.

20

A. The minute hand moves forward -5, +10, -5, +10, -5 minutes, etc. The hour hand moves back 1 hour on each clock.

Test 12

01

A.

02

The scale is balanced by one:

03

25 + 11 / 9 x 35 - 19 - 28 = 93.

04

1 →	11 →	5 ↓	2 ↓	12 ↓
8 ↓	17 ↙	6 →	15 ↙	7 ←
18 ↓	10 ↑	16 ↖	14 ↑	13 ←
9 ↗	21 ↘	4 ↑	3 ←	24 ↓
19 →	20 ↑	22 →	23 ↗	25 ●

05

C.

06

B. (Congeries is rearranged, then a larger circle added to it.)

07

29. (In each circle, the numbers in diagonally opposite segments total 66. 37 + 29 = 66.)

08

1	0	5	9	1		9	7	8	3	7	
9		7			5			4		5	
4	3	1	5	5	2		4	4	9	6	
1					1		3			6	
7	7	5	6	7	9	2	3	8		2	
5			2		2		1			2	
9			3	2	8	7	0	6	2	8	9
	5	8	4		7		1		6		8
	0		6	1	7		5		0		3
7	7	8	3		4	5	9	9			2
6			4				4		8	1	6
8	9	5	2	5	6	1					

09

56. (For each position number n in the sequence, value is n^2 + n).

10

E. (Shape inside has greater number of sides.)

11

B. (Shape with n sides then has n+2 sides.)

12

A circle.

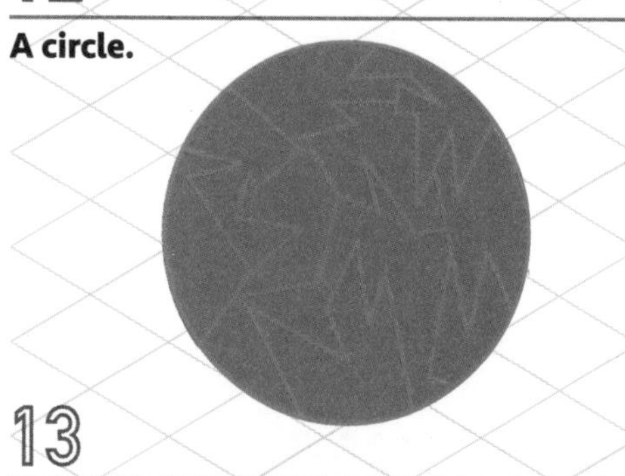

13

(One possible solution.)

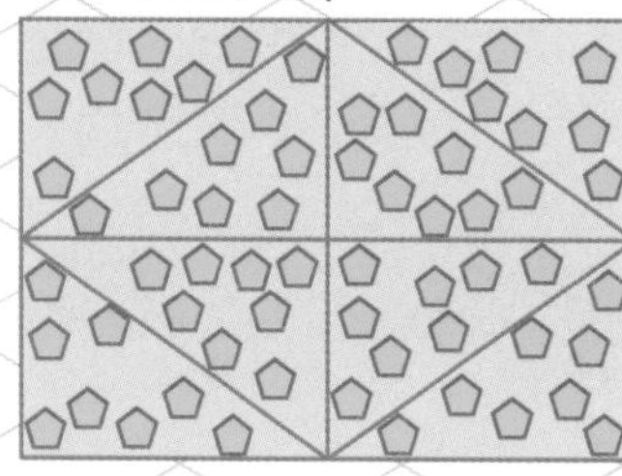

14

9 x 10 / 18 = 5.

15

▲ = 2, ■ = 3, ● = 3, ★ = 4

16

5 x 13 - 19 = 46 (number in lower right is not used.)

17

4:20. (8 / 2 = 4, 40 / 2 = 20.)

18

Sigourney Weaver, Jason Biggs, Vin Diesel, Tom Cruise, Will Smith, Emma Watson, Bruce Willis, David Tennant, Denzel Washington, Jim Carrey

19

(2 x 5) = 10. (0 x 4) = 0. (6 x 4) = 24.
Taking final units = 0 0 4.

20

A 13-symbol sequence runs horizontally from bottom left, rising and switching directions at the end of rows.

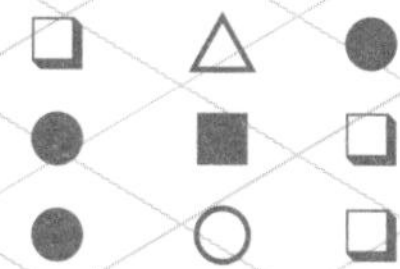

Test 13

01

E. Different positioned circles in adjoining pentagons on the same row are carried into the pentagon between them on the row above. Similarly positioned circles are omitted.

02

24. ● = 1 ■ = 4 ▲ = 10.
Remove ■ from both sides of scale 2:
■ = ●●●●[1]. Multiply both sides of scale 1 by x 2: 2▲ 4● = 6■[2]. Subtract the result[1] from result[2]: 2▲ = 5■[3]. Substitute as result[3] for the 2▲ in scale 3: 6■ =. From result[1] each ■ = 4●, 6■ = 6 x 4●, 6■ = 24●.

03

32. 6 is $^{24}/_{4}$ which is 8 x $^{3}/_{4}$,
therefore 4 (x 8) = 32

04

A.

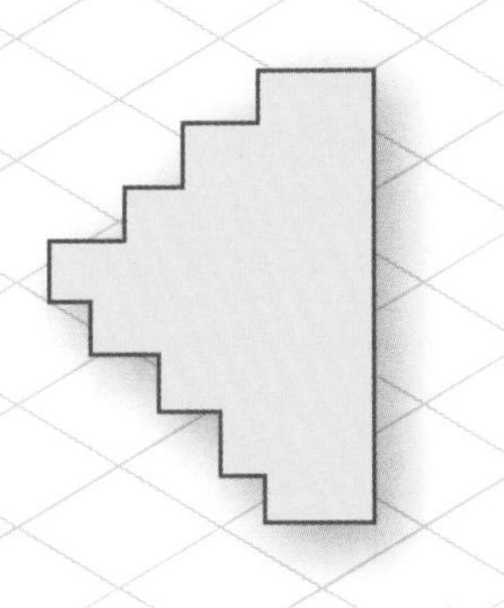

05

3.

06

12	**13**	**8**
7	**11**	**15**
14	**9**	**10**

07

2C.

08

13. The others are all square numbers.

09

E. A + F, B + G and C + D are pairs.

10

6. ▲ = 4, ★= 6, ● = 7, ■ = 9.

11

13. The sum of opposite numbers is 26.

12

D.

13

C. The others all share the same digits (2, 3, 4, 5, 7, 7).

14

150.

15

56 and 92.

1 2 6 15 31 56 92

Examine the differences:

1 4 9 16 25 36

These are square numbers.

16

10:15 a.m. on Wednesday in Dublin.
6:15 a.m. on Wednesday in New York.

17

68. For each square, multiply the numbers on the diagonally opposite corners and add the products, ie., (6 x 8) + (4 x 5) = 68.

18

B.

19

C. Multiply together the individual digits of the larger (left) number to obtain the smaller (right) number.

20

A. The minute hand moves forward +15, +10, +5, 0, -5 minutes etc. The hour hand moves 3, 4, 5, 6 hours, etc.

Test 14

01

A pentagon.

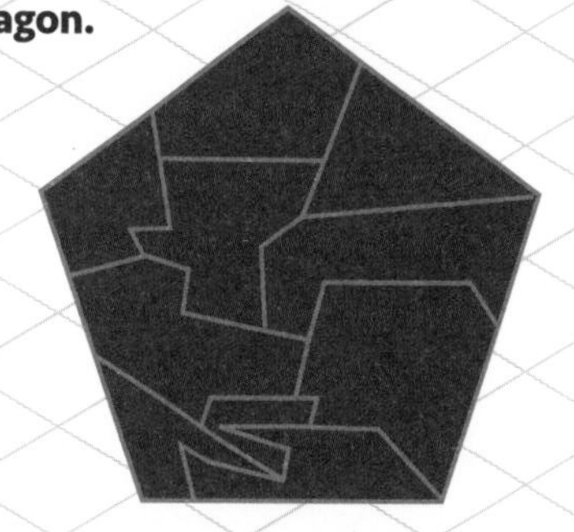

02

The scale is balanced by five:

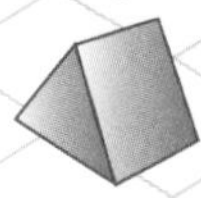

03

17 – 1 – 16 x 20 + 17 – 4 = 13.

04

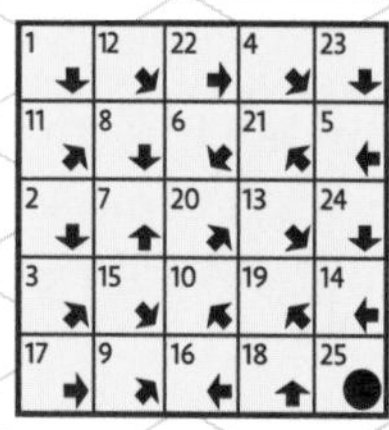

05

A.

06

C. (group is rearranged and gains a shape, alternating between a circle and a square).

07

29. (Adding equivalent sectors in both circles totals the square numbers in sequence. 35 + 29 = 64).

08

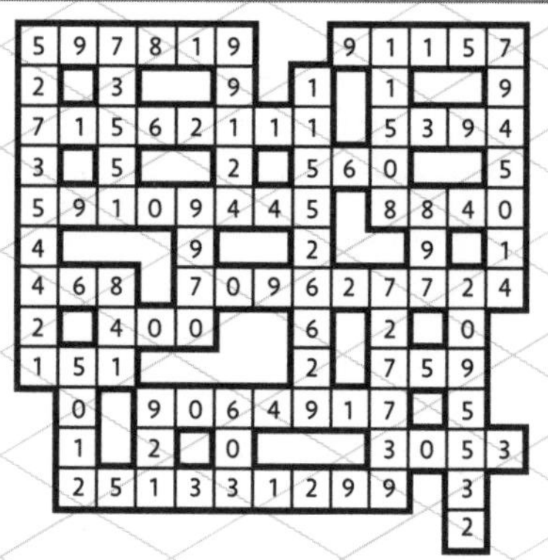

09

1956. (Each term at position n = (previous term + 1) x n).

10

B. (One of the small circles is not placed orthogonally with respect to the center of the larger circle).

11

D.

12

D.

13

(One possible solution.)

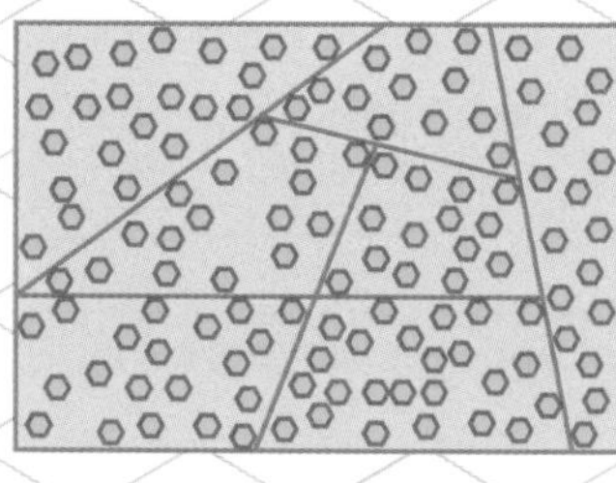

14

(14 x 2) + 11 - (26 / 2) = 26

15

▲ = 13, ● = 17, ■ = 23, ★ = 27

16

The 20th number in the sequence of primes is 71.

17

6:40. (The hours -2 each clock, the minutes are the total of the previous clocks hours and minutes added.)

18

Zach Galifianakis, Cameron Diaz, Kate Beckinsale, Heath Ledger, Tom Hanks, Rowan Atkinson, Chris Hemsworth, Tommy Lee Jones, Brendan Fraser, James McAvoy.

19

87 / 07 = 12 quotient. 74 / 29 = 02 quotient. 71 / 15 = 04 quotient. So missing numbers are **2, 0, 4**.

20

A 13-symbol sequence spirals anticlockwise from bottom right.

△ ○ ❄
● ● ■
○ △ ●

Test 15

01

A. Different positioned circles in adjoining pentagons on the same row are carried into the pentagon between them on the row above. Similarly positioned circles are omitted.

02

4▲. ● = 1 ▲ = 3 ■ = 4.
Remove ▲● from both sides of scale 1: ■ ■ = ● ● ▲▲[1]. Add 2▲ to both sides of scale 2: ▲ ▲ ▲ ▲ ■ = ●●▲▲■■[2]. Substitute result[1] for ■■ = in result[2]: 4▲ ■ = 4■. Subtract common element (■) from both sides: 4▲ = 3■.

03

60. 8 is $^{40}/_{5}$ which is 10 x $^{4}/_{5}$,
therefore 6 (x 10) = 60.

04

D.

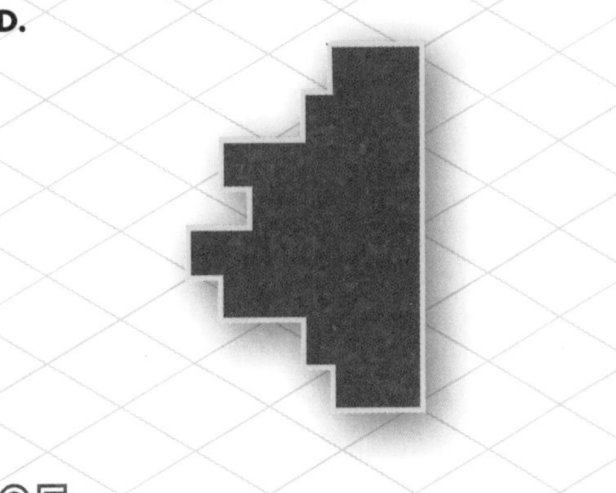

05

6.

06

6	**5**	**10**
11	**7**	**3**
4	**9**	**8**

07

2B.

08

44. The others are all multiples of 9.

09

D and E.

10

3. ■ = 1, ● = 3, ★ = 7, ▲ = 9.

11

1. The product of opposite numbers is 54.

12

A.

13

A. The digits of the other numbers are arranged in order of lowest (left) to highest (right).

14

35.

15

299 and 597.

5 9 19 37 75 149 299 597
(-1) (+1) (-1) (+1) (-1) (+1) (-1)
Examine the differences: 4 10 18 38 74 150 298
If you spot that the differences are alternately (-1) smaller and (+1) larger than the first of each pair of terms, you can deduce that the rule for this series (x2 - 1), (x2 + 1), (x2 - 1), (x2 + 1), (x2 - 1) etc.

16

1:35 a.m. on Friday in Islamabad.
4:35 p.m. on Thursday in Havana.

17

19. Add the three outer numbers and divide by 3, i.e., (16 + 18 + 23) ÷ 3 = 19.

18

A.

19

D. Multiply together the individual digits of the larger (left) number to obtain the smaller (right) number.

20

A. The minute hand moves forward 5 minutes. The hour hand moves -1, +2, -3, +4 hours etc.

Test 16

01

B. (The dark shape does not have the most number of sides).

02

The scale is balanced by four:

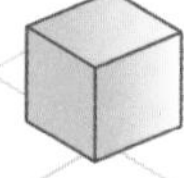

03

36 - 24 ^ 1 + 29 + 20 - 36 = 25.

04

05

D.

06

E. (number of squares in group increases by one).

07

18. (Diagonally opposite sectors summed and added to the total of their equivalent sectors in the other circle always come to a grand total of 81. 23 + 33 + 7 + 18 = 81.)

08

1	7	3	6	5	1	2	4	1		9	7	7
7		8			9		6			4		2
8		9	2	9	7	0	4	9	3	6		4
0		3			5		1		2			0
		7	1	6	6	1	6	4	1	2		0
9	6	1		1			1			4	3	2
0		1		2	3	7	8			4		2
8	7	6		3			5			2	0	4
8		9	7	6	3	6	2	4	1	1		
				0		4		5		7		
4	5	3		8	8	5	3	0	7	2	4	7
3		4			5		7			9		2
9		8	4	0	9	6	9	5	7	0		7

09

60. (Increasing numerical sequence of numbers that are both 1 more and 1 less than a prime integer.)

10

A square.

11

D. ("A" is to "B" as "H" is to "I").

12

(6 + 7)^2 = 16**9**. (5 + 2)^2 = 4**9**. (8 + 3)^2 = 12**1**. So missing numbers are **9, 9, 1**.

13

(One possible solution.)

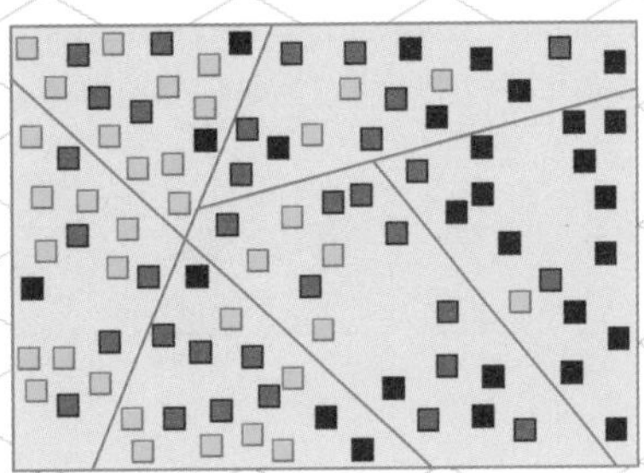

14

144. (Numbers are Fibonacci sequence running right to left along top corner, then bottom left corner, then bottom right corner, and finally center)

15

▲ = 2, ■ = 3, ● = 5, ★ = 7, ▲ = 11,

16

7. ((14 + 7) - (12 + 6) = 3 (Center + top right) - (top left + bottom left) = bottom right).)

17

5:40 - 160m = **3:00.**

18

Owen Wilson, Mel Gibson, Robert De Niro, Al Pacino, Orlando Bloom, Christian Bale, Rachel McAdams, Jessica Alba, Clint Eastwood, Samuel L. Jackson.

19

B.

20

A 17-symbol sequence runs vertically from bottom right, reversing direction each time it moves back a column toward the left edge.

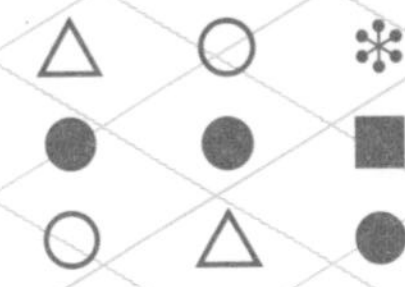

Test 17

01

D. Different positioned circles in adjoining pentagons on the same row are carried into the pentagon between them on the row above. Similarly positioned circles are omitted.

02

10■. ■ = 1 ● = 3 ▲ = 5.
Remove ▲▲● from both sides of scale 1: ● = 3■. Substitute for ● in scale 2: 4■▲ = 9■. Subtract common elements (4■) from both sides: ▲ = 5■.

03

4. 5⅓ is 16/3 which is 8 x ⅔, therefore ½ (x 8) = 4

04

E.

05

3.

06

2 9 4
7 5 3
6 1 8

07

3B.

08

72. The others are all multiples of 7.

09

F.

10

3. ■ = 3, ★ = 4, ● = 5, ▲ = 7

11

121. Opposite numbers are paired with their square numbers.

12

D.

13

B. The sum of the individual digits of the others = 29. 3 + 1 + 2 + 7 + 6 + 7 = 26.

14

49.

15

68 and 133.

1 4 9 18 35 68 133
Examine the differences:
3 5 9 17 33 65
Examine the second the differences:
2 4 8 16 32
The rule for this series is (x2 + 2), (x2 + 1), (x2 + 0), (x2 – 1), (x2 - 2), etc.

16

2:15 a.m. on Thursday in Buenos Aires.
12:15 p.m. on Thursday in Hanoi.

17

42. Add the three outer numbers and multiply by 3, ie., (4 + 5 + 5) x 3 = 42.

18

D.

19

D. Break down the larger (left) number: (1st digit + 2nd digit) x 3rd digit = smaller (right) number.

20

C. The minute hand moves back 5, 10, 15 minutes, etc. The hour hand moves forward 1, 2, 3 hours, etc.

Test 18

01

A hexagon.

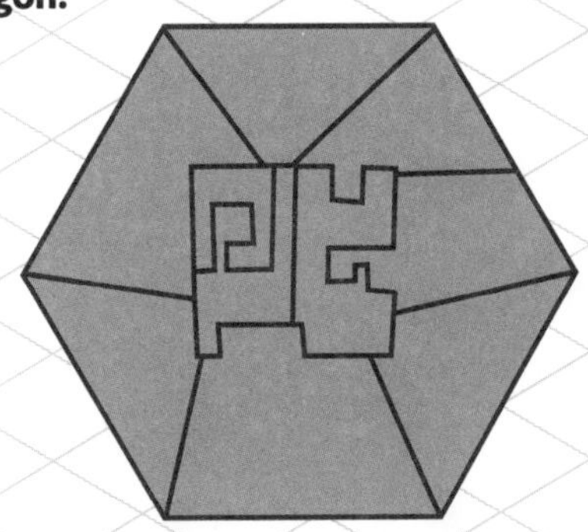

02

The scale is balanced by six:

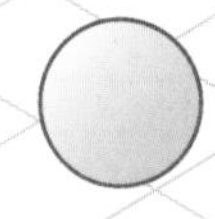

03

16 + 10 - 11 ^ 3 / 9 / 15 = 25.

04

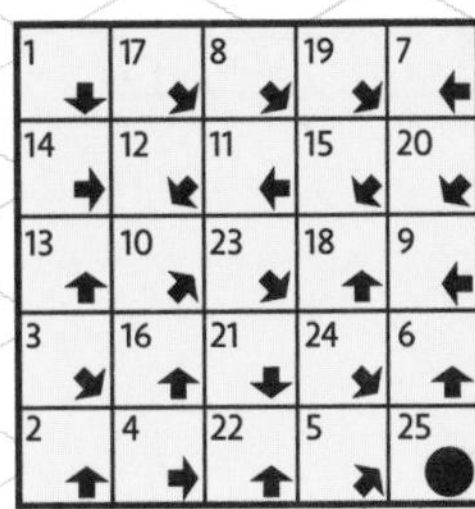

05

D.

06

B. (Ball that starts top left rotates 135 degrees clockwise. Ball that starts far left rotates alternately 15 degrees and 90 degrees anti-clockwise.)

07

26. (A sequence runs across the two circles. Start immediately clockwise of the 12 o'clock position on the left, then move to the mirror-equivalent segment in the right circle (immediately anticlockwise of 12 o'clock). Move back to the left and advance three places clockwise, and continue. So position runs 1L, -1R, 4L, -4R, 7L, -7R, 2L, -2R, etc. Sequence starts at 23, and runs +3, -4, -2, repeating. 23 + 3 = 26).

08

9		4	1	1	6	4	6	1	9	9			
5		2			4			6		4	2	1	0
5	5	9			8			8	0	0		9	
		3	2	8	8	8	2			5	1	0	
3	6	2					8	9	8	0			
4					7		0		0				
3			1	0	8	8	5	5	3	8	0		1
	7	0	1		0		8		8				9
	7		9		1		8		8	0	8		7
	7	9	4	5	3	1	7	2	1		5	8	9
	0		8		4		0		0		8		7
	2	3	0		8	3	3	3	0	1	0	8	3
		7				3		2					1
5	0	4	4	1	3	8	7	5					

09

794. (For each position n, value is 1^n + 2^n + 3^n)

10

B. (Slightly fatter arms, whole shape rotated by 90 degrees).

11

D. (The three polygons in this group do not have n, n + 2 and n + 4 sides – they are n, n + 2, and n + 6).

12

The square numbers are written in reverse, starting top right. Tenth square number is 100 = **001.**

13

(One possible solution.)

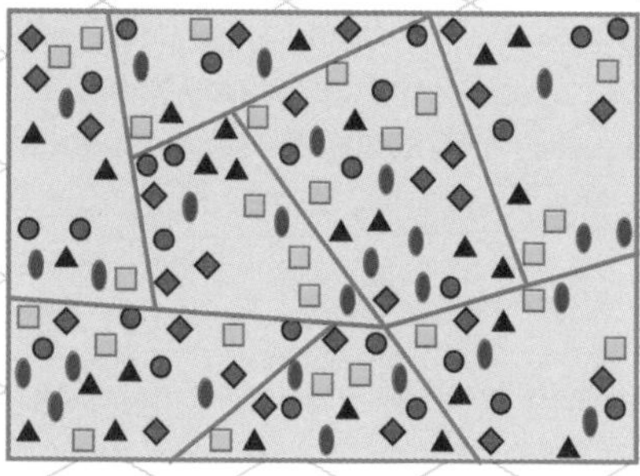

14

(13^1) - 7 = 6.

15

▲ = 14, ▲ = 15, ■ = 17, ● = 19, ★ = 20

16

3. (12^3) / (18 x 6) = 1728 / 108 = 16. ((top left^center)/(bottom left*bottom right)=top right.)

17

6:05. (Multiply the hour by the number of minutes to get 30.)

18

Adam Sandler, Emma Stone, Matt Damon, Bradley Cooper, Peter Sellers, George Clooney, Edward Norton, Scarlett Johansson, Mark Wahlberg, Daniel Craig.

19

A.

20

A 17-symbol pattern runs horizontally from top left, but line 2 is moved to row 9, line 3 is in row 2, line 4 in line 10, and so on, finishing with line 15 in row 8.

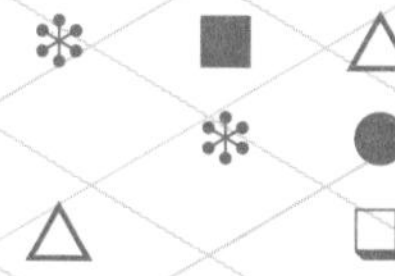

Test 19

01

C. Different positioned circles in adjoining pentagons on the same row are carried into the pentagon between them on the row above. Similarly positioned circles are omitted.

02

4▲. ■ = 4 ▲ = 5 ● = 7.
Remove ▲ from both sides of scale 2:
●● = ▲▲■ or, ● = ▲½■. Substitute for ● in scale 1: (▲▲■)▲■ = (▲½■)■ ■ ■ ■ or, 3▲2■ = ▲4½■. Subtract common elements ▲2■ from both sides: 2▲ = 2½■ or, 4▲ are needed to balance 5■.

03

30. 7½ is $^{30}/_4$ which is 10 x ¾, therefore 3 (x 10) = 30.

04

B.

05

4.

06

45. The others are all multiples of 6.

07

1B.

08

8 1 6
3 5 7
4 9 2

09

E. With the claws at the bottom, image E is the only one in which the tail leans to the right.

10

3. ▲ = 3 ● = 5 ■ = 7 ★ = 9.

11

9. For each segment, the outer number is the sum of the inner two numbers of the opposite segment.

12

C.

13

C. 133597 is a prime number, the others are all divisible by 3.

14

196.

15

129 and 513.
Examine the differences:
17 33 65 ? 257 ?
16 32 ? 192 ? this could be 64 and 128, i.e., differences doubling. By observation it can be seen that the rule to find the next term in the series is (x2 -1), i.e., (2 x 65) – 1 = 129 (2 x 129) – 1 = 257 (2 x 257) – 1 = 513.

16

8:25 p.m. on Saturday in Cairo.
1:25 a.m. on Sunday in Hanoi.

17

16. (top left – top right) x (bottom left – bottom right) = (6 - 2) x (9 - 5) = 16.

18

D. The minute hand switches between 00 and 30 each time. The hour hand moves forward by +2, +3, +4, etc.

19

B.

20

B. Break down the larger (left) number: (2nd digit + 3rd digit) x 1st digit = smaller (right) number.

Test 20

01

Two interlinked circles.

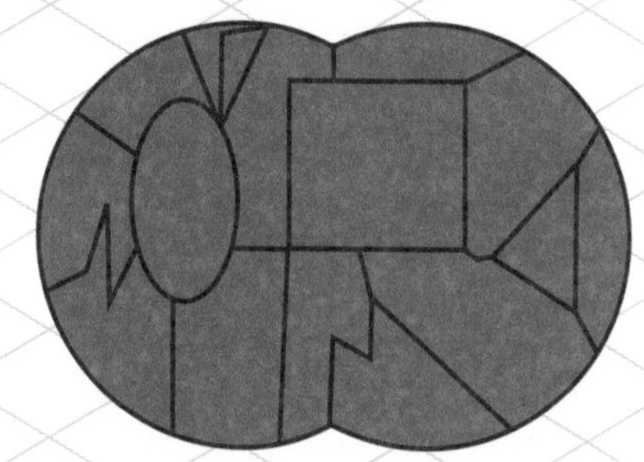

02

The scale is balanced by one:

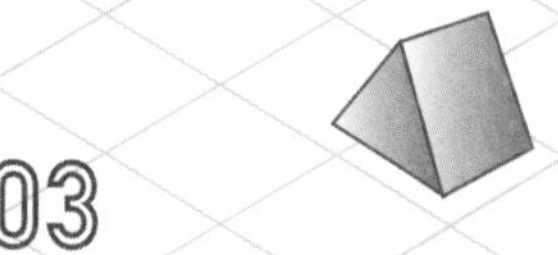

03

15 / 5 x 30 / 6 x 5 - 27 / 16 ^ 4 - 1 = 80

04

1 ↓	22 ↘	6 ↙	21 ←	15 →	16 ↓
27 →	13 ↘	28 ↓	26 ←	25 ←	17 ↙
12 ↗	20 ↗	34 →	24 ↗	7 ↓	35 ↓
2 →	19 ↑	5 ↑	33 ↖	4 ←	3 ←
10 ↓	30 →	18 ↖	31 ↓	14 ↑	23 ↖
11 ↑	9 ↖	29 ↖	32 ↑	8 ←	36 ●

05

B.

06

A. (Each stage = a forty-degree rotation clockwise. Each turn, gray ball advances 1, 2, 3, then 4 stages. Yellow ball alternates +2 and -1 stage. Green ball advances 3 stages. After all advances have been completed, the balls are recolored. Ball on—or nearest to, proceeding clockwise—the 12 o'clock position is recolored gray, next one yellow, and final one green. In overlaps, gray, then yellow, take precedence. Then the turn ends.)

07

25. (For each circle, the total of the uppermost two segments plus the lowermost two segments = the total of the leftmost two segments plus the rightmost two segments = 126. 46 + 28 + 27 + 25 = 126.)

08

		3						3	4	7				
4	5	0	6	8	5	3				9	2	4	1	
		2		7						0		9		
9	9	2	7	3	9	5	3	3		3		7	4	4
4		0		0		2		7	6	5	4			2
9	8	8	3	7	8	3		9				3	9	9
8		2		7		4	9	4	2	1			3	
7	2	0	6	5	0	6		6		2			3	
2				3		9		1	8	3	9	5		1
1	5	3	0	8	9	9	3	9		0		9	1	2
6		3				2				7		4		4
		2	2	9		3	3	6	6	0	3	2	9	0
7	1	7		0			5		2			0		6
0		2		5	7	4	0	3	6	8	3	8		3
1	9	4	5	0								3	8	8

09

2208. (Prime numbers in sequence, starting from 23 [23, 29, 31, 37, 41, 43, 47], are squared and the result has 1 subtracted.)

10

B. (H molecule is to H_2 as O is to O_2).

11

A. (Not a Morse Code vowel: A = m, as opposed to B = a, C = i, D = o and E = u.)

12

868637 - 495201 = 373436. Each successive row starts two positions to the right of the one above, and wraps around, so third row is offset by 4. So missing numbers are **6, 3, 7**.

13

(One possible solution.)

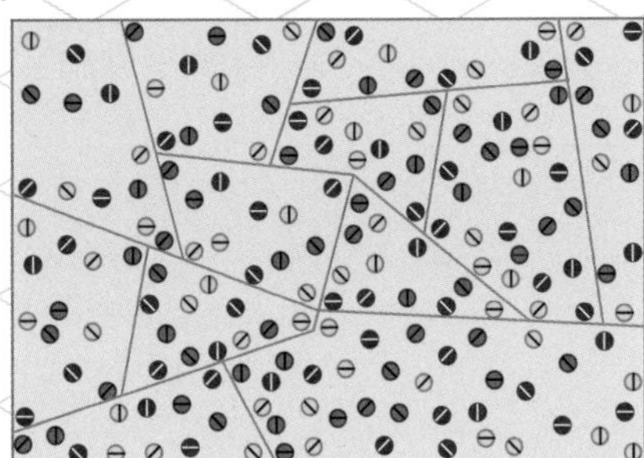

14

(1 ^ 4) + (16 ^ 2) = 257. (Arrange numbers of each triangle in ascending order, i.e., S, M and L, then (S^M)+(L^2)=center.)

15

▲ = 3, ● = 4, ■ = 6, ▲ = 7, ★ = 8, ★ = 9

16

20. (The 20th element of the periodic table has 20 neutrons.)

17

9:25. (Subtract hour from minutes to give next hour. Minutes increased by 5.)

18

Brad Pitt, Ian McKellen, Ben Stiller, Pierce Brosnan, Julia Roberts, Alec Guinness, Keira Knightley, Peter Jackson, Liam Neeson, Sean Connery

19

D.

20

A 15-symbol pattern spirals clockwise from the top left.

Puzzle Notes

286

Puzzle Notes

Puzzle Notes